OLD AGE
ON THE NEW SCENE

Robert Kastenbaum
Editor

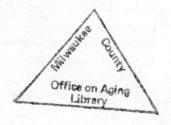

SPRINGER PUBLISHING COMPANY
New York

The International Journal of Aging and Human Development *has established a tradition of introducing new methods, new approaches, and new areas of investigation. We are grateful to Baywood Publishing Company, Inc. for permission to reprint here articles that first appeared in this journal.*

Copyright © 1981 by Springer Publishing Company, Inc.

Springer Publishing Company, Inc.
200 Park Avenue South
New York, New York 10003

81 82 83 84 85 / 10 9 8 7 6 5 4 3 2 1

Library of Congress Cataloging in Publication Data

Main entry under title:

Old age on the new scene.

  (Springer series on adulthood and aging; 9)
  Includes bibliographies and index.
    1. Aged—Social conditions—Addresses, essays, lectures.   2. Aged—Psychology—Addresses, essays, lectures.   3. Aging—Addresses, essays, lectures.   4. Old age—Addresses, essays, lectures.   I. Kastenbaum, Robert. [DNLM: 1. Aged.   2. Aging. W1 SP685N v. 9 / WT 30 043]
HQ1061.039   305.2′6   80-39728
ISBN 0-8261-2360-0
ISBN 0-8261-2361-9 (pbk.)

Printed in the United States of America

Contents

Contributors

Steven Artt, Department of Psychology, Wayne State University, Detroit

Jeanne E. Bader, Hubert H. Humphrey Institute of Public Affairs, University of Minnesota, Minneapolis

A. Harvey Baker, Department of Psychology, Queens College, The City University of New York

Elaine M. Brody, Department of Social Work, Philadelphia Geriatric Center

Sandra E. Candy, Department of Psychology, University of Kentucky, Lexington

Valerie Derbin, Department of Psychology, Wayne State University, Detroit

J. Scott Francher, John Jay College of Criminal Justice, The City University of New York

Hyman Hirsch, Institute for Retired Professionals, New School for Social Research, New York

Gregory Johnson, Department of Sociology, University of Massachusetts, Boston

Richard A. Kalish, California School of Professional Psychology, Berkeley

J. Lawrence Kamara, Department of Sociology, University of Massachusetts, Boston

Michael M. Katz, Veterans' Administration Hospital, Allen Park, Michigan

Morton H. Kleban, Philadelphia Geriatric Center

Margaret E. Kuhn, Gray Panthers, Philadelphia

Calvin J. Larson, Department of Sociology, University of Massachusetts, Boston

M. Powell Lawton, Philadelphia Geriatric Center

Renaldo Maduro, Human Development Program, Langley Porter Neuropsychiatric Institute, University of California, San Francisco

Victor W. Marshall, Department of Sociology, McMaster University, Hamilton, Ontario

Brian L. Mishara, Department of Psychology, University of Quebec, Montreal

Evelyn S. Newman, Institute of Gerontology, School of Social Welfare, State University of New York, Albany

Claire Myers Owen, Author and Counselor

Beverly Patnaik, Philadelphia Geriatric Center

Paul Sabatini, Department of Psychology, Wayne State University, Detroit

Edmund Sherman, Institute of Gerontology, School of Social Welfare, State University of New York, Albany

Ken Stone, School of Public Health, University of California, Los Angeles

Mary Ann P. Sviland, Sepulveda Veterans' Administration Hospital, Los Angeles

Thomas Tissue, Research Bureau, California Department of Social Welfare, Sacramento

A. T. Welford, formerly of the Department of Psychology, University of Adelaide, South Australia

Harold J. Wershow, Department of Sociology, University College, University of Alabama, Birmingham

About This Book

When we were all about 17 years younger, there appeared a book titled *New Thoughts on Old Age*. It was unusual for its day in that readers on the topic of growing and being old had not yet proliferated. It was even more unusual in the book's insistence upon venturing beyond the narrow limits of practice and theory that comprised much of psychosocial gerontology in the early 1960s.

The venturing beyond was not entirely a matter of preference. Many of the contributors to *New Thoughts* were associated with a facility for the ill and vulnerable aged that was attempting to find its way toward a broad, humane, and effective spectrum of care. My colleagues and I at Cushing Hospital (Framingham, Massachusetts) had relatively few guidelines either in our personal education and experience or in the clinical literature. We had to improvise and learn as we went along. This was also the situation of a growing number of other clinicians, researchers, and educators in a variety of settings. Even the least adventurous of us could not remain securely within the established tradition. Not only was this tradition limited in scope, but the ordinary performance of one's responsibility to the hospitalized aged and their families often required knowledge and techniques for which there seemed to be no tradition at all.

Some of our experiences were shared through *New Thoughts,* and the innovative ideas and techniques of several other people not associated with Cushing Hospital were included as well. The spirit of the book as a whole was not to offer an "instant" psychosocial gerontology but simply to encourage fresh thinking about the experience of aging and the challenge of providing relevant, high-level care for those in need. It has been a pleasure, however, to see some of the concepts and procedures first conveyed through this book take hold. That instructors have also found it useful in a wide variety of courses in liberal arts and professional programs has also helped us feel that the book was worth its while. Furthermore, both the contributors themselves and others in the field continue to dip into *New Thoughts* for ideas that still have not yet had their day.

Nevertheless time has passed. A wealth of new talent has developed in and around psychosocial gerontology. There are more men and women devoted to problems of adult development and aging, and there are more resources in the form of agencies, professional societies, journals, and books. The establishment of the National Institute on Aging and the appointment of the superbly qualified Robert N. Butler as director is one of the most visible indexes of a new scene for old age. The Administration on Aging, also blessed with experienced and dedicated leadership, has added stature and resources to advocacy for the aged. The Gerontological Society has continued to mature; in addition to continuing its basic role in the encouragement of scientific and clinical progress, it is now responsive to many public-policy and value issues as well. Physicians participate in the Gerontological Society but also have been cultivating their interests through the American Geriatric Society. Several states and regions have developed effective local organizations such as the Western Gerontological Association and the Massachusetts Gerontological Association.

Titles of organizations make for dull reading, but the ever-increasing roster of groups dedicated to understanding and improving the situation of the older American represents an exciting trend for those who recall how unusual it once was to find even one receptive colleague or bureaucrat. The fact that we now have an Association for Gerontology in Higher Education evidences a new attention to old age on college campuses. The National Caucus on the Black Aged proved its worth through impact on the 1970 White House Conference on Old Age and has since consolidated and further pursued objectives that had been sadly neglected only a few years ago. It has been even more impressive to see the development of well-informed and vigorous group efforts on the part of older Americans themselves. The Gray Panthers, led by Maggie Kuhn, have done much to challenge the lazy stereotypes that many have held about the later years of life. Other valuable self-advocacy programs have been initiated by the National Council of Senior Citizens, the National Retired Teachers Association, and the American Association of Retired Persons, to name some of the prominent organizations in this field. Suborganizations and committees have developed within a number of existing groups, including churches, unions, and professional and scientific societies.

In short, there now *is* a scene for old age that existed only in rudimentary form a few years ago. Service, administrative, scientific, and peer organizations confirm that there is a place in society for the older American, and further, that this place is less than satisfactory and that something can be done about it. There is also a new scene for old age in the sense of increasing awareness of the potential of the later years—potential both for the individual and for society. The scene is new in another sense as well; with the passage of time there is a constant freshening within the ranks of the elderly. As we graduate into old age, each of us brings distinctive life experiences and skills. The character of society's senior echelons continually reshapes itself as some reach the end of life and others cross that perhaps mythical threshold into old age. In this sense the scene will always be new. Society will continue to change, and our children and grandchildren will follow us through the cycle of life.

Today at least some of the "newness" can be seen in a reevaluation of the old man and woman as complete people. There is less inclination to see old age itself as a problem or to reduce the dimensions of the person to fit tired stereotypes. This spirit is represented throughout this volume. I have culled and invited contributions by a variety of observers and researchers that expand our view of growing and being old. The variety of viewpoints and methodology is intentional. On a more personal note, variety has also continued to flourish within my life. I was just beginning to learn about old age from the aged themselves in a newly developed psychology department at Cushing Hospital. After 6 years of such experience I went off to profess hither (Wayne State University) and yon (University of Massachusetts-Boston) and recently returned to the cradle of my gerontological education with the opportunity to serve as its superintendent. There are probably many others throughout the nation who have also moved from one type of involvement with the aged to another in the years between *New Thoughts* and *New Scene*. We are continuing to learn that if there are many problems, there are also many pathways to their resolution. It is to be hoped that the expanding scope and resourcefulness of gerontology will ever more faithfully reflect the richness of human personality from youth through old age.

Robert Kastenbaum

I

Act Your Age!

This familiar admonishment is but one of the ways we attempt to control each other's behavior. "That's not lady-like!" and "Boys don't cry!" express another angle from which the shape-up process sometimes operates. These socialization or control maneuvers usually attempt to limit the options available to an individual. Certain behaviors, even certain thoughts and feelings, are ruled out of bounds. In return for surrendering some degrees of freedom, the individual is rewarded by acceptance as a "good" student, worker, or citizen, or as a "sweet little woman" or a "real man." Something is gained: social acceptance and security. Something is lost: range of behavior and expression.

The message, "Act your age!" has different implications for personal gain and loss at different points in the life-span. Throughout the earlier phases of development there is a strong directional bias in the admonition. The child is urged to abide by the expectations of the present sociodevelopmental age with a decided leaning toward even more advanced maturation. It is no longer acceptable, for example, to throw a tantrum or behave like a baby. The "good" child lives up to the current age-related expectations and moves toward the yet more stringent expectations that are coming up.

In adulthood "Act your age!" comes to represent pressure for stability. Ways of behaving, thinking, and feeling associated with youth are off limits, although not uniformly. The admonition now means that one should take up the full responsibility of this station in life. It is less important to move ahead in age-related expectations than to avoid slipping back and thereby sidestepping present responsibilities.

The same admonishment has a more peculiar and cruel effect when applied to elderly men and women. As with younger individuals, it tends to rule out many past ways of functioning. When the old person acts his or her age, there is no out-of-character sexuality, risk taking, aggressiveness, or competitiveness. Because the person has in fact lived longer, this means that more areas of previous functioning are excluded. But what does the old person receive in return for giving up not only youthful but also mature orientations toward life? What, in other words, is the "good" old person good for? It is the precarious, questionable place of the old person in our culture's hierarchy of values coupled with the insistence that he or she renounce previous ways of being that makes pressure to "Act your age!" so noxious.

The situation improves when we are able to recognize new and valuable qualities that can be cultivated as we move into mid-life and beyond. Elaine M. Brody offers an important illustration in her discussion of filial behavior. The adult

1

child has the opportunity and perhaps also the responsibility to offer support and comfort to the elderly parent. This requires a kind of etiquette but also a kind of continued interpersonal development that has not often been examined.

Sexual intimacy often has been considered quite inappropriate for the elderly. Unfortunately this attitude is sometimes shared by elderly men and women themselves even though pleasurable and meaningful sharing of affection remains well within their power. Mary Ann Sviland dissects some of the myths associated with sexuality in the elderly and offers suggestions based on her own counseling experience.

The unfamiliar images of the middle-aged person as a child and the elderly couple as lovers are joined by the role of the old gambler. Ken Stone and Richard A. Kalish note that many elderly people in the United States and Canada continue in the forms of gambling that prevailed in their countries of origin, while all ethnic groups have a high proportion of poker players. Their exploratory study has some provocative findings and awakens interest in the meaning of voluntary risk taking for people who already seem to have lost some of their decision-making opportunities in society.

One of the most persistent reinforcers of age stereotypes (and other kinds) is the glowing tube of the television set. The commercial can be singled out for particular attention because its messages are often highly focused yet evocative and come at us with relentless frequency. J. Scott Francher finds that television commercials participate in the disenfranchisement of the aged from society. *Young* is the only age worth being. The older person is thought to experience "conflict, anxiety, and anger" in the mixed message that she or he should aspire to, but cannot really expect to achieve, the valued status of the young.

An even more direct approach to understanding what it means to "Act your age" would be to study people's self-interpretations of their ages. An "Ages of Me" interview procedure distinguished *personal age* and *interpersonal age* from *chronological age*. Even young people make private distinctions between how old they feel and how old they believe they look to others. This exploratory study by Robert Kastenbaum, Valerie Derbin, Paul Sabatini, and Steve Artt prepares the way for more extensive inquiries into our personal perceptions of age.

1

The Etiquette
of Filial Behavior

Elaine M. Brody

Background of the Problem

Contemporary American cultural and social attitudes prescribe what may
be characterized as an "etiquette" of filial behavior toward the elderly.
While the social conventions which comprise the rules of etiquette generally arise in the context of society at a particular time, the formalities often
persist over time and are perpetuated as ritual behavior and stereotyped
attitudes unrelated to changing social conditions. Such a lag has occurred
with respect to the community's expectations of the adult children of our
aging population, in a manner which severely disadvantages *all* the generations.

We subscribe to the value of family, but the ways in which we attempt
to foster family feeling and ties are not consonant with current socioeconomic realities. Our attitudes were developed in relation to other groups of
people, for other purposes, and during an earlier phase in history. The
inappropriate social attitudes toward the "responsibilities" of adult children are institutionalized and reflected by clinical approaches and goals in
every sphere of treatment, in planning, policy, legislative enactments, and
in patterns of service delivery. Confronted with a new situation in which
change is the only constant, we still adhere to forms of a long-outmoded
etiquette.

The dramatic increase in the aging population during the twentieth
century has had a profound effect on society as a whole and on the family.
Never before in history have families included so many old people numerically and proportionately, nor have they been so old. At the turn of the
century, the over-65s represented 4% (3 million individuals) of the total

Reprinted with permission from *International Journal of Aging and Human Development*,
1970, *1*, 87–94.

population compared with 10% (20 million individuals) at present; life expectancy at birth has increased from 47 to about 70 (Brotman, 1968a and b). In addition, earlier marriage, earlier parenthood, and fewer large families have narrowed the spanning years between generations (Townsend, 1968), so that the trend is for three generations to develop in the time period that formerly produced two generations (Chilman, 1966).

The family members on whom old people depend are also older. The vast majority of adult children are in the middle years. Those whose parents are in the very oldest stratum of the elderly population are approaching or engaged in the aging phase of life. Therefore, they themselves are experiencing the "insults" of aging such as loss of spouse and peers, mental and physical impairments, enforced retirement, and reduced income.

The dimensions of the situation may be measured in part by the fact that 82% of the elderly have at least one surviving child and most have three or more. Of those, 93% have grandchildren and 40% have great-grandchildren. Thus, most old people belong to three-generation families and "the four generation family is now a common phenomenon" (Townsend, *op. cit.*). Generations two and three—those in the middle—are often caught in the bind of multiple emotional, financial, and instrumental obligations to their own children and to the increasing number of elderly family members. Townsend has pointed out that the emphasis may shift "from the problem of which of the children looks after a widowed parent to the problem of how a middle-aged man and wife can reconcile dependent relationships with *both* sets of parents" (Townsend, *op. cit.*). Reid sums it up by stating that people in their 50s may well "be faced with the responsibility for taking care of as many as four parents and anywhere from one to eight grandparents" (Reid, 1966).

Since the "Good Old Days"

Against that background, what are the facts about adult children? What are their relationships to the elderly? How do they behave? And have they changed since the "good old days?"

The underlying misconception about adult children is the stubbornly persistent myth that they are alienated from and, in general, have neglected the elderly. This is reminiscent of the condemnation of parents (mothers in particular) earlier in this century in relation to the problems of young children. The trail tracing the etiology of Johnny's problems invariable ended on his mother's doorstep (Brody, 1967). Similarly, the present generations of middle-aged and young-aged are now the recipients of blame for abandoning the older generations.

Despite the statistical odds confronting adult children, there is incontrovertible evidence that they behave *responsibly* toward their old parents. A long series of definitive research studies has documented that ties between the generations are strong and viable (Sussman, 1968; Shanas, 1960; Shanas, 1961; Rosow, 1965), that adult children do not abdicate their responsibilities (Reid, *op. cit.*; Streib, 1968), that continuing contacts and services are the rule, and that when they are unable to care for the elderly, a constellation of personal, social, and economic factors may be at work (Townsend, 1965; GAP Report, 1965). Thus, the collective social and cultural rejection of the aged has *not* been acted out on the individual or family level.

Behavior, of course, is not identical to qualitative psychological relationships. However, the clinical evidence also refutes the notion of abandonment (Goldfarb, 1965; GAP Report, 1965; Brody & Gummer, 1967; Brody 1966). At this sophisticated stage in understanding of human psychodynamics, it is a rather peculiar premise that qualitative emotional bonds are severed as the family grows older. The importance of family as the chief formative influence on the young child has long been understood. While the delicate balance of family relationships shifts as the family grows older, the basic psychological patterns and links are carried forward unbroken by time. These patterns persist to the aging phase of the family life cycle. Healthy or not, they are the natural outgrowth of qualitative relationships in the early phases (Brody & Spark, 1966).

Rules of Filial Etiquette

Accepting the ethic of the value of the family ties, how does the contemporary etiquette of filial behavior reflect the realities?

A first rule of filial etiquette concerns living arrangements. Judgmental attitudes expressed by professionals as well as the public are epitomized in the bitter saying, "One mother had room for all her children, but none of them has room for her." Available information shows that "the three generation family to which contemporary commentators often point with nostalgia, in some cases, may have been forced on poor families for lack of any palatable substitute" (Rosenheim, 1965). Donald Kent has characterized as the illusion of the "Golden Past" the fact that "the three generation family pictured as a farm idyl is common, yet all evidence indicates that at no time in any society was a three-generation family ever the common mode, and even less evidence that it was idyllic" (1965).

Where the multigeneration household did exist in the past, it was likely that a young couple, on marrying, lived in the home of the parent. The modern pattern is for the young couple to set up a separate home. By

their own account the elderly prefer to live *near* but not *with* their children
(Shanas, 1962; Beyer & Woods, 1963). Financial problems limit choices
about living arrangements; as income permits, more prefer to live separately (Beyer & Woods, *op. cit.*). Yet the social expectation is that a
middle-aged or aging couple introduce an old parent into their home,
sometimes after half a century of separate living, and often in the crowded
quarters of an urbanized industrialized society.

Such expectations come into sharp focus with regard to families of the
institutionalized elderly. A long inventory of studies in relation to all kinds
of institutions has shown that when such care is requested, it is most often
the last resort (e.g., Lowenthal, 1964; Friedsam & Dick, 1963; Brody,
1969a). In general the children have exhausted all other alternatives,
enduring severe personal, social, and economic stress in the process.
Nevertheless, the superintendent of a large state hospital was recently
quoted in a national magazine as stating that "everyone is sending Grandma to the funny-farm." A rash of articles in popular magazines, deploring
the plight of the institutionalized aged, leaped with *non sequitur* reasoning
to indictment of their hard-hearted children. There is clearly a need to
improve institutional programs and to create new models of care, but to
imply that families should invariably assume the burden is an abdication by
society of its responsibility to carry out that task.

Let us take a close look at the 4% of the elderly who are in institutions
of any kind, the factors leading to their placement, and at their "responsible" family members:

> More than half of the institutionalized elderly are over 80 and the chances of
> becoming a resident increase progressively with advancing age. Only 2% of
> those between 65 and 75, but more than 10% of those over 80 are in institu-
> tions (Brotman, 1968b). Four-fifths have seriously impaired mental function-
> ing and the multiplicity of their physical impairments has been thoroughly
> documented (Goldfarb, 1961; Goldfarb, 1962; Lowenthal, 1964; Simon, 1968;
> Ward, 1967). Family composition is an important factor: proportionately there
> are many times the number of widowed and unmarried people in institutions
> than in the total elderly population, and more with only one adult child.
> Careful research has revealed that "many old people with children continue to
> live at home to an advanced stage of infirmity before seeking admission"
> (Townsend, 1965), and that the death or sudden illness of close relatives are
> the most common events precipitating admission (Townsend, 1965; Beattie &
> Bullock, 1963; Brody & Gummer, *op. cit.*). A study at the Philadelphia
> Geriatric Center showed that some of the "children" of applicants for institu-
> tional care are as old as 74, and forty percent of the applicants have at least one
> child over 60 (Brody, 1966).

The appropriate question is: for which *family* is institutional care of its
oldest members the plan of choice? It is important to view such a service as
one point along the continuum of care in the community to be utilized

when appropriate. For the right person, the right family and at the right time, it is the right service and can represent positive change—security, permanence, medical care, increased comfort and well-being, and relief for all family members from emotional, physical, and economic strain (Brody, 1969).

The assumption is often made that a sophisticated network of community services will eliminate the need for institutional care. But there will probably always be an irreducible number of people requiring comprehensive services which can be offered only on a congregate basis. Hopefully, community services will grow. They will avoid or delay institutionalization for some and help community dwellers to function at a better level of health and well-being, but their growth will be offset by other factors. First, the proportionately greater increase is in the oldest segment of the elderly. The over-85 population is growing at twice the rate of the total elderly population (Grier, 1964). It is that group which is most vulnerable to the convergence of physical and mental impairments demanding round-the-clock supervision and care, and it is often the incapacities of their aging or aged children which operate to make congregate care necessary for the frail very old parent.

Secondly, simply counting the number of persons in institutions, like counting the number who receive services in their own homes, may reflect the quality of existing facilities and their availability to specific groups (e.g., the poor and nonwhites) rather than the need. Long-term care will be made more readily available by implementation and expansion of coverage by Titles 18 and 19. It is to be hoped that the situation of nonwhites will be improved both as to longevity and accessibility of facilities. For example, Negroes now represent 12% of the total population but only 8% of the elderly population. Further, only 4% of the 800,000 people over 65 who are institutionalized are Negro (Brotman, 1967)

To deprecate institutional care per se can only disservice both the elderly and their children—reinforcing their guilt and anxiety even when there clearly is no alternative.

A second rule of filial etiquette, related to the first, is the expectation that adult children provide the services needed by old people in the community. Impaired old people living in the community far out-number those in institutions. The current thrust for community care is exemplified by policies and procedures in many states designed to return elderly psychiatric patients to the community and to intervene to prevent their admission. Assuming the validity of this strategy, we have failed to provide either qualitatively or quantitatively the health and social services needed to enable them to function at a decent level of health and well-being in the community. This responsibility has been left to adult children. Parenthetically, it must be noted that "community" in this context is often a euphemism for placement in other types of institutions, some of which do not provide appropriate care.

The major cross-national study by Ethel Shanas and Associates (1968) revealed that proportionately about 40 times as many older people in England and Denmark are served by public or nonprofit home-help services than in the United States. Less than .5% of elderly community dwellers are served by home nursing in the United States compared with between 1% and 2% for the other two countries. Yet Shanas estimates that one old person in every seven requires health services in his or her own home (Shanas, 1969). The study stated, "In all three countries, the total role of domicilliary and residential services is small. The number of old people actually helped in their housework, provision of meals and care during illness is dwarfed by the number . . . helped . . . by relatives." In this country, however, of the estimated 350,000 bedfast old people in the community (2% of the total over-65 population), between 80% and 90% depend mainly on the family. A critical point is *that where services were provided they supplemented but did not substitute for the services provided by adult children*. Other services, such as day care for impaired old people, temporary care to permit family vacations or to tide families over temporary crises, are practically nonexistent.

A large British study compared the effects of community care of psychiatric patients with the effects of traditional hospital-based services. The burden on families was found to be much more severe when the patient was over 65. The study concluded that effective community care depends on the availability of social supports *to the family* and that the total family situation must be appraised carefully. "Unless this is done, the adverse effect on members of the family may add to rather than subtract from community mental health problems" (Sainsbury, 1969). In short, we talk glibly about "rejection" and "responsibility" but have not provided adult children with the assistance they need in their struggles to care for old people. These struggles are often endured beyond the saturation point, so that they have the very human desire to be relieved of the burdens they carry.

A third rule of filial etiquette concerns financial support of the oldest generations. Support laws in this country (which stem from the Elizabethan poor law) are archaic carry-overs from the time when they were directed at the occasional neglectful child of the occasional older person. Yet the overwhelming majority of states still have legislation requiring support. Kreps has pointed out that the middle generation now supports the other two generations via taxes. In the foreseeable future, this may well be three generations (1965). Despite the economic bind of the middle generation, to quote Schorr's classic monograph, the adult child is often expected to "sacrifice his own, his wife's and his children's resources to assist his parents before the community will accept responsibility" (Schorr, 1960). It is a specious argument that giving money even at the cost of deprivation to self and family, is good for moral fiber and increases love for the needy parent. Love and morality cannot be legislated, and severe economic pressure strains family relations. The consequences of support requirements are to "impose on some old people a standard of living lower than public assistance levels," since they are reluctant to deprive their children and grandchildren. Where support is procured the deprivation is shifted to the younger generations, impeding their own struggle for a better standard of living (Schorr, *op. cit.*). In Pennsylvania, to obtain a reduction in the expected contribution, it is necessary for the old parent to take court action—legally an adversary proceeding. Is this a method of fostering warm family feeling? Hardly.

The hardships of support requirements are most acute when the elderly parent needs long-term health care. The recent working paper of the U.S. Senate Special Committee on Aging states flatly that assurance of adequate income for the aged can "best be provided, or can only be provided through governmental programs." And it notes that "at the oldest ages, the need is especially great for the types of health care not covered by Medicare, notably long-term nursing home care . . . drugs" (Economics of Aging, 1969).

Medicare has been an immense step forward in relieving families of the crushing costs of health care for the elderly with acute illnesses. Yet in many states, long-term care is funded through public assistance programs with punitive LRR (legally responsible relatives) scales of expected contributions. In Pennsylvania, for example, two elderly patients may be side by side in a nursing facility. Patient 1 is receiving 100 days of extended care and his children are not required to contribute. The children of Patient 2 will need to contribute, perhaps for years. A third patient, as sick as the others, is not in a nursing home at all. If his children cannot afford the required contribution, he may be sleeping on a sofa in the adult child's home, or depriving a school child of a room and privacy, or straining beyond endurance an adult daughter's capacity to provide care for both the elderly parent and her sick husband.

The Total Family

What the elderly value most from their children is affection, not money (Schorr, *op. cit.*); caring, rather than the particular method by which it is expressed. It is the task of professionals in all disciplines to exercise leadership by challenging, rather than reflecting, existing attitudes and approaches.

If we want to help the elderly, and if we subscribe to the value of family, it is essential to look to the needs of the total family. The impact of aging is felt by all generations—individually and collectively. At this juncture, the systems of care and service are stretching family ties thin, rather than supporting them. The pseudoethical question of priorities— that is to choose between the old and the young in allocating resources–can only result in disadvantaging all of society. The well-being of each genera- tion is inextricably linked to that of the others, and the etiquette of filial behavior requires revision.

References

Beattie, Walter M., Jr., and Bullock, Jean, *Preface to a counselling service*. Health and Welfare Council of Metropolitan St. Louis, St. Louis, Miss. unpublished, 1963.

Beyer, Glenn H., and Woods, Margaret E. Living and activity patterns of the aged (Research Report #6). Ithaca, N.Y.: Center for Housing and Environmental Studies, Cornell University, 1963.

Brody, Elaine M. The aging family. *Gerontologist, 6,* 4, Dec. 1966.

Brody, Elaine M. Aging is a family affair. *Public Welfare,* April 1967.

Brody, Elaine M. Follow-up study of applicants and non-applicants to a voluntary home. *Gerontologist, 9,* 3, Autumn 1969.

Brody, Elaine M. Institutional settings: Nursing homes and other congregate care facilities. Lecture prepared for Institute on Community Mental Health and Aging: An Overview, University of Southern California, 1969 summer Insti- tute for Advanced Study in Gerontology, July 1969b.

Brody, Elaine, and Gummer, Burton, Aged applicants and non-applicants to a voluntary home: An exploratory comparison. *Gerontologist, 7,* 4, Dec. 1967.

Brody, Elaine, and Spark, Geraldine. Institutionalization of the aged: A family crisis. *Family Process 5,* 1, March 1966.

Brotman, Herman. *National population trends as of July 1, 1966.* (Useful Facts #15). Admin. on Aging, U.S. Dept. of H.E.W., Jan. 6, 1967.

Brotman, Herman. Every tenth American. Presented at State Conference, Iowa Commission on the Aging, Des Moines, Iowa, Oct. 1968a.

Brotman, Herman B. Who are the aged: A demographic view. Paper presented at 21st Annual University of Michigan Conference on Aging, Ann Arbor, Michi- gan, Aug. 5, 1968. Paper appears also as *Useful facts #42,* Admin. on Aging, H.E.W., mimeo, 1968b.

Chilman, C. S. Popluation dynamics and poverty in the United States. *Welfare in Review,* 4:3, U.S. Dept. of H.E.W., Washington, D.C., 1966.

Ecomonics of aging: Toward a full share in abundance. A working paper prepared by task force for the Special Committee on Aging, U.S. Senate, U.S. Govern- ment Printing Office, March 1969.

Friedsam, H. J., and Dick, H. R. Decisions leading to institutionalization of the aged. (Final Report). Social Security Administration Cooperative Research and Demonstration Grant Program Project 037 (C1) 20–031, unpublished, 1963.

GAP (Group for the Advancement of Psychiatry) Report #59, *Psychiatry and the aged: An introductory report*. New York, 1965.

Goldfarb, Alvin I. Current trends in the management of the psychiatrically ill aged, in P. H. Hoch and J. Zubin (Eds.), *Psychopathology of aging*. New York: Grune & Stratton, 1961.

Goldfarb, Alvin I. Prevalence of psychiatric disorders in metropolitan old age and nursing homes. *Journal of the American Geriatric Society, 10,* 77–84, 1962.

Goldfarb, Alvin I. Psychodynamics and the three-generation family, chap. 2 in Ethel Shanas and Gordon F. Streib. (Eds.), *Social structure and the family: Generational relationships*. Englewood Cliffs, N.J.: Prentice-Hall, 1965.

Grier, G. W. Goals and objects in aging; creating opportunities for older people. *Selected papers*. 4th Annual Conference of State Executives on Aging, U.S. Dept. of H.E.W., Washington, D.C., 1964.

Kent, Donald P. Aging—fact or fancy. *Gerontologist 5,* 2, June 1965.

Kreps, Juanita M. The economics of intergenerational relationships in Ethel Shanas and Gordon F. Streib (Eds.), *Social structure and the family: Generational relationships*. Englewood Cliffs, N.J.: Prentice-Hall, 1965.

Lowenthal, Marjorie. *Lives in distress,* New York: Basic Books, 1964.

Reid, Otto M., Aging Americans, a review of cooperative research projects. *Welfare in review,* U.S. Dept. of H.E.W., Vol. 4, 1–2, 1966.

Rosenheim, Margaret K. Social welfare and its implications for family planning, in Ethel Shanas and Gordon F. Streib, (Eds.), *Social structure and the family: Generational relationships,* Englewood Cliffs, N.J.: Prentice-Hall, 1965.

Rosow, Irving. The aged, family and friends. *Social Security Bulletin, 28,* 11, U.S. Dept. of H.E.W., Social Security Administration, Nov. 1965.

Sainsbury, Peter. Paper presented at symposium on Regression and Dependency in the Aged, sponsored by the Boston Society for Gerontologic Psychiatry, as reported in *Geriatric Focus, 8,* 11, June 1, 1969.

Schorr, Alvin L. *Filial responsibility in the modern American family*. U.S. Government Printing Office, Washington, D.C. 1960.

Shanas, Ethel. Family responsibility and the health of older people. *Journal of Gerontology, 15,* 1960.

Shanas, Ethel. Family relationships of older people (Health Information Foundation Research Series 20). Oct. 1961.

Shanas, Ethel. *The health of older people: A social survey*. Cambridge: Harvard University Press, 1962.

Shanas, Ethel. Health and incapacity in later life, chap. 2 in Ethel Shanas and Associates(Eds.), *Old people in three industrial societies*. New York: Atherton, 1968.

Shanas, Ethel. Measuring the home health needs of the aged in five countries. Paper presented at Eighth International Congress of Gerontology, Washington, D.C., Aug. 1969.

Shanas, Ethel, and Associates. *Old people in three industrial societies*. New York: Atherton, 1968.

Simon, Alexander. The geriatric mentally ill. *Gerontologist, 8*, 1, spring 1968.

Streib, Gordon F. Family patterns in retirement. *Journal of Social Issues, 14*, 2, 1958.

Sussman, Marvin B. Relationships of adult children with their parents, chap. 4 in Ethel Shanas and Gordon F. Streib (Eds.), *Social structure and the family: Generational relationships*. Englewood Cliffs, N.J.: Prentice-Hall, 1965.

Townsend, Peter. The effects of family structure on the likelihood of admission to an institution in old age: The application of a general theory, in Ethel Shanas and Gordon F. Streib (Eds.), *Social structure and the family: Generational relationships*, Englewood Cliffs, N.J.: Prentice-Hall, 1965.

Townsend, Peter. The structure of the family, chap. 6 in Ethel Shanas and Associates, *Old people in three industrial societies*, New York: Atherton, 1968.

Ward, Morton. Medical care of the elderly. *Proceedings, Institute on the Significance of Medicare: A System for the Delivery of Comprehensive Medical Care*. Philadelphia Geriatric Center, May 1967.

New Thoughts on Filial Behavior

This chapter was written for presentation in October 1969 at the conference Old Age: Values and Prospects sponsored by the Philadelphia Geriatric Center and the Stephen Smith Home for the Aged. I was left entirely free to choose my own subject within that framework. At the time I had been a social worker at the PGC for about 14 years. During the early years I had been responsible for client intake and had seen and tried to help thousands of older people applying for institutional care and their families. My choice of topic was stimulated by the suffering, often the agony, experienced by the total family. The painful experience of applying for institutional care was (and is still) exacerbated by inappropriate social values and by social policies that expressed those values. Not only were the adult children the targets of the myth of the "dumping" of old people, but they were their own targets, having internalized the same values. To compound the problem, supportive community services were practically nonexistent.

My talk, then, was an angry one. It was a plea for understanding of the realities that were not synchronous with values and for psychological and concrete relief for the members of families of older people. My perspective was the family *including* the older person, and it assumed that a focus on the older individual alone was incorrect and self-defeating from both the theoretical and practical standpoints. I was particularly concerned with the stress on those I characterized as being "in the middle," that is, the middle generation of middle-aged and young-aged adult children confronted with multiple obligations to the younger and older generations.

Now, 12 years later, as might be expected, some things have changed and some have not. Overall, the *myth of family abandonment* has persisted stubbornly despite the continuing accumulation of research evidence to the contrary. The reality is that demographic developments have exceeded projections; that is, the proportion of very old (and therefore vulnerable) people has increased dramatically proportionate to the care-giving generations. Yet the work of Ethel Shanas (nationwide), the General Accounting Office (in the Cleveland area), Barry Gurland (in New York), Steve Brody (in Luzerne and Wyoming, Pennsylvania, counties), and others document that the high level of family care giving has continued despite the increased pressures. There has been a growing emphasis on developing community services, but the needs far exceed the supply.

It would be fascinating to explore the roots of that tenacious myth of abandonment. It probably has multiple sources including the now-disproved theory of the primacy of the isolated nuclear family; the negative view of institutions, so that even appropriate and necessary placement is considered "dumping"; the fear of taxpayers that community services will encourage family withdrawal and increase the tax load; the need of a neglectful society for a scapegoat; and an expression of fear on the part of older people (and younger ones) of abandonment or loss of one's home. As we all know, losses of various kinds are often experienced psychologically as abandonment. As Ethel Shanas's research indicated, among the blamers of families are professionals who generally see the families who are in trouble and childless old people. The myth may also be reinforced by the illusion of professionals that we are the principal caregivers to the old—this in the face of evidence that 80–90% of all health and social services are provided by the family.

Among planners and researchers there has been in recent years an increasing recognition of the role of the family and an increasingly insistent call for family-focused services. But such approaches have not yet been operationalized in social policy. For example, day care services for the impaired aged are sparse, unevenly distributed, and in many states not reimbursed. Respite care (temporary care for relief of families) is not reimbursed at all. The new emphasis on family care cheers the family on but does little to support and strengthen its care-giving activities. One suspects that it often flows from the assumption that family care is cost effective, though the social and economic effects of overburdening the family are rarely considered. Elsewhere I have asked, "At what point does the expectation of filial responsibility become social irresponsibility?"

Parenthetically, since the etiquette chapter was written, there has been a step forward in one aspect of social policy: Medicaid has resulted in families being relieved of the crushing economic burden of paying for long-term institutional care. That is, the LRR requirements no longer obtain for nursing home care. It is ironic, however, that the relief afforded is often only a paper relief because in many areas the low reimbursement rates make Medicaid beds unavailable and little or nothing has been accomplished in improving the quality of life for institutional residents.

In the past 10 years a broad major social trend has occurred with a direct bearing on the subject of filial responsibility and it intensifies my concern for the care-giving generation. I am referring to the rapid rate of entry of women into the work force—not only young women but middle-aged women who are working for the first time or resuming interrupted careers. This development inevitably will affect their capacities and availability to meet the needs of the dependent elderly. The evidence so far is that they have not substituted work for parent care but have added to their responsibilities.

My interest in recent years therefore is focused more sharply on middle-aged and young-old women, for it is they who are the primary caregivers. I consider that they are emerging as a high-risk group who now and in future will increasingly be subjected to the multiple and often competing demands of their roles as workers, parents, spouses, and responsible filial caregivers. They also, I suggest, will be caught between potentially conflicting values: the value of women doing out-of-home work vis-à-vis the traditional value that care of the elderly is a family responsibility. My colleagues and I at the Philadelphia Geriatric Center are involved in research on these matters, hoping ultimately to develop recommendations for policy, planning, and clinical approaches that would relieve the stresses and strengthen the family as care-giving unit.

In closing I should note that, though much remains to be done, things in general are significantly better for older people themselves than they were 10 years ago. We have certainly experienced a process of consciousness-raising, and there have been advances in income maintenance, housing, community services, professional and public interest, and so on. There has not been parallel progress in making knowledge about families speak to their current and future conditions. If we are to make things better for older people, we must help their families as well, or we will increase and perpetuate problems down through the generations.

2

Sexuality and Intimacy in Later Life

Mary Ann P. Sviland

This chapter describes a therapy program for helping elderly couples become sexually liberated and some critical age-related sexual problems of which the counselor must be aware in working with the elderly. To provide an adequate context for the objectives and methods of the treatment, it is necessary first to describe some psychosocial issues that influence sexuality in the elderly. These issues include: negative social attitudes toward elderly sexuality, knowledge of sexual behavior in the elderly, and cultural-physiological factors interacting to restrict elderly sexuality.

Negative Social Attitudes

Sexual discrimination against the elderly still exists in this era of expanding sexual understanding and corresponding liberalization of attitudes. Until recently, society has found the sexual needs of elderly persons amusing; insignificant jokes involving old people and sex brought inevitable laughter. The insignificance of elderly sexuality is reflected in sexual research. Only 3 out of 1,700 pages in the two Kinsey reports are devoted to the older age group (Claman, 1966). The Masters and Johnson (1966) study of sexual response included only 31 men and women beyond age 60 in a total population of 694 people. Part of this inadequate study population may reflect difficulty in eliciting active cooperation from the elderly. Apparently societal strictures make the elderly defensive regarding disclosure of their sexual life. But many people are terribly confused and vitally interested in information about the norms of sexuality in the elderly population (Feigenbaum et al., 1967).

The general social belief that sexuality is the domain of the young has resigned many senior citizens to premature impotence, frustration, self-depreciation, or loneliness. The cultural myth that impotence is a natural phenomenon of aging is so entrenched that even aging physicians are

This article was originally published as, "Helping Elderly Couples Become Sexually Liberated" in *The Counseling Psychologist*, 1975, 5, 1, 67–72.

capable of becoming panicked at one or two erectile failures. More pathetic is the elderly patient seen in counseling practice who is laden with guilt and shame at his or her continuing sexuality and masturbation because of partner unavailability. Since feelings and behaviors are related to societal expectations, many elderly people feel guilty about healthy feelings because they are unacceptable to themselves, the physician, or other people with whom they live (Newman & Nichols, 1966). Counselors, too, may need to examine their own social biases regarding the aged and increase their understanding of elderly sexual function to foster a supporting climate for the resolution of healthy sexual function in their elderly patients.

Counseling elderly patients in improved sexual function and adjustment is not an end in itself but a means of fulfilling a deeper core: the timeless need of all humans for intimacy and love. Sexuality is one avenue of facilitating trust, affection, and caring. As Dean observed: "We know that old people do not cease to be human just because they are old; they have many of the desires of the young, and their need for companionship is even greater. Nor does the desire for romance, intrigue or even sex necessarily disappear with advancing years" (1966).

Thwarted sexuality may be a greater contribution to depression in the elderly than previously assumed. The lack of an intimate and empathic relationship may account for much of the clinical depression currently diagnosed as involutional. Loneliness and feelings of not being attractive or wanted or needed create depression irrespective of age. The positive value of companionship to general physical health is seen in the higher illness and morbidity rates of older single persons.

Primary opposition to sexuality in the aged arises from adult children who view their aged parents' normal urges for intimacy and romance as a threat of social disgrace or as signs of second childhood (Dean, 1966). The negative attitude of the children toward their parents holds much more strongly for the mother than the father, which then generalizes to all elderly women. Claman (1966) describes the identification of parent ideals with old people which blocks acceptance of their sexuality thus:

> Our aversion to serious discussion about sex in older people may be based on the fact that we identify old people with our parents, and therefore are made uncomfortable when we think of our parents in this connection. Sam Levinson, the school-teacher-homespun philosopher of television fame, once said: "When I first found out how babies were born, I couldn't believe it! To think that my mother and father would do such a thing! . . . " Then, after reflexion, he added: "My father—maybe, but my mother—never!"

Mateless parents who express loneliness are told to take up a hobby and are pressed into household service, thereby adding to their social isolation, instead of being encouraged to reenter the mainstream of life through another marriage. The horror toward parental sexual "acting out" is readily observed in the strict nursing home sexual prohibitions designed to appease the bill-paying adult children. Cognizant of the positive value of sexuality in the aged, Kassell (1974) advocated as humanistic the free acceptance of sexuality in homes for the aged.

Research Findings on Physical and Circumstantial Effects on Elderly Sexuality

Contrary to popular mythology, the greater sexual interest, activity, and capacity in earlier life, the greater the interest, activity, and capacity in later years (Claman, 1966). This supports the concept of continuity of lifestyle. Early termination of sexual activity occurs where sex is not important in life (Pfeiffer & Davis, 1972).

Male sexual function shows a steady decline after peak responsiveness attained around age 18, whereas female sexuality reaches peak responsiveness in the late 30s and early 40s and maintains this level into the 60s (Kaplan, 1974). After the 50s frequency of orgasm and length of refractory period has changed significantly in the male; in sharp contrast to men, elderly women remain capable of enjoying multiple orgasms (Kaplan, 1974). Between 50 and 60 years of age the wife may want sex more than the husband is able to give (Kinsey, Pomeroy & Martin, 1948; Kinsey, Pomeroy, Martin & Gebhard, 1953).

Partner availability and good health are crucial variables to sexual continuence. Any acute or chronic illness lowers male sexual responsiveness; and if his wife is ill the aging male is restricted in sexual opportunity (Masters & Johnson, 1970). Swartz (1966) found 7 out of 10 healthy married couples over 60 years were sexually active, some into their late 80s. In contrast, only 7% of the single, divorced, and widowed over 60 years old were found to be sexually active (Newman & Nichols, 1966).

Surveys undertaken at the Kinsey Institute (Kinsey, Pomeroy, & Martin, 1948) and at Duke University (Newman & Nichols, 1966) have disclosed that 70% of married males aged 70 remained sexually active with a mean frequency of .9 per week with some males maintaining a frequency of 3 times per week. By age 75, 50% of married males are still sexually active (Claman, 1966).

Regarding female sexual incidence, 70% of married women and 12% of postmarried women aged 60 engaged in coitus. The incidence of masturbation was higher for postmarital women, with 25% of single females aged 70 still masturbating (Christenson & Gagnon, 1965). Sexual abstinence in the elderly women is not primarily biologic but is influenced by social and psychological factors, for they do not seek partner replacements unless they are unusually attractive and secure, with exceptional personal assets (Kaplan, 1974).

Worry over sexual failure can create secondary impotence. Culture-induced unconscious sex anxiety may cause premature sex abandonment; therefore the supernormal frequencies found in some elderly males may more accurately reflect innate capacity and could become the average expectation in a more guiltless, biologically natural culture (Stokes, 1951). Abnormal sex behavior in the elderly cannot be described when normal sex behavior is still unknown owing to lack of published research (Hirt, 1966). We are realizing that the decline of sexual activity in the elderly is less a factor of physiology than an artifact of social prohibitions and lack of willing partner availability.

Interaction of Restricting Cultural and Physiological Factors

If it is true that sexuality in the elderly is primarily spouse-related and that companionship increases life expectancy and self-worth, then elderly patients who miss intimacy and sexual expression should be directed in counseling to finding a mate. Counseling should also be directed to increasing their sexual satisfaction. Given that sex and companionship are important for the elderly, the interacting physical and cultural limitations to their sex adjustment must next be examined.

Although the culture imposes some restrictions on the elderly male, his sexuality is primarily limited by physical factors. In contrast the elderly female, where physical capabilities and responsiveness have not been depreciated, is primarily limited from sexual expression by cultural factors. Understanding of this distinction is necessary for a more rational approach to sexuality in the aged.

The elderly man experiences reduced sexual stamina, which adversely affects his sex life. Biologic changes include: decreased orgasm frequency, longer refractory periods following orgasm, loss of awareness of pending orgasm, and greater need for direct stimulation for arousal (Kaplan, 1974). Sexual adjustment and satisfaction in the elderly male may require shifts in the sexual pattern. The woman may need to take a more active role in sexual situations, and both partners may need to learn new behaviors to increase compatibility and minimize the functional effects of aging on male sexuality.

Since aging does not substantially affect sexual capacity of elderly women compared to elderly men, cultural factors such as the double standard impede sexual actualization in elderly females. Women are faced with approximately 11 years of matelessness, for they tend to marry males 4 years older and the life expectancy for males is 7 years shorter. Females outnumber males 138.5 to 100 at age 65 and 156.2 to 100 at age 75 (Pfeiffer & Davis, 1972), which makes it easier for widowed males to remarry.

To avert the problem of protracted widowhood, solutions from prolonging the vigor and life of the male to polygamy have been proposed (Pfeiffer & Davis, 1972; Kassell, 1966). Dean (1972) proposed a more parsimonious solution:

> It is an irony of fate and an anatomico-physiological paradox that a male-oriented society has propagated the custom of a man's marrying a woman younger than himself. Many a woman, after reaching the menopause and being freed of the fear of pregnancy, is more desirous of sex than ever before, but it is precisely at such a propitious time that her husband, who is five or ten years older, may begin to show impotence. Many think there would be much less sexual frustration in later years—and perhaps fewer widows—if the chronological trend were reversed so that women marry younger men to begin with.

If not initial marriage, at least dating in older life should allow elderly females access to younger males without social censure based on mother-son incest taboos. There is no need to view sexual contact with an older person as physically repugnant; the attitude stems from our cult of youth as beauty. Many of the physical signs of aging, the paunch and the wrinkles, are due to poor body care, not the aging process. Many elderly people who lived prudently are remarkably attractive without the physical signs we attribute to old age. People, both male and female, should be allowed to pick their life partners on the sole basis of compatibility. This would make acceptable the relationship of the younger male with an older female. Age-discrepant relationships do not necessarily indicate psychopathology for either party. Since the younger man would benefit from the experience of the older woman, the positive sexual and psychological benefits afforded each party would make this combination as rewarding as a liaison with a partner of one's same age. In dealing with the expanding geriatric population and their sexual needs, society will have to take a more liberalized view of alternate lifestyles. People should be allowed to choose their mates on the basis of psychological compatibility, not preconceived standards of propriety or normalcy.

Sexual Therapy to Help Elderly Couples Become Sexually Liberated

Many therapists and sexual therapy programs are now directing themselves to enhancing sexuality (Kaplan, 1974). Therapy modalities that range from weekend sexual workshops directed to body awareness and nondemand mutual pleasuring to the more traditional techniques are helping elderly people obtain a more fulfilling sexual adjustment.

I have been involved in a therapy program to help elderly couples become sexually liberated (Sviland, 1974). This included couples over the age of 60 with a basically sound marital relationship and no sexual dysfunction who wanted to decrease their inhibitions and expand their repertoire of sexual behaviors to conform to recently liberated mores. Raised in a more prohibitive era they wanted to erase still-prevalent internal taboos toward such activities as oral-genital sex or sex for pleasure.

The primary therapeutic goal is increased sexual satisfaction. A universal subgoal is permission to accept one's sexuality without guilt or shame. The therapist then hooks the superego and becomes a stronger authority figure, granting permission for sexual curiosity and exploration. The therapist must remain flexible throughout the therapy, shifting from exercises to psychotherapy with insight as needed. Assignments are always in "the here and now" of what the couple currently feels comfortable to work on. Exercises proceed slowly, with patients in control, to prevent anxiety or negative emotional response. The basic attitude put across is that sex can be playful and enjoyable and another way of expressing affection. One does what one wants when one feels like it. Sex is not a ritual.

Procedure

Voluntary treatment occurred in a hospital setting with referral from medical services. The flood of applicants attests to the needs of elderly couples in the community at large for this type of counseling. The outpatient treatment consisted of weekly 1-hour sessions with homework assignments. Treatment combined educational materials, sexual exercises, assertion training, and traditional psychotherapy techniques according to the needs and goals of each couple. Since the whole issue of sexuality is highly personal, varying with value systems, the therapist never advocated specific behaviors but helped the couple achieve self-stated goals.

First sessions focused on exploration of: (1) current sex life, (2) subjective feelings about current sex life, (3) marital dynamics, (4) degree of attitude change mutually desired, and (5) definition of goals and approximate number of sessions required. In the conduct of therapy with the aged it is very important to recognize that the sexual values, attitudes, and especially capabilities may differ markedly among the elderly. Therefore the rate of progress of introducing various information and techniques requires astute pacing to fit the characteristics of the clients.

Educational materials may be introduced at this point for the purpose of: (1) desensitization to previously taboo behaviors, (2) technique learning, (3) increasing eroticism, and (4) increasing sexual fantasy. Couples may be sent into the field to view X-rated movies, self-selected, and to peruse sexual handbooks such as Comfort's *Joy of Sex* (1972) and Otto and Otto's *Total Sex* (1973). Couples generally experience a sense of naughty intrigue with these assignments. Their responses to these materials are then explored and used to establish sexual exercise goals. Increasing the fantasy system and general level of eroticism facilitates later homework sex assignments. The wife may especially need help with integration of increased explicit sex fantasies and her self-ideal—in other words, to understand that a woman can enjoy and think about sex and still be a lady.

At this stage, increased physical attractiveness and flirtation techniques may be included where the relationship is dull because the couple take each other for granted and do not satisfy each other's romantic needs. Each spouse defines explicit attire and mannerisms that would increase erotic attraction. The husband is told, "If your wife were a young secretary, how would you have to look and what would you have to say to get her to take you seriously as a potential lover?" The wife is told, "If you were widowed and wanted to trap this man in a field of rough competition, how would you have to dress and act and talk to turn him into an ardent suitor?" Simultaneous homework exercises to replicate the playfulness, intrigue, and joy of dating may include candlelight dinners, unexpected love notes, and flirtatious conversations.

Couples write in detail their ideal sexual fantasy before body contact exercises are introduced. The couple exchange their fantasies and behavior to supplement each party's fantasy. Frequently the wife's fantasy indicates a need for more romantic behavior to enhance nurturance and tenderness rather than specific sex acts.

Next sessions involve selected sexual exercises. Sensate-focus exercises involving hand, foot, and head caresses may be initially employed. Opening communication is vital so partners can frankly convey without shame or anxiety what their sexual needs are, which may not agree with what the textbooks state is normative. To this end, the nonthreatening pleasuring exercises developed by Masters and Johnson and by Hartman and Fithian are very useful. Specific sex techniques are approached in a graduated series of steps to prevent anxiety or negative emotional response.

This treatment was markedly successful in changing behavior and attitudes within weeks. Following goal attainment of increased sexual happiness, therapy is extended with minor variations on the exercises to insure a stable system of consistent positive response to recently acquired behaviors with absence of ensuing marital or intrapsychical conflict.

Special Considerations
Critical to Sex Therapy with the Aged

Depression and sexual avoidance following goal success. Some couples who were delighted with their new-found sexual liberation, experi-
mentation, and enjoyment developed a marked avoidance of sexuality
shortly after treatment success. Exploration disclosed that this avoidance
was a psychological defense against depression elicited by sexual liberation
in confrontation with sexual limitations resulting from the physiological
changes of aging. In essence, this was like giving them the keys to a new
sports car, then rationing the gasoline to Sunday driving only. For some,
sexual expansiveness, then, brought a closer identification with the dying
process than with the vitality of youth.

Although this phenomenon has not been previously reported, a major
shortcoming of short-term sexual therapies without follow-up is that therapy concludes before later dynamic shifts occur. In sexual therapy with
elderly couples it is imperative to continue treatment until both partners
have integrated mutual self-acceptance of their age-bound capacities without devaluation or wistful regrets to regain the lost capacity of youth.

*Shifting stereotyped roles and techniques to minimize the differential
effects on aging.* Although the female does not experience much shift in
her sexual capacity with aging, the male undergoes distinct performance
changes. Both partners must understand and accept these changes and
alter their sexual techniques accordingly to minimize the effects so both
partners are left feeling mutually satisfied.

With aging the male experiences a decline in orgasm, although frequent and enjoyable erections can still be maintained (Kaplan, 1974). The
male must be helped to understand without loss of self-esteem or anxiety
that not every erection can result in orgasm. Elderly couples must be
taught to enjoy each sexual encounter for what it brings without performance demands. The female can remain multiple orgasmic throughout her
life. Therefore Masters and Johnson (1970) suggested that the elderly man
enjoy love play with the wife without the ultimate goal of orgasm each time
sex play is initiated. If he is not competitive with his wife and is secure in his
own sexuality he can find pleasure and stimulation in helping her achieve
her capacity for orgasm. Both must understand that the touchdown mental-
ity of our culture requiring end-product orgasm impedes sexual pleasure.
Neither partner should require orgasm from themselves or their mate to
consider the sexual relationship successful. This relieves the necessity of
faking an orgasm.

The aging male may have distinct loss of feeling of ejaculatory inevitability. Where this occurs, the couple must forego simultaneous orgasm as

the ultimate satisfactory act since the male is unable voluntarily to prolong copulation to await the female orgasm. In essence, elderly couples must be shifted to acceptance of tandem nondemand pleasuring. The elderly male may also experience a paradoxical reaction wherein, in prolonged sexual activity, should he lose erection, he is unable to obtain another for 12–24 hours, which is the same as if he had an orgasm (Kaplan, 1974). It is psychologically better for the male to allow himself to experience orgasm freely at any stage of love play, then continue pleasuring the female, rather than concentrating on maintaining the erection and losing it.

As the male becomes older he requires more intense direct stimulation of the genital region to obtain erection and ejaculation. The female may need to become a more active participant in the sex act. This can be highly threatening to couples with rigidly stereotyped, narrowly defined sex roles. I have seen couples who viewed as mutually satisfactory their sex style wherein the wife never touched the male genitalia. As a first step to desensitization of direct stimulation of the male genitalia, the female must understand that this need is not a reflection of her lessening physical attractiveness to stimulate her mate but part of the aging process of the male. Both must be helped more actively to give and receive pleasure without shame or fear that this is shifting their stereotype of what is acceptable or should be reasonable for the male or female role in sexuality.

Working through obstructive marital dynamics. Before sexual therapy can begin, it is necessary first to work through any negative transactions and remove hidden resentments. Many times the bedroom is a battleground for hostilities and resentments arising elsewhere in the relationship. Improved sexual adjustment is improbable where the partners are occupied in power struggles, uncooperativeness, and withholding of behaviors that would satisfy the partner's sexual desires.

One case comes to mind wherein the couple was locked into a repetitive, destructive transaction in which the wife, following a transactional analysis script of "Rapo" (Berne, 1964), would be extremely seductive until the husband took the bait and made a sexual overture, when she would angrily reject him. This script was comparable to the husband's script of "Kick Me." The wife repeatedly requested sexuality in the context of romanticism while the husband was consistently blunt, sabotaging directed homework assignments. The sexual script outcomes of outrage in the wife and anger at rejection in the husband served as fuel for revenge in a more pervasive marital power struggle. Although this couple were easily able to liberate attitudinally and expand their repertoire of sexual behavior, sexual adjustment could not take place until this transactional dynamic was broken through and there was a loosening of the competitiveness and power struggle in the sexual scene.

A major shortcoming exists in sexual therapies that focus narrowly on specific acts. Sexual behavior must be examined from the wider perspective of the total marital relationship. Increased sexual gratification requires a shift in positive feelings for the partner and will not automatically occur from technique improvement alone. There are various types of marital and sexual dynamics occurring in ongoing relationships. These must be examined individually in treatment programs specifically designed either to maintain this balance or to shift the balance constructively for both parties, or the program will be defeated.

Mutuality in sexual goals. Another problem in sexual therapy with the elderly involves mutual acceptance of liberated sexual goals. Typically, in cases of goal incompatibility, the husband wants his wife to become more sexually expansive while the wife wants to avoid any form of sex. The wife's disinterest in sex may be based on years of lack of enjoyment and orgastic dysfunction owing to the husband's insensitivity to the wife's needs or to a chronic deteriorated relationship. Therapy directed to opening communication and marital dynamics must precede sexual expansion techniques. Sexual therapy is contraindicated over traditional psychotherapy where deeper intrapsychical conflicts result in sexual avoidance.

In general, where elderly couples have a good relationship and no sexual problems but want to become sexually liberated, they are given permission to experiment with as wide a range of sexual behaviors as desired. Later they discard or incorporate these behaviors into their sexual patterns according to their own values. It is a mistake for one partner to engage in any specific act to please the other if unconscious aversion is not extinguished. In one case the wife was highly motivated to become more sexually liberal. She expressed conscious enjoyment of recently learned fellatio. Yet loss of voice occurred 4 days following a dream of gagging to death on a penis. When this was interpreted and she was given permission to permanently discontinue fellatio, her voice rapidly returned. Since the couple now enjoy a wide range of other learned pleasuring behaviors, discarding fellatio was no significant loss to the husband.

Summary

For maximum long-lasting therapeutic benefit, sexual therapy should focus beyond specific training of sexual behaviors to treating the total interpersonal relationship. With the elderly couple, therapy must extend to working through depression at the confrontation of age-related physical limitations and to integration of acceptance of current sexual capacity. Sexual therapy directed to helping elderly couples become sexually liberated not only has positive social value but has enabled elderly couples to open communication, increase intimacy and self-esteem, and enjoy without guilt sexual pleasures society accords as acceptable to its youth. Society should provide more such services to elderly couples and publicize their availability.

References

Berne, E. *Games people play*. New York: Grove, 1964.

Christenson, C. V., and Gagnon, J. H. Sexual behavior in a group of older women. *Journal of Gerontology*, 1965, *20*, 351–356.

Claman, A. D. Introduction to panel discussion: Sexual difficulties after 50. *Canadian Medical Association Journal*, 1966, *94*, 207.

Comfort, A. *Joy of Sex*. New York: Crown, 1972.

Dean, S. R. Sin and senior citizens. *Journal of the American Geriatric Society*, 1966, *14*, 935–938.

Dean, S. R. Sexual behavior in middle life. *American Journal of Psychiatry*, 1972, *128*, 1267.

Feigenbaum, E. M.; Lowenthal, M.F.; and Trier, M. L. Aged care confused and hungry for sex information. *Geriatric Focus*, 1967, *5*, 2.

Hirt, N. B. The psychiatrist's view. Panel discussion: Sexual difficulties after 50. *Canadian Medical Association Journal*, 1966, *94*, 213–214.

Kaplan, H. S. *The new sexual therapy*. New York: Brunner/Mazel, 1974.

Kassell, V. Polygamy after 60. *Geriatrics*, 1966, *21*, 214–218.

Kassell, V. *You never outgrow your need for sex*. Presented at 53rd Annual Meeting New England Hospital Assembly, Boston, March 27, 1974.

Kinsey, A. C.; Pomeroy, W. B.; Martin, C. I. *Sexual behavior in the human male*. Philadelphia: Saunders, 1948.

Kinsey, A. C.; Pomeroy, W. B.; Martin, C. I.; and Gebhard, P. H. *Sexual behavior in the human female*. Philadelphia: Saunders, 1953.

Masters, G., and Johnson, V. E. *Human sexual response*. Boston: Little, Brown, 1966.

Masters, G., and Johnson, V. E. *Human sexual inadequacy*. Boston: Little, Brown, 1970.

Newman, G., and Nichols, C. B. Sexual activities and attitudes in older persons. *Journal of the American Medical Association*, 1966, *173*, 33–35.

Otto, H. A., and Otto, R. *Total sex*. New York: New American Library, 1973.

Pfeiffer, E., and Davis, G. C. Determinants of sexual behavior in middle and old age. *Journal of the American Geriatrics Society*, 1972, *20*, 151–158.

Stokes, W. R. Sexual functioning in the aging male. *Geriatrics*, 1951, *6*, 304–308.

Sviland, M. A. P. *Helping elderly couples become sexually liberated*. Presented at Western Psychological Association Convention at San Francisco, April 28, 1974.

Swartz, D. The urologist's view. Panel discussion: Sexual difficulties after 50. *Canadian Medical Association Journal*, 1966, *94*, 213–214.

3

Of Poker, Roles, and Aging

Ken Stone

Richard A. Kalish

"Goals based only on power or acquisitiveness, which were compelling in an earlier phase of life, are no longer appropriate. New ways must be found to use time and to enhance satisfaction and self-realization."[1] The White House Conference on Aging background paper on retirement roles and activities was expressing a frequently held assumption. They overlooked, albeit understandably, a role for the elderly that does lead to a goal based in large part upon power and acquisitiveness, an old—indeed ancient—way of enhancing satisfaction: gambling.

McLuhan[2] makes an interesting pronouncement in contrasting gambling and the use of alcohol. He states that alcohol leads to "festive involvement" in the Western world of highly individualistic and fragmented relationships. On the other hand, "in tribal societies, gambling . . . is a welcome avenue of entrepreneurial effort and individual initiative to the point of mocking the individualist social structure. The tribal virtue is the capitalist vice" (p. 249).[2] And a little later, "when we, too, are prepared to legalize gambling, we shall, like the English, announce to the world the end of individualist society and the trek back to tribal ways" (p. 249).[2] The authors are not quite ready to join the McLuhan trek back to tribal ways, but we have observed considerable movement toward the legalization of gambling in this country.

Our presentation is divided into four sections. First, we briefly discuss gambling itself. Second, we describe a specific setting where gambling proceeds with full legal sanction and where older and retired persons constitute up to half the clientele. Third, we present some new research findings, and fourth, we attempt an analysis of role satisfactions for the older gambler, a highly speculative venture at best.

Reprinted with permission from *International Journal of Aging and Human Development*, 1973, *4*, 1–13. The authors wish to express their thanks to the late Harry Stone, Mark Landsberg, Marina Chapman, and Pat Cannon, who provided advice and work, depending upon which was needed at the time.

Gambling: A Few Comments

"Gambling has existed in every known society from the most primitive to the most complex."[3] Gambling has been noted in Stone Age cultures, among the South African bushmen and Australian aborigines, and the pre-Columbus American Indians. Dice have been found in an Egyptian tomb; a gaming board was located at the Acropolis; additional evidence of gambling was found in the Roman Empire. Casting lots is mentioned in Joshua 18:10.[3] *Newsweek* (of April 10, 1972) estimated that gambling is a $50 billion annual business in the United States and growing steadily.

Regardless of laws or community pressures, gambling does occur. Our own nation is an excellent example of the confusion of laws and mores. Some states permit some kinds of gambling under some kinds of conditions on certain days at certain places . . . but outlaw everything else. Nevada, of course, has extensive legal gambling. State-run lotteries have come into being in New Hampshire, New York, New Jersey, Pennsylvania, and Massachusetts; California and Virginia are studying off-track betting while Connecticut and Pennsylvania have already made the decision to proceed; casinos have been proposed in the New York legislature and already exist in New Jersey and California. At least 34 states permit some form of gambling, and the number appears to be increasing.

Academic writing about gambling is sparse. A collection of articles that appeared in 1967 drew from the literature of the previous 25 years, but most were descriptive and none presented any sort of research data (other than financial). A more recent volume suggested more sophistication,[5] and the same author also developed a bibliography for distribution.[6] But academic researchers still appear reluctant to become involved with the topic. One hopeful sign: An article on card hustlers in *Trans-Action* mentioned that the senior author had been a professional gambler prior to the academic career that was leading to a doctorate in communications.[7] An earlier article in the same journal, a rather convincing analysis of why people play poker, was also co-authored by a person with experience working in gambling establishments.[8]

To our knowledge, there is no meaningful epidemiology of age of gamblers available. However, we can make a crude estimate from statistics for arrests provided by the FBI.[9] The overwhelming preponderance of persons over 65 who are arrested are charged with drunkenness (61.5%). Of the remaining causes for arrest in this age group only disorderly conduct (8.4%) accounted for more arrests than gambling, with 4.5% of all arrests of persons over age 65 being for gambling. Comparable percentages at 25–34 and 45–54 are 1.0% and 3.2%, respectively.

Many elderly persons in the United States and Canada have continued the kinds of gambling that prevailed in their country of origin. Thus, older Italian men are found playing dominoes; elderly Filipinos and Puerto Ricans often find ways to put on cockfights, in spite of their illegality; mah jong is still popular among elderly Chinese; and all ethnic groups seem to have a high proportion of poker players.

Lest the reader assume that geriatric gambling is restricted to the low-income and foreign-born, we suggest that a trip to stockbroker's office will change their thinking. One Los Angeles brokerage office is well known locally for its "standing room only, wall-to-wall old men's gallery, and that after recent expansion." Some of the men observing the tape and the changing numbers on the wall have substantial investments, while others may have only a few hundred shares altogether. Some probably have no money invested at all but come to partake of the company and of the feeling that they are part of some meaningful activity. These elderly observers according to the brokers themselves are no more likely to make a sale or purchase than are their counterparts sitting at home. However, they will sit and watch the board for hours at a time, frequently with little discussion. Some readers may reject the assumption that playing the market is like playing the horses, but it is difficult to deny the element of gambling.

Gambling, in company with drinking, drugs, and sex, is a victimless crime that seems to be here to stay. Yet it is not unknown for a back-porch poker game to be raided through the efforts of a district attorney on the rise. For example, several years ago, police in a major west coast city cracked down on a pinochle game that had been going on openly in a park for several months. Six or seven elderly men had gathered that day for camaraderie and fresh air to participate in the low-stake game, and one died immediately of a heart attack. Nonetheless, on a recent Sunday the senior author visited several parks and found some 40–50 older men playing and kibbitzing, as they do every Sunday. They are careful not to exchange money openly. One of them quipped that "90% of us here are under doctor's orders not to play cards."

Ignoring the cost in physical and emotional health, there is serious question as to whether the financial cost of breaking up such kinds of gambling is a useful public investment. In New York City it cost $3,500 in police expenses to bust one "bank" (the numbers or policy racket in the ghettoes), which consisted of two people. In 1970, 356 arrests occurred, with an average fine of $177 per person. During a 10-year period, one individual was imprisoned for 1 day. (Based upon Mary Minone, Ph.D., Research Director, Policy Sciences Center, New York City, on National Educational Television broadcast, *The Advocates*, December 22, 1971.) No data regarding age were provided, but we suspect the proportion of elderly was not negligible.

Today's elderly were reared in an era when gambling was probably more discussed and less professionalized than it is now. Slot machines, pinball games, punchboards, bingo games, pinochle and casino, all these were part of the scene 50 and 60 years ago. Gambling was often seen as a sign of sin and debauchery, but with an aura of romance. The autobiographical novel, *The Gambler,* by Dostoevski, the short stories by Bret Harte, Mark Twain, O. Henry, Stephen Crane, and so many others, the characters of Damon Runyon, the man who broke the bank at Monte Carlo—all became part of the cultural folklore. Gambling is still big business, bigger than ever, but it seems less romantic. Whatever romance exists in Las Vegas must compete with the big-business image of the entrepreneurs and corporations that ostensibly run the city.

Many gamblers are persons in their 60s and beyond,, yet—except for bridge and bingo, plus an occasional "Gamblers Night" with scrip—programs for the elderly have taken little heed. This is not because the elderly are anatagonistic or uninterested but perhaps because the program planners are concerned that these older persons not lose the little money they have in gaming—and perhaps because of a lingering feeling that gambling is immoral. While the planners hesitate, the California senior citizen clubs charter buses for Nevada gambling centers and make their way to the California poker casinos in large numbers (see Figure 3.1).

The Setting

Gardena (population, 50,000) is contained within a few square miles of the flatlands of Greater Los Angeles, undifferentiated from the surrounding communities except for the existence of six poker palaces clustered within a few blocks of each other. These six clubs—bright, well lit, heavily neoned, garish, comfortable, an almost inaudible level of hum and bustle broken primarily by the soft clatter of chips—provide tables, cards, chips, services, supervision, and some protection against being cheated for a charge, collected twice an hour, ranging from $.75 to $4.00 per player—all for the privilege of sitting there and playing poker.

Draw poker has been legal in Gardena since 1936, in spite of six attempts to vote the law out. At one time, 40% of the city's revenue was generated by the clubs, but this has slowly diminished to 13%. Gardena is the only community in Los Angeles County with legalized poker, although some 175 other California communities permit this through local option.[10] The clubs are in business for the long haul, and their management is careful not to violate the numerous city restrictions or to anger either local citizens or customers. Licenses for three of the clubs are held by veterans organizations, which receive around $25,000 for this formality.[10]

Wed. Apr. 5th.	FANCY HOTEL
$30. Twin (3 days, 5 nights)	This fabulous new hotel invites our Senior Citizen members to enjoy a 3 day holiday. Your cost includes transportation, twin bedroom, one buffet breakfast, one buffet dinner, $3.00 in nickels, one free cocktail and lounge show. Also included is a trip to the Xyzabs with cocktail, a trip to Hahaha-Hohoho with free nickels and booklet, and one breakfast at Le Sucker with fun book. One suitcase per person. Twin accommodations only. No deposits.

Figure 3.1 An almost uncensored, verbatim excerpt from a mimeographed mailing by the Blank Tours for Senior Citizens, in Southern California.

By regulations, each club has 35 tables, seating eight persons each. They are open from 9:00 a.m. in the morning until 5:00 a.m. the next morning, with somewhat shorter hours on Sunday. Each club closes down one day a week, with the days rotating so that at least four clubs are functioning at any given time, and six on Friday, Saturday, and Sunday. During the evening, 100% occupancy is standard for the game tables, and each club probably has an additional 100 or so persons on the premises— waiting for a table, lounging, watching television, talking, or eating in the very reasonably priced dining rooms. From opening to closing, there are seldom fewer than 200 people playing in each club.

It works very simply. The prospective player enters, leaves his initials with the "board man" as he tells him the game he wants to play (five-card draw or low-ball) and the stakes ($.50–$20.00). He is called when the right opening appears. Greetings are given, if at all, perfunctorily, whether an old and familiar face or a new participant. He is as anonymous as he cares to be—nicknames seem even more common than other identifications. As soon as he sits down the play continues, with the deal rotating as in most private games at home. A woman, usually youngish, and probably sporting a complicated wig or bouffant hairdo, comes around every 30 minutes to collect the rent—in cash. No one at the table represents the house. The house cut is strictly from the table charges.

A quarter-million patrons come annually from all over southern California, but mostly from Greater Los Angeles area.[10] And they leave behind—a little in the restaurant, but primarily in table charges—over $15 million a year to support their pleasure. An indication of the profitability is that a 1% interest in one club reportedly sold in 1970 for $65,000, as against an initial 1949 investment of $5000.

The Study

Actual studies of the gambling behavior of any population are rare. To our knowledge, no one has attempted to study the participants of the Gardena poker clubs since 1953,[11] nor has anyone had much luck in surveying the feelings, beliefs, and attitudes of any group of gamblers. Neither did we.

Questionnaire

Based largely upon the experience of the senior author, a 52-item questionnaire was devised. The information requested included demographic data, involvement in Gardena and other gambling opportunities, experiences with gambling, and relevant attitudes. It was pilot-tested on a handful of players, and changes were made accordingly.

Procedures and Sample

Initial attempts to distribute the questionnaire in the clubs were firmly rebuffed, although our explanations were sufficient—and our attitudes appropriate—so that we were not "hassled" when giving the forms out to people as they left the clubs. Some 250 forms were distributed. An attempt was made to avoid including respondents below age 50.

Place, hour, and day were randomized, and every eligible person leaving the selected club was given a questionnaire. It was explained that the project was under the supervision of the School of Public Health, UCLA, and that all responses would be anonymous. A stamped, addressed envelope was attached to each questionnaire, returning it to the university. About half the persons approached refused to take one.

The first indication of our probable rate of return came the day following the distribution of our initial 100 questionnaires. Three envelopes had arrived within less than 24 hours after distribution; they were all apparently mailed from the same postal station and were assumed to belong to three elderly women who engaged the research assistants in pleasant conversation. All three were blank. Eventually, the total return was 44 questionnaires (18%) of which 29 were usable (12%); 10 women and 19 men returned these forms. Of the 15 returned manuscripts that we did not include, 9 were dropped because of too many omitted items.

Results and Discussion

That the elderly of the area make substantial use of the clubs is apparent. Although their proportion of the total assemblage varies as a function of the time of day, with many more being around during daylight hours, they are never absent. The senior author made a careful estimate of the percentage of players he perceived as being 65 or older. These estimates were conducted at all of the clubs and were made at various times and days. During each 3-hour period the clubs were open, one count was made, with the checks rotating among the clubs and among the days of the week. These counts were carefully done but subject to the obvious bias of lack of external validation. During the daylight hours 40% of the players were over the age of 65; this dropped slightly in the late afternoon; by early evening, the percentage was closer to 20%, where it remained until closing time. A *Los Angeles Times* article estimated that 60–70% of the regular players—those who play three or four times a week or more—are over 65;[10] our own estimates would be similar.

One club is even referred to as "the old folks home" because they have done so much to encourage older people to attend.[10] This club probably also has the largest number of group cab arrangements (see below). A recent advertisement in the *Los Angeles Times* announced their Tuesday special: Chicken in the pot, along with carrots, potato noodle, matzo ball chicken broth, vegetable, roll, low calorie cheese cake, and coffee, for $2.00. Nowhere on the 5-inch, two-column advertisement was there any mention of poker.

The elderly were not equally distributed among tables but clustered at the less expensive ones where the stakes and the table costs were both lower. For this, they would pay $1.50 to $2.00 per hour, and they could buy in for $5.00 or $10.00. A rough guess of the proportion of the $15 million plus take of the clubs contributed by older persons would be $3.5 to $4 million. The ratio of the cost of playing to the stakes was highest for these less expensive tables meaning—as usual—that the elderly pay relatively more money for what they receive.

Of equal interest, we found that between 50 and 90% of the nonplayers were estimated to be in the 65+ age group. Thus, the restaurant, bar, and informal meeting places were more likely to be inhabited by the older customers, suggesting either less endurance (both physical and financial) or greater needs to socialize.

To look at our data: Our 29 respondents had a mean age of 62, ranging from 47 to 75; 10 were 65 or over; 5 were between 60 and 64; 13 were under 60 (one did not state). Over 80% were native born; roughly two-thirds were Jewish; political views tended to the middle-of-the-road Democratic. There were 21 who had living children; 18 had living grandchildren; 1 was a great-grandparent; 16 saw their children and/or grandchildren at least once a month. Though 11 were retired, 11 were employed (3 of them part time), and 4 were housewives. The median annual income from all sources, of the 12 who responded to that item, was about $6,000.

These are not casual players—over 60% of our respondents visited

Gardena for poker at least two or three times a week, with half of those coming at least four times a week, and one person playing almost every day. Since we did not include "Daily" as an alternative (the respondent penciled it in), we probably underestimated the number of daily patrons.

When asked how long they usually stayed, the mean response was 5.7 hours, with a range of between 3 and 12 hours; the respondents over age 65 did not differ from the younger persons. Most drive to Gardena either by themselves (14) or with a friend (10), while a few (3) make use of a group cab arrangement that many customers—especially the elderly—use; only one arrives by bus.

With an average of about 2.5 visits per week, for an average of 5.7 hours per visit, each individual spends 14 hours each week at the clubs. Assuming as much as 1 hour per visit for eating and socializing, since two-thirds of our sample eat one meal per visit on the average (this is much longer than most persons spend away from the tables, as anyone familiar with Gardena will attest), we still end up with better than 11 playing hours a week. Based upon the stakes they say they play for, i.e., an average of about $1.25 per *half*-hour (less for the older), average table costs amount to about $28 per week per individual, somewhat lower for the 65+ group (and we have been erring on the side of caution). Add to this a median roundtrip of about 30 miles, with expenses not usually shared, and our respondents begin their gambling stint well over $30 behind. It is doubtful that the older gamblers average much less than this. Undoubtedly the observation that attendance of the elderly shrinks during the later part of the month reflects the wait until the next social security check.

The obvious explanation for the willingness of these older persons to continue to play against such high odds would be that they expect to win. Strangely, this is not the case. Of the 10 persons over 65 who responded, 7 expected to lose at Gardena, 2 anticipated breaking even, and only 1 expected to win; of the 15 under 65, 10 thought they would win, 3 believed they were breaking even, and only 2 assumed they would lose. When asked about all gambling efforts, the results were comparable—none of the oldsters believed they came out ahead, 5 were losing, and 2 were breaking even (the others did not respond); among the younger gamblers, 8 thought they ended up ahead, 2 broke even, and 1 lost. Even back in 1954, psychologist William McGlothlin concluded that most of the 31 women gamblers he interviewed expected to lose.[11]

Therefore, in addition to transportation costs of several dollars a week and table costs of $25 a week or so, our geriatric gambler does not expect to win. The implications are quite clear; his gambling will cost him a substantial portion of his income from all sources, perhaps as much as 20–25% in many instances—perhaps more.

And still he makes the trip two or three times a week. Why? Nearly

75% state they just like to gamble. Slightly over half think that "Gardena is a good gamble." A similar number like the people and almost as many like the atmosphere. One-third admit to having nothing better to do, and one-third feel they need to get away from where they live. Fewer still—and almost none of the elderly—figure they can win some money. Only 2 feel compelled to come. Not only do they like to gamble, but they prefer poker to all other kinds (18), although they also enjoy pinochle (9), blackjack (9), horseracing (8), bridge (5), pan (5), craps (5), keno or bingo (3), and the slots (2). But the enjoyment of gambling is the most important reason they give for coming and the most important reason they assume others will give for coming. Only one person gives winning money as his most important reason for playing.

These poker players are not new to gambling, even though two-thirds admitted to playing cards more often for money now than 20 years earlier. Nonetheless, the mean age of initial interest in gambling was 31. And they have supportive spouses. Of the 16 married respondents, only 5 have spouses who never play, and only 2 show any disapproval—and only 1 admits to having a child showing any disapproval.

Personal observations during the period of the study, plus at other occasions, suggest that the regular "oldsters" comprise something of a clique, where they are well known and sympathetic to each other, in contrast to the clubs' usual atmosphere of anonymity and every man for himself.

The older players will frequently allow each other to save money and will extend otherwise rare courtesies in game situations. For example, one oldster may indicate to another that he is beat and should not call. Informal arrangements are made to avoid bluffing each other; this is known as "soft-playing" and is often costly to the participants, because other players "pick up on it" and utilize the information. Other methods of mutual support include defending each other in disputes, protecting each other's hands from being "fouled," i.e., rendered unplayable, usually by having other cards touch it, keeping the pots from being short-changed, loaning money, returning a few chips for luck or giving the ante, providing a rundown on opponents' styles, advising of minor cheating going on. (Although the older players are normally oblivious to the more expert cheater, the saving grace is that even "sharps" could hardly afford the size of the collection at the small games where most elderly play.)

The gambling losses of colleagues—as they come to see each other—are frequent topics of conversation, as is the illness or death of a playing companion. Although the casual observer would not notice anything that passes for conviviality among the players, even the older players, a sense of camaraderie apparently does develop and may occasionally sustain itself beyond the club parking lot.

An Attempt at Analysis

We had no hypotheses to test in a formal sense—only a wish to explore a matter of personal interest. However, we feel that the implications of Gardena's success in drawing the elderly of Los Angeles to its poker tables should not remain unnoticed. Given the physical difficulties of getting to Gardena, the immense (relative to the average income of the elderly) table costs, and the generally "bad name" that gambling has, something is taking place that is worthy of attention. What is the attraction of gambling and how does this relate particularly to older persons in the United States?

Bergler attributes gambling to unconscious motivation.[12] For him, gambling unconsciously revives childhood fantasies of grandeur and activates rebellion against the reality principle, in favor of the pleasure principle. According to Bergler, the gambler has a great deal of unconscious aggression which is acted out through self-punishment. Many gamblers have read Bergler—few if any see themselves in his analysis, although his descriptions of behavior often elicit a positive response. This, obviously, is not an ultimate criterion for the validity of Bergler's insights. For what it is worth, the authors are in strong agreement with the gamblers.

We trying to explain the behavior of only a few individuals. However, we firmly believe that, given the opportunity, they would be joined by many, many more. That is, were it not for limitations of money, for the lack of transportation facilities, and for the moderately high skill level of the present players against whom they would need to compete, vast numbers of elderly would join the parade to Gardena.

Some of the reasons are obvious. First, there is always the chance of winning, with the possibility of riding a streak of luck and skill into substantial financial reward. Even though the elderly realize that they lose overall, the chance for a big win is possible. Second, they enjoy the social life of the poker palaces more than that of its alternatives, e.g., senior citizen recreation centers (which are much more accessible to most of the players), the Santa Monica shuffleboard games, walking and sitting on benches, observing the passing parade of hippies and tourists on the beach at Venice. Third, the mere fact that he is participating in a program that is *not* planned for senior citizens is motivation enough for some of the elderly.

Martinez and LaFranchi describe the "loser," i.e., the gambler who ends up fairly consistently behind at the end of a month or of 6 months or a year, as being a social isolate. "Neither job, nor friends, nor leisure activities and hobbies are as meaningful to the loser as is poker" (p. 35). "For losers, poker is sought as a form of compensation or escape from anoic social relations" (p. 35).[8] Martinez and LaFranchi may well be correct—we suspect that they are. Unfortunately their analysis only skims lightly on the surface, the major query being: Why poker? If they are social isolates, why come to a crowded club when they might arrange a game at home without having to give a cut to the house? Their article is among the best available, but it helps only a little in understanding the older "loser."

We sense another element that is too readily overlooked. Older people are losing their decision-making options and their ability to rely upon their own instrumentality. Their income is from a source that, although stable and assured (ignoring, for the moment, the importance of inflation), has little or nothing to do with their own capabilities and is beyond their power to influence. Increasingly, others—their children, their physicians, various social planners, and others—are making decisions for them. Long-range payoffs are impractical and short-range payoffs are unavailable. Not only has disengagement taken place in the social sense, i.e., reduced numbers of contacts, but the available challenges are much less engaging on a psycological basis, i.e., ego-involvement. The excitement of facing success or failure on a job, in a sexual or affective encounter, with a variety of athletic activities—all these are now either greatly diminished or absent.

Gambling changes this. First, the payoff in gambling is real—it matters, it affects what the gambler eats or drinks or wears. And the game is part of the real world and not of planned programs.

Second, the gambler is pitting his skill and his good fortune against that of others without being patronized or planned for because he is old; the poker table is a total leveler of age. One wins or loses because of skill (John Scarne, the noted gambling expert, considers poker to have the greatest element of skill of all card games, bridge included), not because of age-related factors. The older player, even though he expects to lose, can decide himself whether or not to play, how to play, when to play. The locus of control does not reside in outside forces but within himself. The gambler is an active agent in his own fate, even in games of pure chance, because he must still decide whether to take the chance. We are suggesting, then, that it is not the winning that counts so much as the possibility of winning on one's own decisions, whether through skill or chance.

Third, gambling is engaging, in the sense that it provides the opposite of disengagement. For the most part the elderly person can anticipate a predictable income, with minor fluctuations from the erosion of inflation or the politics of election year. At the poker table, each draw, each bet, each grimace or grin has meaning. Not only is the player socially engaged in that he is interacting in meaningful fashion with many individuals, but he is immensely psychologically engaged—he is absorbed, involved, caught up in the action of the moment. (In *A Poker Game*, Stephen Crane says of poker, "Here is one of the most exciting and absorbing occupations known to intelligent American manhood; here a year's reflection is compressed into a moment of thought".) No artificial barriers of age limit, no reminders of lack of power because of age status, no helpful middle-aged person trying to shelter him against the real pains of a real situation.

To add a bit of icing to the cake, all this is conducted in an atmosphere where—at nearby tables—thousands of dollars are changing hands, where a touch of sin is suggested, where a bit of the tawdry quality of the gambling den rubs off.

And, finally, the payoff is now, today, this minute, not in building for some potential future that, for the elderly, may never come to pass. Although these elderly assume they will lose during the course of a year, there are days when they go home winners. How many nongambling friends can say the same?

Conclusion

The authors are not program planners and yet cannot help but feel that one conclusion stands out over all others: Here is a role for the elderly based— for better *and* for worse—on power and acquisitiveness. Isn't there something that can be learned by this?

References

1. Streib, G. F. *Retirement roles and activities*. Background paper for the White House Conference on Aging. Washington, D.C.: Government Printing Office, 1971, p. 1.
2. McLuhan, H. M. *Understanding media*. New York: Mc-Graw-Hill, 1964.
3. Morehead, A. H. Gambling. In *Encyclopedia Britannica, IX*, 1968, 1115 ff.
4. Herman, R. D. *Gambling*. New York: Harper & Row, 1967.
5. Kusyszyn, I. (Ed.). *Studies in the psychology of gambling*. Toronto: Author, 1972 (unpublished).
6. Kusyszyn, I. Psyhology of gambling, risk-taking, and subjective probability: A bibliography. *Journal Supplement Abstract Service Catalog of Selected Documents in Psychology*, 1972, 2, 7.
7. Mahigel, E. L., and Stone, G. P. How card hustlers make the game. *Transaction*, 1971, 8(3), 40–45.
8. Martinez, Thomas M., and LaFranchi, Robert. Why people play poker. *Transaction*, 1969, 6(9), 30–35, 52.
9. Riley, M. W.; Foner, A.; and Associates. *Aging and society, Volume I*. New York: Russell Sage Foundation, 1968.
10. Shaw, D. Gardena. Poker draws young and old to the tables. *Los Angeles Times*, March 28, 1971, Section B., 1–3.
11. McGlothlin, W. A psychometric study of gambling. *Journal of Consulting Psychology*, 1954, 18, 145–149. Cited also in the (Los Angeles) *Herald Express*, June 1, 1953.
12. Bergler, E. *The psychology of gambling*. New York: Hill & Wang, 1957.

4

"It's the Pepsi Generation": Accelerated Aging and the Television Commercial

J. Scott Francher

"You've gqt a lot to live and Pepsi's got a lot to give" are words that reached our ears and eyes via the medium of television advertising. The jaunty melody, which served as the vehicle for the Madison Avenue catch phrase, lured us into listening. Supposedly, the majority of us were made to feel that we can become part of this "brave new world" simply by imbibing Pepsi-Cola. There are among us, however, those who no longer "have a lot to live"; namely, the elderly among us who are subtly, but surely, disenfranchised by this message and others of the same genre.[1]

External Stress

Our society pressures the individual to assume a certain physical and mental attitude once he has acquired a specified number of years to his life. At an arbitrarily chosen point in the life cycle individuals are put out to pasture, told they have become obsolete, and forgotten about by those who will soon follow them (but would rather not think about it). Within the system there are subtle reinforcers which condone these actions and which dictate that we shall perceive them as the inevitable course of human existence. The commercial messages produced by the mass media are among the reinforcers which foster individual images and attitudes of senility. Perhaps an analysis of these media messages will bring a new awareness to the problem of aging in American society.

For the purpose of this article it was decided to limit the analysis of commercials to those seen on television. Because of the popularity of the television medium, commercials are almost universally seen in American society and have become a part of our visual culture. Support for this

Reprinted with permission from *International Journal of Aging and Human Development*, 1973, *4*, 245–255.

contention can be found in the fact that the Federal Trade Commission has restricted tobacco manufacturers from advertising cigarettes on commercial television, whereas no such restriction has yet been imposed on other media—such as magazines. Television constantly emits messages which are geared to shaping, molding, and influencing the behavior of the individual. It is, therefore, a potent and critical force in terms of its impact on the individual and his behavior alternatives. The originality and novelty employed in their productions make them a highly popular and enjoyable quasi-art form. It is not unusual to hear audiences comment that they enjoyed the commercials more than the feature show! With such a wide audience and range of public appeal it can be assumed that the impact of these commercial message productions is as great or greater than competing forms of advertising.

But what is the nature of the messages emitted in the television commercial? Beyond the manifest content, what relationship do these seemingly innocuous message productions have to one's self-image? Can any relationship be inferred between these message productions and the plight of the aged in American society?

Procedures Utilized

In order to answer these questions the following set of procedures was utilized. First, 100 television commercials were randomly sampled and closely monitored. Second, a viewing schedule was devised and the following categories were noted for each commercial:

   A.   Type of product advertised.

   B.   Major characters—Here each character used in the message production was recorded and the physical characteristics such as age, sex, degree of attractiveness were quantitatively described.

   C.   Tone—How are the advertisers attempting to sell the product: through serious advertising, humorous appeals, or some other form of attention-getting mechanism?

   D.   Target group—What age, sex, or interest group is the commercial directed toward?

   E.   Scene—What is the dramatic setting for the commercial message?

   F.   Promise implied by the commercial—What benefits can the user expect from the product?

Third, the verbal lines of the commercials were recorded verbatim.

It was hoped that the above procedures would offer some sort of evidence as to whether or not these television messages did affect the self-image of the aging person. Did the commercials reinforce the society's prescription of when to get old?

The commercials exhibited the following general characteristics:

A. *Type of product*. The range of products advertised was impressive. Few tendencies regarding the products advertised and their bearing on attitudes toward the aging can be discerned at this time. Time of day, however, seems to bear some relationship to the products advertised. Midmornings and late afternoons evidence a large number of products intended for children. Afternoons show a tendency to emphasize the housewife as the target group. Detergents, beauty aids, and food products are especially popular during this time slot. The widest range of products is seen in the evening hours. Presumably, this is the time when television is viewed by the working members of the population.

B. *Characters*. Significant variation exists with reference to the characters used in the television commercial. When a single character carries the message of the advertiser a young, attractive, modishly attired, often sexy female is utilized. This trend was documented in 33% of the sample. LaBarre noted this tendency in 1946 when he stated:

> Advertisements, movies, popular fiction, and other vehicles of publicity, amusement, and fantasy unite in demonstrating to us that in our society it is the nubile young female who achieves the most attention, who is the cynosure of all eyes.[2]

Next in order of frequency (14%) is the single character who is, to some degree, a celebrity. Age and physical attributes seem irrelevant here except when the product advertised is intimately associated with one of the sexes. Such is the case with the feminine hygiene products. It is assumed that the celebrity status is sufficient to lend weight to the product advertised. Single men account for 10% of the characters. Invariably they are young, handsome, and dressed according to contemporary canons of fashion. Age seems to be more flexible in the case of the male character, reflecting the inclination in American society of holding the woman more accountable for physically aging than the man. Men are permitted graying temples and a certain cragginess of face so long as the image of virility and sexual appeal is maintained.

In 9% of the sample no human characters were used; they relied instead upon animated figures or still photos. In these cases the voice describing the product becomes of prime importance. Invariably the voices can be identified as youthful.

Of those commercials using two characters (15%), either a couple or two members of the same sex were employed. Here the characters were young, attractive, and stylishly dressed. In only one instance is the couple older or middle aged. It is significant that in this particular case the product advertised is a vitamin especially designed for older people, promising "a younger, more active you."

Of the commercials viewed, 11% showed a number of people in montage fashion. In only two instances did the group contain any older characters. The general tone of these two commercials using the older characters was decidedly humorous.

What is significant here is that the overwhelming number of commercials utilize young, attractive people. Older people are used when a product especially designed for them makes more sense when advertised by a member of this age group or when the commercial is humorous in tone. It appears, therefore, that the tendency in America to elevate youth to a primary position is reflected in the primary visual position they enjoy in televsion advertising.

C. Tone. The tone of the commercial refers to the nature of its appeal to the viewing public. Three distinct categories emerged: serious; serious imbued with a high degree of sexuality; and humorous. Significant differences exist between the three categories in terms of products advertised and the characters used in the commercial message. Serious commercials relied heavily upon celebrities or attractive young models (73%). Products in the serious category ran the gamut from breakfast cereals to automobiles. In the serious-sex-imbued category, 100% of the major characters could be characterized as young and attractive, while 45% of the products advertised in this category emphasized the body as their major focus. An interesting inversion exists in the humorous category. In 80% of these cases the characters were classified as average, man-in-the-street types, blatantly comical in some aspect of the presentation of self, or clearly middle aged or old. In only one case did the character described as "older" advertise products for the body. They seem to be restricted to less personal products such as household detergents or food products.

D. Target group. No general characteristics can be attributed to this aspect of the viewing schedule. Suffice it to say that multivarious interest groups are reached—i.e., denture wearers, automobile owners, parents, women, housewives, and so forth.

E. Scene. The scene enacted in the commercial message proved to be too integral a part of the whole message production to be studied as a separate entity. What can be said at this juncture, however, indicates that the scene, pace, setting, drama, and motif provide an essential vehicle for the transmission of the commercial message.

F. Promise implied. The promise implied by the commercial is, of course, intimately bound up with the product itself. It is not surprising to learn that a popular laundry detergent promises a "cleaner, whiter wash." Yet important secondary messages or cues are implied by the age, sex, and physical attributes of the major character, the tone the message assumes, the setting in which the drama is acted, and the final outcome of the "commercial drama." Thus, an otherwise neutral commercial for a popular soft drink which utilizes all youthful people engaged in action-oriented scenes such as tennis or hiking becomes restricted to a youthful action-oriented population while at the same time promising to supply the energy needed for these activities. Of the commercials monitored, 57% pledged youth, youthful appearance, or the energy to act youthful. Often this pledge was coupled with the promise of increased sexual appeal and conquest, a phenomenon well documented in the history of American advertising.

Analysis of a Popular TV Commercial

The following analysis of a Pepsi-Cola commercial illustrates the principle and the method of analysis employed for each commercial monitored.

The commercial lasts for 1 minute. During its duration a number of short film clips are rapidly flashed upon the screen in a photomontage fashion. In all, seven such clips appear. They are in the order of their appearance:

1. A handsome young man with modishly long blond hair is bending over a river bank drinking water from his cupped hands. The scene is one of bucolic isolation and peace. Private sensory gratification and delight in nature are highlighted here.

2. A handsome young couple are seen walking arm in arm along a river bank. The young man draws the girl closer to him and they embrace. They are laughing and enjoying both the physical and emotional closeness of the relationship.

3. A young, athletic-looking man is seen in a high dive. The camera angles beneath him revealing a perfection of physical form and adroit execution of a difficult physical maneuver. Here action orientation, physical prowess, and the beauty of the body become cues suitable for emulation.

4. A group of young children is pictured at a birthday party. One jubiliant youngster blows out the candles, and the other children gathered around him are caught up in the excitement of the group activity. Thus, sociability, sharing, and delight in group experience are of primary importance in this film clip.

5. A young, althletic-looking man is seen climbing down a mountain side. Action, youth, and physical prowess are lauded here.

6. A tall, young man holding a toddler (female) on his shoulders is pictured walking down a long stretch of deserted beach. Father enjoying his child and the mutual closeness of the family are implied here.

7. The camera moves in for a close-up of a young, attractive girl in a group of young people. She is laughing and obviously enjoying herself. Joy, impulse release, and contentment within the group confines are expressed here.

8. A bottle of Pepsi-Cola fills the screen. The verbal message is carried by a youthful sounding male chorus which sings the following song for the duration of the commercial:

> There's a whole new way of living,
>   Pepsi helps supply the drive.
> It's got a lot to give for those who like to live,
>   'Cause Pepsi helps them come alive
> It's the Pepsi generation,
>   Coming at you, going strong.
> Put yourself behind a Pepsi
>   If you're living, you belong.
>
> You've got a lot to live and
>   Pepsi's got a lot to give
> You've got a lot to live and
>   Pepsi's got a lot to give.

During the 1-minute duration of the commercial the viewer is bombarded with a constant stream of cues. First, one notices that the pace of the commercial is lively. This effect is created by the photomontage technique of rapidly changing visual images and the spirited rhythm of the musical line. Such an animated pace provides an appropriate setting for the action-oriented scenes in the film clip. The lyrics of the music line provide yet another reinforcement for action orientation as a major cue. Such phrases as "helps supply the drive," "coming at you, going strong," articulate what is implied by the pace and visual content of the scenes.

All of the characters in the scenes are young and attractive. Youth as a major cue is reinforced by the lyrics which announce that "there's a whole new way of living" and "it's the Pepsi generation." Thus, we are told that a new lifestyle has displaced the no longer fashionable lifestyle of the older generation. Indeed, the bearers of this new culture are the young who seek sensory gratification and impulse release either through private experience, or under the aegis of the group. Action-oriented behavior is not only an end in itself but an indispensable means of attaining the pleasure of the "good life."

Triumph of New Over Old

A threefold manifesto emerges based on the triumph of new over old,
action over intellect, impulse over moderation. Through this edict, a
product otherwise general in its appeal and consumption becomes specifically directed toward youth as a target group and all those who aspire to
emulate the youthful modes of behavior. The first part of this threefold
manifesto may be called "emphasis on the body." The body is portrayed as
young and svelte if female; lean and muscular if male. The variety of
messages here charge the individual to pay close attention to the inevitable
signs of aging of the body. One is instructed to maintain a youthful
physique at all costs. If this fails, one is cued to mask the telltale indicators
of aging. Face, hair, and hands become objects of special concern and are
all-important indicators of aging. The second part of the manifesto is "The
Age Phenomenon." Youth is depicted as the object of social concern and
admiration. One is directed to measure both his or her body and range of
activities by the barometer of age. A ready maxim emerges: What is or
appears to be youthful is good and desirable; all that is otherwise, is not.
The new canon concludes: "You've got a lot to live." A lifestyle based on
action and sensory gratification is held up as the ideal pattern to follow.
Here the "good life" is one both rich in material accouterments and
symbols of youth. Henceforth, the "youth complex" is used to refer to this
threefold testament: emphasis on the body, emphasis on youth, and emphasis on action orientation and sensory gratification.

It is perhaps not surprising to learn that in the Western world the
disorganizing effects of aging on the human personality are physiologically
defined and explained. Arteriosclerosis and chronic brain syndrome, two
diseases commonly associated with the elderly, are credited with robbing
the individual of viable social contacts with the outside world. The idea that
senility and its attendant maladies is caused by actual physical changes and
deterioration of the brain is deeply rooted in the American consciousness.
Like the younger person defined as mentally ill, the older person labeled as
senile is "cracked in the head."

Despite the fact that this notion persists, there are those who have
transcended its limitations, providing us with unique insight into an otherwise tradition-bound area. One such innovator is Dr. Muriel Oberleder of
the Bronx State Hospital, Bronx, New York who believes the phenomenon
we label "senility" is not caused physiologically but is a function of the
anxiety related to the cultural stresses placed on the aging in our society.
Oberleder states:

> In my belief, anxiety is the extra stress of aging; indeed, old age is anxiety. Old
> age occurs when external stresses overtax the older person's ability to func-

tion, and if you remove the stress, the person can again function. I feel that anxiety underlies all senile symptoms, and causes them. In old age you have more anxiety-evoking situations and fewer anxiety-reducing opportunities; that formula in itself could account for senility, or emotional breakdown in the aging. (pp. 191–196)[3]

Oberleder identifies the fear of loss of sexuality, of loss of status, of loss of a sense of security and the trauma caused by body changes as major focuses of stress in the individual. She points out that these anxieties do not blossom into full flower at the age of 65 but find their roots in the unresolved stresses of middle age. These anxieties not only have an incremental value for the individual but when juxtaposed with the common life crises of older years (forced retirement, loss of spouse, loss of role, etc.) the individual often turns to the culturally prescribed role of senility. Quoting Oberleder, "I believe that people bring senility on themselves . . . When you are really old and feeling stress, you grab at the senile symptoms to end the tension" (p. 194).[3] These factors which cause the anxiety, moveover, are largely cultural factors. No absolute cultural rule exists which determines 65 as the age of forced withdrawal from society. Indeed, even though the changes brought about by aging in the human body are inevitable, and part of the physical "program" to which all species are heir, society's attitude toward these changes is the crucial element—not the changes per se.

TV Commercials and Their Effect on the Aging

It is suggested here that an important causal relationship exists between the major messages which have been identified in television advertising and predispositions toward aging and the symptoms which are commonly called senile. These cues create anxiety and anger, two factors which Oberleder has identified as causal in the emotional breakdown of the elderly.

The major impact of this commercial is undoubtedly a visual one. The viewer is presented with a rapidly changing series of scenes depicting young people in action poses or scenes depicting sensory gratification. The three elements which we have termed "the youth complex" constitute a message grouping. The messages charge one to take note of youth, action, and sensory gratification in a favorable way. This does not, however, operate on only the visual plane. It charges one to *feel* youthful, to *act* youthful, and to *believe* that youth, action, and sensory gratification as a focus has a universal validity, to hold youth in awe and to use youth as a role model.[4]

In the data gathered, youth is the model after which one is directed to measure oneself. Such culturally sanctioned role models constitute a crucial element in the socialization process. One can easily discern the functional character of such role models when observing the behavior of children. By imitating role models children "practice" adult roles, modes of dress, and even styles of body deportment. Much has been written which illustrates how this imitative behavior facilitates the acquisition of appropriate cultural behavior. The data show that in 43% of the commercials monitored, the characters used were both young and attractive. Moreover, these youthful models are depicted in action postures, espousing sensory gratification. We can readily comprehend how this visual preoccupation with the youth complex serves the young. But what of the rest of the population which is no longer young; which can never again hope to realize the attributes of youth as depicted in the television commercial? Like the young viewer, the older one is charged through this message grouping to perceive, to feel, to do , to believe, to emulate, and to hold in awe—the youth complex. He or she is told that this is the cultural model par excellence, the self to which he or she must aspire. The gap between the physical and social self as experienced in reality and the television self, the model the viewer is directed to incorporate may be so great, that a loss of self-esteem is a natural consequence. Such occurrences as thinning hair, failing eyesight, dentures, and a more measured, less action-oriented lifestyle are not accounted for by the social model; indeed, their very existence is met with denial.

The "Youth Complex"

The "youth complex," a system of messages accentuating youth, action orientation, and sensory gratification was identified as a major message grouping in television advertising. This message grouping directs the individual to invest positive emotion in these phenomena and, at the same time, further charges the individual to incorporate them into a variety of behavioral patterns. Individuals are charged to see this youth complex favorably, to perform in accordance with its dictates, to incorporate these values into their system of beliefs, and to reverently hold persons, objects, or events which symbolize or contain them. When the reality of one's physical person and social self roughly corresponds to the image projected by and contained within this youth complex, the possibility of conflict arising among the various aspects of this message system is markedly reduced since an agreement is reached between the self-image and the projected image of the idealized self of the advertisement. Understandably, this conflict-free arrangement is most available to the young in our society. But what of the older person, the person who has long since passed the age when the attainment of this projected idealized self is no longer possible, the person whose body has long since passed the stage of the young, attractive model of the television screen? Speculatively, there can be little doubt that older individuals find conflict, anxiety, and anger in this arrangement. For them the conflict lies at the very heart of this complex. On one hand they are directed through the message grouping to perceive the youth complex in a favorable fashion, while on the other hand it does not allow them the possibility or even the hope of bringing their own feelings and image of self in line with these perceptions.

The field of gerontology offers myriad possibilities for innovative research. We now know that the aged in our society are confronted with many anxiety-inducing and tension-provoking situations. This research suggests the necessity of our understanding the importance of the mass media and its role in shaping the aging person's awareness of self with respect to both social models and the rest of society. Until we know the extent to which popular heroes, celebrities, and fictional characters of the mass media influence the origin of lifestyle models, we cannot hope fully to understand or appraise their impact on the individual's image of self. Yet, we do know more precise inquiry is needed in this significant area.

References

1. Francher, J. Scott, American values and the disenfranchisement of the aged. *Eastern Anthropologist*, XXII, *1* January–April, 1969, 29–36.
2. LaBarre, W. Social Cynosure and Social Structure, in D. G. Haring (Ed.), *Personal Character and Cultural Milieu*. Syracuse, N.Y.: Syracuse University Press, 1956, p. 535.
3. Oberleder, Muriel. Emotional breakdown in elderly people. *Hospital and Community Psychiatry*, July 1969, *20* (7), 191–196.
4. Nelson, B. Actors, directors, roles, cues, meanings, identities: Further thoughts on 'anomie.' *Psychoanalytic Review*, spring 1964 (1), 135–160.

Bibliography

Gerbner, G. Cultural indicators: The case of violence in television drama. *Annals*, *338*, March 1970, 69–81.
Goffman, E. *The presentation of self in everyday life*. Garden City, N.Y.: Doubleday, Anchor, 1959.
Kluckhohn, F. R., and Strodtbeck, F. L. *Variations in value orientations*. Evanston, Ill.: Row, Peterson, 1961.

5

"The Ages of Me": Toward Personal and Interpersonal Definitions of Functional Aging

Robert Kastenbaum
Valerie Derbin
Paul Sabatini
Steven Artt

How should a person's age be established or judged? One popular answer is that a person is "as old as he feels." Perhaps an even more popular rejoinder is that a person is "*only* as old as he feels." While the personal definition is unlikely to replace all other approaches, it does appear reasonable to include self-report as a legitimate and potentially useful entry. In this chapter we report on the early stages of an attempt to define and assess age from the personal frame of reference. The study also includes a quest for an interpersonal definition of age and an exploration of the relationships between personal and interpersonal frames.

Background

Three strands of interest have been interwoven into the present research sequence:

1. The attempt to *induce* and *modify* behavior syndromes characteristic of the aged;

2. The attempt to expand and refine the concept of *functional age;*

3. Curiosity about the way in which gerontologists view their own development and aging.

Reprinted with permission from *International Journal of Aging and Human Development*, 1972, 3, 197–211. This report derives from a study supported in part by the Institute of Gerontology, University of Michigan/Wayne State University.

Induction and Modification of
"Old" Behavior

Gerontological research has been more descriptive than experimental. The imbalance is most extreme in the social and behavioral branches. We have not mounted a systematic effort to induce, modify or reverse the behavioral syndrome that is taken to be characteristic of "old age." How has it happened that the classic experimental approach, so crucial to the advancement of other scientific disciplines, has not been pursued here? We do not know the answer to this question. It is likely, however, that the following factors have influenced our disinclination to experiment:

1. Descriptive knowledge is valuable and perhaps deserves priority in so new a field of inquiry.
2. There are neither suitable concepts nor techniques available for the experimental induction and modification of aging in the psychosocial sphere.
3. It goes against our grain to contemplate a program of deliberately inducing or simulating aging: Should we not bend our efforts to prevent old age or bring back youth?
4. Moral and ethical problems arise when we even begin to consider the possibility of inducing "old age."
5. There is no guarantee that a vigorous experimental program would actually result in the induction of "old" behaviors, or their modification or reversal even if induced.

We do not wish to convey the impression that the feasibility and desirability of an experimental program has been thoroughly evaluated and subsequently set aside. The fact is that the issue has seldom been aired even as a possibility.

One cannot easily dismiss the (guessed-at) inhibiting factors mentioned above. In our opinion, however, these points do not compel indefinite paralysis. We will never know if the conceptual, methodological, temperamental, and ethical problems can be solved unless the challenge is taken up. It would seem a pity to lose by forfeit!

Previous articles and reports have introduced theoretical, procedural, and empirical material relevant to the experimental induction or simulation of "old" behavior (Kastenbaum, 1968, 1969a, 1969b, 1971). This material will not be repeated here. Essentially, our strategy has been to attempt to induce a syndrome of "old" behavior in adults who are not aged—but to do so by psychosocial means only, and in miniaturized forms that would produce transitory, self-limiting effects. Pastalan (1971) has recently reported an independently conceived project in which young adults moved through their daily activities under the handicap of age-simulating sensory impairments. Neither Pastalan's work nor ours has "proven" anything yet, but the preliminary experiences have been on the moderately encouraging side.

There are many ways one might go about attempting to induce "old" behavior. There are even more ways in which each attempt could fail. To anchor our experimental efforts more securely we decided to pursue the following research sequence:

1.   Develop means of differentiating among people who have distinctly different views of their age status although all sharing the same chronological age. The rough categories would be "younger than my age"; "older than my age"; and "neither younger nor older than my age."

2.   Determine the relationship between subjective or personal age and objective measures of functioning. Do people who "feel" younger, for example, also "test" younger?

3.   Explore biographical-developmental factors associated with being a person who is "younger" or "older" than his or her chronological age.

4.   Determine the relative susceptibility of "youngers" and "olders" to an experimental program of inducing "old" behaviors, and study the strategies they employ to cope with the experimental situations.

The present study is directed toward the objectives stated in the first point above. It has also been designed to explore functional aging from the personal and interpersonal frames of reference.

Functional Age

Physicians are well acquainted with the fact that people may have "young arteries" or "old kidneys" in relation to the norms of bodily functioning expected at certain chronological age levels. Many employers appreciate the fact that work output declines markedly for some fifty-or-sixty-year-olds while others at the same age show no decline at all. It appears both reasonable and useful to augment (or challenge) chronological age with functional criteria in all spheres: biological, psychological, and social. The emergence of functional aging as a powerful concept obviously would influence theory and research in gerontology. Many political, economic and personal repercussions might also follow if the concept gains more general acceptance. Clearly, then, the concept of functional aging and its supporting evidence must be cultivated with both diligence and caution.

Heron and Chown helped to energize research in this area with their little book on *Age and Function* (1967). Perhaps the most extensive ongoing research effort is the one that has been undertaken by a multidisciplinary team at the Boston Veterans Administration Out-Patient Clinic. Methodology and early findings are reported by Fozard, (1972), Rose, (1972), and Damon, (1972). While the VA Normative Aging Study has concentrated upon external and objective assessments of functional age, we have delved into the subjective frame.

Viewed as a contribution to functional aging, the present study is an attempt to develop instruments, concepts, and preliminary data that would lead to recognition of personal and interpersonal age as useful components of total functional aging.

Subjective Age Perceptions of Gerontologists

Other people may permit their preconceptions, insecurities, and needs to influence their observations of aging and the aged. Gerontologists are the exception. Their own relationship to the aging process is neutral, objective, normal, under control. Perceptions of their own age do not enter into their work as sources of potential error.

The proposition stated above may be true. But it has not been proven true—indeed, it has never been put to the test. We know very little, in systematic fashion, about the personal characteristics of those who study aging. Lacking data to the contrary, it may be most prudent to forego assumptions about the possible uniqueness of gerontologists as "neutral" or "objective" scientists. Donahue (1965) has called attention to a possible bias factor in the age match-up between researcher and subject. On a broader front, it might be worth pondering the relationship between gerontologists' total relationship to their own aging process and their scientific and professional activities. At present we do not know whether people who are attracted to gerontology are either more or less concerned about problems of personal aging than people in general. We also do not know enough about future gerontologists' personal orientation to select appropriate learning experiences for them or capitalize upon their special strengths and sensitivities.

We decided to indulge our curiosity in this area by including a sample of gerontologists-in-training in the present study.

Terminology

Confusion is an ever-present danger once we step beyond the familiar guideline of chronological age. The definitions that follow are intended only to tag and differentiate those concepts that are most basic to the present study. More appropriate terminology can be formulated as our knowledge increases. Each of the terms proposed below is considered to be a component or dimension of the broader concept of functional age.

By *personal age* we mean the individuals' self-reports of their age status: how old they seem to themselves. By *interpersonal age* we mean the age status of an individual as evaluated by others.

Each of these terms can be further differentiated as appears useful. We could speak either of personal age or personal ages. The plural form opens the possibility that even within the subjective realm there might be multiple dimensions along which age should be assessed. It also opens the possibility that the number and types of subjective dimensions might be related systematically to the individual's developmental level. Interpersonal age also could be treated either as a unitary measure or as a confederation of specific ages (e.g., "She looks like such a young thing, but she is wise beyond her years"). Additionally, interpersonal age could be constructed from the perspective of one or of several observers. Both personal and interpersonal age could be evaluated either on a one-time, situational basis or over a more extended period of time (characteristic or baseline age).

The relationship between personal and interpersonal age might be expressed in terms of *consensual age*. Close agreement between self-perception and perception-by-others would constitute a firm consensual age. Two components are involved in establishment of consensual age: a measure of inter-rater agreement, and the actual age or age direction for which agreement has been found. It should be made clear that neither interpersonal nor consensual age is concerned primarily with the ability of others to guess the individual's chronological age. The ratings often will involve estimates of chronological age. The point, however, is to establish the degree of consensuality concerning the personal component of functional age. The observer might know for a fact that he is observing a man who is 30 years of age. If he believes this man looks 10 years older, and the man himself believes he looks 10 years younger, then we have an instance in which no consensual age can be established.

Personal and interpersonal age are each established on the basis of direct reports (e.g., "I have the interests of a man of 50," or "He has the interests of a man of 35"). By contrast, consensual age is determined by logicostatistical operations performed on two or more sets of observations, e.g., the two statements quoted above.

The terms that have been introduced here should be distinguished from other functional age constructs whose verbal labels are somewhat similar. (Eventually, perhaps, it will be possible to formulate a standard table of functional ages in which agreed-upon symbols take the place of ambiguous, vague-edged terminology.) Perhaps the most similar-sounding concept to those introduced here is that of *social age*. Rose (1972) has defined social age "as the predicted age yielded by a multiple regression equation composed of weighted social variables and a constant. Individuals whose social life styles are the same as those of their age peers would have a social age the same as their chronological age." Social age differs from personal and interpersonal ages in the following ways: (1) Social age is the outcome of statistical manipulations of multifaceted data, while personal and interpersonal age essentially come from one source each and are more direct "sources" or "ratings"; (2) social age is constructed from a mix of both objective and subjective data, while personal and interpersonal age rely entirely upon subjective appraisal, whether by self or other; (3) social age is based upon a set of prespecified criteria, while appraisal of personal and interpersonal age require (or allow) the perceiver to exercise his or her own judgment as to what constitutes salient and admissible evidence: (4) personal and interpersonal ages are devised to serve as checks upon each other (consensual age) and thus contribute to our understanding of human interaction dynamics, while social age provides a sort of affiliation index between the individual and his or her chronological age cohort. Perhaps the distinction can be put another way: social age could be read as "sociological age," and personal-interpersonal age could be read as "phenomenological" and "intersubjective" age.

It is unfortunate that terminology is such a burden at this stage in functional age research, but one must run the risk of seeming overly pedantic at times—or take the consequences of tenuous connections among concepts, methods, and findings.

Statement of the Problem

The basic aim of this study is to uncover the problems that must be worked through before the concepts of personal, interpersonal, and consensual age can be introduced fruitfully into the general domain of functional age. Broadly stated, the major questions are:

1. Is personal age adequately represented as a unitary construct?
2. What is the general relationship between personal and chronological age?
3. Is interpersonal age adequately represented as a unitary construct?
4. Is consensual age generally capable of being established, or must personal and interpersonal age generally be treated as two very distinct constructs?

There are many other specific questions and hypotheses involved, but the above are basic in the sense that future research pathways will be strongly influenced by the way in which these questions are answered. As the study is still in progress, we will be able to report upon only a few aspects of the total range of data being obtained.

Procedure
Instruments

"The Ages of Me." A structured interview format was developed to study personal age. The basic procedure is administration of a 49-item interview schedule which has been designated "The Ages of Me." It is given on an individual basis for purposes of this study but can also be administered to groups. The individual interview format, although more effortful and time consuming, was preferred for this first study because of its potential for teaching us more about both the subject matter and the directions in which the instrument might be usefully modified.

Participants are told:

"Most people have other 'ages' besides their official or chronological age. We may feel or look younger or older than our chronological age. The questions we are asking you here all have something to do (directly or indirectly) with the various possible ages of you.

"We appreciate your cooperation in this study. Any comments or suggestions you would care to offer about these questions would be most welcome."

The first set of items requests comparative ratings. There are five fixed-alternative questions:

Most of the time I *feel:*
Most of the time I *look:*
My *interests* and *activities* are most like those of:
People who know me *casually* regard me as:
People who know me *very well* regard me as:

The following response choices are provided:

Quite a bit older than most people my age.
A little older than most people my age.
Neither older nor younger than most people my age.
A little younger than most people my age.
Quite a bit younger than most people my age.

(The wording is slightly different for the *interests* and *activities* question, e.g., "People who are quite a bit older than myself.")

This set of items also includes three open-end questions, requesting the respondent to specify the interests and activities he had in mind, and to indicate the probable basis upon which other people judge his or her relative age.

The second set of items includes four questions that request specification of an absolute age instead of a comparison:

I *feel* as though I were about age:
I *look* as though I were about age:
I *do* most things as though I were about age:
My *interests* are mostly those of a person about age:
There are also two open-end items in this set:
If there is anything about me that is "young for my age," it is probably:
If there is anything abut me that is "old for my age," it is probably:

The third set consists of nine items dealing with the respondent's past. These questions are included to obtain clues for more systematic study into antecedent conditions of those who classify themselves as younger or older than their current chronological age (e.g., "When I was a child, my parents tended to treat me as though I were: quite a bit more grown up than most other children my age . . . a little more grown up . . . neither more nor less grown up . . . a little less grown up . . . quite a bit less grown up than most other children my age").

The fourth set is concerned with the respondent's comfort with her or his age and also with her or his sense of comfort with people of various ages. The items alternate between fixed-alternative and open-end responses. Among the items most relevant to the present report are:

(No. 25) If I could pick out the age I would like to be right now, I would select age:
(No. 26) Why? Please explain your answer.
(No. 27) At this time in my life I am (five fixed-alternatives from "entirely comfortable with my present age" to "very uncomfortable with my present age"):
(No. 28) The reason I gave this answer:
(No. 29) I would like to stay at my present age, if this were possible (five fixed-alternatives from "as long as possible" to "prefer to move to the next age a lot sooner"):

The fifth set is comprised of open-end questions inquiring into the criteria respondent uses to appraise a person's functional age. An example is (No. 43): I can imagine two people who are each 50 years of age. One of these people seems "old" to me, the other does not. The important differences between these people are:

The sixth set consists of three more self-classification items:

> If I had to classify myself according to age, I would choose to describe myself as a (examples: teenager, adolescent, young adult, middle-aged, elder, old, aged, etc. If you have a better term to describe your own age, please use it):
> I feel as though my rate of change (growing up or growing older) is now (speeding up/continuing at its previous rate/slowing down).
> In general, my body is (five fixed-alternatives from "very young for my age" to "very old for my age"):

Some of the Ages of Me items contribute directly to personal age scores, while others of the items provide a context for interpretation and hypothesis generation.

Age-Appropriate Attitudes Technique. The research interview also includes administration of the Age-Appropriate Attitude Technique (AAAT). This procedure consists of a gallery of six fictitious people who each have a distinct outlook on life. The original form (Kastenbaum, 1963, Kastenbaum and Durkee, 1964) employed masculine names only; for this study, female names were employed when administered to females.[1]

The AAAT characters are presented in Table 5.1. The outlook listed for each character is given here to clarify the items' intent but is not presented to the respondents.

Respondent is asked several questions about each AAAT character: "About what age would you say_____is? Why did you choose this age for_____? Now that you know how_____feels, what would you say to him by way of a reply? Using a 5-point scale, would you strongly agree, agree, agree somewhat, disagree, or strongly disagree with this view?"

Additionally, when the respondent has responded to all the characters individually, he or she is asked to indicate which of them holds a view that is most similar to his or her own outlook at the present time. (By comparing his or her choice with the dialogue he or she previously invented, we are provided with a possible insight into the respondent's inner relationship to his or her own age.)

The AAAT data do not contribute directly to the personal age determination but provide helpful contextual information.

Time perspective questionnaire. A brief time perspective questionnaire (Teahan & Kastenbaum, 1970) is also administered. The questionnaire inquires into past and future outlook, including specification of age range of "happiest years," assessment of role in the future (agent vs. recipient), and both expected and desired length of life-span.

Observer rating forms. The most relevant questions asked of the respondents about themselves are also asked of the interviewer. At the

TABLE 5.1. Age-Appropriate Attitudes Technique

Character	Sketch	Outlook
Harry/Carol:	is feeling very blue. He has decided that the future holds nothing for him.	Null future
Phil/Ann:	wonders if he is really getting any place. He does not know whether he should be hopeful or pessimistic about his future.	Uncertain future
Charlie/Susie:	is feeling great. He feels that his life is just beginning, that nothing can stop him.	Exuberant future
Grant/Christine:	feels that he has everything he wants. He is completely satisfied with his life, and desires nothing more.	Satiated present
Ted/Pamela:	does not like new things. He prefers the old way of doing things, feeling that things are not as good as they used to be.	Beloved past
Sam/Gwen:	has no use for the old way of doing things. He prefers everything new, believing that things are getting to be much better than they used to be.	Despised past

conclusion of the interview, the respondent's "looks," "interests," and so on are rated by the interviewer. The respondent is also asked to provide the name of somebody who knows him or her well. This person is then contacted to make a parallel rating of interpersonal age (with the respondent's knowledge and permission).

Participants

Two subpopulations were utilized in the present study. Students supported for advanced studies by the Institute of Gerontology (University of Michigan/Wayne State University) comprised one sample. The gerontology specialists included 27 women and 16 men with an age range from 20 to 60 years. While the number of women and men was almost equal in the 40-and-under range (16 women; 14 men), only 2 male students over the age of 40 could be located as compared with 11 women. The other sample was comprised of men and women roughly matched with the gerontologists in that they also are pursuing studies and careers involving many personal interactions, but they do not manifest any special interests in or commitment to gerontology. Most of these people were recruited from employees of a state agency. The nongerontological or general sample included 10 women and 21 men. The age range was comparable, with the exception of 3 women in the 60–65 age bracket. The total number available for analysis was 75: 38 women, 37 men.

Results

The response to the age-focused interview deserves brief comment. Typically, the respondent begins with a matter-of-fact, slightly aloof orientation. The interview is something he or she is prepared to "handle" in professional rather than personal terms, not surprising in view of the background of most of the participants. Before long, however, the respondent tends to be deeply immersed. The questions seem to strike home. Some make use of the interview to launch a probing self-examination of their developmental history and prospects; few seem to remain unaffected by the experience. In future studies it would be useful to objectify type and intensity of involvement in the interview per se. The gerontology specialists do not appear to be immune to the challenges of age-oriented inquiry. Several gerontologists are among those who expressed the greatest amount of perturbation during and after the interview. (This reaction tends to confirm earlier impressions by the authors that gerontology training programs do not invariably prepare specialists to cope with age-related problems on a personal basis.)

Personal Age

Respondents are asked to rate their own age status in two ways: by comparing themselves with others at the same chronological age (Item Set 1), and by specifying the absolute chronological age that most closely matches the way they look, feel, think, and act (Item Set 2). This analysis was limited to the absolute age mode of response which, on available evidence, appears to be a more sensitive index. The following illustrative data bear on the questions of unitary versus multidimensional structure of personal age and on the relationship between personal and chronological age at various levels of chronological age.

One obvious question concerns the general level of agreement between personal and chronological age. The percentage who gave their actual chronological age in response to each of the four personal age questions considered here was computed. This provides percentage-of-agreement data on "feel age," "look age," "do age," and "interests age" for five chronological age categories: 20s, 30s, 40s, 50s, and 60s (the latter with such a small number that no conclusions are warranted).

Inspection of the results indicates that agreement between personal and chronological age occurs only to a moderate extent. Of the 20 figures displayed in Table 5.2, only one shows as much as a 50% agreement (*interests* age at chronological age 30). The range of agreement percentages scales all the way down to 0% (*look* age at chronological age 50). The lack of comparative data from other populations severely limits our ability to specify how "high" or "low" these consistency percentages might be. It is clear, however, that knowledge of a person's chronological age cannot be substituted for direct knowledge of age status in his or her own eyes. Personal age, in other words, does appear to be a concept distinct enough from chronological age that they cannot be interchanged without the likelihood of gross error.

Next, one can turn to the same set of data for information concerning age trends. The mean percentage of agreement between personal and chronological ages declines steadily throughout the adult decades (but one must not lose sight of the fact that these data are cross-sectional). While men and women in their 20s express 41% agreement (across specific personal age items), this figure dips to 12.5% for those in their 50s. The decline in agreement decade by decade shows a 6% drop between 20s and 30s, another 9% for the 40s, and 13.5% for the 50s. The declines for the 40s and 50s are especially striking when it is understood each is subtracted from a progressively lower agreement figure for the preceding (younger) decade. (Data on the 60s are indicated for sake of completeness but are not included in further analysis and interpretation.)

This pattern suggests what might be characterized as an increasing personalization of personal age with advancing chronological age. If we wished to arrive at a general expression of agreement between chronological and personal age, then we would have to qualify the usefulness of this term very heavily, or incorporate an age-correction term. The mean percentage of agreement for the present sample turns out to be 32.7% (computed on the basis of the actual number for each decade, rather than taking

TABLE 5.2. Percentage of Respondents Expressing Agreement between Chronological and Personal Age

Decade	Look Age	Feel Age	Do Age	Interests Age	Mean
20s	44	41	41	38	41
30s	20	30	40	50	35
40s	35	30	20	20	26
50s	0	20	20	10	12.5
60s	33	33	16	16	

the mean from the percentages given for unequal numbers in Table 5.2).
While this figure happens to come close to the consistency shown by
30-year-olds between their personal and chronological ages, it would prove
more misleading than helpful in evaluating the general relationship between personal and chronological age. Unless subsequent data reverse the
present trend, it will be necessary to recognize a widening disparity
between personal and chronological age throughout the adult years.

Of equal interest to percentage of agreement is the question of direc-
tionality. Do people tend to regard themselves as younger or older than
their chronological ages, or can any generalization be made? On the basis of
the limited data currently available, this problem can be addressed directly: (1) Personal age tends to be younger than chronological age, and (2) the
bias toward a younger personal age is found in an increasingly conspicuous
form as we move upward in the chronological age scale. In other words,
most of the increasing gap between chronological and personal age already
noted can be accounted for in terms of a bias toward self-reported youthfulness.

One of the ways in which the directional trend can be expressed is in
terms of algebraic mean for inconsistencies between personal and chronological age. A deviation toward older personal age arbitrarily was recorded
as positive, deviation toward younger personal age as negative. Equal
inconsistencies in both directions would result in an algebraic mean of 0. As
can be seen in Table 5.3, all of the 20 item-by-decade computations show a
bias toward personal age being reported as younger than chronological age.
The bias begins in a modest way with the 20-year-olds whose algebraic
means favored youthful self-evaluations by differentials such as –.66 (*look*
age) and –.72 (*feel* age). By the time we reach the 50-year-olds, however,
all discrepancies between personal and chronological age are in the youthful direction, with means ranging from –7.6 (*look* age) up to –13.2 (*interests*
age).

TABLE 5.3. Direction and Extent of Inconsistencies between Chronological and
Personal Ages

Decade	Look Age	Feel Age	Do Age	Interests Age
20s	–.66	–.72	–.69	–.83
30s	–.80	–2.90	–4.30	–1.20
40s	–2.85	–6.30	–6.40	–7.80
50s	–7.60	–8.30	–12.60	–13.20
60s	–4.66	–9.33	–16.60	–15.50

Negative sign = personal age younger than chronological. Positive sign would = personal age
older than chronological, but no such instances were found.

The data already presented have implications for the dimensional structure of personal age. The age a person believes that she or he *looks* tends to be that aspect of personal age which is closest to chronological age. In Table 5.3, for example, *look* age shows the smallest youthward bias for every decade represented, while *interests* age shows the greatest youthward bias. The gap between *look* and *interests* also appears to widen with every decade (from a –.17 differential in the 20s to a –5.80 in the 50s). Given this trend toward systematic difference among personal age dimensions, it might be premature to treat personal age as a unitary variable at this time.

It is perhaps even more relevant, however, to examine directly the internal consistency of personal age responses apart from their relationship to chronological age. Simple inspection of the data revealed that only 13 of the 75 respondents specified the same personal age for each of the four items—in other words, about 80% of the sample expressed some internal inconsistency. (Inconsistency is not intended to be a negative value term here; it also could be said that people who give more than one age have a more highly differentiated view of their personal age.) Incidentally, 4 of the 13 consistent individuals specified a personal age that was different from their chronological age. At the opposite extreme, there were 11 respondents who gave a different age for every item. Another 25 respondents specified three different ages for the four personal age items. In other words, almost half of the sample (36 of 75) showed a high degree of internal variation on the personal age items. Another interesting group was the set of 19 respondents who gave three identical ages but one that was different. It turned out that *look* age was clearly the most often "out-grouped" dimension: 9 respondents were internally consistent for the other three items, with the remaining 10 respondents distributed randomly in their choice of an item to break the consistency pattern.

Further information can be obtained by counting the number of instances in which a particular personal age item received the same response as another item. Percentage of consistency among the four personal age items is shown in Table 5.4. One of the most striking results is the low

TABLE 5.4. Consistency Percentage among Personal Age Items

	Look Age	Feel Age	Do Age	Interests Age	Mean
Look age		45.33	28.00	33.33	35.55
Feel age	45.33		49.33	44.33	46.22
Do age	28.00	49.33		45.33	40.89
Interests Age	33.33	44.33	45.33		40.89

ceiling for interitem agreement. No pair of items was given the same age more than 50% of the time. How old a person *feels* was in agreement 49% of the time with the response to "I *do* most things as though I were about age: ___." The lowest agreement also involved *do* age. This item showed only 28% consistency with *feel* age.

Overall, when respondents specified their *look* age, they were giving a response that had only a 35.55% mean consistency with their other personal age items. How old they *feel*, however, provides the best clue to general personal age with a consistency percentage of 46%. *Do* and *interests* age fell almost exactly halfway between *look* and *feel*.

It is interesting to see that while a person's evaluation of her or his *look* age is closest to chronological age, it is her or his *feel* age that most nearly approaches an index to her or his broader view of personal age.

Interpersonal and Consensual Ages

There are two sources of interpersonal age data in this study: interviewer ratings and ratings made by an acquaintance of the respondent. We consider here only the ratings made by the interviewer on two items: how old the respondent *looks* to the interviewer and how old interviewer thinks of respondent as being in *general*. About two-things of the time, the interviewer was consistent in rating *look* and *general* for the same respondent. As can be seen in Table 5.5, consistency was relatively high for the 30s and 50s (80% agreement), and relatively low for the 20s and 40s. Consistency of interviewer's ratings exceeds the average internal consistency of respondent's self-ratings (Table 5.4). The mean *interpersonal* age consistency (65%) is well above any of the agreement percentages found between pairs of *personal* age items. Within the limits of these data, it would appear that the interviewer is more apt to take *look* age as an index of *general* age than is the respondent.

TABLE 5.5. Interpersonal Age Consistency Percentage by Decades

Decade	Look/General Age
20s	62
30s	80
40s	55
50s	80
60s	67

Mean interpersonal age consistency: 65%.

Illustrative data on *consensual* age are presented in Table 5.6. Two *personal* age items *(look* and *feel)* are each paired with the two *interpersonal* age items *(look* and *general)* given above. Interviewer and respondent are furthest apart when we match "I *feel"* with the interviewer's rating of *general* age. Perhaps this is consistent with a finding presented above, namely, that *feel* is the component of *personal* age that is least predictable from knowledge of chronological age, a more inward dimension than *look*.

A number of age trends are suggested by the data in Table 5.6, but none are clear enough to seize upon at the moment. The usefulness of various items for establishing consensuality seems to depend upon respondent's chronological age. Respondent and interviewer agree 70% of the time, for example, if respondent is in the 50s and the comparison is between personal *look* and interpersonal *general*. The same comparison, however, yields only a 44% consensus if the respondent is in the 20s. At some age levels (30s and 40s) consensus is virtually identical no matter what specific ratings are being compared—but marked differences are found at other age levels (20s and 50s). The consistently low agreement between respondent and interviewer for the 30s opens a problem area that will be explored in more detail in later studies and reports. People in their 30s were the only respondents in the present study who showed any substantial trend toward seeing themselves as both younger and older than their chronological age. The youthward trend is already established for the 20s, as reported above, and accelerates from the 40s onward. While the person in the 30s tends to be a participant in the "younger-than-my-age" movement, he or she also has some thoughts in the opposite direction as well.

Contextual Data

Only a few illustrations can be given here of data emerging from the AAAT and the time perspective questionnaire. "Charlie/Susie," the exuberant future character of the AAAT, was easily the most popular choice as character-identified-with by the respondents in general (38 of 75). This

TABLE 5.6. Consensual Age Consistency Percentages by Decades

Decade	Look/Look	Feel/General	Look/General	Decade Mean
20s	72	45.0	44	53.66
30s	40	40.0	40	40.00
40s	55	50.0	55	53.33
50s	50	50.0	70	56.66
60s	50	83.0	100	77.66
Mean	56	46.7	55	

finding appears consistent with the youthward bias that pervades so much of the personal age data. The parallel also holds true when chronological age by decades is added to the picture. Older respondents tended to select Charlie even more often than did the younger respondents. Charlie was the choice of 38% of the 20s, 50% of the 30s, 65% of the 40s, and 60% of the 50s (as well as by two of the six 60s). In other words, the older the respondents the more likely they are to identify with a person who believes that life is "just beginning," and that "nothing can stop him."

Who did *not* identify with Charlie? There were no Charlies at all among respondents who *wanted* to live much longer than they *expected* to live on the time perspective questionnaire. This suggestive finding points up the importance of considering respondent's orientation toward death along with attempting to understand personal age. As a number of observers have remarked, it might be more useful to reckon age from date of death backward, rather than date of birth forward. Relationship between personal age and life-death expectation will be examined more intensively in future reports.

Discussion

The methodological limitations of this study are numerous. As the first stage of a new research program, it was intended to replace itself as soon as possible. Apart from problems that should be readily apparent to the reader, it should be noted that the interviewers were all in the 20s age range and were not provided with special training in estimation of interpersonal age. Both the age match-up between interviewer and respondent and the criteria established for interpersonal age ratings might be expected to influence the results. We did opt deliberately for the untutored rating of interpersonal age at this stage in the research, with the variables of interviewer age and specificity of criteria to be explored further later. It also bears repeating that our data are cross-sectional and thus do not establish anything about changes with age in the same respondent.

A thorough discussion is probably out of place at this stage. There are a few points, however, which deserve mention here.

1. We had not expected the bias toward a youthward personal age to show itself even in the youngest subsample. It seems traditional to assume that young people want to be "grown up" in their own and others' eyes. If so, at what age level does the switchover toward youthward self-perception begin? Is it possible that young people are less interested or less ready to see themselves as grown ups than in past generations? Or do people now

feel "old enough" before their 20s, and believe that subsequent years bring little in the way of further maturation?

2. With advancing adult age we have found an increasing tendency to express a personal age that is much discrepant from the chronological. Is it "healthy" or "pathological" to embrace an ever-more-youthful self-conception as one grows older? What are the critical differences between those who give personal ages consistent with the chronological and those who so resolutely think (themselves) young? Will, in fact, the most youth-ward-biased respondents prove to be correspondingly youthful when tested on objective measures of functional age?

3. As a corollary to the above, it appears somewhat unusual to find a person who considers himself "old for his age," especially in the upper age brackets. Will this trend be extended or reversed when we include people in their 70s, 80s, and 90s? The strong general youthward bias, if supported in subsequent studies, would have implications for the experimental-modification line of research sketched earlier in this chapter. Fairly clear-cut samples of people who consider themselves young for their age should be easy to obtain, but perhaps not so easily for those who classify them-selves as older than their age. The entire classification system may have to be shifted to the youthward side (e.g., "much younger than my age," "somewhat younger than my age," and "not younger—but not older—than my age").

4. The present data imply that how old people *look* and *feel* (both from their own frame of reference) represent appreciably different aspects of their total personal age. At least these two facets should be differenti-ated, and perhaps others, as research continues. Future efforts might be directed toward obtaining more adequate measures of *looks* and *feels* components of personal age, and to determine the relationship of each to other measures of functional age. Would the more inward dimension show a stronger relationship to subtle measures of biologic age? Would the more "exposed" component of *looks* age prove more strongly related to social age?

5. At this point, there is an impression that gerontology specialists share in the general trends that have been reported for the total sample. It is possible that this impression will be modified when all analyses have been performed. The lack of conspicuous differences, however, does sug-gest that involvement in specialized gerontology training (or choice of this specialty in the first place) cannot be assumed to create a cadre of adults with distinctive orientations toward their own personal age. The possibility of including age role playing and other self-confrontation procedures in gerontology training might be worth serious consideration.

6. The results allow for cautious optimism concerning the possibility of establishing interpersonal and consensual age on a footing that is at least as secure as that of personal age.

Conclusion

Three concepts have been introduced: *personal* age (how old a person seems to her or himself), *interpersonal* age (how old he or she seems to others), and *consensual* age (degree of agreement between personal and interpersonal ages.) This initial research report indicates that the structure of these three ages must be considered in relation to chronological age level. The most general finding was an increased bias toward youthward evaluation (and, thus, discrepancy with chronological age) as we ascend the age ladder from the 20s through the 50s. Individuals tend to take a more differentiated view of their own age status than do interviewers. This includes a moderately clear distinction between the age a person *feels* and the age that he or she believes he *looks*. Interviewers had particular difficulty in assessing how old a respondent *feels*. The overall results suggest that personal and interpersonal age can be developed into sets of concepts useful in the more general domain of functional age and might also serve as basis for experimental attempts to create and manipulate "old" behavior. Advanced students of gerontology who participated in the study appear to share the same orientations as the population in general.

References

Damon, A. Predicting age from body measurements and observations. *Aging and Human Development*, 1972, 3, 169–174.

Donahue, W. Relationship of age of perceivers to their social perceptions. *Gerontologist*, 1965, 5, 241–245; 276–277.

Heron, A., and Chown, S. *Age and function*. Boston: Little, Brown, 1967.

Fozard, J. L. Predicting age in the adult years from psychological assessments of abilities and personality. *Aging and Human Development*, 1972, 3, 175–182.

Kastenbaum, R. Cognitive and personal futurity in later life. *Journal of Individual Psychology*, 1963, 19, 216–222.

Kastenbaum, R. Perspectives on the development and modification of behavior in the aged: A developmental perspective. *Gerontologist*, 1968, 8, 280–284.

Kastenbaum, R. What happens to the man who is inside the aging body? An inquiry into the developmental psychology of later life. In F. C. Jeffers (Ed.), *Duke University Council on Aging and Human Development. Proceedings of seminars, 1965–1969*. Durham, N.C.: Duke University Press, 1969a, pp. 99–112.

Kastenbaum, R. Toward the experimental induction of "old behavior." NIMH project proposal. Detroit, Mich.: Wayne State University, 1969b.

Kastenbaum, R. Getting there ahead of time. *Psychology Today*, 1971 (December), pp. 52–54; 82–84.

Kastenbaum, R., and Durkee, N. Young people view old age. In R. Kastenbaum (Ed.), *New Thoughts on Old Age*. New York: Springer, 1964, 237–249.

Pastalan, L. Testimony to U.S. Senate Special Committee on Aging, 1971.

Rose, C. L. The measurement of social age. *Aging and Human Development*, 1972, 3, 153–168.

Teahan, J., and Kastenbaum, R. Future time perspective and subjective life expectance in "hard-core" unemployed men. *Omega*, 1970, *1*, 189–200.

II

The Inner Life

The external signs and emblems of old age are important for the effects they have on society and on older people themselves. It is easy to become so preoccupied with the externals that we neglect the person inside. Gerontology in general has not given very much attention to the inner life of old people, although a gradual arousal of interest can now be seen. Our understanding of old age on the new scene would be severely limited if the inner dimensions of experience were ignored.

One of the most interesting contemporary explorations, however, comes from a rather old scene: the traditional place of the creative artist in India. Renaldo Maduro explains the relationship between artistic creativity and the various phases of the Hindu life cycle before turning his attention to a direct study of the old man as a creative artist at an ancient pilgrimage center in Western India. An interesting link can be seen between folk theories of creative process and Carl Jung's view of the life cycle. The close and subtle relationship between the cultivation and expression of the artistic impulse in the individual and what the host culture expects and values is well illustrated in this study. The results stand in marked contrast to previous studies of age and creativity conducted in our own society.

"I am 80 and have never been happier" is a statement that flows naturally out of the experiences of Claire M. Owens. She has found that meditation offers a path to self-realization for people of all ages. In particular, Owens believes that meditation, "discovering the universe within," is an ideal way for elderly men and women to attain a sense of purpose and a higher level of consciousness. It is interesting to see how she interweaves ancient Eastern philosophy with modern research and speculations on the relative functions of the right and left cerebral hemispheres. Different from the other contributions to this book in tone and perspective as well as content, Owens's essay needs no proof outside itself to demonstrate the ability of elderly people to explore the riches of inner life.

How a person organizes his or her entire life along the time dimensions is another significant clue to the nature of inner experience. The life perspective of older people is examined by Robert Kastenbaum within the larger context of our relationship to time from infancy onward. Attention is also given to the variety of time perspectives among old people and the influence of social attitudes and pressures.

These are but a few of the ways in which the inner experiences of older people can be approached, revealing a richness and variety that might otherwise escape the attention of those who are unduly impressed with the external emblems of age.

6

The Old Man
As Creative Artist
in India

Renaldo Maduro

The Problem

Although there has been general interest in both aging and creativity, a
more focused consideration of artistic creativity in relation to different
phases of the life cycle has been neglected. Anthropological studies of
culture and aging have not stressed the expressive symbolic dimensions of
human existence (creativity). In fact, the whole field of aging is rather new
to anthropology. Except for the early work of Simmons and a few others,[1]
cross-cultural investigations prior to the 1960s merely mentioned old age in
connection with other more traditional cultural categories. In the 1960s
anthropologists turned with increasing enthusiasm to the interdisciplinary
study of aging in other cultures and in American minority-group subcul-
tures. New life and direction have come from a growing awareness of the
pressing need to study problems of human development covering the
entire life-span, and mainly from work stimulated by Clark, Clark and
Anderson, Clark and Mendelson, Cowgill and Holmes, Erikson, Kiefer,
Shelton, and Spencer.[2-12]

Outside the purview of anthropology, little has been done to elucidate
the complex interrelationship between creativity and middle age and
aging. Most researchers have not defined what they mean by "creativity,"
so that a confused reader gropes among a welter of possible meanings and
associations. We are not told if the term refers to artistic creativity,
scientific creativity, or creativity as a generalized personality trait. For
example, the well-known work of Lehman vaguely lumps together all
forms of creativity and fails to distinguish between "achievement" and

Reprinted with permission from *International Journal of Aging and Human Development*,
1974, 5, 303–329. Support for research and the preparation of this article was generously
provided by the Foundations' Fund for Research in Psychiatry (Grant 72-538) and the
National Institute of Child Health and Human Development Grant No. HD 00238.

other possibilities. [13] Yet we are told that maximal creativity occurs during youth, a commonly held but unsubstantiated notion. Lehman refers in the same work to "creative production rates . . . high quality research . . . achievement . . . creative acheivements . . . [and] . . . creative achievements of the very highest order." Likewise Dennis writes of "creative productivity,"[14] and Taylor of "achievements" and "creations" of noted American pianists. [15] Previous creativity-and-aging research designs have shared a common (perhaps American) bias: a preoccupation with creativity as product, output, achievement, or contribution. Nearly always the locus of evaluation of such products is external to the individuals under study. Thus one may argue that what is studied has more to do with aesthetic value systems or economic incentives than with creativity per se.

This chapter is based on 18 months of anthropological field work in Nathdwara, a small pilgrimage center in arid Rajasthan, Western India. Nathdwara town is the headquarters of Pushtimarga, an influential Hindu Vaishnava sect devoted to the worship of Shri Nathji, the statue of a 7-year-old Divine Child form of Lord Krishna on earth, believed by Pushtimarga followers to be "living" (swārūpa). Some 155 Brahmin folk painters (110 men, 45 women) belonging to two different subcastes live and work around this numinous cult institution; as a community within a community, they form an integral part of the sacred temple complex. Painting in this ritual context, the artist reports his role as "sacerdotal" and his artistic endeavor as "a part of sacred mystery of the temple precincts." For a comprehensive psychocultural account of this group and analyses of symbolic expressive behavior, readers are referred to Maduro. [16]

It is my contention that in dealing with creativity as a research domain, we must distinguish between at least three distinct yet tightly interwoven perspectives: (1) creative *products*, (2) creative *personality attributes,* and (3) creative *process*. At the same time, however, we have an obligation to look at *sociocultural* factors that either foster or inhibit the manifestation of a specified kind of creativeness in a particular setting.

Here discussion is limited to Hindu folk theories of *creative process* in relation to traditional art styles: How is the notion of creativity defined, regarded, and personally experienced? Where does creative energy originate and how is it thought to be utilized? Data which bear on these and other related questions are presented—data which are "emic" because they are part of Hindu world view and refer to processes which folk painters themselves regard as significant and say they experience. Indigenous theories of art and the psychogenesis of creative energy are here related to recent theoretical interest in ego boundary maintenance, [17] disengagement theory, [18] and creative mid-life introversions of libido posited by Jungian analytic theory. In connection with the latter, Neugarten has noted the "increased interiority of the personality" in the second half of life.[19] As such, this is an attempt to get at kinds of artistic creativity not easily measured—creative *process* as it applies especially to Hindu male folk painters in India.

It will become clear that artistic creativity does not decline with chronological age, or more precisely, that it can often peak in early middle age and remain actively vibrant into later life. It will be demonstrated that relationships exist between stages of the Hindu life cycle and creative activity and that the concept of ego boundary permeability or impermeability can help to explain disengagement theory in a new and less confusing framework for analysis. Because orthodox Hindu customs made it impossible for a male investigator to remain alone with a woman for any length of time, intensive life history research was, perforce, limited to male painters. However, three of the 45 female painters in Nathdwara were frequently cited as "highly creative" by men. Although much of what is said here about male painters and creativity throughout the life cycle also applies to women, this study is unfortunately limited to data collected from men. As such, it does not systematically explore possible sex differences in creativity through the life-span in India.

The Hindu Concept of Aging

Hindus divide the life cycle into childhood and four later overlapping stages: the *āshramas* (literally: halting or resting places, milestones). Prabhu has aptly referred to these as the "psycho-moral bases of society."[20] Hindu world view holds that by successfully passing first through childhood, and then these four stages, one may repay all his obligations or debts to the gods, ancient seers, and forefathers. Only then is salvation or liberation *(moksha)* from the vast timeless ocean of deaths and rebirths made possible.

When Brahmins in Nathdwara speak of the *āshramas* it is with a sense of idealism. For example: "It is my duty to try as hard as I can to attain balance in my life and to live according to the ideals *(ādarsh)* of each stage along the journey of life." In the discussion to follow it will be important to keep in mind that we are listening to male Brahmin painter informants, for the stages of life are believed to be especially applicable to only the three highest caste *(varna)* rankings of the Hindu ritual hierarchy—Brahmins at the very top (ideally the priests and teachers), Kshatriya (ideally warriors, rulers, and landlords), and Vaishya (merchants and men of commerce). These three highest orders of the orthodox Hindu caste system are known collectively as "the twice born." Lower castes are not permitted to participate in the same symbolic death-rebirth initiation ceremonies designed to demarcate the serious life transition from "childhood" to the four stages proper.

While four ashramas (*Brahmacharya, Grihastha, Vānaprastha,* and *Sanyāsa*) are generally acknowledged, "spiritual life" is not thought to begin with physical birth but with the symbolic rebirth *rite de passage* alluded to above. This "second birth," involving the investiture of a sacred thread, can occur at or after puberty, although the modern trend among Brahmin painters is to combine marriage and sacred thread rites at a time in later adolescence or young adulthood. It is crucial to note also that at each life-cycle stage certain developmental tasks or roles are expected to be performed and particular states of self-awareness attained. Stages are, therefore, more task defined than strictly age-specific. Moreover, Brahmins are popularly believed to be inherently "ready" to pass on to the next stage sooner than Kshatriya or Vaishya. As one painter put it: "It is their inherited predisposition to be more interested in these things and to develop more rapidly along these lines. They are very intelligent and make faster progress."

For men, the sacred thread investiture ushers in the first ashrama, that of the *Brahmacharya*. This is a student stage in which there is a great emphasis on celibacy, the conservation of semen, and strict obedience to one's teachers. For folk painters it is a period of apprenticeship and "the time of patient preparation." The young painter is enjoined to submit to authority, to learn diligently exactly as he is taught, and to accept wholeheartedly an external locus of self-evaluation. Only much later, it is said, can he hope "to go his own way just as he pleases doing his own thing." The young painter is *guru-bound*. To quote from two painters:

(1) The creative painter must practice frequently from childhood on; he needs the guidance of the guru, especially when he is in the brahmacharya stage. He may have a guru after he is a householder for some time, but the guru's special place is early when the young painter is acquiring self-control. This is before sex life—I mean having a wife and family—and during this stage the creative painter must be of a peaceful nature. His nature must be cool *(thand)*; he musn't get angry or aggressive *(gussa)*, because if he angers quickly he will not be able to learn anything from a guru. The guru will say, "This is not a good piece of work!" and the student will have to listen to suggestions and follow instructions calmly. If he is creative, some religious bent is also needed at this stage, but generally this can only develop later. Now he follows instructions and is disciplined. He learns the rules for what comes later.

(2) The creative painter must also have guidance from a guru. He cannot do it alone. He must be persistent and take great care in his work. It is not a question of the young brahmacharya painter being religious all the time. This occurs when he is ripe after being a householder. I will tell you about that too.

But I want to say that the brahmacharya painter can begin to learn—if his guru is spiritually advanced—how to paint sacred subjects like Shri Nathji. He begins to learn how to concentrate with all his mind and heart on the gods within—on Him—the feeling of Shri Nathji must be manifested in the artist. Those who will become creative later know of these experiences, even from childhood.

In the second life-cycle stage, the *Grihasthāshrama*, one is expected to marry, procreate, participate actively in social affairs, and work hard to acquire material goods and economic wealth. Early in this stage, emphasis is on progeny and a measured appreciation of Eros, the life force, sex; at this point younger painters speak of being under the dominance of Kamadeva, the god of love, and of the significance of this symbolic identification in their creative efforts. The householder stage is a period in which libidinal demands of utmost importance slowly give way to a dawning consciousness of maturity and eventual death. This stage blends into middle age—a time spanning the summer and autumn of life. But by the end of this stage a man is well entrenched in later life, and painters have already begun to speak of "ripening" and maturity. A young painter in this stage of the life cycle explains:

PAINTER: A man should not be shy and anxious after he leaves his guru-father. If his guru experience has been good—and mine wasn't because I never could apply myself to studies!—then the creative artist will develop his own personal style by experimenting with all the things he has been shown and taught. He will concentrate hard, be very interested in his work, and apply himself diligently to his work, since he has a great need for money in this householder stage—feeding his old parents and caring for them if he has some, and taking care of his own wife and children too . . . (pause ending in laughter) . . . You know—suppose—this is the time when the painter does everything, tries all techniques and paints in all styles because he suddenly gets tied to or comes into relationship with *(sambandh mē ānā)* Kamadeva. This is what we believe here in our locale. This god is for the erotic life, sex, and creativity. The householder uses this . . . I mean, in this time over and over again the creative man feels the powerful influence of this god. The old painter X is very creative, and he says it is very important to let it be . . . (pause) . . . it means that . . . well, I know you ask me to tell you whatever I am thinking, so I mean to say that Kama means sex, and the creative painter in this stage will be going here and there with friends, earning money, trying all new things in his art, and eating, drinking, and enjoying sex. That's it. Moving about here and there. . . .

QUESTION: Do you mean to say that there's a strong connection between sex and creativity during the householder stage?

PAINTER: Yes, friend. That's it. Kamadeva. It is an environment of pleasures, not like the strict life of the Brahmacharya. They are very strict. From pleasure springs art.

QUESTION: How is the creative painter's work different during this stage?

PAINTER: Well, as I said to you, the creative man wants to be on good terms with his castefellows (jāti-wāti log) and make money. His style mixes everything from all styles—colors and linework—but he is not really so deep inside himself or mature (paripakva) yet. We have a saying here that it takes everything its own time to become ripe. Well, the householder is getting ripe. Ha! Ha! But he is still young at first. Only later with ripeness can he be really creative and teach others. It is his duty then to be a very religious man and teach others, not to lock up the secrets of meditation and self-discovery in his heart. Only after he has lived fully in the householder stage can a painter come into his own and be creative. Moving out of the householder stage brings forth what we call here "divine mental vision" (gyāna chakshu). A creative painter now becomes very reflective (vicārvān).

Ideally the third phase, "Vānaprasthāshrama of the elders," is characterized most by the attainment of some degree of psychological wholeness and integration. This "forest hermit" stage always occurs slowly, never abruptly. One painter reports with feeling: "When a man begins to see that his skin is wrinkling, his hair has turned or is turning white, and there are sons of his sons, then he can feel good that he has met his family obligations and performed his duties to caste and society. He can then turn inward and contemplate the inner light. At this time of life a man's powers of imagination increase fourfold because he has learned to reach into himself for light, bliss and balance."

In ancient times, men and women are said actually to have departed from their families and vanished into the forest during the third ashrama. In 1970 this did not occur, but the idea had strong symbolic meaning for painters in this stage. Many retired to a corner of the family compound to think and paint in solitude; others separated from their usual sleeping quarters and lived generally more introverted lives. A few became near recluses or actually set up shop in the woods and hills outside town, refusing to work with sons and pupils on days when they were particularly in touch with inner subjective states and painting. A common remark from painters of later middle age was: "I feel the need to be alone in the hills to take in the clear cool mountain air for creative inspiration and psychological health." However this expressed need to be alone more often for psychological work does not preclude all social engagement; within the family and to some extent the subcaste, many individuals remain powerful and active, yet this stage may include a relative lack of social interaction with members of the wider Hindu community.

Beginning near the end of the householder stage and continuing into the ashrama of the elders, middle age is a time in which one kind of mental activity and power is gracefully relinquished for another. Turning inward with discipline is believed to gradually replace an urge to acquire more power and securities in the external world. Growing old brings augmented comprehension of new psychological direction and emergent symbolic life inhibited previously by a preoccupation with the development of ego mastery over self and environment. With increasing years creative artists say they are "more open" to the nuances of internal chaos and pure intuition, to "conceiving," and to "the unfolding of the self" than to reinforcing the ascendency of the ego's executive functions over the entire psychic apparatus. It is as if ego is expected to give up control from the top down for the rewards of a more wholeness-fostering dialogue with creative unconscious processes. To quote one highly creative painter who in 1970 was 67 years old (see Figure 6.1):

> Now the truly creative painter—as a man in the elders' stage—he is unconventional (navīn), original, and somewhat less sociable (sāmājik). He is really different from others because of his age and because of his mind which remains very sharp-witted (tēz budhi wālā) and especially sensitive (samvēdanshīl) to messages from within for his artistic work. He listens more carefully for messages from inside, from the gods, from the world of māyā rūpa, and he is less outgoing (bāhar jānē wālā). But he is able to be more original (mautik) and creative now—also more individualistic (vyaktivādī). He paints whatever he likes. He doesn't give a hoot sometimes about other people, including providing for his own family. He happily does his own thing (āpnē masti sē) just like the water buffalo. This means he is more imaginative (kalpanāshīl), mature/ripe (pakka) and religious (dhārmik ādmī)—not religious with mantras and tantras and temple service here and there, but with self-development and independence (svatantrata). He is closer to the power of the gods within him now; and closer to root emotion. This is a man who is strange (ajīb), but he is not so pleasure-seeking (sukh khōji wālā) as during his householder stage.

Whereas the main task of the first half of life is seen as the development of strong (other-directed) ego mastery skills, the second half is characterized by inner self-development. This increased interiority or active creative introversion with age is not the same as increased religiosity or orthodoxy, but rather a heightened sense of autonomy, completeness, and system of personal ethics experienced as internally centered and evaluated. The mature creative painter has plunged into the chaos; he has asked questions at depth and challenged the structure and "roots" (jarh) of human consciousness.

In the last or Sanyāsa stage, one is ideally a wandering ascetic who has cut all bonds with family, society, and worldly pleasures. Unlike previous stages where psychological work coupled with artistic activity is prescribed, this period can be one of relative locomotor passivity and life-avoidance: the confrontation of nothingness from which new life will

Figure 6.1.   Shri Gulabji Chandra Sharma was a painter, sculptor, jewelry design-er, goldsmith, and architect of great fame in the region. He was cited by many as being an "all-around creative artist and master craftsman." In his 60s he retired to the outskirts of town to paint and pursue other artistic activities in contemplation—usually alone near an old ruin and surrounded by a clump of scrubby trees filled with parrots. Although he withdrew more and more from social engagements, he continued to produce artistically and to explore his inner world by sketching these and other fantasies for his work. The other person in this photograph is a visiting caste fellow.

eventually spring, i.e., the wheel of reincarnations. One painter in this life stage remarks:

> I am a very old man and people say I am very creative. I agree with them. I try to look at things in a different way—a new way all the time. I have lost interest in everything external to my artistic efforts, in all other things except my special interests. Even though I stand before darkness and death—ready—

still I try to incorporate everything that is natural in my paintings. I therefore try to get closer to God. We are all just a part of Him. I have an awareness of the world when it concerns my paintings. My mind is always aware of the surroundings—clothes, sky, buildings, etc.—with a keen eye to incorporate these things into my paintings. Otherwise I take no notice and give no importance to other things. It is a special kind of vision which creative painters have in old age, though I have had these propensities since my childhood days. For example, the truly creative painter is not so involved with friends when he's older, although he says "Jai!" to everyone. It means he is more independent, and he turns to look deeply inside. The mind of the really creative painter is different from others. And I tell you clearly: after the householder stage he who is the creative painter is equal to God—he performs the highest acts of creation.

In reality, few men live long enough to become sanyasi, and those who do withdraw totally from life generally elect this course of action long before extreme old age (i.e., they renounce the world for a great variety of reasons during the two preceding stages). Brahmin men over 70 are rare and considered very old. They may remain actively painting; often they are inactive, physically disabled, senile, but always attended to with formal respect and in many cases great admiration. In this period one faces death and darkness, "the eternal womb," and the few who live to be over 70 or 80 engage in even more active contemplation than before—except that they do not often continue to paint and work concretely with fantasy material.

The four ashramas form a carefully thought out philosophy of the life cycle. For each stage various behaviors, ethical standards, levels of creative activity, and stages of ego consciousness are prescribed as ideals. That not all men and women achieve the ideals associated with each ashrama and that stages overlap are important considerations to keep in mind. Yet the traditional model is familiar to the popular mind and affords a degree of psychological security and coherence to everyday life and creative activity among painters. It is telling that four colors, also corresponding to the four caste orders (varnas), are associated with the four stages of the life cycle. In sequence they are white, red, yellow, and black.

Folk Theories of Creativity as Process

The Tension of Psychic Opposites

According to Hindu folk psychology, he who possesses the creative faculty in all its fullness is in touch with the realm of "divine forms" and "affect images" (bhāvana, rūpa) of the unconscious or unmanifest mind (avidyā, māyā). He is also said to be of practiced vocational excellence. Moreover this special kind of artist—the creative artist-yogi—often is believed to be under the influence of the mother goddess *Saraswati*.

Artistic tradition teaches that it is only through his self-discipline and contemplative searchings that the Hindu painter can at last reach a stage, where as subject, he merges with an inner object or emotional state he would like to render into concrete form. He may then experience what is considered psychic wholeness, the transcendence of all opposites and life contradictions, "balance." The artist is believed to experience the mystical penetration of an artistic reality which exists independent of him alone.

Thus for the artist, beauty exists in the abstract and in ideal form. Painters often say with a sense of urgency that it is the "duty" of a really creative artist to contact this level of reality within the depths of himself, to strive to make it manifest, and indeed to become one with it, integrate it through meditation and self-actualization. In a real sense the artist is enjoined to re-create or reactivate what is already latent in his unconscious mind *(adrashta*, the *samskāras)*. This is recognized as a task for middle and later life.

It is not surprising to learn that Nathdwara painters recognize a special group of creative men who, in one artist's words, "are innately endowed with the quality of"*saraswata*," when we remember that the daughter and female consort of Lord Vishvakarma, god of creativity, is the popular mother goddess Saraswati herself. For while Vishvakarma is the Seer, an Eternal Awareness and Male Witness *(Mahā Purusha)*, Hinduism argues that it is always the divine mother—a female component of the personality—whose natural energy *(prakrati)* actively creates. It is the female energy or cosmic principle which *does* the work—creating blindly in the sense of mother nature, receiving, incubating and giving birth to new life and originality.

Thus while stressing identification with the father figure, Lord Vishvakarma (see Figure 6.2), Nathdwara painters seldom fail to mention the significance of "mataji" or "devi" (the mother goddess) and her creative energy and influence *(shakti)* too. Matriarchal consciousness is cited as an important source of inspiration and as creative energy available from a creative unconscious. For example: "He gets his creativity from the mother goddess. Her power works in him and it is this energy which creates."

Artists say the creative potential is actualized or activated when this female power or energy *(shakti)* can be integrated symbolically with the male principle. Therefore the concept of Vishvakarma-Saraswati, expressed so often by Nathdwara painters, contains one of the most important psychological principles related to artistic creativity and its popular conceptualization in India: that energy made available to the human psyche for creative expressive symbolic behavior comes through the union of oppo-

भगवान विश्वकर्मा

आर्टिस्ट द्वारकालाल शर्मा
नाथद्वारा (राजस्थान)

Figure 6.2   Line drawing of Lord Vishvakarma, God of Creativity and patron of all the arts and crafts from whom all Nathdwara painters claim to be descended.

sites, or more precisely, from the tension caused by the polarization of psychic opposites contained *simultaneously* in the mind. Symbols of polarity are well known in every art form the world over: male-female, light-dark, good-bad, right-left, heaven-earth, father-mother, sun-moon, thinking-feeling. In Hindu psychological theory there is a concern with the idea of the duality of one, and for this reason the female element is never left out or discarded intentionally for a strictly patriarchal model of human consciousness and personality dynamics. Nor is the satanic dismissed in religious art, as though it could be banished.

The role the mother goddess identification plays in art and during the creative process is clearly and positively stressed in this folk model of creativity based on uniting the opposites in oneself. As in life, so also in art: the goal is to achieve a balance and harmony *(sattva)* between two inherent tendencies of the mind, the inert *(tamas)* and the active *(rajas)*.

According to this model of creativity, any mental life producing energy for art must involve psychological growth and transformation through the confrontation of differences, the opposites. The cultivation of an artistically creative personality implies no less than this. Informants very often summed up the whole concept with a shrug: "Pleasure and pain *(sukhdukh)* will always, naturally, accompany each other!" From the moment a sperm fertilizes an ovum, something new—a third original something—has emerged. It is believed to be the same with artistic creativity: the confrontation of differences and polarities gives rise to a previously hidden symbolic third factor, something which is of greater importance than the two opposites from which it sprung. Nathdwara painters call this *dhvani* and *dhvanit*.

In order to sustain this process as a life-long experiment in psychological growth and integration, the artist must undergo a long and arduous period of training which can involve no small amount of personal suffering. As one of the most perceptive and creative painters put it: "In order to have success, the creative artist must confront and unite the psychological opposites in himself, no matter how antagonistic to each other they are." And he adds: "How can this be possible except in later years—after a painter has become somewhat wise."

Psychocultural evidence suggests that only in cultures which include an appreciation of the female principle or deity do we find any impressive profusion of images and richness of fantasy in pictorial religious art. For example, in Islam, Judaism, and major Protestant denominations where God is by definition an all-powerful father figure, there is a dearth of artistic elaboration of anthropomorphic religious imagery. There are, instead, proscriptions and taboos against the artistic "conception" and representation of deity in anything but very abstract and nonhuman forms. The Hindu model would seem to suggest, then, that for men there is something basically feminine, passive, accepting, or if not feminine, perhaps bisexual which strongly correlates with artistic creativity in a very general sense, and with all pictorial art stressing the articulation of the human form in particular.

Hindu psychology has for centuries given philosophical shape to this idea in its detailed elaboration of the Tantric *Shiva-Shakti* cults where male-female energies unite in cosmogonic procreation (*ardhanārīshvara*). That creative artistic energies originate from the tension generated by the polarization of psychic opposites is a widely accepted notion among Nathdwara painters, many of whom claim to have experienced just that in their lifetimes. To be descended from God, "the Heavenly Father and Architect of the Whole Universe," Vishvakarma, is to be infused at the same time with inspiration from the creative unconscious comprised essentially of power from the Divine Earthly Mother, *Mahā Devi*, or *Mahā Māyā*.

"Artistic capacity is in part inherited from the creator god Vishvakarma," say the painters, cultivated through psychological individuation begun in early adulthood, revealed in dream and vision, and expressed as part of sacred ritual. Any Nathdwara painter will tell you that this essential quality or propensity of the mind to entertain simultaneously and then unite the opposites is his solemn birthright. The process must be seriously pursued in the householder stage but is believed to flower later with age. In later life Indian folk culture not only permits, but encourages, the creative individual to concentrate and telescope his psychic energy on less immediate and more transpersonal goals.

The Reservoir of Māyā Rūpa

In talking about creativity and the power of imagination, painters often return to the idea of *māyā rūpa*, a kind of inner reservoir of creative power in the form of "affect images" (*bhāvana*) at man's disposal. This particular theory of the source of creative energy and artistic form is very frequently voiced by nonartists as well. In his *Transformation of Nature in Art*, Coomaraswamy also takes note of this notion of creativity, but in the fine arts of the Hindu Great Tradition: "Maya is not properly delusion, but strictly speaking creative power, *sakti*, the principle of manifestation."[21]

At the popular folk level *māyā rūpa* is an active force and potential which refers to a reservoir of creative power. The interior world of *māyā rūpa* has specific meaning for painters who conceptualize it as a source or fountain of ideal energized affect images. The theory of *māyā rūpa*, the forms of illusion, delusion, imagination, and the creative unconscious or unmanifest mind, speaks to the question of where actual forms, images, and contents come from. Two examples are here provided from field notes:

1. The potter shaman *(bhōpa)* Lalu Ram told me with conviction about his powers of imagination and creativity. He said—pointing to his chest-heart region—that:

> The imagination is located here. All originality (mauliktā) and imagination *(kalpnā shakti)* come from the forms thrown out by māyā. It is all inside each of us. We can call forth every kind of image and imagination from this *māyā rūpa* deep inside. Each man has it all inside him, if he only tries to see it and use it, and if it is the pleasure of God to allow him this maturity.

2. The 67-year old painter Babu Lal squinted his eyes and sighed:

> Creativity? Oh—it's all *māyā rūpā*—everything. This *māyā* which I have inside me is thrown out into my art. This is a sacred truth and something which grows with age. All imagination and the things of worldly appearance and form exist there first. They are not real when they come outside. These appearances in art are confused thinking, fantasies, and like the dream world. All outside forms are determined by this very same *māyā* force. They are all from *māyā (sub ēk hī māyā sē hain)*—from the inside—the whole world is, furthermore, nothing more than God's own *māyā* creation. It is the dream of Brahman, and we painters contain a part of that force in us too because we are all part of Brahman (i.e., the One Universal Soul or Light, of which everything else in the world is thought to be a shadow).

The men cited above tell us about the nature of symbolic content, as well as creative psychic energy. Both tell us something about the mechanism of projection in art. According to this view of creativity, the artist reflects another order of psychic awareness, the world of *māyā rūpa*. In the words of these two men there is a deep respect for meditation, introversion, and diving into the unconscious. The artists point to the necessity of symbolism and its crucial role in all art. For them symbols are "alive," moving from inside to outside, and called up from the depths during the creative process.

The whole question of what a symbol is, can be, or is not, will not be raised in this context, but it will help us to understand what Nathdwara painters mean when they talk about the world of *māyā rūpa* and creativity if we briefly make one important distinction, as they do, between a sign *(nishāni)* and a "living" symbol *(pratika)*.*

A symbol is something which is always transitive in the sense that it points to referents beyond our daily conscious lives. A sign, however, is

---

*In the West, Jung[48] and later Langer[49] have highlighted the differences between a "living" symbol as transformer of energy from the unconscious to consciousness and a conventional sign lacking in such energic force and numinosity.

something already known to consciousness; a mere sign is "dead" as is a red "stop" sign that has a fixed meaning and fails to stir one deeply, affectively. Investigation shows that the etymology of the word *symbol* in English comes from ballistics and means *something which is thrown out*. Because in India the word for symbol refers more specifically to this psychologically dynamic and transitive quality, we find with reference to a symbolic work of art that Hindu painters inquire: "Does this transcend itself? Does it awaken us to archetypal energies of the spirit, or is it only an imitation of nature? Does it evoke affect and content from the unconscious?" If it does not, then it is not truly art imbued with the universal creative force of *māyā*. All true art is thought to be essentially symbolic since it draws on the deepest springs of the world of *māyā rūpa*. Most important, symbols brought up and thrown out point beyond the immediate material world of signs and are believed to evoke what is known as *rasa*.

Rasa is the spirit, sentiment, essential affect or "taste" of a work of art. Because for Hindu artists beauty is something of an ideal and abstract quality, it is felt to exist *in potentia*. As we have pointed out before, it is the duty of the creative artist to realize or re-create this potentiality in himself, to aspire to attain and to become it by opening his consciousness to the world of *māyā rūpa*. Theoretically the artist never paints anything which is external to himself. The identification of the subject with the inner object is the goal of the artist: "To worship the god one must become the god."

Something which is *rasāvat* possesses *rasa*, the quintessence or flavor of some innate aesthetic or emotional experience which gets projected into the outside world in living symbols from the unconscious. The symbol not only connotes or denotes, but it suggests a hidden third something, the *dhvanit* referred to previously: "The *dhvanit* which appears is a vehicle for one of the nine specific rasas." These nine permanent moods of the human condition are said to be the erotic, the joyful, the heroic, the odious, the sad or pathetic, the wondrous, the peaceful, the angry or furious, and the terrible or fearful.

The symbol, then, allows the spectator of art to "taste" *rasa*, a vision of beauty evoked from another realm, from the world of *māyā rūpa*, by aesthetic contemplation.

But there is also a negative side to *māyā rūpa*. Painters explain that too much *māyā* may entangle a person hopelessly, throwing him into a confused world where he has little grip on social reality, and where he accepts fantasy and delusion for objective facts. In such an ego-fragmented state the artist moves psychopathologically further and further away from knowing his true self—his unique inner nature (*ātman*). It is in this sense that Hindus may speak disparagingly of *māyā*: "Oh, that fool is all caught up in *māyā!*" Unfortunately Western interpretations, paralleling the fear of primary process in many psychoanalytic circles, have tended to dwell on these negative associations, failing to see *māyā* in its positive light, as creative power and potential in the unconscious. *Māyā* then stands out as the dynamic, emerging, and revitalizing force behind all truly symbolic art and culture—a reservoir of teeming life, images, and affects, all struggling to be manifest, all manifested to different degrees.

The Creative Experience

The *Yoga Sutras* speak of four main stages of the creative act in which the artist temporarily blends his ego with objective images evoked from deep within *(antar drshya)* during concentration. Very briefly stated, the four stages of the creative process spelled out by yogic tradition and experienced by Nathdwara painters are:

1. Selecting or fixing on an inner object,
2. Effort to achieve union or self-identification with the object,
3. An interval of suspense and incubation, and
4. The creative climax or solution.

There is first a period involving preparation; this can be long or short, but in any case, the artist attempts to contact by self-will and ceaseless effort the subjective region of his mind thought to be located "near the heart." It is here that all reality and truth are supposed to exist in "ideal forms." During this phase of the creative process, the Nathdwara artist removes himself symbolically from the normal world by burning incense to Lord Vishvakarma, the playful Divine Child, a mother goddess, and other deities. He prays for inspiration from Vishvakarma, his patron *(Ishta Deva)*, and assumes a posture conducive to the reception of ideas and impulses from within himself.

Since painters believe that everything is already inwardly known, the creative act is seen more as an attempt to contact the numinous realm of the psyche and to reflect it with force and unusual vigor. In most cases the artist is not in the market for creating completely new images, but he hopes to demonstrate his ability to re-create and reinvigorate inner images in a divergent and unusual way. The acquisition of this kind of "knowledge" would be enough to make him "original" in the eyes of his fellow artists and in his own eyes. He need not face a blank canvas to feel challenged. Instead he is perfectly content to work within the requirements of his traditional styles. The cult of originality which demands that an artist create something *ex nihilo* every time he involves himself in his work is a much more Western and modern idea.

Nathdwara painters who are more creative, agree they should reveal subjective reality or feeling experienced as the manifestation of inner life—emerging forms from the world of dream and vision. In the creative process the painter effects a self-identification with what he is about to paint. During this process, or perhaps we should say "dialogue" between the painter and his unconscious, there are insights and joyful intuitive leaps similar to what Western artists have described. The creativity Nathdwara painters describe would appear to be more a matter of new and original experience for the painter than the creation of some new theme, product, or subject.

From his immediate experience "deep inside" the painter brings back energized forms, the symbolic material from the unconscious. The artist has thus engaged spontaneously in self-expression through self-discovery, *and* in social communication because he concretely represents *rasa* affect, something invisible which is assumed to exist, and therefore to resonate, in everyone. The last stage of the creative process, as Hindu tradition sees it, meets not only a subjective need related to the artist and his own psychological individuation but also some social end. Personal myths and symbols are also fantasies.

In different terms Nathdwara painters describe roughly the same stages of the creative process that Western artists do: (1) preparation, (2) incubation, (3) insight, and (4) verification.[22] But unlike most Western artists, Hindu painters all seem consciously to share a strong belief in the existence of a reservoir of creative potential, affect images, the collective forms of *māyā*. In Nathdwara, painters often refer to this rich fund of images and symbols as a body of water—usually "a vast ocean," but sometimes "a lake or a pond." Others say the images come simply from "mother nature."

Asked to define creativity, a very sensitive and intuitive young painter replied:

> The older creative painter paints for pleasure—out of personal desire—it is he who paints in order to bring peace to his soul, and not just for money, or because he is forced to paint by other people in society. The creative painter will try to learn everything and be responsive to everything that is around him. He will attempt to draw from the vast ocean of ideas and images. There is a story told about keeping one's finger in the pond. The creative man should be interested in self-creation, in the growth of his own mental powers. He should follow the religion of humanity, not only one narrow path.

The way in which Nathdwara painters view creative process presupposes a certain amount of technical competence as part of the artist's preparation, although this is not often made explicit by painters in their responses. It is possible that this oversight reflects the generally accepted idea that even an image or a painting which has been badly executed has spiritual merit. It can be symbolically and functionally "beautiful" in-asmuch as all art is divinely inspired; everything honestly produced and experienced through internal struggle is equally valid on one level of appreciation.

To be creative means to participate in an overall act of becoming or manifesting interior contents of the psyche, a process which may take weeks, days, or hours. Painters recognize that each stage of the creative process is beset with its own problems, insights, and demands. What for one painter passes quickly and easily can be a lengthy state of disequilib-rium and tension for another.

Ego Boundaries: Relative Permeability or Impermeability

Hindu folk theories of artistic creative process in painting, as outlined above, imply an inordinate capacity for psychological growth in the work-ing through of complex symbolic processes late in the life cycle. Although the creative painter may often distinguish himself early in life from others and his creativity reach one peak in the householder stage, he continues to maintain and further develop his inner resources. Introspection and attempts to integrate symbolic opposites may proceed with ruthless ded-ication into old age. The truly creative painter is expected to achieve a growth-fostering dialogue with unconscious mental processes in the second half of life. Painters say a decisive change in the quality and content of creativeness takes place near the end of the householder stage.

In an effort to avoid imposing preconceived Western notions of creativity on the Indian setting, this study attempted to replicate the format of work done on creative American architects by MacKinnon[23-26] by having all painters in Nathdwara rank each other into one of three groups along a creativity continuum:

1. "Group I, *most* creative,"
2. "Group II, less, or *moderately* creative," and
3. "Group III, *least* creative."

After explaining that he should categorize in terms of three groups, I asked each full-time male painter over 20 to "name all those painters in Nathdwara who you feel fall into Group I, the most creative, and then all those who you think fall into Group II, the less creative." All remaining painters were placed into Group III.

There was wide and clear consensus among painters about who were the most creative men in their community. Of the 101 painters asked, only 8 did not respond; 7 outrightly refused to rank anyone, and 1 psychotic was unable to deal with the task. When tabulated the remaining 93 responses were divided into three main groups according to percentage recognition. I decided to include in Group I 13 painters who were recognized as "most creative" by at least 30%, of all respondents. Group II included 12 men recognized as "most creative" by less than 30%, but not less than 4%, of the total respondents.

Although I kept up social relationships with all other painters in the community, I now began to focus more intensively on 38 individuals ranked into three different groups: Group I "most creative" with 12 members, Group II "moderately creative" with 10 painters, and Group III with 16 "least creative" men. Of the 16 painters selected from Group III for intensive life history study, none were ever ranked into Group I or Group II. Further, an attempt was made to include in Group III only painters who were frequently called "hack artists" by others.

Table 6.1 shows clearly that creativity tends to increase with age in Nathdwara. Although one can not argue logically that age causes creativity, Table 6.1 suggests a correlation. Since painters ranked into all three groups were both old and young—there is a wide range of ages within each subgroup in the study—respect for the aged in India alone cannot account for the higher mean and median ages of Group I painters.

While growth and expansion facilitated by the organizing (synthesizing and differentiating) functions of the ego may play a crucial role in the development of creative adult personalities beginning with mid-life crises sometime between the ages of 30 and 40, a gradual disengagement from the widespread social relationships previously enjoyed in the community at large is at the same time considered "ideal" and socially approved. It is as if the creative painter, in perceiving these social role expectations, responds directly and becomes even more open to psychological change and individuation in later life. However, it would be wrong to equate the Hindu ideal of progressive renunciation of the mundane, or the high evaluation of a contemplative approach in later life, with the well-known disengagement theory,[18] for the latter does not adequately explain what may occur intrapsychically. Moreover, aging in India does not carry with it the weight of deviancy, stigma, and negative identity so familiar in youth-oriented cultures; the old in Nathdwara are highly regarded; age may increase personal prestige and social power; and "wisdom of the elders" is still honored. The aged do not say they feel "powerless," and their roles are not as limited and marginally defined as in American culture.[cf.58]

The older creative painter does not disengage passively into a do-

TABLE 6.1. Ages of Male Painters Ranked by Percentage
Recognition into Three Groups According to Degree of
Creativity

	Group I	Group II	Group III
Number	13	12	77
Mean	52.2	44.7	36.2
Median	55	40.5	34
Range	33–73	30–76	20–87

nothing. He is given space for increased inner growth, and very *actively*
engages in an arduous process of self-exploration and the scanning of inner
resources. There is much more to be said for his positively valued introversion beginning in mid-life than simply a decrease in social participation,
which may not often be the case. For example, creative Hindu painters in
the second half of life were found to be distinguished by: (1) an extremely
rich fantasy life and rapport with deep inner states of nonego awareness; (2)
a great tolerance for ambiguity; (3) a noteworthy capacity to form very
complex symbolic identifications, fusions, displacements, and condensa-
tions in a striving toward wholeness and balance; and (4) more fluid and
permeable inner ego boundaries with a strong ego core requiring less
unconscious defensive maneuvers (e.g., repression, projection, isolation of
affect, denial, etc.) than less creative painters. [16,27-29] The older painter who
has maintained his creativity is marked by greater intrapsychic freedom
than those who have not accepted the challenge of individuation in mid-
life, and it is here that the Jungian "ego-self axis" formulation assumes
importance.

Among the early founding depth psychologists, we may turn to Jung
for insights into the dynamics of creative personality and process. Since the
earliest days of his split from Freud* in 1914, Jung and his school have

---

*To my knowledge Butler is one of the very few psychoanalysts writing from a Freudian
position who attends seriously to the relationship between aging and creativity as process and
personality. [50] In his stimulating work he recognizes the importance of "the qualitatively
different tasks of later life as a field of investigation," and he is not excessively reductionistic.
Butler asserts that many people in middle and later life continue to be highly creative and very
cogently illustrates this point. His work clearly discredits a contemporary Western belief that
creativity decreases as a function of chronological age. Nevertheless, Butler also fails to clarify
what he means by creativity—something he finds to be "persistent" in later life. For example,
he considers Titian, Verdi, Freud, Saint Augustine, Jung, Darwin, Eisenhower, and others
together. Butler's important work also calls our attention to the limitations and inadequacies
of classical Freudian theory where questions of creativity and adult personality formation in
later life are raised. [51-53] I have discussed at length the limitations of a theory of art and
creativity based on the concept of "regression in the service of the ego," [54] "narcissism," [55] and a
depreciation of primary process per se based on what is essentially pre-1920 Freud
elsewhere. [16,30]

insisted that creativity is an instinct *sui generis*. As deeply rooted in the human psyche as sex, aggression, and the will to power, creativity is subject to the same vicissitudes and transformations as any other instinct and may not be simply reduced to something psychosexual. Jungian analysts have consistently grappled with the complexities of ego adaptation in the creative process and with the symbolic transformations through which individuating creative personalities pass.[31]

Moreover, Jung distinguished himself clearly from Freud by outlining and stressing "the normal stages of life,"[32] psychological transition, conflict or crisis in middle age that could, under growth-fostering circumstances, lead to a very active striving toward wholeness and individuation (self-actualization). Jung's autobiography is a testimony to what he called "the work" of later life: active struggle for increased psychic differentiation and synthesis. It remains one of Jung's major contributions to depth psychology that he first widened and deepened the Freudian perspective to include, among other things, the life-cycle perspective. Many Jungian and neo-Jungian insights and theoretical formulations (e.g., "the ego-self axis") have yet to be systematically applied to data on aging and creativity; psychological analyses of artistic products alone, in comparison, have tended to be overly causal-reductive, oriented to psychopathology, and therefore extremely limited in scope.

Jung recognized early that perhaps the most important developmental task in the second half of life is to let the ego go, to relativize it in relation to the larger self. His use of the word *self* differs from current psychological usage, since the concept is not interchangeable with the term *ego*. In 1921 Jung wrote: "Inasmuch as the ego is only the centrum of my field of consciousness, it is not identical with the totality of my psyche, being merely a complex among other complexes."[56] Later, in 1939, he wrote: "For this reason I have elected to call it the 'self,' by which I understand a psychic totality and at the same time a centre, neither of which coincides with the ego but includes it, just as a larger circle encloses a smaller one."[57,]* The individual may need to experience a degree of disintegration (ego boundary diffuseness) in an attempt to acquire a more well-rounded perspective and an ability to tolerate *nonrational* inner promptings. In this sense a greater overall tolerance for ambiguity among creative painters after mid-life would seem to go hand in hand with increased creative potential—the strength to tolerate and integrate psychological opposites occurring in the mind simultaneously. During the first half of life, according to Jung, a man has been busy winning his freedom from the mother,

---

*In my opinion, we are indebted to the Freudian school for major advances in the field of ego psychology and to the Jungian school for its theoretical emphasis on a whole human personality growing—on a psychodynamic self.

dying to childhood, being assimilated to the society of males, and forming a strong, well-integrated ego identity with a *"rational"* orientation to life. But with the transitional mid-life introversion/crisis a reluctance to let youth and ego defenses go becomes the central problem. One older painter relates with feeling: "Old age is the time of turning inward and getting back to the roots—to the root emotions and to exploring all the branches. It is a different pathway when we are older."

The ego boundary construct is complex; it was insightfully conceptualized by Jung as early as 1916 and extended by Federn.[48,33] Jung considered two kinds of ego boundaries: an unconscious demarcation between ego and nonego within the personality, and the ego's separation from nonego external to the personality. Later "the fluidity of ego boundaries" was discussed by Bychowski and the "constriction and expansion of ego boundaries" by Rose.[34,35] In general, however, the psychological literature reflects an overall bias by inclining to view fluid ego boundaries as deficit rather than creative adaptation. Hindu folk theories of creative process do not make the same philosophical distinctions between subject and object, nor does Jungian theory as it relates to the ego-self axis. Jung observed that the conscious portion of the ego complex exists to assist in the growing awareness, integration, or manifestation of the total psyche or self. This occurs as psychodynamic process involving fluid ego boundaries around a strong organizing core and nucleus, an adaptive capacity to endure flux—the expansion and contraction of boundaries to further synthesis, individuation. Jung stressed the vital role of ego attributes and functions such as "definiteness and directedness . . . continuity and reliability" but without overlooking the adaptive significance of regression and ego boundary permeability during creative process.[48] In 1916 he wrote: "Great artists and others distinguished by creative gifts are, of course, exceptions. . .The very advantage that such individuals enjoy consists precisely in the permeability of the partition separating the conscious and the unconscious."[48]

Students of Jung have referred to creative introversion of libido later in life as the process of "centroversion."[36] Centroversion is the reverse of any passive acceptance of the seemingly inevitable; it is an active life process offering potential wholeness, centering, dialogue between conscious portions of the ego-complex (consciousness) and the deepest layers of the self (unconscious). In short, it is the reestablishment of the ego-self axis, a connection generally thought already to exist in earliest infancy.[37–39] The ego is said to evolve out of the more archaic self matrix.[40,41] In a most trenchant and elaborate discussion of the ego-self axis, Edinger writes:

> Clinical observation leads one to the conclusion that the integrity and stability of the ego depend in all stages of development on a living connection with the

Self... Thus ego and Self have a close structural and dynamic affinity... The ego-self axis represents the vital connection between ego and Self that must be relatively intact if the ego is to survive stress and grow. This axis is the gateway or path of communication between the conscious personality and the archetypal psyche. Damage to the ego-self axis impairs or destroys the connection between conscious and unconscious, leading to alienation of the ego from its origin and foundation.[42]

Only recently have we begun to study "open" ego boundaries from a less biased point of view. In his comprehensive study, for instance, Landis is concerned with *"the relative dominance* of permeability or impermeability of ego boundaries."[17] In describing the nature of inner and outer ego boundary articulation, Landis makes no value judgments. Permeability and impermeability are considered summary concepts that express an overall degree of ego openness or closedness. These two qualities are found in everybody and vary situationally, yet one tends to predominate and characterize the way in which a personality organizes the sum total of its experience. Thus degrees of permeability-impermeability exist along a bipolar continuum: "Permeability is conceptualized as a relative openness of demarcation between ego and non-ego . . . Impermeability of boundaries is conceptualized as entailing a relatively solid, impenetrable 'wall' between ego and non-ego." It is important to point out that inner and outer ego boundaries may be either similar or incongruent with regard to properties of permeability-impermeability.

In his extensive treatment of ego boundary concepts, Landis does not address himself in any serious way to the issue of personality change throughout the life cycle. From this perspective we would want to know if and when permeability-impermeability change over the entire course of human development. For example, to what extent might increasing inner boundary permeability in old age necessarily indicate or reflect social disengagement?

From what we know of the Hindu life cycle, at least two hypotheses related to creativity and ego boundary permeability-impermeability may be formulated and tested against psychological test data collected in rural India:

1.   Outer ego boundary permeability remains high with advancing age in creative personalities. These men continue to recieve and actively process responses to complex stimuli from the external world, yet actual time spent in socioeconomic other-directed interaction *outside* the immediate contexts of extended family and subcaste (*jāti*) may decrease.

2.   Inner ego boundary permeability is high and increases with age in

creative personalities. Older creative painters are able to tolerate larger doses of perceptual and emotional ambiguity in the service of what Jung described as individuation (ego-self axis in later life), self-actualization, growth.

Painter Group Differences:
Psychological Test Results

In an attempt to test for insights gained from life history data and everyday participant observation over 18 months of field work in Nathdwara, various psychological tests were administrated to all three groups of artists participating in the intensive comparative study of artistic creativity. Among these, the Barron-Welsh Revised Art Scale of the Welsh Figure Preference Test was employed.[43] This test is simple, direct, objective, and verbal; since a respondent only states whether he "likes" or "dislikes" each of a series of 86 black-and-white figures presented to him rapidly in a test booklet, the task does not require literacy, nor is there anything inherent in the items to make a person think there must be some "correct" or "wrong" answer. Moreover, scoring is completely objective, the highest possible test score being 60 points. The test has been standardized on American artists who score a mean of 40 points. More creative and original artists in the West have been found to score higher.

Scores and scales on the Barron-Welsh Revised Art Scale have been devised to meet a large number of research needs.[44-47] Among other things, the test is designed to discriminate between personality preferences for: (1) perceptual clarity or ambiguity, (2) simplicity or complexity, and (3) symmetry or asymmetry. In the present study, use of the test was based on the hypothesis that older, more creative Group I men, said to be in close contact with the hidden feeling life's of extremely complex unconscious mental processes, would obtain higher point scores.

That painters continue to be perceived as artistically creative into later life has already been documented. These men are noted for their predispositions to rich fantasy life, rapport with the unconscious, and preferences for complex symbolic associations and identifications. Because of a strong capacity to maintain the ego-self axis, they are able to deal more resourcefully with the psychic disorder inherent in all creative introversion. They can allow psychic opposites to exist simultaneously and brook relatively permeable, fluid inner and outer ego boundaries (expanding and contracting) without permanent or prolonged ego-loss and fragmentation. This ability is strikingly reflected in test scores reported in Table 6.2. Creative

TABLE 6.2. Barron-Welsh Revised Art Scale for Creativity Groups

	Groups		
	I (N = 12)	II (N = 11)	III (N = 16)
Mean (points)	45.5	37.6	36.1
Standard deviation	7.7	9.6	11.6

Group I painters prefer complexity, disorder, asymmetry, and ambiguity to simplicity, geometric order, symmetry, and clarity of design. Older creative painters identify more readily than others with unbalanced figures, suggesting they have a higher tolerance for perceptual ambiguity.

In contrast to many Group II and Group III men, Group I painters never blocked on this test or appeared to be flooded with anxiety. Creative men could always cope with the ambiguous stimuli in nonconstricted ways. They often departed momentarily from the easy "like" or "dislike" format to supply rich personal associations and symbolic transpersonal material. In Rorschach and TAT-like fashion, Group I painters frequently provided a wealth of imaginative descriptive detail—often in story form.

To get directly at the concept of ego boundaries and an assumed propensity for an individual to project unconsciously his perception of these onto unstructured ambiguous stimuli (cf. Landis for Rorschach scoring techniques[17]), painters were asked to go back and consider three particular figures in the test booklet once they had finished with the first part of the test. Figures 21, 68, and 85 of the Barron-Welsh Revised Art Scale were selected by the investigator because they met "sufficient ambiguity" criteria needed for projection. Each painter was instructed as follows: "Please say anything that comes to mind about the picture. There are no right or wrong answers to this. I would like to know all that you see." More frequently than Group II or Group III painters, Group I men were able to enjoy this task and provide a greater amount of comprehensive detail related to the figure as a whole.

Figure 68 of the scale (see Figure 6.3) relates directly to our present interest in a projected sense of ego boundaries onto ambiguous stimuli. In coded responses to this figure, individuals tended to see parts of the whole as either solid or relatively diffuse substances. It is suggested here that these differences may well be related to the projection of quite different ego boundary perceptions and states of being. Taking only one part of Figure 68 for study (marked "a" on Figure 6.3), it is hypothesized that: (1) a subjective state of relatively high ego boundary permeability would be expressed by responses citing objects we might call amorphous, inherently fluid, penetrable, soft, moving, open, readily permeated, insubstantial, and having unclear or changing boundaries; and (2) relatively high ego boundary impermeability would be reflected in responses citing objects we might call solid, impenetrable, hard, stationary, closed, and having clearly defined and not readily permeated boundaries.

In describing Figure 68, many painters spontaneously considered portion "a" an island or a cloud. Many also saw it as wooden or as water. This suggested to me that, when quantified, qualitatively different responses from group to group might reflect personality differences between ego boundary impermeability-dominated subjects and permeability-dominated subjects and that these differences were related to both creativity and age. Months after the test had been given the first time, painters who *had not* mentioned portion "a" as either an island or a cloud were asked to consider Figure 68 again briefly and to report "which it most feels like in the picture as a whole—a cloud or an island." The results of this small experiment are presented in Table 6.3.

For purposes of analysis, a cloud response is taken to mean the projection of a sense of ego boundary permeability, attributes of a cloud being that it is highly permeable, fluid, constantly changing shape, and insubstantial. An island response, in contrast, is assumed to mean quite the

Figure 6.3.   Figure 68 of the Barron-Welsh Revised Art Scale.

TABLE 6.3. Painter "Cloud or Island" Responses to Portion "a" of Figure 68 on the Barron-Welsh Revised Art Scale

	Cloud	Island	Block/Rejection
Group I "most creative" (N = 12)	11	1	0
Group II "moderately creative" (N = 11)	5	3	3
Group III "least or noncreative" (N = 16)	6	8	2

opposite: a projection of a sense of relatively impermeable ego boundaries, the attributes of an island being that it is usually more stationary, clearly defined in outline, solid, impenetrable, and tightly bounded than a cloud. Results indicate clearly that creative Group I painters, almost to a man, see portion "a" of Figure 68 as a cloud form, whereas less creative men of the other two study groups more often see it as an island.

It is possible that the overall gestalt qualities of Figure 68 could account for Group I preferences for "cloud" or "island" in Table 6.3. Because "a" is located in the upper portion of the whole, it might be argued that, as was true for Rorschach responses not reported on here, less creative men more frequently failed to integrate isolated details into a whole-card response than did creative men. However this would fail to explain why over half (i.e., 7) of the Group I painters originally saw portion "a" of Figure 68 as "water."

Admittedly these data are very limited, and one would not want to rely on them alone to prove a statistical point which would call for much greater elaboration and consideration of additional test results. However, it has not been my purpose to demonstrate this kind of statistical analysis here. I present these findings because they are highly suggestive and consistent with ethnographic findings. In combination with reports extracted from life history interviews where stages of the Hindu life cycle are related to painter-perceived levels of creativity, we may posit with greater certainty that older Group I painters do indeed remain flexible and open into later life. To develop and maintain a strong ego-self axis (rapport between ego consciousness and the unconscious), special capacities for creative introversion and the persistence of relatively permeable ego boundaries are required. Both clinical and anthropological data combine to suggest that older creative painters share a capacity to meet these internal demands.

References

1. Simmons, L. W. *The role of the aged in primitive society*. New Haven, Conn.: Yale University Press, 1945.
2. Clark, M. The anthropology of aging, a new area for studies of culture and personality. *Gerontologist*, 1967, *7*(1), 55–64.
3. Clark, M. Changing value systems and intergenerational conflict: American subcultural comparisons. *Proceedings of the Eighth International Congress of Gerontology*, Washington, D.C., 1969, *1*, 425–427.
4. Clark, M. Patterns of aging among the elderly of the inner city. *Gerontologist*, 1971, *11*(1), Part 2, 58–66.
5. Clark, M., and Anderson B. *Culture and aging: An anthropological study of older Americans*. Springfield, Ill.: Thomas, 1967.
6. Clark, M., and Mendelson, M. Mexican-American aged in San Francisco: A case description. *Gerontologist*, 1969, *9*(2), Part 1, 90–95.
7. Cowgill, D., and Holmes, L. *Aging and modernization*. New York: Appleton-Century-Crofts, 1972.
8. Erikson, E., *Childhood and society*. New York: Norton, 1950.
9. Kiefer, C. W. Notes on anthropology and the minority elderly. *Gerontologist*, 1971, *11*(1), Part 2, 94–98.
10. Shelton, A. J. Igbo aging and eldership: Notes for gerontologists and others. *Gerontologist*, 1965, *5*, 20–24.
11. Shelton A. J. Igbo child-rearing, eldership, and dependence: A comparison of two cultures. *Occasional Papers in Gerontology*, 1969, *6*, 97–106.
12. Spencer, P. *The Samburu: A study of gerontology in nomadic tribe*. Berkeley: University of California Press, 1965.
13. Lehman, H. C. The creative production rates of present versus past generation of scientists, in B. L. Neugarten (Ed.), *Middle age and aging*. Chicago: University of Chicago Press, 1968, pp. 99–105.
14. Dennis, W. Creative productivity between the ages of 20 and 80 years, in B. L. Neugarten (Ed.), *Middle age and aging*. Chicago: University of Chicago Press, 1968, pp. 106–114.
15. Taylor, C. Age and achievement of noted pianists. Mimeo, 1972.
16. Maduro, R. *Artistic creativity in a Brahmin painter community*. Berkeley: University of California Center for South and Southeast Asia Studies, Monograph 14, 1976.
17. Landis, B. Ego boundaries. *Psychological Issues*, 1970, *6*(4), Monograph 24.
18. Cumming, E., and Henry, W. E. *Growing old: The process of disengagement*. New York: Basic Books, 1961.
19. Neugarten, B. L. Adult personality: Toward a psychology of the life cycle, in B. L. Neugarten (Ed.), *Middle age and aging*. Chicago: University of Chicago Press, 1968.

20. Prabhu, P. H. *Hindu social organization*. Bombay: Popular Prakashan, 1940.
21. Coomaraswamy, A. K. *The trasformation of nature in art*. New York: Dover, 1934.
22. Wallas, G. *The art of thought*. New York: Harcourt Brace, 1926.
23. MacKinnon, D. W. The personality correlates of creativity: A study of American architects. *Proceedings of the XIV International Congress of Applied Psychology, Copenhagen 1961*, 1962, *11*, 11–39.
24. MacKinnon, D. W. The nature and nurture of creative talent. *American Psychologist*, 1962, *17*(7), 484–495.
25. MacKinnon, D. W. Creativity and images of the self, in R. W. White (Ed.), *The study of lives*. Englewood Cliffs, N.J.: Prentice-Hall, 1963.
26. MacKinnon, D. W. Personality and realization of creative potential. *American Psychologist*, 1965, *20*(4), 273–281.
27. Maduro, R. The Brahmin painters of Nathdwara, Rajasthan in N. Graburn (Ed.), Ethnic and tourist arts: Cultural expressions from the fourth world. Berkeley: University of California Press, 1976, pp. 224–244.
28. Maduro, R. El pintor tradicional en la India: Su estatus y papel social. *Estudios Orientales*, 1973, *8*(2), 162–195.
29. Maduro, R. Symbolic equations in creative process: Reflections on Hindu India. *The Journal of Analytical Psychology*, 1980, *25*(1), 59–90.
30. Maduro, R. Notes on the adaptive significance of regression in analytical psychology, in R. Davidson and R. Day (Eds.), *Symbol and realization: A contribution to the study of magic and healing*. Berkeley: University of California Center for South and Southeast Asia Studies, Monograph No. 12, 1974, pp. 116–131.
31. Neumann, E. *Art and the creative unconscious*. New York: Harper Torchbooks, the Bollingen Library, 1959.
32. Jung, C. G. The stages of life. (Originally published 1930.) *The structure and dynamics of the psyche, Collected works, 8*. New York: Pantheon, 1960, pp. 387–403.
33. Federn, P. The ego as subject and object in narcissism. *Ego psycology and the psychoses*. New York: Basic Books, 1952.
34. Bychowski, G. *Psychotherapy of psychosis*. New York: Grune & Stratton, 1952.
35. Rose, G. J. Creative imagination in terms of ego "core" and boundaries. *International Journal of Psycho-analysis*, 1964, *45*, 75–84.
36. Neumann, E. *The origins and history of consciousness*. Princeton, N.J.: Princeton University Press, 1954.
37. Fordham, M. Some observations on the self and the ego in childhood. *New developments in analytical psychology*. London: Routledge & Kegan Paul, 1957.

38. Fordham, M. *Children as individuals*. New York: Putnam's 1969.

39. Fordham, M. Primary self, primary narcissism, and related concepts. *Journal of Analytical Psychology*, 1971, *16*(2), 168–182.

40. Jung, C. G. Transformation symbolism in the Mass. (Originally published 1940.) *Psychology and religion: West and east, Collected works, 11*. Princeton, N.J.: Princeton University Press, 1958, pp. 201–298.

41. Neumann, E. Narcissism, normal self-formation and the primary relationship to the mother. *Spring*. New York: The Analytical Psychology Club of New York, 1966.

42. Edinger, E. F. *Ego and archetype*. New York: C. G. Jung Foundation for Analytical Psychology, 1972.

43. Welsh, G. S. *Welsh Figure Preference Test: Preliminary manual*. Palo Alto, Calif.: Consulting Psychologists, 1959.

44. Barron, F. Some personality correlates of independence of judgement. *Journal of Personality*, 1953, *21*, 287–297.

45. Barron, F. Complexity-simplicity as a personality dimension. *Journal of Abnormal and Social Psychology*, 1953, *48*, 163–172.

46. Barron, F. The disposition toward originality. *Journal of Abnormal and Social Psychology*, 1955, *51*, 478–485.

47. Barron, F., and Welsh, G. S. Artistic perception as a factor in personality style: Its measurement by a figure-preference test. *Journal of Psychology*, 1952, *33*, 199–203.

48. Jung, C. G. The transcendent function. (Originally published in 1916.) *The structure and dynamics of the psyche, Collected works, 8*. New York: Pantheon, 1960, pp. 67–91.

49. Langer, S. *Philosophy in a new key*. New York: Pelican, 1948.

50. Butler, R. The destiny of creativity in later life: Studies of creative people and the creative process, in S. Levin and R. Kahana (Eds.) *Psychodynamic studies on aging*. New York: International University Press, 1967, pp. 20–63.

51. Freud, S. On psychotherapy. (Originally published 1905 [1904].) *Standard edition, 7*. London: Hogarth, 1953, pp. 257–268.

52. Freud, S. Dostoevsky and parricide. (Originally published in 1928 [1927].) *Standard edition, 21*. London: Hogarth, 1961, pp 177–194.

53. Freud, S. Leonardo da Vinci and a memory of his childhood. (Originally published 1910.) *Standard edition, 11*. London: Hogarth, 1957, pp. 59–137.

54. Kris, E. *Psychoanalytic exploration in art*. New York: Schocken, 1952.

55. Kohut, H. Forms and transformations of narcissism. *Journal of the American Psychoanalytic Association*, 1966, *14*, 243–272.

56. Jung, C. G. Psychological types. (Originally published 1921.) *Collected works, 6*. Princeton, N.J.: Princeton University Press, 1971.

57. Jung, C. G. Concerning rebirth. (Originally published in 1939.) *The archetypes and the collective unconscious, Collected works, 9*, Part 1, Princeton, N.J.: Princeton University Press, 1959, p. 142.

58. Wheelwright, J. Some comments on the aging process. *Psychiatry*, 1959, 22(4), 407–411.

Related Readings

Maduro, R. and Wheelwright, J. Analytical psychology, in R. Corsini (Ed.), *Current Personality Theories*. Itasca, Ill.: Peacock, 1977, pp. 83–123.

7

Meditation As a Solution to the Problems of Aging

Claire Myers Owens

Old age poses one of the greatest unsolved problems of our contemporary society. "The joy of aging" sounds like a contradiction in terms. Today, however, data are emerging that suggest it is perhaps psychologically unnatural or at least unnecessary for old age to be a time of depression, fear of death, and purposelessness. This chapter attempts to demonstrate that activation of the right cerebral hemisphere through meditation offers unique solutions to many of the problems of aging. In fact it suggests that it may be more natural for old age to be the happiest period of human life.

What are the major problems of aging? Illness and sometimes neurosis. Fear of aging and death. Loneliness. Impairment of faculties. Poverty. Inactivity. Meaninglessness of life. Depression.

What is the cause of these painful difficulties? One cause seems to be the absence of *wholeness*. This condition involves almost exclusive dependence on the left cerebral hemisphere and failure to activate the right hemisphere and later to integrate the functioning of both to create the whole person. We are endowed with two arms, two eyes, and two hemispheres of the brain. It is inconceivable that nature did not intend for us to utilize both of each pair. This wholeness often is attainable through the practice of meditation.

In recent centuries science and reason have dominated Western culture and have asserted they were able to solve all problems, answer all questions. Even Christianity has often maintained that God could be known through reason. Ironically enough it is science itself that has destroyed the dominance of science and the exclusivity of the left hemisphere—the center of which seems to be the ego. The self is the center of the right hemisphere. Science has operated on the hypothesis that the left hemisphere is equated with the conscious mind and the right with the unconscious. The growing awareness in science of the nonrigid nature of this distinction has led to general questioning of its validity.

In *The Spectrum of Consciousness* (p. 91) Wilber says that it was the discovery of quantum mechanics by Schroedinger and the uncertainty principle by Heisenberg that obliged science to recognize the existence of two modes of knowing: the intellectual and the intuitive-phenomenological.[1] In the *Meeting of East and West* (p. 439), Northrop describes the components of these two modes as "the empirically verified scientific theoretic" and "the immediately apprehended aesthetic."[2] Each component is equal and ultimate because irreducible.

In Europe the analytical psychology of Jung recognized the necessity of the second way of knowing. It ran counter to the prevailing culture in general and to Freudian theories in particular. Jung's psychotherapy penetrated not only the individual level of the unconscious as the Freudians had done but the deeper level, the collective unconscious, where self-realization of the religious experience occurs. Wilbur, however, suggests that Jungian therapy penetrates only to the transpersonal band in the spectrum of consciousness.[1] He believes that the Eastern religions with their meditation techniques are the methods that penetrate the deepest level of universal mind. In other words, it is possible to encounter reality without becoming one with it and possible to suppress the ego without extinguishing it.

During the eruption of the 1960s counterculture, youth rejected our prevailing rationalism and found that psychedelic drugs were able to induce glimpses of higher states of consciousness—if not the highest—but drugs were injurious. This left a vacuum into which there quietly flowed the various Eastern religious systems. Supply responding to demand, Buddhist meditation centers, Hindu ashrams, and humanistic growth centers sprang up like mushrooms all over the country.

About this time science lent its support to youth's belief in the validity of experiencing the second mode of knowing. The California neurosurgeon Joseph Bogen, operating on the injured brains of soldiers, uncovered a startling fact.[3] The two hemispheres of the brain perform entirely different functions. The left hemisphere is concerned with reason, language, mathematics, and analysis. The right is concerned with intuition, imagery, creativity, synthesis, and apparently, the spiritual experience. The right hemisphere seems capable of awakening to its own immanent good and contacting or uniting with transcendent energy with which it was "already always" one—usually without being aware of it. The left hemisphere erects a barrier to both; therefore the need for meditation.

This scientific recognition of the functioning of the right hemisphere and its ability to produce altered states of consciousness was revolutionary. It meant such states could be measured and verified scientifically to some extent. In short, the mystical experience became respectable in the eyes of scientists. Employing yogi and advanced meditators as subjects, scientific research in this area burgeoned in a few university laboratories.

Some scientists accepted the theory of actualizing man's noblest potentials by means of meditation. The younger generation flocked to the religious centers to practice meditation, while the middle aged were inclined to seek the humanistic growth centers. Those who needed inner transformation most urgently—the older generation—ignored and feared what seemed to them a revolutionary new religious philosophy. They assumed it undermined everything Western culture had taught them to believe, even though this very culture had left them stranded high and dry with an empty, unproductive old age. The number of gray heads, however, is increasing today in meditation centers—certainly in the one where I have trained for the last 7 years.

The Path and the Goal

The majority of the people of the world live in a continual state of ordinary consciousness, or dualism, plagued by the conflicts between opposites: I and the universe, I and others, subject and object, love and hate, intellect and intuition. Of the thousands who strive for enlightenment, Ramakrishna estimated that only 5% succeed. Travelers on the path far outnumber the enlightened.

To the novice much of the classic religious literature of the East is confusing because it seems contradictory. It may simplify matters if we appear to refute the great accepted truths by making a distinction between the experience of the *path* and the experience of the *goal* of self-realization. Most enlightened authorities maintain that "the path and the goal are the same," that to search for the truth is never to find it because this implies duality, that effort in meditation is self-defeating, that the senses are the enemies of enlightenment, that sleep should be dreamless, meditation imageless. If, they contend, the truth is within you, why embark on a long journey to find it?

These contentions are all true, but there is an *awareness* of them only during full realization or in the fleeting "moments of being" experienced by beginners. The complete actualization of the noblest human potentials is rare. The practitioner may be told that there is a unity of all things but does not *experience* an awareness of this oneness except periodically and briefly. For struggling aspirants to be informed that to search for Truth means they never will find it destroys their incentive. The search for reality is the very work to which they are dedicating their lives, and even though they may know intellectually that the search is actually within, it feels as if it is also external. The novice is told by one master that, in meditation, effort will accomplish nothing; while another, such as Po Shan, in Chan's *The Prac-*

tice of Zen,[4] advises that "one never reaches enlightenment by merely waiting for it. He must press forward with all his mind to get [it]" (p. 97). Such contradictions may cause frustration.

The senses—much denigrated by the enlightened—may serve as a vehicle to convey unenlightened practitioners to the very threshold of reality—though they never quite open the door. To those only intermittently in higher states of consciousness, dreamless sleep would be injurious, judging by experiments that have been conducted in various laboratories on the stages of sleep, especially the necessary REM stages. If dreams are compensatory, as Jung maintains, it is only the fully realized person who does not require compensation for his or her unconscious to balance the self-deceptions and mistakes of the conscious mind. Dreams also frequently suggest solutions in a crisis.

During periods of intense and prolonged meditation (8–10 hours a day) the abundance of images projected by the unconscious are sometimes meaningful guides if we accept the interpretation offered by Jung in his *Collected Works*[5] or Huxley in *Heaven and Hell*[6] or accept our own interpretation. Apparently it is only when the adept is purified of all defiling residues in her or his unconscious that meditation is imageless.

To discover experimentally that the universe is *within* usually requires many years of arduous practice. The experience of the search for ultimate reality actually *feels* like a long journey through the world and through the universe with a return to the self and the beyond within. Experience of the cosmic principle often feels like a welcome invasion from without until the happy day when there comes awareness of the unity of all things. It requires years before the meditator becomes permanently one with the universe. Many of the most profound Eastern books on enlightenment appear to be written by the enlightened for the enlightened—not for struggling students.

I can find no adequate analogy for the novice and the experienced. The nearest similarity is the caterpillar in the chrysalis and the free-flying butterfly. The caterpillar is a potential butterfly but is *not* a butterfly, as the aspirant is a potentially enlightened person but is *not* enlightened. They are the same entity in very different forms. The greatest difference is that the meditator is granted periodic flights as a butterfly, then returned to the worm stage, while the caterpillar is not. After we experience fully the actualization of our finest potentials, we know that the path and goal are the same. But the struggle to ascend a mountain and standing on the peak do not *feel* like the same experience to those who have not known both. This chapter explores the rewards that accrue all along the path known to the many rather than those of the shining peak known to the few. That is another story for another day.

However joyful the inner growth produced by meditation, it is not continuous every hour of every day; it is periodic and brief. The meditator returns repeatedly to the lower level with its doubts and disappointments. As his or her practice advances, however, the trainee's character, behavior, and hierarchy of values change radically. Meditative practice, however, does not endow the practitioner with any new virtues. All it does is allow him or her to become what he or she potentially already is. It is the activation of these buried virtues that may resolve many of the problems of the aging.

Illness and Neurosis versus Natural Health in Old Age

Illness seems an inevitable problem of aging. The old suffer from organic, psychosomatic, and neurotic ailments. Often there is a daily battle with arthritis, hypertension, asthma, severe indigestion, and countless other disabilities. Fears of aging and of death are psychological accompaniments for which there appears to be no satisfactory solution, though there actually is.

Many of the physical and mental dilemmas of aging in particular, and modern life in general, are caused by being in conflict with the inevitable laws of the human body, the mind, and the universe. We wish *not* to be ill, *not* to grow old, *not* to die. We think we wish to live by reason alone, suppressing emotion and intuition. But that is against the principles of health and wholeness. Suppressing emotion, the doctors inform us today, may cause physical or psychological illness.

Meditation, however, offers an opportunity to live in harmony with the laws of body and mind and even with what appear to be the laws of the universe. The difficulty is that our egoistic conscious mind thinks it knows what is good for the body even better than the body itself. We seldom listen to the faint warnings of our body and of our intuition. Physical relaxation aids the body in hearing itself; the mind, according to Jung, is a self-regulating mechanism when given the opportunity. The process of thinking creates tension within the body. Any meditator becomes aware of this when her or his hard-won physical relaxation is destroyed by random thoughts.

Scientific experiments conducted in various laboratories, using yogi and advanced Western meditators as subjects, reveal that in deep, relaxed meditation the heart rate decreases, but apparently the muscles of the walls of the blood vessels relax. This allows blood to flow more abundantly to all organs including the brain. There are those who believe that meditation possesses the power to raise human vibrations and thereby empower the meditator to draw on cosmic energy, which purifies the mind and heals the body. Others believe everything is already within the mind, waiting for our awakening.

One day a woman who was in her first year of meditation practice found that four small rivers were streaming down her face from her eyes and nostrils. The doctor diagnosed it as hay fever and said it would eventually disappear. She had never had hay fever in her life and did not intend to have it now, thank you. Nor could she wait for "eventually." She returned home, sat on her cushion, and meditated more arduously than ever before in her life. After 2 hours the ailment disappeared and never returned.

I have observed meditators who have been suffering from minor arthritic pains, serious indigestion, or congestion of the sinuses rise up after a 2-hour sitting free from pain, gas, and congestion. Meditation is also a preventive measure as well as a curative process. When in an elevated mind state meditators feel a sense of remoteness from their own bodily pain. It is as if it were happening to someone else at a far distance and were not very important. They transcend pain, and this detachment makes it endurable. Concentrated practice and prolonged relaxation often leave the body with the feeling of a well-oiled machine. There is abundant evidence in meditative groups of improvement in the health of the body. In fact, the hyphenated term *body-mind* is regarded as a single word by aspirants.

Sometimes the illness is mental. What effect, if any, does meditation exert on a neurosis? Neurosis is usually thought to be a problem of youth up to approximately the age of 35. In *C. J. Jung Speaking,* however, Jung states: "In the second part of life those people who flunk the natural development of the mind—reflection, preparation for the end—they get neurotic too" (p. 108).[7]

Is it also true perhaps that Americans are immature? In Europe, Americans are often referred to as brash children. Be that as it may, the prevalence of older persons in the United States who adopt surrogate mothers and fathers—with disappointing results as a rule—is obvious.

During the meditative process is the neurotic level of the unconscious penetrated? Are the same four levels activated during meditation, and in the same order, as when psychedelic drugs are administered expertly, for instance by Masters and Houston (pp. 142–314)?[8] I borrow Masters's and Houston's terminology to designate the four levels of the unconscious: the *sensory,* where images are seen; the *recollective-analytic,* where subjects become aware of their own neuroses and sometimes see solutions to them; the *historic;* and the *integral,* where self-realization and the religious experience may occur.

While counselor to members of a meditation group, I listened to many of them, both young and old, describe their inner experiences. They rather enjoyed the first parade of images projected like motion pictures by their unconscious. The imagery arose, it may be assumed, from the sensory level in the right hemisphere. In the next level, however, confrontation with memories of a miserable childhood frightened them so badly they sometimes abandoned all meditation forever.

Meditation is a therapeutic process. It is necessary for trainees to live through their original neurotic situations painfully if they are ever to be rid of them or be able to penetrate the deepest level and attain their goal of spiritual awakening. Sometimes during the meditative process the practitioners gained intuitive insights into their own neurotic problems for the first time and even envisioned solutions. Relations with their estranged parents or siblings improved so markedly they cheerfully left the training center at the first stage of their inner development, to the dismay of their teacher and to their own loss.

Distinction must be made between the different varieties of awakening: shallow and full, transient and permanent. Some meditators attain shallow and transient enlightenment, others full but transient. Most teachers, gurus, and yogi, presumably have both fully and permanently realized the self, even transcended it. Everything in the whole long process of actualizing the self is a matter of degree—degree of intensity, frequency, duration, depth, or height.

The example of the penetration of the fourth and deepest level with which I am most thoroughly acquainted was not induced by meditation but occurred spontaneously. The underlying principles, however, are the same. The sequence of stages are different, but they produce similar results. A traumatic incident triggered a painful climax to a woman's neurosis. She was confined to bed for several months, and her rational mind strove to discover the cause and cure for her incapacities. Frustration, suffering, and defeat caused the conscious mind to surrender its usual dominance. This surrender promptly provided an opportunity for the right hemisphere to plunge her directly down to the deepest level of the unconscious. She experienced a mystical awakening that revolutionized her life. In her new-found love of the whole human race, she felt compassion for her mother.

The human unconscious apparently responds in a similar manner to different stimuli, whether psychedelic drugs expertly administered, Jungian therapy, meditation, or a spontaneous awakening. Each of the methods appears to alleviate, if not cure, a neurosis. The quality, duration, and effects of the experiences are another matter altogether.

Fear of Aging versus Inner Growth

Almost everyone over 50 dreads old age. Wrinkles and gray hair, loss of attractive face and figure are regarded as major catastrophes. This is especially true among women. Aging, however, is inevitable in everyone. Are we suffering unnecessarily because we are attempting to reverse that law? Is it not perhaps a law of the human mind that physical aging is naturally a time of inner psychological and spiritual growth?

In lives dedicated to internal development, physical appearance painlessly ceases to be of prime importance. A new hierarchy of values gradually emerges, based not on youth and beauty; not on social status, wealth, or intellect; but on inner development, selflessness, readiness to serve others, joy, purity, and moral radiance. Gradually over the years a mysterious purification of mind and world view is engendered by meditation.

This purgative process may occur during work, even intellectual work. So incredible is the transforming power of meditation that, between sittings, the practitioner's work may become his or her practice. In other words, if concentration on the task is so complete that the practitioner is one with it, then benefits and joys may result from work like those that emerge from actual meditation. For example, two trainees were collaborating on writing an article on meditation and cosmic consciousness.[9] The young man was in his 20s and I was in my 70s. It was my third year of training. Suddenly one day our ideas commenced to flow without effort, without ratiocination. Work became play. Effort became effortless. We laughed and laughed from sheer spontaneous joy. A mysterious wave of purification swept through us. We felt a strange new innocence as if we were two children walking in the morning of the world. After the young man's departure I felt so buoyant I feared my body might levitate to the ceiling.

This experience of purification and innocence sometimes suffuses the face with a faint pink glow that lends a deceptive youthfulness even to the aging. One feels eternally young—ageless. Most older Americans were brought up on the well-known words, "Unless you become as little children, you cannot see the kingdom of heaven." No one ever explains its meaning.

Occasionally an embarrassing charisma envelops a self-realizing person to her or his dismay. I witnessed this phenomenon last winter in Florida. An elderly woman, staying at the same hotel as I was, confessed she preferred solitude in order to maintain the fragile mind state induced by her meditation practice. Despite this or because of it, she was besieged by strangers younger than herself. They urged her to dine with them every evening, to lunch with them, to talk with them about their troubles.

In our extraverted, overactive culture, it seems eccentric—or worse—for a person to devote several hours a day to inner development. Yet no one considers it strange that athletes who compete in the Olympics practice 6 hours every day to perfect their bodily skills. In other cultures, however, it is considered a natural law of life to devote youth to education; middle age to bringing up a family, to working and making one's contribution to society; and later years to spiritual training. The process of physical aging can be suspended by the process of internal renewal, transformation, and final rebirth. Instead of being the unhappiest time of life, it is possible for old age to become the happiest period—by our own efforts. I know: I am 80 and have never been happier.

Fear of Death versus Intimations

Most people spend their lives in unspoken fear of death. The human instinct for survival is in silent conflict with the loss of precious personal identity, with final extinction. People begin to feel the ultimate futility of all life's work and love and courage. Today many people fear there may be no life after death, no ultimate reality, no justice in this world or any other.

These fears are dissipated—not by the opinions of others, not by cults or books or authoritative leaders, or by institutions. They are dissipated by activating the second mode of knowing, by intuitive and experiential knowledge awakened through serious and prolonged meditation. This mode of knowing taps a cosmic energy, and this energy—if that is what it is—is "already always" there, to borrow an apt phrase from Wilber in his *The Spectrum of Consciousness*.[1] It is we who lock the door against it. Meditation is a battering ram that breaks through this iron door at unexpected moments. Then transcendent energy feels as if it is always immanent.

How do contemporary scientists view this form of energy other than ordinary human energy? Cautiously. Tart writes, "It is wise to distinguish between consciousness and basic awareness. . . . Basic awareness is something added to the brain from outside rather than something that arises from within. . . . Awareness may have functions in a wider universe than man is able to comprehend" (pp. 208, 214, 116).[10] Or perhaps only once, but that is enough; the serious meditator may be visited by intimations of mortality—like Wordsworth (though his was spontaneous, not induced).[11] Whether meditators believe in reincarnation or not, they gradually come to feel that death is but a transition to another state. Death loses its terror, especially if we are granted a glimpse of life after death. Gradually meditators learn that, for the young, meditation is a beautiful preparation for a beautiful life; for the old, a beautiful preparation for a beautiful death— preceded by a few very happy years.

Loneliness versus Inner Companionship

Loneliness plagues the lives of many older persons like an incurable malady that can neither fight nor escape. In our culture the old suffer from lack of respect; from the humiliation of growing old in a youth-oriented society; from the feeling of being unwanted and unloved by family, friends, and society. Many of the aging suffer from living alone. Nowhere to go. No one to see. No one will come. The phone may never ring again. Sometimes panic sets in. They fear losing all contact with the living world of people, drowning in a sea of nothingness, unneeded, unmissed. It is a kind of living death.

There exist, however, inner resources that are inherent in all human beings—often unsuspected but waiting. Meditation merely uncovers the treasure house within that often has been locked away for a lifetime. In other words, meditation enables practitioners to become themselves, their true selves, as the Buddhists say.

This true self when awakened becomes a frequent though not constant companion. It is like a twin sister or brother who possesses the virtues one's own personality lacks. When in doubt one can be guided, encouraged, and supported by it. This is the very dualism, of course, of which one is striving to free oneself by meditating; but in the early period of self-development, dualism is inevitable. The true self is particularly efficacious in harmonizing relationships with other people—one of life's worst unsolved problems at all ages. The awakening of the original nature through meditation muffles the ego temporarily, so one can be fully aware of the other person's welfare in a controversy instead of only of one's own precious ego.

This may effect startling results in altercations with a husband or wife, friend or employee. Appreciation works magic. For example, a woman who had been meditating for 3 years flew down to Williamsburg, Virginia, for her spring vacation. The staffs in all the hotels and restaurants and the drivers of the shuttle buses were black. Everywhere she went she was confronted by what appeared to be a silent conspiracy among all blacks to be coldly, almost insolently hostile in manner and tone of voice but polite in word and act to all the whites they served. My friend described it as a cold blast, but it was like walking into a refrigerator.

In an ordinary state of consciousness she would have felt affronted, complained to the management, and terminated the visit immediately.

Instead she was surprised to feel nothing but deep compassion for the embattled blacks. She was astounded to find herself smiling and friendly, to hear herself complimenting those who served her everywhere. It thawed out the ice of resentment in all cases except two, which appeared to be frozen into a state of permanent animosity.

In addition to the true self, another invisible companion may present itself to the lonely mediator. It is even more mysterious and more helpful. The chief role of the awakening self is to prepare the way for this elusive companion: the cosmic principle of oneness. During meditation training, teachers will explain that meditation is a long process of liberation from all attachments—even to teachers. To achieve the freedom can make one feel guilty, frightened, relieved, and elated. The cosmic principle can be agitating, frightening, puzzling, reassuring, but purifying above all. It is a "moment of becoming." This presence, though perhaps newly recognized, has always been there waiting. Never need the older person feel alone again.

Secondary companions may also appear. During the actual practice of meditation, sensory input is distracting and discouraged. In full self-realization sensory perception is transcended. But between the sittings that induce merely higher states of consciousness, sensory perception is intensified. Often the barrier that isolates one from nature is dissolved. One may even merge with it briefly. One experiences the meaning of Hegel's statement, "Beauty is a manifestation of infinity in sensuous form." Nature then becomes a living, breathing companion and a more reliable avenue to reality than human beings.

Also the beauty of the great human-made arts ceases to be merely a source of a moment's titillating pleasure. It agitates, elates, purifies. It can convey the meditator to the very threshold of the absolute, because that is its primary source. Great art is always there to be a companion. It never tires as long as one is receptive.

After years of practice even solitude ceases to be a painful deprivation. Passionate meditators never need to be lonely; they find companionship in their own awakened selves, in the mysterious presence, in nature and art, and even in solitude.

Poverty versus Internal Riches

Poverty is an affliction worse than any disease, the economist Galbraith said recently. Of course the basic necessities of life are essential to everyone. Maslow writes that basic needs—food and shelter, self-esteem, love, and self-expression—must be fulfilled before anyone is receptive to higher needs.[12]

Does meditation aid in securing a livelihood? It may, in ways too subtle to investigate here. But it does diminish the desire for material possessions, often awakening a preference for simplicity or a greater longing for beauty. It frees the aspirant from the bondage of attachment to unnecessary things that usurp energy, distract the mind, and absorb the emotions. It transforms the whole hierarchy of values from the seen to the unseen. The chief riches valued by followers of the Eternal Way are inner wealth: certitude, courage, creativity, honesty, love, desire to serve others, selflessness, purity, and joy.

Inactivity versus
the Work of Internal Development

Many women and men in their 60s, 70s, and 80s are moldering away in inactivity—physical and intellectual, creative and spiritual. They have already accomplished their work in the world, brought up their families, and made their contribution to society. People who retire at 65 or 70 suddenly find that society has relegated them to the shelf like an old shoe. Women in their 50s discover that their major task in life of childbearing and child rearing is behind them. What will they do with the 20 or 30 remaining years? Society offers retired people little occupation but playing shuffle board in the sun or playing with their grandchildren.

Did not nature design these years of forced inactivity for a purpose? Is it not perhaps a natural time for actualizing their noblest potentials through some practical technique such as meditation? Inner development is strenuous, continuous work requiring much time and effort. It requires a minimum of 2–3 hours every day of actually sitting motionless in concentration on a cushion. Also, every minute of every day and every circumstance is a challenge, a battle to conquer the ordinary state with the higher states of consciousness. Every incident can serve as another means to growth.

We live in a society with an unwritten law that no work is worth doing unless it produces hard, cold cash. Meditation is, according to seasoned meditators, the most strenuous work imaginable and the most rewarding that life has to offer.

Impairment of Faculties versus
Stimulation

Deafness in the aging is common, cataracts more so. Food tastes tasteless to the old who are living in the ordinary state of consciousness. My 92-year-old grandmother complained that the cook never put any seasoning in the food; so she blackened her vegetables with pepper.

In the high*est* state of consciousness the senses are transcended but in the high*er* states all sensory responses, including taste, are intensified to a rapturous degree. Colors suddenly acquire a vibrant life and power of their own, music opens the door to infinity, though it does not convey the listener over the threshold. Beauty is a force. It stimulates all reawakened faculties.

One meditator who had been practicing for 2 years was informed by her doctor that she must have the cataracts in both eyes operated on within the next 6 months. She redoubled her efforts of concentration and increased the time she spent in meditation. This stabilized her cataracts for several years. Apparently the daily practice of sitting motionless, concentrating, quieting the discursive intellect, suppressing sensory input, relaxing the body, and emptying the mind does not prevent the eventual impairment of the faculties in age, but it does delay it for a few delightful years.

Usually old people tire easily. Today, in a meditation center when trainees of all ages emerge from a week-long session of intensive meditation (9–10 hours on the mat daily), they are so filled with an excess of energy they feel they can move a house. Hundreds of years ago in Japan a famous Zen Buddhist master said that at 70 he lectured daily to 500 obstreperous students, had little sleep, and yet never grew tired. He attributed his abundant energy to his daily meditation. The effects are the same in any country.

What happens to the intellect? Does the direct arousal of the right hemisphere indirectly arouse the left hemisphere? This is a controversial point. Some researchers maintain that the intellect is not stimulated by the mystical experience. Informal study of famous persons reveals that in some cases the fully enlightened appear to experience little activation of the intellect. What of Blake and Beethoven, Whitman and Millay? On the other hand the biographies of Dante, Jung, Socrates, and Buddha seem to prove that the intellect was stimulated to more brilliant heights after realizing the self. Eastern teachers, however, maintain that in the advanced stage one no longer desires to know but only to be.

What of creativity? Do meditation centers attract the creative types? Or does meditation awaken the dormant creativity apparently inherent in all people? Many self-development centers are crowded with painters, sculptors, writers, and cabinetmakers, as well as doctors and teachers. My best book was written when I was 80—700 pages in 7 months. It flowed like the Mississippi River at the flood. I had very little to do with it except to enjoy every word of it.

So it appears that meditation delays the impairment of some faculties and stimulates others—for a few more happy years at least.

Purposelessness versus
the Purpose of Living

Western culture proclaims that the purpose of a man's life is to make money, pursue a professional or business career, be aggressive, competitive, and strong. Traditionally, before the women's liberation movement, a woman's main purpose had been to rear a family of normal, healthy, happy children and to serve and nurture others. When men are 70 and women 50, occidental society considers their chief goals in life to have been attained. The implication is that once people are old they have no purpose in living. Intuitive insights released through meditation reveal the purpose of life: that human beings should perfect their inner beings as nearly as possible, actualize their finest potentials, attain self-realization, and eventually transcend the self. Every definite step toward this perfection seems to involve confrontation with the purifying force of cosmic energy, whether believed to be internal or external or both.

Meditation is like learning to play the piano. One must play the same piece over and over again in order to perfect one's skill. The senses, so denigrated by the enlightened human being, often serve the neophyte as a means toward elevating oneself to higher mind states. Smith in *Religions of Man* (p. 142) explains that the aspirant must arrive at the state where he or she is able to look at a commonplace tree in the backyard and see into its true nature, see it as it is: a manifestation of infinity.[13]

Thoreau, though not a meditator in the formal sense, devised his own method when walking through the woods. Keller states that it is evident from Thoreau's *Journals* that he sought "a course in self-purification so that he [might] finally live completely in the Reality he [had] perceived" (p. 44) intermittently.[14]

To be motivated by a noble purpose is to know that the journey is no longer aimless, life no longer useless. A purpose in living is revitalizing at any age.

Meaninglessness versus
the Meaning of Life

What is the meaning of life? Everyone asks that question at some time. The answer is especially important to the aging. In the Western world too often too many of the old feel their lives have been disappointing: children rebelling against parents, dreams unrealized, hope for wealth unfulfilled, life in undying love shattered. All the struggle and love of a lifetime gone for nothing; and, all around, society frightening and disillusioning, rife with crime, corruption in government and business, human rights everywhere violated, humans destroying humans and the environment, and no visible proof of any omnipotent, benevolent power over all. The logical conclusion often is that life is meaningless.

In the other half of the world, however, the culture of the ancient East provides old and young, poor and rich with an inner purpose in life, a distant but high goal to work toward, and a practical method through meditation for attaining it. When this Eastern technique of meditation is applied in the West, the same religious philosophy emerges from personal experience, with or without instructions of an organized system. The psychological principles governing the activation of the right hemisphere of the brain are the same in both East and West.

A Western meditator has testified that in the experience of deep meditative relaxation she saw into her own mind. Everything had stopped. She felt no driving, no compulsion, no needs. She was free. Free of all her desires—for the moment. She was intensely aware that she needed nothing. She had everything she needed within herself. She knew beyond doubt that everything was in her mind, that everything she needed was in her own small mind—even universal Mind itself—impossible as that sounded. She knew experientially the meaning of life: all is one; one is all. The very next day she smiled when she read a headline in *The New York Times*, Sunday, November 13, 1977, above a drawing of a human brain: "1,000 Scientists in California Find the Universe in the Brain."

Depression versus a New Kind of Happiness

Depression is inevitable for anyone afflicted by any or all of the problems of aging. It has been suggested in this essay, however, that sustained meditation solves or alleviates these problems to a surprising extent. Meditation induces better physical and mental health, internal growth, and intimations of immortality. It brings together the true self and ultimate reality briefly and periodically. It stimulates the faculties, accumulates inner riches, and motivates the strenuous activity necessary for personal development. It awakens a purpose in living: self-perfection. It reveals experientially the meaning of life, that all is one and one is all and that the meaning of life is vibrant awareness of our oneness with ultimate reality.

Meditation is such a natural healthy process it occasionally occurs spontaneously almost without effort. Inner development is not easy. To those on the path, dramatic results following the activation of the right hemisphere are not continuous in the early years or even frequent. Arid days, even months, may occur. The precious ego is diminished gradually but may often reassert itself until its dissolution in reality during final realization and transcendence of the self. The small personal identity vanishes. Awareness of identity with the universe surges up periodically at first but continuously later, in successful cases.

The joys of meditation are as nothing, of course, compared to the quiet bliss of final self-transcendence. But to all who have experienced it, the accumulation of meditative benefits that accrue along the path brings a happiness deeper and more enduring than that produced by success or social status, wealth, power or fame, love or passion, beauty or youth—or even sports, cocktails, gambling, or fornication.

Tomorrow

What of tomorrow? Today the conclusion seems tenable that meditation alleviates many of the problems of aging even though the data are based on meager empirical evidence. The ideal meditator awakens the self, identifies with humankind, and returns to his or her source. He or she has intuitive insight into the nature of humanity and the nature of the universe; experiences the unity of all things; is prompted to sacrifice his or her life in service to others; and becomes more loving, honest, creative, unpossessive, and unafraid. Psychologically the ideal meditator penetrates the deeper and sometimes the deepest levels of the right cerebral hemisphere or the unconscious mind and releases its inherent virtues. But is this wholeness?

What of the intellect? In the Eastern literature, thought is condemned as the great enemy of enlightenment. Ironically enough, intellect is the greatest obstacle to inner awakening, even in the West. Must, then, thinking be neglected? Certainly not in the West. We regard reason as one of the triumphs of evolution. Logic, science, mathematics, and philosophy are deemed essential to a balanced society just as to a balanced human being. But any virtue when carried to the extreme becomes a vice. Not only individuals but whole societies suffer from lack of wholeness. In the East, neglect of the left hemisphere has resulted in famine, death of millions, disease, illiteracy, and catastrophic overpopulation unchecked by science. In the West, neglect of the right hemisphere has resulted in nuclear destruction, amorality, materialism, fear, and emptiness. The person of intuition is only half a person. The person of reason is only half a person. The two must be integrated if people are to be healthy and happy, wise and whole.

After all, the work of the world must be performed: shelters built, food grown, clothes manufactured, money made, and ideas evolved. Already the fact is emerging from the meditation and religious centers in America that the ideal person of tomorrow in the West will not be a saint with a begging bowl or even a monk in a monastery, as in the East. It appears more likely that the role of the West will be to integrate reason and intuition, to create the whole person with indebtedness to the spiritual East for its indispensable and unique contribution to the new world citizen.

Today meditation promises a way to bring happiness and greater health to many, especially the aging. Tomorrow it may be the only way to save humanity from destroying itself. It may be the only way to ensure that the Aquarian Age will be what it promises to be: a Golden Age.

The modern physicists are wiser than all the governments, politicians, and philosophers who decide the fate of nations. In the *Tao of Physics*. Fritjof sums up our present problem: "Modern science does not need mysticism and mysticism does not need science but man needs both" (p. 297).[19]

References

1. Wilber, K. *The Spectrum of consciousness*. Wheaton, Ill.: Theosophical Publication House, Quest Books, 1977.
2. Northrop, F. S. *Meeting of East and West*. New York: Macmillan, 1946.
3. Bogen, J. The other side of the brain. *Bulletin of the Neurological Societies, 34*, July 1969.
4. C. Chan *The practice of Zen*. New York: Dutton, 1959.
5. Jung, C. *Collected works*. Princeton, N.J.: Princeton University Press, 1953–1978.
6. Huxley, A. *Heaven and hell*. London: Chatto and Windus, 1956.
7. Jung, C. *C. G. Jung speaking*, W. McGuire and R. Hull (Eds.). Princeton, N.J.: Princeton University Press, 1977.
8. Masters, R., and Houston, J. *Varieties of psychedelic experiences*. New York: Dell, 1967.
9. Owens, C. M. "Zen Buddhism," in *Transpersonal Psychologies* C. Tart (Ed.). New York: Harper & Row, 1975.
10. Tart, C. *Psi: Scientific studies of the psychic realm*. New York: Dutton, 1977.
11. Wordsworth, W. Ode on intimations on immortality in *Narrative and lyric poems*. New York: Holt, 1909.
12. Maslow, A. *Towards a psychology of being*, 2nd ed. Princeton, N.J.: Van Nostrand Reinhold, 1968.
13. Smith, H. *Religions of Man*. New York: Harper & Row, 1965.
14. Keller, M., Henry David Thoreau, transpersonal view. *Journal of Transpersonal Psychology*, 9,(1), 1977, 43–82.
15. Capra, F., *The tao of physics*. New York: Bantam Books, 1977.

8

The Foreshortened
Life Perspective

Robert Kastenbaum

The elderly person is marked in more ways than one. His face, hands, and all those body parts which are significant in social communication have become unmistakably engraved with age. Before he speaks, he has already identified himself to others as a person who occupies an extreme position in the spectrum of life. Should his words and actions also betray those features we associate with advanced age, then we are further encouraged to mark him down as one who is strikingly different from ourselves.

He is also marked by numbers, of course. In the case of the elderly person, the statistics relentlessly intersect and pursue. Begin any place. Begin by tracing the declining function of this organ system or that one. Begin by measuring changes in the musculoskeletal system or the speed of central nervous system activity. Begin by locating the elderly person within the actuarial charts. Wherever we begin, it is clear that the numbers have a common bias: they are all against him.

These markings, however, do not tell the whole story. As a matter of fact, they provide only the background and props. It is true enough that any of us might contrive the story of any elderly person's life, based upon these externals. We could manufacture suppositions about what he is experiencing within these biologic and statistical markings—how he regards the past, how he views the future, and all the rest. The pity of it is, we do this sort of thing much of the time without realizing that what we are hearing is not his story but merely the sound of our own voices. It is so easy to suppose that he feels the way we think we would feel if we were in his situation, or simply that he must feel the way we think it proper for an elderly person to feel. Any time we begin with such a misstep we are likely to accumulate even further distortions. We are likely to generalize without correctives. We are likely to develop set ways of dealing with the way we think he is.

From *Geriatrics*, 1969, *24*, 126–133. Reprinted with permission of *Geriatrics*.

How does the elderly person actually view his own life? What is his perspective and how did he happen to develop it? What functions does it perform for him? In what ways might his perspective affect the course of his own life and the lives of others? Of his total life experiences—past, present, and potentially future—what has he included? What has he excluded? Has he settled upon this perspective as a fixed, permanent vantage point, or are other orientations to come? Most basically, has he managed to create a symbolic structure that comes to terms with his total existence at the very time that this existence itself has become so vulnerable?

To gain perspective on the life perspective of aged people, it might be helpful to back up all the way to infancy. Does the infant have a life perspective? Quite on the contrary—he is almost totally engrossed in life. He experiences the moment. He does not reexperience the past or preexperience the future, at least not in that sense which depends upon the development of symbolic structures. One of the most profound differences between infant and adult is the raw experiencing of the moment, an experiencing that lacks the protection afforded by perspective. Although this point may be an obvious one, it should be emphasized because it is important in a different light in the phenomenological world of the aged.

Very quickly, the infant comes to appreciate the difference between a presence and an absence. At first this awareness does not distinguish between temporal and spatial dimensions. Either something (for example, smiling-mother-presenting-lunch) is both here-and-now or it is absent—totally absent. By contrast, the adult differentiates "absence" into several alternatives that have differential meanings to him: something exists now, but not here, in this space; or something will be in this space at a later time; or something has been in this space, but at a previous time; or again, something is neither here nor there, now, then, or ever.

Such distinctions, and many others that are crucial to the development of a life perspective, come later in life, but the first gropings toward a perspective begin in infancy. There is a clear directional movement. The infant becomes increasingly liberated from its biology, on the one side, and its immediate environment, on the other. The directional thrust is a general process that must be distinguished from what might be called the solidified achievements of human development. This is perhaps the most fundamental basis for challenging the notion that the aged person and the child have a great deal in common. Although certain similarities do exist, the fact remains that it is only the child who is being carried forward on the tide of psychobiologic development. All of his behavior and experience is marked by the directional thrust.

The surge of general development continues with great vigor throughout the childhood years and is manifested in physical, social, and psychological changes. Although all of these developments contribute to the emergence of life perspectives, two of the most salient psychological discoveries that children make are:

1.   *The discovery of futurity*. This discovery has several components. First, there is the discovery of future time in the sense that "when this moment is over, there will be some more time coming." Second, there is the discovery of future time as qualitatively different from any other kind of time—it is fresh, unused time that can bring forth new experiences and events. This discovery implies a dawning appreciation of possibility and uncertainty. Third, there is the discovery of world, or objective future, time. Implied in this discovery is the realization that one does not really possess magical control over the universe and cannot really "take time out." Additionally, this is one of the insights that prepares the child to appreciate that, for all his precious and self-evident individuality, he is simply one of many fellow creatures, all of whom dance (or drag) to the music of time.

2.   *The discovery of mortality*. Some rudimentary appreciation of nonexistence may be achieved in early childhood, perhaps even before the conquest of language, but many additional years of development are required before the child can frame the concept of personal mortality. The proposition "I will die" is intimately related to the sense of futurity. It will be the continuing task of the adolescent and the adult to define the nature of this relationship for himself, to integrate the concepts of more time—fresh, new time—possibility, hope, trust, and uncertainty with the concepts of certain death.

The available evidence suggests that adolescence is usually the time during which the developing person begins seriously to create his life perspective. He has had many of the elements previously but now, for the first time, he also has the intellectual equipment to forge these elements into a perspective—and the psychosocial readiness to venture forth as his own self. Children have their notions—but it is adolescents who have ideologies. It is the transformation in thought that underlies the adolescent's changes in social behavior. He now can think about thought, compare ideal with reality, shatter the world as it is presented to him with his new tools of intellectual analysis, and at least try to put the pieces together again in a new and more satisfying manner. Adolescence, then, is the time of life in which the act of trying to develop perspectives is dominant.

Other characteristics of adolescence are: First, the adolescent has a strong sense of moving into the future. This is not at all the same thing as planning for or visualizing the future; rather, it is a restless experiencing of the developmental current running within oneself.

Second, the adolescent typically projects his thought and feeling intensively into a fairly narrow sector of the future. It is the proximate future that counts, that decisive and eventful time which is just around the corner. Old age is so remote and unappealing a prospect that it hardly can be located at all on his projective charts.

Third, the adolescent often neglects the past, especially his personal past. Neglect may be too passive a word to describe this phenomenon. I have the impression that many adolescents are waging an active battle against the past, trying to put psycological distance between who-I-used-to-be and who-I'm-going-to-be.

Finally, there is the adolescent's way of coming to terms with finality. The prospect of death, like the prospect of aging, often is regarded as a notion that is so remote as to have no relevance to one's own life. Death is avoided, glossed over, kidded about, neutralized, and controlled by a cool, spectator type of orientation. This is on the level of what might be called self-conscious, socially communicated thought. However, more probing and indirect methods of assessment suggest that many adolescents are extremely concerned about death—both in the sense of attempting to fathom its nature and meaning and in the sense of confronting the actual prospect of their own demise. We are no longer surprised when we come across an adolescent whose behavior is influenced by the expectation that he may die at an early age. Indeed, a foreshortened life perspective is by no means the special prerogative of the aged person.

What happens to life perspective during the adult years? We know less about mature perspectives than any other sort, but I think the life perspective of a mature adult has the following characteristics:

It is, first of all, a genuine perspective. This means that the individual has been able to subdivide his life-space into multiple points which stretch away in both directions from the present moment. He is able to locate himself at any one of these points and utilize the other points to achieve the effect of perspective. He might, for example, evaluate the immediate situation in terms of its possible future consequences. A more complex perspective consists of evaluating the immediate situation in terms of both past and future circumstances. More complex still is the perspective in which the individual flexibly shifts the emphasis among past, present, and future standpoints, with all three orientations always involved but varying in relation to each other. At one moment his pivotal concern may be with past events; thus he calls upon his immediate observations and future projections to provide a context of meaning around the past. At another moment he locates himself in the future and scans his past and present for what clues they can yield that would help him to comprehend his future self.

Upon closer inspection, his perspective will prove to be a structure that includes a variety of subperspectives. These might be visualized as operating in an umbrella type of arrangement. Opened slightly, the perspective system permits the individual to gain coverage of his proximate past and future. This could be called the yesterday-and-tomorrow framework. Opened more broadly, he now has perspective on a larger period of time, but this is still only a small range within his total life-span, where he has been and where he is going, relative to where he is now.

A mature use of the life perspective involves good judgment in deciding when it is appropriate to use a particular subperspective. It involves the ability to scan time in two distinctly different ways—the axiological and the probabilistic. In projecting the future, for example, the individual identifies his hopes, fears, and values, This is the axiological orientation. But he also is capable of reading the future in a more objective style, trying to establish the most likely pattern of expectancies. The ability to sweep through time in both axiological and probabilistic styles seems to be one of the hallmarks of a mature life perspective that is maturely employed. Furthermore, there will be an optimal balance between perspectives already established and fresh perspective-seeking activities. A flexible life perspective makes it possible to identify and integrate the novel or unexpected event without scuttling the more enduring perspectivistic structure.

Just as important as the life perspective itself, however, is the ability to let go, to know when it is in one's best interests to become totally engrossed in a situation. All perspective and no engrossment makes for a barren, abstracted sort of life.

A mature life perspective is the type that permits a person to make constructive use of his past experiences without becoming enslaved to them and to confront his future, including the prospect of death, without capitulating in that direction either. Many people fail to develop a functional and versatile life perspective, however. In some cases we see a distorted or dysfunctional perspective; in other cases we are struck by the absence of perspective. These different psychological orientations cannot be expected to lead to the same situation when the individuals involved reach advanced age.

In exploring what has been learned and what has yet to be learned about life perspectives in the aged, we should examine the disengagement theory. This is not just a courtesy call to respect the contributions of Elaine Cumming and William E. Henry—it happens that the disengagement theory is one of the few conceptual orientations to make something of life perspectives in later adulthood. Everybody knows by now that the hypothetical process of disengagement involves a gradual and mutual withdrawal of the aging individual and his society. It is said to be an inevitable and normal developmental process. It is said to occur universally, or at least to occur universally under favorable conditions. Obviously, this is an important proposition. Is it also a true proposition? That is another question and one which would take us beyond the scope of this discussion.

But there is a relevant question here. How does the disengagement process itself get started? Cumming and Henry have suggested that disengagement begins with an event that takes place within ourselves, or more specifically, within our life perspectives. As we approach the later years of our lives we come to realize that our future is limited. There is not enough time left to do everything we had hoped and planned. Eventually we also realize that time is not only limited; it is running out. Death comes into view as a salient prospect. Do Cumming and Henry mean that without this altered life perspective there would be no disengagement? They say: "It seems probable that disengagement would be resisted forever if there were no problem of the allocation of time and thus no anticipation of death. Questions of choice among alternative uses of time lead to curtailment of some activities. Questions of the inevitability of death lead to introspective reflections on the meaning of life."

Although this formulation emphasizes the importance of the individual's inner framework for organizing his experience and, in particular, the role of death anticipations, the formulation appears to be at variance with the facts. Although our knowledge of life perspectives is far from adequate, I believe that enough has been learned to indicate that the disengagement hypothesis has only limited application.

The disengagement hypothesis assumes that everybody has just about the same kind of perspective as they approach the later years of life. This generalization is not tenable. It is already clear that there are significant individual variations, even within particular subgroups in our own society. Some people, for example, never develop the complete umbrella of perspectives described earlier. They move through their life-span within a narrow shell of time, almost day by day. This kind of person does not wake up one morning and gasp, "My God, I have only a finite number of years ahead; I had best reallocate my time." The sound of distant drums never had much influence over him, and it may not get to him now, either. Many people in their seventh, eight, and ninth decades maintain a well-entrenched narrow perspective.

By contrast, there are other people who have been brandishing a wide-open perspective umbrella ever since their youth. The use of time and the prospect of death are factors which have influenced their lives every step of the way. Such people confront different challenges than do those who may be first awakening to intimations of morality or those whose limited perspectives have been little influenced by the passing years.

Many people do not experience the altered outlook on time and death that Cummings and Henry proposed as the psychological trigger for disengagement; but even among those who do confront this prospect within their life perspectives, there are important variations. The disengagement theorists have stated that "the anticipation of death frees us from the obligation to participate in the ongoing stream of life. If there is only a little time left, there is no point in planning for a future and no point in putting off today's gratification."

On the contrary, many people intensify their participation in life in order to obtain the greatest possible yield from the time remaining to them. This orientation can persist well beyond the sixth and seventh decades. In studying the psychology of dying and death within a population of very aged patients in a geriatric hospital, we have encountered many who came to terms with approaching death by investing themselves solidly in the network of interpersonal life.

Furthermore, there is reason to believe that the aged person who does clamber out of "the ongoing stream of life" may be doing so for a different reason. Our research interviews suggest that in many cases the individual is not gracefully disengaging to enjoy today's gratification because the future is too short to support long-range plans. Rather, he is more likely to feel that he is no longer capable of making good use even of the limited time that is available to him. It is a sense of inner depletion, impotence, and frustration coupled with the appraisal that his environment offers very little that is inspiring or rewarding.

Perhaps Cumming and Henry have projected into the minds of elderly people the sort of outlook on time and death that they themselves believe to be reasonable and appropriate. This is one of the pitfalls of those who deal wih the aged, but most aged people are not theoreticians and simply do not develop the kind of perspective that comes naturally to a theoretician's mind.

Also, we have learned from a number of aged people that they are likely to experience a double-bind regarding time—there is an awareness that future time is scarce but also a heavy sense of oppression at the hands of the clock, too much time that they cannot put to satisfying use. Even a heartfelt lament about the uselessness of future time is not identical with a will-to-die.

Finally, for at least some aged people, the qualitative nature of the future has changed radically. It is no longer the time in which exciting, fresh, novel events are to be expected. The future, in a sense, may be regarded as "used up" before it occurs. The past wends its way forward into the future.

Other points that have emerged from research and clinical experience include:

1.   A foreshortened perspective at any age is likely to increase the probability of premature death. The specific pathway of lethality may be through suicide or accident, but particular attention should be given to what might be called psyhosomatic or subintentional suicides, in which the individual's physical vulnerabilities are self-exploited to hasten his death.

2.   The balance between perspective and engrossment becomes increasingly difficult to maintain with advanced age. An environment that truly shelters the aged person, that truly protects him during his periods of special vulnerability, would make it possible for him to enjoy the spirit-replenishing experience of engrossment more frequently. We become more vulnerable when we are engrossed. We could help our elders if we developed ways of enabling them to drop the burden of their perspectives from time to time without excessive physical or social danger.

3.   The perspective of the aged person may become more diffuse or even collapse. Changes in the direction of simplification may be appropriate and beneficial to some people. But there is the danger that the entire perspective may become dysfunctional and contribute to an unnecessarily steep decline in social integration and behavioral competency. There are things we can do that are likely to have a bolstering effect on the aged person's perspectivistic system. For example, we could enter his past as an active force, a sort of participant-observer. Too often, the aged person's preoccupation with his past chases us away—he is snubbing us by focusing upon a scene in which we had no role. We can develop a sort of semirole in his past and, through this, help him to link his past with the present that all of us share and the future that most of us expect. We are also likely to gain something ourselves through this interpenetration of life perspectives.

4.   Both our formal and informal socialization processes emphasize personal growth and expansion during the early years of life. "The system" ill prepares us for living within limits, living with losses, and living with the prospect of death. When the achievement-oriented socialization system gets to work on a person who is growing up in a deprived or ruptured environment, he is alerted to the incongruity between the ideal and the reality. His reaction may take the form of a refusal to accept the socially sponsored perspective in the first place, or a rapid aging of the perspective if he does try it out. The person who is growing up in an environment that makes the goals of "the system" appear attractive and feasible is, of course,

more likely to develop a life perspective that is centered around individual achievement in the usual sense of the term. Both kinds of people would be better served if our socialization processes—including the classroom— offered a broader, more versatile, and more humane model from which the individual could fashion his own life perspective.

Related Readings

Cumming, E., and Henry, W. E. *Growing old*. (Originally published in 1961.) New York: Arno, 1980.

Kastenbaum, R. Time, death and ritual in old age, in J. T. Fraser and N. Lawrence (Eds.), *The study of time, II*. New York, Heidelberg, Berlin: Springer-Verlag, 1975, pp. 20–38.

Kastenbaum, R. Memories of tomorrow: Interpretation of time in later life, in A. Wessman and B. Gorman (Eds.), *The personal experience of time*. New York: Plenum, 1978, pp. 194–214.

III

From Youth to Old Age

I remember a 3-year-old boy who gathered with the other local folk to watch Boston Marathon runners pass through the little town square quite early in their race. Other children and all available dogs bounced along with the runners for a few strides. But David had a mind of his own. He bucked the current to run in the opposite direction, and he had a perfectly lucid reason to offer his father when he was finally apprehended running away from the flow: "I want to see where they're all coming *from!*"

This is also a perfectly lucid reason for turning some of our own attention to the years of youth; this, after all, is where the old people are coming from. Until the day when people are born old, there is much to learn from examing the antecedent personality and social factors that contribute to old age being what it is, and what it isn't.

Sociologists Gregory Johnson and J. Lawrence Kamara recognize that both getting into and being squeezed out of the race have significant political dimensions. They analyze and discuss our society's trend toward artificially compressing the "productive" years of life. This social policy seems to have broken loose from its psychobiologic moorings, for the older generation has greater psychological and physical vitality than ever before. A *biosocial paradox* is posed by society's political exclusion of both young and old from productive life when both age subpopulations actually have the necessary competence. Johnson and Kamara provide a concise and well-integrated approach to the question of enabling people to be full participants in society from youth through old age.

With Michael Katz's study we enter an experimental situation in which old people are asked to perform self-control tasks that had previously been studied in children. This experiment draws on the Russian psychologist A. R. Luria's theory of the verbal regulation of motor behavior—how words affect actions. The study is of more than theoretical interest; there are substantial implications for physical and social activity of the elderly. We see here an example of how the simplification of "real-life" processes often required by experimental psychology can lay bare some of the difficulties that a person encounters in daily life.

By contrast, Brian Mishara and Harvey Baker remind us of the individual differences we see among residents of the same nursing home or, for that matter,

129

among any adults of the same age. They suggest that there may be a continuity of underlying characteristics throughout the life-span that can be understood in terms of a *stimulus intensity modulation* (SIM) phenomenon. SIM is studied through a fairly simple perceptual-cognitive task that differentiates between people who "reduce" and those who "augment" the intensity of incoming stimuli. There are implications here for both theory and practice.

Loneliness and problems in new learning are among the major difficulties often associated with old age. It is seldom, however, that efforts have been made to see these phenomena in relation to each other and to the individual's entire life history. The distinguished gerontologist A. T. Welford steps outside the laboratory to examine the links between *motivation, learning,* and *values* as an individual ages. He brings with him insights from a broad spectrum of research, including *signal detection theory*. Apart from Welford's specific suggestions, it is stimulating to see in general how one can both make use of existing scientific knowledge and also be sensitive to the realities of everyday life for the elderly.

These studies can but illustrate the heightened interest in the antecedents of the old person's life situation. Pursuing this problem to its limits will itself be a sort of marathon!

9

Growing Up and Growing Old: The Politics of Age Exclusion

Gregory Johnson

J. Lawrence Kamara

> For as I like a young man in whom there is something of the old, so I like an old
> man in whom there is something of the young; and he who follows this maxim
> in body will possibly be an old man, but he will never be an old man in mind.[1]
>
> > Cicero

> The generations at the extreme poles, the really old and the emancipated
> teen-agers . . . already have one foot in another world, and they can indulge in
> their separate dreams and thoughts.[2]
>
> > Edgar Morin

In the agrarian society of the nineteenth century, the work life of the young
and old was dictated by biologic rather than social definitions. The young
commonly worked on the farm as soon as they were physically able, and the
aged often worked until the day they died. By contrast, the twentieth
century has created a series of social definitions which have gradually
excluded the young and old from the productive process. For the young,
these definitions include successively new "stages of life" such as "adolescence" and "postadolescence" or youth.[3] For the aged, arbitrary exclusion
from work at age 65 has created a "postretirement" stage.[4] An earlier
preretirement, postparental stage has been identified as the "young-old."[5]
These stages of life indicate how modern society has prolonged youth and
old age into lengthy stages of growing up and growing old.

The mutual nonproductivity of the young and old is portrayed demo-
graphically by the term *dependency ratio*. This term refers to the number

Reprinted with permission from *International Journal of Aging and Human Development*,
1977/78, 8, 99–110. This chapter is a revised and modified version of a longer one presented at
the S.S.S.P. annual convention, August 1975 in San Francisco.

of persons in the nonworking years (defined as under 20 and over 65) to each 100 persons in the working years (20–64). In 1975 the dependency ratio for the United States was 86—that is, there are 86 dependent persons who must be supported by each 100 of those of working years. Of these dependents, over three-quarters are presently youths, and less than one-quarter are old.[6] Moreover, the dependency ratio has dropped slightly since 1900—from 94 to 86. Rather than the total dependency ratio, the important historical change has occurred in the nature of its age structure. As Table 9.1 indicates, our society is gradually changing from one which was largely comprised of young dependents to one which will be almost half comprised of old dependents.

Rather than supporting one end of the life cycle, our society is coming to the point where it is characterized by the shared dependency of the young and old. Considered together, the two extremes account for a significant segment of the total life cycle. The increase in life expectancy at one end, coupled with the prolongation of adolescence at the other, means that nearly 50 years of a person's entire life may be at stake. Young persons now spend nearly three decades in a *preproductive* stage of life. Simultaneously, old persons now spend nearly as much time in a *postproductive* stage. The gradual exclusion of the young and old from productive roles is indicated by the data on employment in Table 9.2.

One consequence of these developments is the "compression" of the productive years of middle age (the stage of life generally associated with child rearing, economic production, and consumption). The "compression" of middle age is partly a reflection of the declining significance of the extended family, the one institution which traditionally linked the three generations. Of particular importance has been the gradual shift of the family from a productive unit (family businesses, for example) to a consuming unit. Early retirement at one end and the extension of adolescence through schooling at the other are recent developments which have "compressed" the productive years. When combined with the fact of increased human longevity, an unprecedented short portion of one's entire life is now

TABLE 9.1. Changing Structure of Dependency

	Dependency Ratio	Percentage under 20	Percentage over 65
1900	94	90	10
1975	86	75	25
2025	79	60	40

Adapted from Shanas and Hauser.[6]

TABLE 9.2.   Labor Force and Participation Rate and Projections to 1985 by Sex and Age

	Total Labor Force (in Thousands)			Participation Rates		
	1900	*1972*	*1985*	*1900*	*1972*	*1985*
Male total	22,641	55,671	66,017	85.7	78.5	78.3
16–19	2,834	4,791	3,962	62.0	59.2	55.5
20–24	3,302	7,795	8,496	90.6	88.8	88.4
25–44	10,560	23,450	34,017	94.7	95.7	94.6
45–64	4,958	17,614	17,460	90.3	85.8	84.9
65+	987	2,022	2,082	63.1	23.3	20.0
Female total	4,999	33,320	41,699	20.0	42.3	45.6
16–19	1,230	3,576	3,203	26.8	45.7	46.4
20–24	1,179	5,337	6,523	31.7	58.9	64.9
25–44	1,791	12,549	18,899	17.5	49.7	52.9
45–64	672	10,974	13,755	13.6	47.3	51.4
65+	127	1,085	1,319	8.3	8.8	8.5

Sources: Statistical Abstract of U.S. (1973) and Statistical History of U.S. (1965).

spent in the productive years. These developments can be historically visualized by the following paradigm (Figure 9.1).

The separation of the young and old from productive life is especially visible now because both groups are numerically more significant than ever before. Population figures indicate that in 1970 there were nearly 40 million persons in the United States between 14 and 24 or approximately 19% of the total population.[7] Correspondingly, there were roughly 22 million persons 65 and over, or approximately 10% of the total population. Thus, the combined total of the two groups in 1970 was roughly 29% of the total population.

Especially paradoxical is the fact that the young and old are excluded from productive life *despite* their increased biologic capacities. For the aged, human longevity is increasing every year. Estimates for 1975 are 69.5 for males and 75.8 for females. Correspondingly, psychological and physical vitality seem to be also extended into later years more than ever before.[8] This pattern of physiological advancement holds true for the lower end of the life cycle as well. During the past century, each succeeding generation has reached puberty at an earlier age than the generation preceding it. In terms of adolescent growth spurt, attainment of adult size, and physiological characteristics, each generation is more mature than were their parents at a similar age.[9] For females, this trend is indicated by progressively lower ages at menarche and fertility.

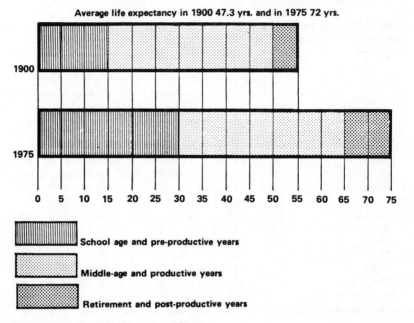

Figure 9.1. Compression of middle age.

Adulthood, however, is defined in social, rather than biologic terms. Although the young and old may be increasingly capable of engaging in productive work, their participation in the work force has been progressively postponed.

This biosocial paradox underlies several questions which we examine in this chapter:

   1.   How is this situation to be understood theoretically? Is the separation of the young and old from productive life a "natural" occurrence, inevitably determined by chronology?
   2.   Which institutions in society that promote and sustain the dependency of the young and old as nonproductive members of society result in similar consequences for each?

By pointing to these issues, we hope to suggest ways in which the entire life cycle is a unitary phenomenon. Developments which influence the aged can have reciprocal effects on the young. Rather than being limited to one end of the life cycle, future researchers and policy planners might usefully study the entire life cycle. This unitary perspective on the life cycle will be especially essential during the next 50 years, when our society will witness dramatic shifts in age composition.

Previous Literature

A considerable body of sociologic research suggests that the disengagement perspective suffers from some basic defects and consequently should be reformulated (see Hochschild, for a comprehensive summary of this research[10]). The implicit value judgment that disengagement is *desirable* for aging persons is certainly a serious defect; as Rose points out, it is often the *engaged* elderly as opposed to the *disengaged* who express the greatest life satisfaction.[11] It is also fallacious to assume that disengagement is a linear phenomenon, inevitably affecting the aged; as Hochschild suggests, disengagement is a variable process and can occur at all ages including youth.

Perhaps the most serious defect of disengagement theory stems from its failure to take into account the role of power in age relations. Much like functionalist political theory, disengagement theory has tended to emphasize the role of consensus in age relations. Thus, the young and old are viewed as naturally excluded from the productive system because they are either dysfunctional (they simply do not contribute to the needs and survival of the system) or they are normatively deviant (they are too "old" fashioned in the case of the old *or* too "immature" in the cases of the young). This perspective ignores the fact that economic and political power is concentrated in the hands of the middle aged, a fact which enables them to exclude the young and old. The inherently economic nature of our conceptions of maturity is noted by Neugarten and Moore:

> The period of economic productivity may be regarded as 'maturity' and the period of economic dependency in the first part of the life cycle is regarded as 'immaturity.' Dependency in this sense occurs also in the last part of the life cycle; and the point at which the individual enters the period of economic old age becomes defined as his age at retirement.[12]

Foner has suggested how age relations might be understood in "conflict" rather than "functionalist" theoretical terms.[13] She states that age is as significant as class, race, and sex in identifying and rewarding members of society. Furthermore, this process of *age stratification* is a significant source of "social inequalities, values, group loyalties and societal conflict." (p. 187).[13] Age stratification is distinguished from other types of stratification (such as economic stratification) in one critical aspect: guaranteed social mobility. By the very process of aging the individual moves from one status (and set of roles) to another. In extending Foner's conflict perspective, we wish to point to some of the causes and consequences of age stratification in the sectors of the life cycle where it is most dramatically visible—old age and youth.

Essential to a conflict perspective of age relations is the view that the productive and powerful middle aged maintain their position by disengaging the nonproductive and powerless young and old. This forced disengagement is largely achieved through retirement from and postponement of entry into middle-aged adult work roles. This process is not a deliberate conspiracy but is the consequence of the workings of the institutional order, especially the institutions of education and retirement.

Age Coalitions and the Consequences of Exclusion

An illustration of the workings of age stratification is provided by the example of implicit age coalitions. The middle aged have maintained power by forming alliances with both ends of the age spectrum. In skilled labor and professional settings, apprenticeship and accreditation procedures delay the entry of the young into the labor force. In such instances, the middle aged and old join forces to hold back and exclude the young; the disparaging terms used include: "You aren't ready" or "you don't have enough experience." At other times, however, the middle aged act in an opposite manner—combining forces with the young to dislodge the old; common rationalizations for this procedure include: "You are too old" or "you can no longer do the job." Kalish described how old persons, because they have internalized the values of society, are likely to see the young (who tend to deny the validity of these values) as enemies rather than natural allies.[14] In fact, the young and old are "generation gap allies" because some of the same values that discriminate against the young also discriminate against the old.

These age coalitions suggest how the shared position of the young and old might be described as a common *structural vulnerability*. By being excluded from meaningful participation in society, the young and old are inherently vulnerable to the workings of power in society. A significant prerogative of such power is the ability to define appropriate conduct. In our society, a person's economic function is strongly emphasized, which means that persons who do not economically produce (such as the young and old) are severely devalued.

The specific consequences of structural vulnerability parallel Shibutani and Kwan's exhaustive analysis of ethnic stratification.[15] In discussing ethnic discrimination they state: "This type of discrimination develops (where) members of the dominant group occupy most the desirable positions and others perform most of the menial tasks." Rather than being intrinsic to "human nature," discrimination on the basis of ascribed traits exists because it justifies a preexisting system of power and privilege. It is likely that a similar process justifies age stratification systems in which the middle aged "occupy most of the desirable positions." Following Shibutani and Kwan's analysis, specific consequences of age stratification can be identified:

1. Economic discrimination;
2. Age stereotyping, and
3. Territorial segregation.

Economic Discrimination

The primary form of age-based economic discrimination occurs in employment. Like racial discrimination, exclusion from employment contains numerous residual economic consequences, including higher insurance premiums and difficulty in obtaining bank accounts, loans, and mortgages.

Examples of employment discrimination against both the young and the old are abundant; an important recent example of job discrimination against the elderly was evidenced by a suit against two railroad companies.[16] This $20 million suit was initiated by the aged employees, who charged that the railroad companies, by their mandatory retirement regulations, had illegally deprived thousands of persons of their livelihood. At the lower end of the age spectrum, young persons frequently complain that they are the last hired and the first fired. For unskilled young in high schools and colleges the problem is especially acute; each summer millions of students face a dwindling job market for unskilled, short-term labor.[17] Intensifying this problem is the present minimum age laws, which prevent the young from obtaining job training through apprenticeship programs.

The economic consequences of exclusion from the labor force are visible at both ends of the life cycle. In 1975, the proportion of all persons living below the poverty line of $3,000 was 22%. The proportion of aged couples living below the poverty line was 21% while the proportion of aged single persons was 25%. Furthermore, the proportion of the aged living in substandard housing was 25% of the population.[18] Although comparable figures for the young are not as readily available, the economic consequences of exclusion are indicated by inferential indicators. Any observations of the number of young persons receiving surplus food, welfare payments, and food stamps indicate that economic hardship has beset thousands of young persons.[19]

Age Stereotyping

Exclusion of the young and the old is rationalized by invidious conceptions of their ability to perform in work roles. Besides being a justification of preexisting power arrangements,[15] these stereotypes enable the middle aged to define appropriate conduct for both the young and the aged.

Thus, both forms of age stereotyping are rooted in the alleged inability of the young and old to engage in productive work. This fact might reveal more about the middle aged (and their immersion in the "work ethic" and its associated values such as dependability, restraint, seriousness of purpose, and frugality) than either the young or old. Thus, by determining that dependability or seriousness of purpose are absent in the young or old, the middle aged guarded against such failings in themselves.

The consequences of such age stereotyping are evident in conceptions of the young. Exclusion of the young is rationalized by conceptions of their conduct as immature, lazy, and overly playful. They are viewed as lacking in the reasoned caution which is acquired with age and are pictured as impulsive, overly adventurous, and likely to be extreme in speech, manners, and political views. Such stereotypes are illuminated by exceptions to the rule, such as the few young persons considered "mature" enough (in terms of self-control, goal direction, and caution) to be acceptable to their elders. The parallels with racial stereotyping are instructive: Just as whites accept those blacks who appear most like them (in terms of values, lifestyles, dress, and demeanor), so do the middle aged readily accept young persons who seem "oldest" or "most mature."

The stereotypes which categorize the elderly also refer to their alleged inability to engage in the productive pursuits of the middle aged. Rather than being dismissed as inadequate owing to a surplus of energy or exuberance (as are the young), the opposite holds true for the aged; they are deemed inadequate because they do not have enough.

Blau's studies indicate several pervasive stereotypes regarding the aged, including an alleged inflexibility toward acceptance of new ways as well as an overconservatism of dress and conduct.[4] Moreover, her research indicates that the aged were expected to associate exclusively with persons their own age. These findings are corroborated by a Harris poll which discovered that the vast majority of Americans under 65 believed the elderly to be weak, feeble, in poor health, in fear of crime, and beset by loneliness.[20] The application and use of these stereotypes indicates the pervasive nature of "age-ism," that is, the systematic discrimination of large segments of the society primarily because of their age. Noted gerontologist Robert Butler described how many United States senators and congressmen in recent years have employed age-ism in an attempt to oust several old, politically conservative committee chairmen.[21] The fact that these committee chairmen were also politically conservative in their youth was overlooked. Instead, their advancing years and alleged inability to perform their work became justifications for attempts to oust them from their posts.

Territorial Segregation

The development of such stereotypes is intensified by age-based territorial segregation. A group's territory, or "turf," is a critical dimension in any stratification system. Territorial segregation is a relatively recent historical development, being virtually unknown in rural nineteenth century America. The urbanization of the past century has witnessed the gradual segregation of class, ethnic, and racial groups into geographical enclaves. Just as age is one of the last of these dimensions to become a source of political conflict, it is also the last to become designated by separate territories. There seems little doubt, however, that present-day America can be viewed as age-segregated. The picture of age segregation is clear in virtually every state in the union, which includes college communities comprised primarily of the young, suburban "bedroom" developments housing the middle aged with children, and retirement communities comprised exclusively of the elderly.

The most significant "youth ghettos" are clustered around the sprawling American "multiuniversities" in such communities as Berkeley, California; Madison, Wisconsin; and Ann Arbor, Michigan. The degree to which these communities are comprised almost exclusively of the young has led Lofland to describe "age territories" as America's "new segregation."[22] Although university students form the population core, those communities also are comprised of thousands of nonstudents and ex-students. Although often physically indistinguishable from their collegiate contemporaries, these young persons have been attracted by the university communities' tolerant atmosphere, which allows them to express a deviant lifestyle.

Age segregation among the aged has developed along somewhat similar lines. There are many examples of communities comprised almost exclusively of the elderly, especially in the Sun Belt, the southern tier of the United States, which includes such "old-age" towns as Sun City, Arizona; Palm Springs, California; and St. Petersburg, Florida.

Such age ghettos, although similar in many respects to ethnic and religious ghettos, bear a significant difference: They are formed with the willful consent of the persons involved. Individuals migrate to Berkeley,

California, or to St. Petersburg, Florida, with the willful intention of associating with persons of their own age and place in life. Although age-based housing discrimination exists, it is not as severe as that practiced against ethnic and racial minorities. Although the sources of age ghettos are different from those of racial and ethnic ghettos, many of the consequences are similar; perhaps most significant is the segregation of conduct which accompanies segregation by age. Geographical separation inevitably implies that age groups will increasingly associate exclusively with age peers. Friendships with persons of different ages will be thereby decreased. When relationships with persons outside one's age group occur, they will be formalized, limited to "instrumental" job and business dealings.

Conclusions

Modern society is witnessing a sharpened awareness of arbitrary collective inequalities, including exclusion based upon sex, race, and class. Like these forms of arbitrary inequality, age exclusion is based upon an inherent power imbalance. Butler described how powerlessness is a condition considered by the middle aged to be synonymous with old age in America.[23] Consequently the old, patronized and infantilized, have like the young come to accept their society's stereotyping of them as helpless and therefore powerless. This inherent vulnerability of the young and old to the workings of power in middle-aged society results in the developments outlined here:

1. Despite increasing biologic capacities, the young and old have been progressively excluded from participation in the productive life of society;

2. This exclusion is accomplished by custodial treatment (including both mandatory schooling and compulsory retirement), which is justified by cultural conceptions equating productivity with maturity; and

3. Arbitrary age-based exclusion has resulted in specific consequences both for young and old, including economic discrimination, age stereotyping, and territorial segregation. Implications of these developments affect both social policy and further empirical research.

Regarding social policy, it is clear that future recommendations might address the entire process of *age exclusion* rather than solely address the problems of one end of the life cycle (such as the Coleman report on confusing youth).[23] Thus, our conclusions suggest that the plight of the young and aged can be understood as a single problem, subject to some of the same recommended changes.

Riley has argued this point persuasively:

Like all life course transitions, these two are interlocked within the lives of individuals as they age, and within the age strata of the dynamics of society. Any change in one evokes a change in the other . . . restructuring institutions in which the young mature [implies] alterations that will also impinge upon the old.[24]

What would be the implication of mutual restructuring of the existing institutions which serve both the young and the old? As a means of lessening the segregation of the young from adult society, the Coleman report (pp. 157–163) suggests an "alternation of school and work." This proposal involves work situations which incorporate schooling and school situations which incorporate work.[23] Examples include work-study programs at universities and educational credit programs in industry. Extending this line of reasoning to the aged, we might suggest work situations which incorporate retirement and retirement situations which incorporate work. Although these programs are still embryonic, examples include:

1.   "R.S.V.P." programs in Boston, Massachusetts, in which the aged are incorporated into work situations and

2.   Preretirement programs for older workers which allow them to anticipate and prepare for the unstructured existence of retirement.

Proposals for large-scale institutional changes will be immediately confronted with an obstacle which is deeply rooted in American consciousness: our productivity-based conception of human worth. This conception, as many of the examples in this chapter indicate, influence how persons are treated at each stage of the life cycle. Any proposals for incorporating youth in work situations will be likely to be opposed by cost accountants who complain that the youth cost the company more than they are worth. Similarly, for the aged, the expenditure of institutional resources on persons about to die seems like an enormous waste in cost-accounting terms. Such a process explains the failure of some continuing education programs for the middle aged and elderly. Educational systems are simply not designed to absorb persons without many years of productivity ahead of them.

Regarding further research, several questions seem evident. Given their shared plight, what are the possible chances for political alliances between the two age groups? What are the attitudes and values of both the young and old which might facilitate or hinder such alliances? What political and economic developments might foster or impede such alliances? A related question refers to the possible political ascendance (in terms of either absolute size or actual political influence) of one end of the age cycle. Is the total power possessed by the young and old a fixed quantity, thus implying that the ascendance of one group would inevitably diminish the power of the other? We may have an opportunity to witness such a development in the next three decades, when the proportion of elderly persons will probably expand greatly. As yet unforeseen dynamics of age stratification will be revealed by the extent to which this expansion also involves a shift in power and prestige from the young and middle aged to the elderly.

References

1. *Cicero's offices*. New York: Dutton, Everyman's Library, p. 236, 1966.
2. E. Morin. *The red and the white: Report from a French village*. New York: Pantheon, p. 121, 1970.
3. K. Keniston. Youth: a new stage of life, *American Scholar, 39*, 631–654, 1970.
4. Z. Blau. *Old age in a changing society*, New York: New Directions, 1973.
5. B. Neugarten. The rise of the young-old, *New York Times*, January 1975.
6. E. Shanas and P. Hauser. Zero populaton growth and family life of old people. *Journal of Social Issues, 30*, 79–91, 1974.
7. N. Ryder. The demography of youth, in *Youth: Transition to adulthood*, J. Coleman (Ed.). Chicago: University of Chicago Press, pp. 45–64, 1974.
8. P. Van den Berghe. *Age and sex in human societies*, Belmont, Calif.: Wadsworth, 1973.
9. D. Eichorn. Biology and psychology, in *Youth: Transition to adulthood*, J. Coleman (Ed.). Chicago: University of Chicago Press, pp. 91–111, 1974.
10. A. Hochschild. Disengagement theory—A critique and proposal. *American Sociological Review, 40*, 553–569, 1975.
11. A. Rose. A current theoretical issue in social gerontology. *Gerontologist, 4*:(1), 48, 1964.
12. B. Neugarten and J. Moore. The changing age-status system, in *Middle-age and aging: A reader in social psychology*, B. L. Neugarten (Ed.). Chicago: University of Chicago Press, pp. 5–21, 1968.
13. A. Foner. Age stratification and age conflict in political life. *American Sociological Review, 39*, 187–196, 1974.
14. R. A. Kalish. The old and the new as generation gap allies. *Gerontologist, 9*:(2) 83–89, summer 1969.
15. T. Shibutani and K. M. Kwan. *Ethnic stratification*. Chicago: University of Chicago Press, 1965.
16. Big age bias suit against two railroads, *San Francisco Chronicle*, p. 2, June 30, 1974.
17. M. Feldstein. The economics of the new unemployment. *Public Interest, 33*, fall 1973.

18. M. Tompkins. 1970 census of population and housing, first court summary tape, Boston Redevelopment Authority Research Department, 1970.
19. *New York Times*, p. 15, June 1975.
20. L. Harris. Senior citizen: More numerous, more militant. *Christian Science Monitor*, p. 2, October 1974.
21. R. N. Butler. Fighting seniority with bigotry. *Washington Monthly*, pp. 37–42, June 1971.
22. J. Lofland. The new segregation: A perspective on age categories in society, in *Youth and Sociology*, P. Manning and M. Truzzi (Eds.), Englewood Cliffs, N. J.: Prentice-Hall, pp. 235–236, 1971.
23. J. Coleman, (Ed.). *Youth: Transition to adulthood*. Chicago: University of Chicago Press, 1974.
24. R. N. Butler. Pacification and the politics of aging (The elderly have been watergated too), Public Interest Report No. 14, *International Journal of Aging and Human Development*, 5:(4) 393–395, 1974.
25. M. W. Riley. The perspective of age stratification. *School Review, 83*:(1), 1974.

10

Self-control in Old Age: An Experimental-Developmental Approach

Michael M. Katz

This study deals with the ability of elderly people to exercise self-control, that is, to produce appropriate behavior and to inhibit inappropriate behavior. Ideas derived from Luria's theory and research on the development of verbal regulation of behavior in children are used to examine the effects of aging on self-control.[1,2]

According to Luria, the development of verbal regulation of behavior follows an orderly sequence of stages. Behavior becomes progressively less influenced by external stimuli and progressively more influenced by self-regulating processes. In the first stage (ages 1–2 years) a child's own speech cannot yet guide his or her behavior. The speech of others can only initiate behavior. Attempts to use verbal instructions to *terminate* ongoing behavior not only will fail but will usually intensify the behavior. During the second stage (ages 2–4½ years) the child is now able to use language to guide his or her behavior but has difficulty inhibiting behavior because the excitatory properties of speech and of environmental stimuli are usually stronger than the child's semantic and inhibitory controls. According to Luria, this excitatory property refers to stimulation of the child's central nervous system, which spreads to areas in the brain that control motor behavior. This stimulation can result in motor behavior even if the behavior is unnecessary, inappropriate, or prohibited. For example, Luria found that when instructed to squeeze a rubber balloon when a blue light

Reprinted, under a different title, with permission from *International Journal of Aging and Human Development*, 1974, 5, 141–156. This study is based on the author's doctoral dissertation at Wayne State University. The author expresses gratitude to Dr. Robert Kastenbaum for his help as doctoral advisor and to the residents and staff of the Carmel Hall nursing home of Detroit for their cooperation in this study.

144

went on, but not when a yellow light went on, most 2–4½ year olds squeezed to *both* lights. When instructed to *say*, "Squeeze" and to squeeze to the blue light and to *say*, "Don't squeeze" and to not squeeze to the yellow light, they made *more* erroneous squeezes than when they were silent. Thus, the light onset, representing an abrupt change in environmental stimuli, and speech overrode the semantic property of the instructions and led to unnecessary motor behavior. In the third stage (ages 4½–5½ years) the semantic property of speech comes to dominate its excitatory influence and the excitatory influence of environmental stimuli. Internal symbolic and cognitive processes emerge as the primary regulators of behavior. By age 5½ nearly all children are able to do the previously mentioned tasks correctly (Table 10.1).

Luria's theory of the development of self-control is consistent with that of Vygotsky, which asserts that verbal experiences between mother and child form the foundation for the development of the ability to direct one's own behavior.[3] For example, the mother directs the child to "Hold the cup with two hands." Growing older the child internalizes her verbal instructions and says, "I will hold the cup with two hands" and does so. Thus, a response initially elicited by another's speech leads the child to direct his or her own actions. Luria's theory is also consistent with that of Piaget, which states that cognitive development proceeds through stages, during which one becomes less dependent on external stimuli and more influenced by internal structures, which he calls "schemata."[4] For example, children who fail Piaget's conservation problems insist that changing the shape of an object also changes its mass, volume, or weight. Their judgment is based on the external physical appearance of the object rather than on the application of internal conceptual operations to the stimuli. With the development of internal structures one becomes better able to

TABLE 10.1. The Development of Verbal Regulation of Behavior (Luria)

Stage	Approximate Age	Influence of Speech
1	1–2 years	Speech initiates but cannot terminate behavior.
2	2–4½ years	Speech guides behavior more, but its ability to "excite" dominates over the meaning-content.
3	4½–5½ years	The meaning or semantic property of speech gains dominance both over its excitation value and over environmental stimuli. Self-control becomes possible.

deal actively with the environment on abstract and symbolic levels and to integrate different aspects of the stimulus situation.

Kagan defines impulsivity as the tendency to respond quickly to problems without giving them enough rational thought.[5] He asserts that impulsivity is an enduring and pervasive personality trait that affects many different kinds of behavior, including learning, problem solving, and reading difficulties. He, like Luria, Vygotsky, and Piaget, found that in children impulse control increases with age.

Luria's research has relevance for theories of child development. For example, psychoanalytic theory maintains that the infant enters the world as a creature of impulses, who reacts to tensions by immediate and diffuse motor activity. With the development of the ego the child learns to control impulses and to delay the discharge of tensions until an appropriate occasion occurs. It is very likely that verbal control of behavior plays an important role in the development of the reality principle and the secondary process, for it facilitates such ego processes as organizing, planning, and delaying. Both theories agree that self-control increases with development, as does the use of internalized processes to guide, regulate, and control one's behavior.

Katz found that most 3-year-olds and many 4-year-olds had difficulty inhibiting motor behavior on a 24-item set of Luria-type tasks, in which the motor behavior was depressing a lever.[6] Luria's finding that light onset and speech can function as impelling stimuli that can elicit unnecessary and prohibited behavior was verified. It was found that saying certain words produced a mild tendency to push the lever; saying the words when the light went on resulted in a stronger tendency to push, which was not reduced when the children were explicitly instructed to refrain from pushing. Observing a model perform each task did not improve ability to inhibit. The 3-year-olds made 3 times as many errors as 4-year-olds. Teachers' evaluations of the 3-year-olds on their impulsivity versus self-control correlated significantly with performance on the tasks. This 24-item set of tasks is used in the present study and referred to as the Katz Impulsivity Scale, (KIS). Bates and Katz found that performance of 4- and 5-year-olds on a modified version of the KIS correlated significantly with performance on another measure of impulsivity—Kagan's Matching Familiar Figures test.[7]

These findings have important implications for child rearing. In many cases, when children are told *not* to do something by their parents but do it anyway, they are punished because the behavior is construed to be the result of negativism, disobedience, or hostility. An alternative interpretation of some misbehavior is that it is not the result of willful disobedience but of the developmental immaturity of neurological and psychological mechanisms responsible for self-control.

Purpose of This Study

This study investigates the elderly person's ability to exercise self-control. The KIS was given to two groups of people ranging in age from 65 to 75 and from 80 to 96 years. Their performances were compared to each other and to those of the children in Katz's previous studies in an attempt to answer the following questions.

1. What happens to self-control in later life? Various alternatives can be supported by different theoretical viewpoints. Some researchers, including Dennis and Mallinger, Pressey and Kuhlen, and Bromley, maintain that regression occurs in old age, implying that, like young children, the elderly may have some difficulty inhibiting unnecessary behavior.[8-10] The physiological degeneration theory, held by Birren, Hinchcliffe, and others, suggests that the elderly may have difficulty inhibiting behavior because of deterioration of cells responsible for self-control.[11,12] The disengagement theory of Cumming and Henry leads to two opposing predictions on how the elderly might perform on Luria-type tasks.[13] According to this theory, normal aging involves a mutual withdrawal or "disengagement" between the person and society, which is inevitable and self-perpetuating. As the withdrawal proceeds, more and more relationships with others are eliminated. Consequently, there is a reduction of social behavior, of the number of roles that society expects from them, and of their conformity to social norms. Being less responsive to social stimuli implies that the elderly may make unnecessary motor responses on the KIS tasks. On the other hand, disengagement theory also maintains that the elderly reduce the frequency and variety of their behavior, so as not to waste what little time and energy they have. This reduced inclination to behave at all (their nonresponse set) suggests that they would not produce unnecessary behavior. Learning theory suggests that verbal control of behavior is extremely resistant to decay as it is a well-practiced and often reinforced behavior. This implies that KIS performance should not deteriorate with age. This proposal is supported by the studies of Botwinick and of Norman and Daley which found little or no decline in verbal skills with age, unless massive brain damage occurred.[14,15] The present study tries to resolve these theoretical discrepancies.

2. At what ages do changes (if any) in self-control occur? Tuckman and Loren found that 100% of undergraduates and 97% of middle-aged people believed that "old age" begins at a particular chronological age, with 60 and 65 being the most often mentioned ages.[16] Calhoun and Gottesman found that many people have a stereotype of old age (over 65) as a period of rapid social, emotional, and physical decline.[17] Calhoun and Gottesman maintain that this stereotype is false: that becoming "old" is a gradual process occurring over a long period of time and that there are wide

individual differences among the elderly. That many people retire (often
against their will) at age 65 may be due, in part, to this stereotype that
decline in functioning will shortly occur. If this stereotype is valid, then the
65–75 year olds should show considerable loss of self-control on the KIS.

3. *How does the verbal control of behavior in the elderly compare with
that found in children?*

4. *Is the behavior measured by the KIS related to performance on
other measures of self-control?*   Pollock and Kastenbaum found that older
people were less able to write the phrase "New Jersey Chamber of Commerce" as slowly as possible.[18] It appeared that they lacked the self-control
to take their time and to suppress the desire to complete the task. Performance on this task is compared with that on the KIS.

5. *What factors account for individual differences (if any) in self-
control among the elderly?*   Knowledge of these factors may facilitate the
understanding of how the individual and society contribute to increases or
decreases in self-control among the aged.

Method

Participants were 48 persons living in a Detroit nursing home; 24 persons
ranging in age from 65 to 75 years ($M = 71.8$) were compared with 24
persons ranging from 80 to 96 years ($M = 85.2$). Each group included 16
women and 8 men. All were white, of middle-class socioeconomic background, and lived in the section of the home restricted to persons judged
by the staff to be nonsenile, alert, well-adjusted people capable of caring
for themselves with minimal or no supervision. They conducted their daily
lives as they wished, including going shopping or walking downtown by
themselves. The few people living in this section who had had mild strokes
or who were hard of hearing were excluded from the study so as not to
confound the effects of aging per se with those of obvious organic damage.

Apparatus

The apparatus for the KIS consisted of a blue 6 × 6 × 7-inch wooden box
with a standard 7½-watt light bulb and a spring-loaded lever mounted 3
inches apart on its top surface. A manipulandum disk 2 inches in diameter
was fitted to the end of the lever to serve as a resting place for the
participant's index finger. The stimulus light was controlled by a switch in
the experimenter's hand.

The apparatus for the slow writing test consisted of a piece of card-
board 14 inches long and 8 inches high on which was printed the phrase

"New Jersey Chamber of Commerce." The letters were in black ink and were 2 inches tall and ½ inch long.

Procedure

Prior to testing, the experimenter spent two mornings at the home being introduced to and chatting with each participant. At the beginning of the testing session, which was conducted in each individual's room, the experimenter tried to establish rapport by asking about the people's health, how they felt, and how they spent their time, and what kinds of things were important to them. After rapport was established, the KIS was administered. The KIS is a measure of the ability to carry out instructions in the midst of impelling physical and verbal stimuli. In other words, when faced with a sudden change in environmental stimuli, such as the light onset, is one's behavior influenced more by the impelling aspects of the situation or by one's internal controls? For testing, the experimenter and the participant sat facing each other, with the apparatus between them on a table. The experimenter gave the following instructions:

> I will tell you to do some things and you try to do them. Sometimes I will tell you to push this stick (the lever) like this (experimenter pushed down the lever with his right index finger). Sometimes I will tell you to don't push the stick; and sometimes I will tell you to just say a word without doing anything. Try to do exactly what I tell you to do and don't do anything else except what I tell you to do.

These instructions were repeated. All participants indicated that they understood the instructions.

The KIS consisted of 24 tasks in which four verbal phrases ("push," "don't push," "sing," and "house") were used in each of six different conditions as described in Table 10.2. The word "sing" is used because it is a task-irrelevant verb whose effects can be compared to a task-irrelevant noun, "house," as well as to the effects of the task-relevant verbs "push" and "don't push" on their tendencies to elicit or inhibit the motor behavior of depressing the lever. The six conditions differ in (1) the presence or absence of the light onset, (2) source of verbalization: self or other, and (3) instructions whether the pushing response should or should not be made. By varying the presence of these three aspects of the stimulus situation, their relative importance can be assessed.

There was a 10-second interval between the end of each task and the start of the next one, the participant being asked to place his or her index finger on the manipulandum at the start of each task. The six conditions

TABLE 10.2.   Outline of Experimental Conditions

Condition 1: Say, "———."		*Condition 2:* When the light goes on say, "———."	
1. "Push"	2. "Don't push"	5. "Push"	6. "Don't push"
3. "Sing"	4. "House"	7. "Sing"	8. "House"
Condition 3: When the light goes on, say, "———," then push the stick.		*Condition 4:* When the light goes on, say, "———," then don't push the stick.	
9. "Push"	10. "Don't push"	13. "Push"	14. "Don't push"
11. "Sing"	12. "House"	15. "Sing"	16. "House"
Condition 5: When the light goes on, I will say, "———," then you push the stick.		*Condition 6:* When the light goes on, I will say, "———," then you don't push the stick.	
17. "Push"	18. "Don't push"	21. "Push"	22. "Don't push"
19. "Sing"	20. "House"	23. "Sing"	24. "House"

were presented in four units, with Conditions 1, 2, (3 and 4), and (5 and 6) constituting the units, because it was felt that shifting from one unit to another on successive tasks would be too confusing. Conditions 3 and 4 were placed in the same unit because in both the participants verbalized the words; whereas Conditions 5 and 6 were grouped together because in both the experimenter verbalized the words while the participants remained silent. The four units were presented in a latin square design to control for any possible order effects. The order of presentation of tasks within units was predetermined on a random basis. The numbering given in Table 10.2 is for reference purposes and does not represent the sequence of tasks as presented.

After these tasks were completed, the participants performed the slow writing test. After reading the phrase "New Jersey Chamber of Commerce," they were asked to write it. After doing so, they were asked to write it again as slowly as they could without stopping. The regular and slow writing speeds were timed by a stopwatch held in the experimenter's hand.

Results

The main effects and interactions of the age, conditions, and words variables were assessed by means of a $2 \times 6 \times 4$ repeated measures analysis of variance, carried out on the number of tasks containing an error. The analysis revealed significant differences with age ($F = 14.66$, $df = 1/46$,

$p < .001$), words ($F = 6.33$, $df = 3/138$, $p < .01$), and conditions ($F = 4.85$, $df = 5/230$, $p < .01$). None of the interactions between factors were significant.

Effects of Age, Conditions, and Words on KIS Performance

The mean number of errors on the KIS was .46 for the 65–75 year olds and 3.37 for the 80–96 year olds. The range was 0–4 in the younger group and 0–11 in the older group. In the older group, 12 people made more than 2 errors; only 1 person in the younger group did. Further breakdown of the data for the older group reveals that the 20 people between the ages of 80–89 had a mean of 2.45 errors with a range of 0–10; the 4 people between 90–96 years had a mean of 8.0 errors with a range of 6–11. Thus, there was a *substantial* decline in verbal control at age 90. Participants had much more difficulty inhibiting inappropriate behavior on the KIS than in emitting appropriate behavior. Errors of omission (not pushing the lever when they were supposed to push) were absent in the younger group and extremely rare in the older group.

The mean number of errors made for each word is shown in Table 10.3. The maximum score is 6, as each word is used in six conditions. The Neuman Keuls analysis comparing pairs of means was performed. Since the insignificant age × word interaction indicated similar effects of words for both age groups, the data from both groups were pooled for the comparisons. The comparisons revealed that "push" differed from each of the other three verbalizations beyond the .05 level. No other differences between pairs of means approached significance. These results indicate that the semantic property of words is important on these tasks. A consistent pattern was that most errors occurred on tasks in which participants were supposed to inhibit the motor behavior after saying or hearing the word "push," that is, when the verbalization was inconsistent with the behavioral task.

The Relationships among Age, KIS Performance, and Writing Speeds

The mean number of KIS errors, mean regular and slow writing speeds, mean difference in seconds between the two speeds, and the mean ratio of slow to regular speeds for each age group are shown in Table 10.4. That the older group made more KIS errors than the younger group, had slower regular writing speed ($t = 1.54$, $df = 40$, p is between .05 and .10), and were less able to slow their speed writing speed, is reflected on the difference between regular and slow speeds ($t = 1.99$, $df = 40$,

TABLE 10.3.   Mean Number of Errors Each Participant Made to Each Word

	Words			
Age	"Push"	"Don't push"	"Sing"	"House"
65–75	.25	.04	.08	.08
80–96	1.17	.79	.70	.70
Combined mean	.71	.42	.39	.39

$p < .01$), and differences between the ratios of the two speeds ($t = 2.59$, $df = 40$, $p < .01$). The relationship between performances on the KIS and on the writing tasks for the older group were assessed by calculating the product moment correlation coefficients. They were $r = .71$ between number of KIS errors and regular writing speed and $r = -.52$ between number of KIS errors and the ratio of slow:regular speeds. The latter correlation is negative because those who made the fewest KIS errors slowed their writing speed the most. It is noteworthy that the people in the older group who made no errors on the KIS wrote twice as fast at regular speed and four times as slow at slow speed than those who made more than 4 errors.

The Relationship between
Interview Responses and Performance

The responses to the questions asked about their health, how they felt, how they spent their time, and what kinds of things were important to them were studied to see if any personality or attitudinal characteristics corresponded with performance on the various tasks. It was the experimenter's impression that some participants spent most of the interview complaining about nearly everything, including their family, the home, the food, the way the staff treated them, their neighbors down the hall, and their aches and pains. They reported spending most of their time in their rooms by themselves in such activities as sitting, waiting for the next meal, sleeping, reading, watching television, praying, looking out the window, and thinking. They said that they preferred solitary activity because it gave them privacy to think about their lives or because they did not want to be around old people, especially those who always complain.

Other people, although stating that they had various aches and pains and that living in their own home would be more enjoyable than living in the home, rarely complained about their personal situation. When they

TABLE 10.4.   Mean Performances

		(Seconds)		Difference between Speeds	Ratio of Slow:Regular Speeds
Age	KIS Errors	Regular Speed	Slow Speed		
65–75	.46	22.05	47.86	25.81	2.30
80–96	3.37	25.81	35.14	9.33	1.44

complained, it was about such topics as the Vietnam war, the teenage drug problem, the rising crime rate, politics, and other social problems. They spoke mainly of their past accomplishments and of the achievements of their children. They reported that the staff was very helpful in assisting them to adjust to life in the home. They reported spending their time in such activities as visiting and going shopping with friends, writing letters to family and friends, playing cards or checkers, helping the crippled elderly, knitting, taking walks outdoors, and playing piano.

On the basis of the interview responses, the experimenter placed the people in the older group into two classes: the "active copers" and the "inactive complainers." There was no overlap between classes, as everyone who spent most of the interview complaining reported leading relatively inactive solitary lives. Table 10.5 shows the mean performances of both classes on the KIS and writing tasks. It indicates that there is a strong relationship between their everyday activity–adjustment level and their performances on the tasks, as the active group did much better than the inactive group. It is noteworthy that the range of KIS errors for the active copers was 0–7, whereas the range for the inactive group was 4–11. In other words, all 10 people with perfect KIS scores were active copers.

Comparisons between the Elderly and Children on the KIS

The performances of the elderly on the KIS were compared with those of children in the author's previous research.[5,6] Table 10.6 and Figure 10.1 show the mean number of KIS errors for people of different ages. They indicate that verbal regulation of behavior, as measured by the KIS, is relatively weak during the 3rd year of life, becomes much stronger during the 4th year, and continues to strengthen in the 5th year, by which time an error on the KIS *rarely* occurs. Verbal control continues to be very

TABLE 10.5.   Mean Scores of Active Copers versus Inactive Complainers

	N	KIS Errors	Regular Speed	Difference in Speeds	Ratio of Slow:Regular Speeds
			(Seconds)		
Active copers	17	1.65	22.81	10.75	1.53
Inactive complainers	7	7.59	35.40	5.80	1.15

strong until around age 80, when there is a *small* decline in its strength in some people. At around age 90, however, there is a *marked* decline in verbal control of behavior.

For the younger children, as well as for the elderly, there were more erroneous pushes with the light onset than without it, explicit instructions to inhibit were ineffective, source of verbalization was an insignificant factor, and the verbalization "push" elicited more erroneous pushing behavior than the other three verbalizations. Thus, some similarities appear to exist between the verbal control of motor behavior at both extremes of the life-span.

Discussion

The results indicate that verbal regulation of behavior, as measured by the KIS, remains strong until very late in life, at which time it weakens. That self-control tends to decrease very late in life is consistent with the observation that older people often have difficulty inhibiting some behaviors. For example, they may have less control over bowel and bladder functioning. A reasonable explanation for decreased control in later life is that cells and tissues responsible for self-control deteriorate. According to Luria, the area in the brain most responsible for the verbal regulation of behavior is in the frontal lobe, which is usually the first lobe of the cortex to deteriorate.[19] Deterioration of frontal lobe cells might explain not only the decline in verbal self-control but also the poorer performances on the writing tasks, as the area in the brain primarily responsible for motor behavior is also located in the frontal lobe. Since the frontal lobe is involved in both the verbal control and the writing tasks, it is reasonable that performances on them had moderately high correlations.

An alternative explanation, of a psychogenic rather than a physiologi-

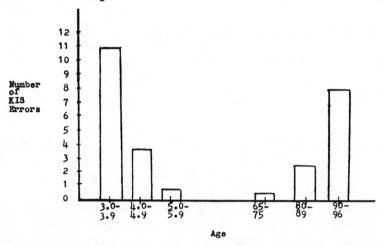

Figure 10.1. The relationship between age and number of KIS errors.

cal nature, for the decline in self-control very late in life is suggested by disengagement theory. Because of the mutual withdrawal between the person and society there is a reduction of interactions between the person and others. This reduction of social behavior leads to the loosening of social controls, which would make one less responsive to the KIS instructions to inhibit behavior. By leading a less active life, one has fewer opportunities to practice verbally controlling one's behavior in the midst of changing environmental stimuli. Through disuse this skill deteriorates. This explanation accounts for the many KIS errors to the light onset, which is a sudden change in environmental stimuli. That those who exhibited the least self-control on the KIS and on the slow writing task were the least socially active (the most disengaged) supports this explanation. On the other hand, the finding that many of the 80- to 96-year-olds engaged in and enjoyed a variety of social activities and made no errors on the KIS suggests that withdrawal from social activities and decreased self-control may not be a rapid and inevitable outcome of aging, especially if one's health is relatively good.

The stages of the decline of verbal control of behavior in later life seem to bear some similarities to the stages of its development in childhood. Between the 3rd and 4th year and after 90, verbal control is weak and unstable. Thus, there were many errors on the KIS. Between the 4th and 5th year and between ages 80 and 89, verbal control is strong, but a few KIS errors occur. From age 5 through age 75 verbal control is very strong, with an error on the KIS rarely occurring.

For both the elderly and the children the most impelling element of the stimulus situation was the light onset, and the most impelling verbal-

TABLE 10.6.   Mean Number of KIS Errors for Different Ages

Age	3.0–3.9	4.0–4.9	5.0–5.9	65–75	80–89	90–96
M	24	24	20	24	20	4
Mean	10.71	3.53	.60	.46	2.40	8.00

ization was "push." That certain verbalizations can lead to unnecessary motor behavior can be accounted for by an explanation based on Osgood, Suci, and Tannenbaum's mediational theory of language.[20] They maintain that words produce internal responses similar to but less intense than the overt responses that would be made to the object or activity that the word symbolizes. For example, the words *eat* and *hamburger* produce unperceived internal gastric, salivary, and chewing responses. Perhaps, under certain conditions, these responses become so strong that they cannot be confined within the person and manifest themselves in overt motor behavior. This explanation accounts for why there were more erroneous pushes to the word *push* than to the other words, as this word would certainly produce more internal pushing responses than *house* or *sing*. It is feasible that the conditions when ordinarily internal responses become overt include (1) when one is stimulated beyond an optimal level by changes in the environment (such as the light onset on the KIS) and (2) when one's central nervous system is in a relatively undeveloped or deteriorating condition, as in the very young and the very old person. That one tends to make unnecessary motor behavior when stimulated beyond an optimal level is supported by the observation that many people, when they are trying to cope with problems, engage in such extraneous activities as pacing up and down a room, tapping their fingers on a table, and making frequent hand gestures and movements when they speak. That a "weak" nervous system may lead to excessive motor behavior is supported by the observation that infants often respond to changes in stimuli with diffuse motor behavior. Thus, the very young and the very old made many unnecessary motor responses on the KIS because they had to cope with a sudden change in stimulation with a relatively weak central nervous system.

The finding that handwriting speed declined in the older group is consistent with the general observation that "the decline in speed of performance is one of the most outstanding characteristics of aging" (p. 183).[10] Writing is a well established skill in most people. The 80- to 96-year-olds wrote neatly and legibly; they just took more time to do so. These findings suggest that the qualitative outcome of performance on well established skills suffers little or no decrement in nonsenile elderly

people, even though there is a decline in speed. This view is consistent
with that of Bromley, who states:

> The decline in speed of performance . . . helps to explain age changes in
> intellectual efficiency, skilled performance, work output, and research
> achievement. It also helps explain the existence of some misconceptions about
> the effects of aging, since in situations where there are no serious time limits
> the effects on performance are negligible until late in life. (p. 183)[10]

One of the misconceptions to which Bromley refers is that a quick, large,
and pervasive decrement in skills inevitably occurs once one is in one's
60's.

The slow writing task required the participants to perform a well
established skill at a speed to which they were unaccustomed. Most stated
that writing slowly was difficult because they were used to writing quickly.
That the 65- to 75-year-olds slowed their writing speed about three times as
much as the 80- to 96-year-olds suggests that the ability to adapt a skill to a
novel requirement decreases in later life. Pollock and Kastenbaum, who
found that college students slowed their writing speeds about six times as
much as people in their 70s, speculated that, because older people realize
that they have little time left, they cannot afford the luxury of taking their
time and of delaying gratification of the desire to complete the task. This
explanation is feasible, as is the thesis that deterioration of frontal lobe cells
contributes to difficulty with this task.

Implications of this Study

That almost all the 65- to 75-year-olds had perfect or nearly perfect performances on the KIS has important implications concerning when "old
age" begins and what changes it produces. It refutes the commonly held
belief that at around age 65 rapid and inevitable decrements in behavior
and skills occur: a belief that is a major reason why 65 is the age at which
most people retire (or are retired against their will). In nonsenile people, it
appears that verbal control of behavior shows very little decline until age 80
and no major decline until around age 90. Therefore, it might be beneficial
to revise the practice of forcing people to retire just because they have
reached a particular chronological age. This suggestion is important because retirement is often the first step in people's disengagement from
society and often contributes to their feelings of inadequacy, depression,
and worthlessness, because they feel that they are no longer as capable,
useful, or needed as they once were.

An important finding of this study is that social inactivity and lack of
meaningful pursuits is associated with and probably contributes to the

decline in verbal control of behavior, the decline in speed of performing
old skills, and the decline in ability to adapt old skills to new requirements.
Therefore, it is suggested that the elderly help themselves maintain their
ability to function effectively by—in spite of all the frustrations, pains, and
losses that confront them—keeping active rather than becoming isolated
and inactive. It is recommended that people caring for the elderly strongly
encourage them to do so. It is also suggested that more research be done on
the elderly person's reactions to changing and stressful situations. A final,
but important, suggestion is that more people who are trained to help
others cope with changing and stressful situations, such as psychiatrists,
psychologists, and social workers, apply their therapeutic skills to the
elderly in an effort to help them lead more productive, meaningful, enjoyable, and fulfilling lives.

References

1. Luria, A. Verbal regulation of behavior, in M. Brazier (Ed.), *The central
   nervous system and behavior*. New York: Joseph Macy, Jr. Foundation, 1960,
   pp. 359–379.
2. Luria, A. *The role of speech in the regulation of normal and abnormal behavior*. New York: Liveright, 1961.
3. Vygotsky, L. Selected psychological papers. Moscow: 1956, as cited in C.
   Stendler (Ed.), *Child behavior and development*. New York: Harcourt, Brace
   & World, 1964, p. 392.
4. Piaget, J. *The child's conception of number*. London: Routledge & Kegan Paul,
   1961.
5. Kagan, J. Reflection-impulsivity and reading ability in primary grade children.
   Child Development, 1969, *36*, 609–628.
6. Katz, M. Effects of semantic and visual stimuli on the development of self-
   control. Unpublished Masters thesis, Wayne State University, 1970.
7. Bates, H., and Katz. M. Development of the verbal regulation of behavior.
   Proceedings, 78th Annual Convention, APA, 1970, pp. 299–300.
8. Dennis, W., and Mallinger, B. Animism and related tendencies in senescence.
   Journal of Gerontology, 1949, *4*, 218–221.
9. Pressey, S., and Kuhlen, R. *Psychological development through the life-span*.
   New York: Harper, 1957.
10. Bromley, D. *The psychology of human ageing*. Baltimore: Penguin, 1969.
11. Birren, J. (Ed.). *Handbook of aging and the individual: Psychological and
    biological aspects*. Chicago: University of Chicago Press, 1959.
12. Hinchcliffe, R. Acting and sensory thresholds. *Journal of Gerontology*, 1962,
    17, 45–50.
13. Cumming, E., and Henry, W. *Growing old*. New York: Basic Books, 1961.
14. Botwinick, J. Wechsler-Bellevue split-half subtest reliabilities: Differences in
    age and mental status. *Journal of Consulting Psychology*, 1953, *17*, 225–228.

15. Norman, R., and Daley, M. Senescent changes in intellectual ability among superior older women. *Journal of Gerontology*, 1959, *14*, 457–464.
16. Tuckman, J., and Loren, I. Classification of the self as young, middle-aged, or old. *Geriatrics*, 1954, *9*, 534–536.
17. Calhoun, M., and Gottesman, L. Stereotypes of old age in two samples. Division of Gerontology, University of Michigan, mimeo. 1963.
18. Pollock, K., and Kastenbaum, R. Delay of gratification in later life, in R. Kastenbaum (Ed.), *New thoughts on old age*. New York: Springer, 1964.
19. Luria, A. *Higher cortical functions in man*. New York: Basic Books, 1966.
20. Osgood, C.; Suci, G.; and Tannenbaum, P. *The measurement of meaning*. Urbana: University of Illinois Press, 1957.

11

Individual Differences in Old Age: The Stimulus Intensity Modulation Approach

Brian L. Mishara

A. Harvey Baker

Two men reside in a nursing home—a deprived environment, relatively devoid of stimulation. One man is constantly seeking stimulation; he seeks out people to talk to and situations where a lot seems to be happening. The second man avoids interpersonal contacts and spends most of his time in a solitary and remote location.

A survey of current research in gerontology would not alert one to the prevalence of such great individual differences nor indicate the importance of differences in lifestyles. Botwinick, in his review of gerontology research, noted that most experimental and theoretical articles have been primarily concerned with similarities among people as they grow old.[1] Relatively little attention has been given to understanding individual differences.

An Approach to Individual Differences

This chapter presents a theoretical approach to individual differences in lifestyle and human-environment behavior. It is based upon our research over the past few years in the perceptual-cognitive style of stimulus intensity modulation (SIM).[2-6] We have become increasingly impressed by the range of attributes predictable from SIM theory and by the diversity of its implications for research, planning, and social action.

The SIM approach encompasses the particular personality character-

We wish to thank Irene Wolk Kostin and Barbara Robertson for their invaluable contributions at various phases of the research.

istics illustrated by these two nursing home residents, namely, their different reactions to an environment. It focuses on people's levels of satisfaction and the amount of additional stimulation they seek out. SIM theory holds that individuals may be classified along a *single* dimension according to how they process incoming stimulation. This is assumed to be a basic and enduring organismic trait that affects the behavior of the elderly in a unique manner only to the extent that the social and physical environments of old people are different from the environments of younger adults.

The two best known theories in social gerontology—disengagement theory and activity theory—each discuss aspects of the social environment. They specify, however, a particular type of social environment which is supposed to be best for all old people. Disengagement theory holds that elders gradually reduce life involvements and contacts.[7] Activity theory argues that, the more elderly people persist in their activities of middle age the better off they will be, as indicated by higher morale.[8-12] More recently, the authors of disengagement theory have tried to disassociate themselves from the value judgments attributed to that approach.[13] Our SIM approach differs from these theories in two ways. First, SIM focuses on individual differences rather than assuming what is best or typical for all old people. Second, SIM theory specifies that people can be characterized according to a general organismic trait that encompasses not only personality attributes (such as desired level of engagement) but individuality in perception and cognition.

A third approach to aging, personality theories, shares our focus on individual differences.[14] Personality theories have usually postulated discrete personality types, however, rather than a single underlying trait, such as SIM. Personality theories of aging have not generally encompassed perceptual-cognitive aspects of the individual.

Our approach derives in part from hypotheses presented by Baker and Mishara, by Petrie, by Sales, and by Silverman.[2,4,6,15-17] They hypothesized that some individuals, called "reducers," attenuate the intensity of incoming stimulation. In other words they perceive external stimulation as relatively *less* intense. Other individuals, called "augmenters," magnify the intensity of incoming stimulation. These researchers used the Kinesthetic Aftereffect task (KAE), a tactual size judgment test, to classify individual tendencies toward augmentation or reduction. Petrie, the forerunner in this area, looked primarily at individuality in pain and suffering. She and subsequent researchers reported findings consistent with the view that reducers show greater pain tolerance than augmenters.[18-21]

In other situations where the external stimulation is minimal one would predict that augmenters fare better, since they "magnify" whatever minimal stimulation there is. It might be expected that reducers would tolerate stimulus deprivation conditions poorly since they perceive the minimal external stimulation as even less intense. To confirm this hypothesis, studies of sensory deprivation found that augmenters (classified by the KAE task) were more able to tolerate sensory deprivation[19] and sought less to increase their perceptual stimulation.[22]*

Under normal circumstances, reducers are subjectively more stimulus deprived than augmenters.[3,4,6,15] Reducers are therefore assumed to seek more stimulation in their daily lives to compensate for this stimulus deprivation. Augmenters, on the other hand, are under normal circumstances, generally overloaded with stimulation and thus avoid stimulation. This augmentation-reduction mechanism is also operative in situations where the magnitude of external stimulations is extreme. For example, reducers reacted more favorably when placed in a "psychedelic" environment with extremely intense and complex visual and auditory stimulation.[22]

SIM theory specifies that individual differences in how people modulate external stimulation affects what is perceived as *pleasant or unpleasant* as well as *how much stimulation* individuals seek out. Augmenters are likely to be pleased by less intense stimulation and tend to avoid seeking more stimulation. Reducers generally enjoy situations where more intense stimulation is available and tend to seek out stimulation. Nevertheless, SIM theory makes no claim that all choices or preferences are based upon individual differences in the modulation of stimulus intensity.

How does SIM theory interpret human-environment interactions? We define *environment* to be *all aspects of external stimulation* available to an individual. Thus, environment includes input from the physical characteristics (for example, the nature of the room around us) as well as from social stimulation (for example, interactions with other people). Our SIM approach postulates that individuals will differ in their reactivity to the total environment according to their characterization along this single organismic dimension. The dimension ranges from extreme augmentation—where the intensity of environmental stimulation is perceived as relatively much greater—to extreme reduction—where the intensity of perceived stimulation is relatively much less. Furthermore, this characteristic may be easily measured using a perceptual-cognitive task, KAE.

In our approach there is no implicit value to being either an augmenter or reducer without considering the nature of the environment. Within a

---

*Some recent studies have been highly critical of KAE as a measure of individual differences in SIM. We have shown recently that these criticisms do not apply to the single-session variant of the KAE procedure used in our research, citing extensive validity support, including a reanalysis of a recent major critical study.[3,4]

specific environment, however, there may be greater or lesser adaptive value for augmenters or reducers. This is particularly true when the environment is extreme in terms of the intensity or amount of stimulation available.

Individual differences in SIM reflect a long-enduring organismic trait. We therefore predict that individuals generally will seek out environmental situations to match their different preferences and thereby maximize their adjustment. The relationship between adjustment and SIM traits becomes more salient, however, when the choices of environments are limited. Elderly people often have less *choice* of social and physical environments in which to live. Relocation and institutionalization exemplify two typical changes in environment wherein the elderly have little choice. In addition, other factors affect aspects of the environment of the elderly, for example; (1) Elders may have a reduced social environment because of deaths of friends, and (2) there are particular stereotypes regarding what types of environment are appropriate for elderly people to inhabit and visit. Also there are common physiological changes often associated with increasing age that reduce the amount of stimulation a person perceives (e.g., auditory, visual, and olfactory deficits).

It is our belief that unless these changes are severe enough to cause an extremely different experiential environment, (e.g., being almost totally deaf), the general SIM tendency will often maintain itself despite the changes. For example, we hypothesize that the reducer will be more likely to move closer to people in order to hear better and maintain his or her current higher level of stimulation, whereas the augmenter (who is seeking a lower level of stimulation anyway) may use this as a convenient justification for avoiding social stimulation.

SIM Applied to Elderly Samples

In the area of social-environmental stimulation, the usefulness of the SIM approach was exemplified by a community study of two elderly samples: people living independently in their own homes and a group of nursing home residents.[4] The first sample comprised 40 people over age 60, ranging in age from 61 to 85 (mean age 71.1, SD 5.3 years), living in housing for the elderly in the Detroit, Michigan, area. Half of the sample was white and half black, and each racial group had an equal number of men and women. The second sample was comprised of 21 nursing home residents (mean age 73, SD 8.29 years).

The elders were interviewed individually and tested on the KAE task. KAE testing involves making judgments while blindfolded by indicating with your left hand how wide a standard-width block of wood held in the right hand seems. Judgments are made before and after going through an aftereffect induction procedure of rubbing with the right hand a block of wood that is wider than the standard. It is well established that a perceptual change generally occurs. After rubbing a larger block the average person judges the standard block as smaller than before. Those who show a maximal decrease in their width judgments are classified as reducers. Those who show a minimal decrease (or even an increase in perceived width) are classified as augmenters (for scoring procedures, see Mishara, Baker, Parker, and Kostin[23]).

In this study we wanted to assess if status on SIM, measured by KAE performance, could predict individual differences in the elderly. We looked at five separate domains:

1. *Engagement*. Since reducers generally seek more stimulation, this should be reflected in greater social involvement, which we measured using engagement questions developed by Cumming and Henry.[7]

2. *VIRO*. To see if actual interpersonal involvement (engagement) with the interviewer would corroborate the results from self-reports of engagement, this behavioral observation scale developed by Kastenbaum and Sherwood was included.[24]

3. *Life difficulty*. Reducers were predicted to minimize the perceived intensity of life's troubles, which was assessed by questions about past and future life difficulty.

4. *Items previously validated*. To see if the elderly sample would replicate findings with young adults, questions about sleep habits, smoking, and planning for the future were included.

5. *Death attitude*. To try to replicate an enticing finding with young adults wherein reducers showed less avoidance of the intense stimulation provided by the thought of death,[6] a death personification procedure was included.

Four domains gave significant evidence of the validity of the SIM approach, but the fifth area, death attitudes, needs further clarification. Reducers tended to lead more engaged lives, behave more responsively in the interview, report less past and future life difficulty, sleep less, smoke more, and plan more. Combining all five domains into a single overall index, augmenter-reducer differences were significant ($p<.005$ one-tail test), and the correlation between KAE scores and the overall index was .47 ($p<.001$).

Results from multivariate analyses of variance gave significant evidence of the validity of the SIM approach with these two elderly samples

$(F=2.73, df = 10/64, p<.01$, and $F=1.95, df = 8/30, p<.10$). This study confirmed our hypothesis that, among the elderly, reducers generally seek out more stimulation.

A Clinical Example

Let us return to the two elderly men cited at the beginning of the chapter, who also happened to be part of our nursing home study. The clinical descriptions of the two elderly men were based on observations made over 1 year by individuals who had no knowledge of the elders' standing on SIM. Both men resided in the same nursing home. Both had long histories of institutionalization and were basically equivalent in their results on medical evaluations and their performances on neuropsychological tests. Yet one man was a SIM reducer, as determined by KAE, and the other was an augmenter—and they differed dramatically in their adjustment to the same environment.

The first man, Nate, had a favorite song he would offer to sing at the least provocation:

> The bear went over the mountain,
> the bear went over the mountain,
> the bear went over the mountain,
> to see what he could see.
>
> Well, they put him in a dark hole
> covered him up with charcoal,
> kicked him in the you know what,
> and left him there to die.

Nate was not terribly impressed with his environment. His case history revealed that he led a stimulating preinstitutional life. In the nursing home he continually sought out any form of stimulation available, often to the consternation of the staff. For example, he once decorated the walls of his room with magic markers. Nate scored on KAE as the strongest male reducer in the sample.

The second man, Will, did not speak unless directly questioned. The staff called him "shy." He never complained but made it known that he did not particularly care for social get-togethers. On one occasion he did not choose to "clutter up his room" by accepting a gift of some wall ornaments. His case history revealed that he always used to maintain this level of relative stimulus avoidance. Will scored on KAE as a SIM augmenter.

Our findings indicate that SIM, as measured by KAE, relates to engagement as well as other aspects of lifestyle. Positive results are evident in both systematic investigation and our own informal clinical observations. The SIM approach may be particularly valuable in gerontology since it stresses that individuals may differ in their reactions to the same physical and social environment. These differences are interpreted as more than just a social preference. They are assumed to reflect a long-term organismic trait that underlies a perceptual-cognitive and lifestyle dimension.

SIM theory may have useful applications to social planning and interventions for the elderly. Assessment of individuals' standings on SIM may help planners design suitable environments which take into account individual differences. Also, interventions may be developed to help match individual differences in SIM to appropriate therapeutic situations.

References

1. Botwinick, J. Geropsychology. *Annual Review of Psychology*. Palo Alto, Calif.: Annual Reviews, 1970, pp. 239–272.
2. Baker, A. H.; Mishara, B. L.; Parker, L.; and Kostin, I. W. When "reliability" fails must a measure be discarded?—The case of kinesthetic aftereffects. *Journal of Research in Personality*, 1978, (Sept.) *12*(3), 262–273.
3. Baker, A. H.; Mishara, B. L.; Kostin, I. W.; and Parker, L. Kinesthetic aftereffect and personality: A case study of issues involved in construct validation. *Journal of Personality and Social Psychology*, 1976, *34*, 1–13.
4. Mishara, B. L., and Baker, A. H. Stimulus intensity modulation: A perceptual-cognitive approach to life style in the elderly. Unpublished manuscript, University of Massachusetts, 1976.
5. Mishara, B.; Baker, A. H.; and Kostin, I. W. Will to live, future planning and kinesthetic aftereffects: Toward a theory of individual differences in the aged. Paper presented at the 1972 Annual Scientific Meeting, Gerontological Society, San Juan, 1972.
6. Mishara, B. L.; Baker, A. H.; and Kostin, I. W. Do people who seek less environmental stimulation avoid thinking about the future and their death?: A study of individual differences in kinesthetic figural aftereffect. *Proceedings, 80th Annual Convention, American Psychological Association*, 1972, pp. 667–668.
7. Cumming E., and Henry, W. E. *Growing old: The process of disengagement*. New York: Basic Books, 1961.
8. Kuypers, J. A. Changeability of life-style and personality in old age. *Gerontologist*, 1972, *12*, 336–342.
9. Maddox, G. L. Activity and morale: A longitudinal study of selected elderly subjects. *Social Forces*, 1963, *42*, 195–204.
10. Maddox, G. L. Fact and artifact: Evidence bearing on disengagement theory. *Human Development*, 1965, *8*, 117–130.
11. Maddox, G. L. Persistence of life style among the elderly. *Proceedings of the Seventh International Congress of Gerontology*, 1966, pp. 309–311.

12. Palmore, E. B. The effects of aging on activities and attitudes. *Gerontologist*, 1968, *8*, 259–263.
13. Cumming, E. Engagement with an old theory. *International Journal of Aging and Human Development*, 1975, *6*, 187–192.
14. Neugarten, B. L.; Havighurst, R. J.; and Tobin, S. S. Personality and patterns of aging, in B. L. Neugarten (Ed.)L, *Middle age and aging*. Chicago: University of Chicago Press, 1968.
15. Petrie, A. *Individuality in pain and suffering*. Chicago: University of Chicago Press, 1967.
16. Sales, S. Need for stimulation as a factor in preferences for different stimuli. *Journal of Personality Assessment*, 1972, *36*, 55–61.
17. Silverman, J. A paradigm for the study of altered states of consciousness. *British Journal of Psychiatry*, 1968, *114*, 1201–1218.
18. Petrie, A.; Collins, W.; and Solomon, P. Pain sensitivity, sensory deprivation, and susceptibility to satiation. *Science*, 1958, *128*, 1431–1433.
19. Poser, E. Figural after-effect as a personality correlate. *Proceedings of the 16th International Congress of Psychology*. Amsterdam: North Holland Publishing, 1960, pp. 748–749.
20. Ryan, E. D., and Foster, R. Athletic participation and perceptual reduction and augmentation. *Journal of Personality and Social Psychology*, 1967, *6*, 472–476.
21. Sweeney, D. R. Pain reactivity and kinesthetic aftereffect. *Perceptual and Motor Skills*, 1966, *22*, 763–769.
22. Sales, S. Need for stimulation as a factor in social behavior. *Journal of Personality and Social Psychology*, 1971, *19*, 124–134.
23. Mishara, B. L.; Baker, A. H.; Parker, L.; and Kostin, I. W. Kinesthetic figural aftereffects: Norms from four samples, and a comparison of methods for classifying augmenters, moderates, and reducers. *Perceptual and Motor Skills*, 1973, *37*, 315–325.
24. Kastenbaum, R., and Sherwood, S. VIRO: A new scale for rating for interview behavior of elderly patients, in D. P. Kent, R. Kastenbaum, and S. Sherwood (Eds.), *Research, action, and planning for the elderly*. New York: Behavioral Publications, 1972, pp. 166–200.

12

Motivation, Capacity, Learning, and Age

A. T. Welford

Motivation as a Factor in Performance and Learning by Older People

It is now traditional to consider problems of old age primarily in terms of changing physical and mental capacities on the one hand, and of flexibility or ability to learn and change on the other. While this approach is fundamentally correct, it is not the whole story. Effectiveness of performance by older people depends not only upon their capacities but also upon that willingness to use them to the full; anyone who has observed older people knows that some individuals use limited powers to the utmost, while others leave much greater powers idle.

As regards learning, it is now well recognized that older people have difficulty with certain processes involved in learning and remembering, especially comprehension of the material to be learned, registering it in some form of enduring memory store and, later, recovering the material from this store for use in recall. The difficulty can in certain cases be largely—indeed completely—overcome by suitable methods of instruction. In particular, the so-called discovery method, whereby trainees discover for themselves correct methods of performing tasks under conditions in which they have little chance of making errors, has been found to be strikingly successful for people in middle age whose learning by other methods was much poorer than that of people in early adulthood.[1-5] Again, however, these cognitive factors are not the only ones which determine learning by older people. There seem also to be important factors concerned with willingness to try new tasks and methods.

These essentially motivational factors that affect performance and learning by older people seem not to arise from any unwillingness to do

Reprinted with permission from *International Journal of Aging and Human Development*, 1976, 7, 189–199.

their best but from various more subtle considerations.[6] In particular, older people seem often to be hesitant about committing themselves to action[7-11] and to be unduly cautious, tending to accumulate more evidence than younger people would before making a decision. These tendencies are, of course, sometimes beneficial in that they can lead to increased accuracy, although at the expense of speed, but in the case of learning they can be a handicap in two ways. First, rapid and effective learning requires the observation of results of positive action and is thus impaired by any tendency to withhold action. Second, unwillingness to commit oneself to a response unless one is sure it is correct will mean that what has been learned may fail to be effectively used.

A Signal Detection Model of Motivation

Let us look at the motivational problem in terms of a model derived from signal detection theory—a theory which has been a powerful tool in the study of several forms of decision making and which seems capable in many cases of indicating more precisely than has been possible hitherto, where to look for age effects.

Consider the tendency to take a particular action in a situation in which it would be possible but is not specifically called for. The tendency will vary in strength from time to time owing to factors such as interest, attention, fatigue, anxiety, and a host of others, operating in the individual at different times. The variation on different occasions can be broadly represented as a distribution such as that shown on the left of Figure 12.1. Whether action actually occurs or not is determined by a cutoff on this distribution; no action is taken unless the strength of the tendency to action rises above the cutoff point.

Normally the cutoff is set at a point high enough (i.e., far enough to the

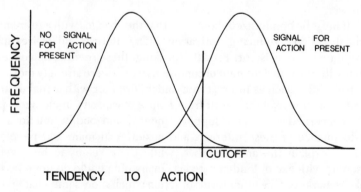

Figure 12.1. The basic signal detection model applied to motivation.

right) to prevent action occurring inappropriately except on rare occasions. Just how high it is set seems to vary between individuals. Some people have a greater tendency to action than others, and much of the seemingly ill-considered or even bizarre actions they take could be regarded as being due to their placing their cutoff point relatively low. It is plausible to suggest that older people's reluctance to take positive action means that they place their cutoff relatively high. It seems likely also that the various tendencies which give rise to the distribution on the left of Figure 12.1 might be more variable in older people, partly because of increasing randomness with age in the operations of the brain[12,13] and partly because tendencies to action must depend to some extent on experience which would be likely to structure and polarize attitudes and interests increasingly as age advanced. Any increase in variability would tend to widen the distribution, so that the cutoff point would have to be placed farther to the right in order to prevent inappropriate action.

A situation which specifically calls for the action, or provides appropriate opportunity for it, can be represented as adding to the tendencies to action in such a way as to shift the whole distribution to the right, as shown on the right of Figure 12.1. The shift means that more of the distribution lies above the cutoff point, so that although action is not certain to occur, it is more likely to do so. How far the distribution is shifted depends upon how strongly the individual regards the situation as demanding action. Here again is a source of variation between individuals, and possibly between ages, as needs change with the passage of years. For example, situations concerned with getting married, building a home, and bringing up a family will cease to be stimuli to action when these tasks have been accomplished. It should also be noted that if the distribution is wider, as we have suggested it may tend to be in older people, any absolute shift will have less effect because it will leave a greater amount of the distribution below the cutoff point than it would have done if the distribution has been narrower.

It must be emphasized, however, that the changes with age are not all in the direction of reducing motivation. Many interests and desires appear to become more insistent. Broadly speaking, these seem to be concerned either with the reinstatement of conditions which were strongly motivating in earlier life—such as interest in grandchildren, or with actual or anticipated problems likely to result from failure of capacity in old age—problems concerned with care, support, money, and bodily functions. The predominance of these interests and anxieties in many old people can perhaps explain the anomaly that, while there seems to be a general lessening with age of tendency to act, many old people do upon occasion make remarks or take other forms of action which show somewhat less than normal restraint. We can perhaps regard their inappropriate statements or other actions as the result of intense interest or anxiety combined with a cognitive inability to distinguish between appropriate and inappropriate occasions.

Adjusting the Cutoff Point

So far I have dealt only with what may happen on a single occasion. Let us now consider events in recurrent situations. The signal detection model was formulated originally to account for performance in experiments where subjects were given a series of trials in which they had to detect a faint signal against a background noise.[14-16] The situation in these experiments can be represented by regarding the left-hand distribution in Figure 12.1 as that of noise in the absence of signal, the right hand as that of noise-plus-signal. If the distribution of noise-alone and noise-plus-signal overlap, some errors are inevitable: The part of the noise-plus-signal distribution which lies below the cutoff will mean that signals are missed, while the part of the noise-alone distribution which lies above the cutoff will lead to false positive identification of a signal when none is in fact present.

Subjects in these experiments who have been given money or other rewards for correct responses and had these deducted for wrong responses, have been found to vary their cutoff points in a way which tends to maximize their gains and minimize their losses.[17-19] The optimum cutoff point for this purpose is defined by the following equation:

$$\text{Optimum } \beta = \frac{\text{Probability of No-Signal}}{\text{Probability of Signal}} \times \frac{\text{Value of correct NO + Cost of incorrect YES}}{\text{Value of correct YES + Cost of incorrect NO}} \tag{1}$$

The quantity ß is defined as the height of the ordinate of the noise-plus-signal distribution at the cutoff point, divided by the height at the same point, of the noise-alone distribution. If the cutoff is at the crossover point of the distributions, ß is therefore 1. If the cutoff is to the right or left of the crossover point, ß is greater or less than 1 respectively. A high value of ß thus means that many signals will be missed but that there will be few false positives, while with a low value of ß the reverse will be true. In terms of this model of motivation, a high value of ß will imply a tendency to refrain from action with many failures to act when needed but few inappropriate actions; a low value of ß will imply that action will be more likely both when it is appropriate and when it is not.

The right hand side of Equation 1 consists of two ratios, both of which seem likely to change with age:

1. Optimum ß is high, and action therefore less likely, when the ratio of No-Signal to Signal is high—in other words when calls or opportunities for action are infrequent. We can see that, because of this, a vicious circle situation could develop for old people. Any restriction of activity, any lessening of demand for action, will make action even less likely to occur when it is required. Thus old people who live in homes where everything is done for them may quickly reach a state in which they are unwilling to do anything, whereas those in situations where they have to act for themselves are, for just that reason, likely to remain active.

2. The second ratio is a *payoff matrix*. For our present purpose, this ratio may be simplified by considering situations, typical of everyday life, when the benefits from inaction are nil and the costs of inaction when action could or should be taken are also nil; the only disadvantage is missing the benefit that would have been gained by taking action. At the same time the cost of taking positive action is appreciable, although when it is appropriate the cost is outweighed by the benefit obtained. To take a trivial example, consider the making of a phone call to talk to a friend. There will be a "cost" in terms of effort in going to the telephone and dialing the call, and this cost will be incurred whether or not the friend answers. If he or she does so, this cost will be more than compensated for by the benefit of the ensuing conversation. No cost or benefit will accrue if no action is taken, whether or not the friend would have answered if one had called. If we regard dialing the call as YES and getting through as "Correct," the payoff matrix becomes

$$\frac{0 + \text{Cost of YES}}{(\text{Benefit of correct YES} - \text{Cost of YES}) + 0}$$

or more directly in terms of motivation:

$$\frac{\text{Cost of action}}{\text{Net benefit of successful action}} \qquad (2)$$

where net benefit means benefit minus cost.

Both costs and benefits are likely to change with age. Any loss of capacity will mean that the cost in terms of effort to be expended in order to attain a given result will rise. At the same time, the achievement in middle age of a well-structured and ordered way of living will mean that the benefits to be gained from many activities will tend to diminish. The overall result will be an increase of cost: benefit ratio leading to a raising of ß and a reduced tendency to take action.

This change is especially relevant to the problem of learning by older people. It is almost always more difficult—"costly"—to work out and learn a new procedure than to apply one already known. Thus, any change of working conditions, whether in factories or offices or elsewhere, will tend to produce a temporary rise in cost: benefit ratio unless the change produces a very great improvement in the cost: benefit ratio inherent in the job. Even then, the need to learn new procedures will mean that the full benefits of the change will not be realized immediately. When one takes these facts together with the known cognitive difficulties associated with age, one can understand why changes are often resisted by older people and only accepted under extreme pressure or necessity.

These considerations apply not only at work but in other areas of life. For example, moving from a familiar home to a unit or room in an old people's home inevitably requires the relearning of many details of everyday life and can thus impose a severe immediate strain whatever long-term benefits the move may confer. Again the rise of cost: benefit ratio with age makes understandable the unwillingness often shown by older people to undertake rehabilitative procedures: These are often laborious and painful, and progress is usually slow, so that while costs are all too obvious, benefits are not.

More generally, changing cost: benefit ratio can account for many shifts of interest in later life as a person moves away from activities such as vigorous games and sports where reduced capacities have raised costs, or from pursuits where altered needs have reduced benefits, and moves toward other concerns, such as for security, where benefits are likely to rise with age. Looking at changing interests and activities in this way is not to be construed as a criticism of older people. It is in line with the sound biologic principle that the organism designs its activities to make the best use it can of its capacities and opportunities. If so, much of the behavior of older people which seems to an outsider to be crabbed, unadventurous, inward looking, or otherwise unsatisfactory needs to be judged with caution. What the old people concerned get out of life may not be what others would choose, but it may be the best they can achieve. Any attempt to change their behavior would seem to be justified only if, at the same time, conditions of living are secured which ensure that the changed behavior has a lower cost: benefit ratio than existing behavior *for the individual concerned*. In short, the new behavior must really "pay."

Value

A complicating factor in motivation is the fact, fairly well supported empirically, that while a high cost: benefit ratio tends to deter action, it seems also to enhance the value subsequently placed on achievement.[20] Why this is so is not clear. Is it that value is a function of cost alone, as when we describe gems or antiques as having values measured by the money required to buy them? Alternatively, does value depend on cost: benefit ratio? If so, we might have an explanation for the high value placed on some trivial possessions. However, many of these, such as souvenirs of children or of journeys overseas, might be regarded as *symbols* of activities which had been costly in an absolute sense, and if so the value placed upon them could be accounted for in terms of cost alone.

Whatever the answer to these questions, values tend to affect willingness to learn and change. We tend to value possessions, skills, and pursuits which have been attained with difficulty, and we are unwilling to relinquish them even when their cost: benefit ratios have ceased to be favorable. Perhaps the best hope for acceptance of change in these cases is to recognize that new possessions, skills, and pursuits which are hard to acquire may, for that reason, be valued highly once they have been achieved.[21] There seems to be a lesson here for those concerned with rehabilitation.

Social Motivation

Adjustment of criteria for action, as represented by the cutoff in Figure 12.1, in terms of cost and benefit must depend on feedback of the kind shown in Figure 12.2. Cost in terms of effort or unpleasantness can be sensed by the organism when taking action, but benefits and any costs in the form of adverse outcomes can be assessed only by observation of the results of action. Such "knowledge of results" is well recognized as necessary for the learning of skill and maintenance of accuracy.[22-23] It can also have important motivating effects.[24] There is some evidence that older people make less use of such feedback than younger (e.g., Szafran, reported by Welford[25]).

Feedback seems to have important implications for social relationships, especially those in old age. The reason becomes clear if we put, in place of the "external object" in Figure 12.2, another person as shown in Figure 12.3. Each person observes the other's reactions and, in turn, reacts to them, in a continuous series of exchanges. If these exchanges yield a favorable cost: benefit ratio, we have the conditions for *friendship:* Each will lower his or her cutoff point so that the tendency to act in response to the other will be increased and mutual exchanges will tend to grow. If, on the other hand, the cost: benefit ratio is unfavorable, tendency to act will decrease, mutual contacts will be reduced and, if one party presses them, the other may make active efforts to prevent them; in short, *hostility* may develop.[26,27] Of course, in many cases relationships may be more

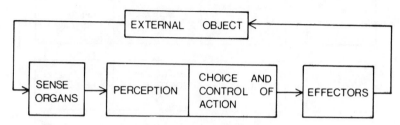

Figure 12.2.   Schematic diagram of information flow in the individual.

complex than these; for example, even in the best friendships, periods of reduced contact may be desirable. Also relationships may apply only in particular settings; for instance we may be able to maintain friendly and beneficial relationships with a colleague at work whom we despise and detest as a person and could never regard as a friend in private life.

The main importance of all this for old age lies in its implications regarding the cause and possible cures for *loneliness*. It is reasonable to argue that loneliness will arise when the circularity of relationship between a person and others is broken. This will obviously occur following bereavement when, say, a spouse who has been the principal source of feedback is no longer there. It may also occur with deafness when communication with others becomes difficult. The most serious problems of loneliness in old age seem, however, to have a different origin. They occur in people who are not physically isolated from others but who are surrounded by relatives, neighbors, welfare workers, and acquaintances. Their loneliness seems to arise either because the communications from these people are ignored or because communications to others are not accepted. In either case, the circular relationship with people around is broken.

The reason, in both cases, seems usually to be that the lonely individual is self-centered. He or she is thus not interested in most of the communications that come from others—the cost of listening to them is regarded as outweighing the benefit of doing so. At the same time, communications to others couched, say, in terms of how clever the lonely person and his or her children are compared with others, has an adverse cost: benefit ratio for listeners. The results are that cutoff levels for acceptance of communications, either by the person concerned, or by others, or by both, are raised.

The personality traits which lead to loneliness in this way seem commonly to be present throughout life, and it may therefore be questioned why they should result in serious loneliness only in old age. The reason is probably that in earlier years communications with others were made rewarding by the exigencies of work and of bringing up children.

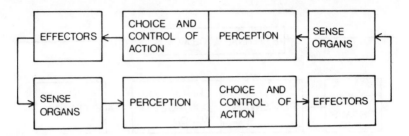

Figure 12.3. Schematic diagram of information flow between two individuals.

Once these tasks are over, the costs of communication with others remain, but the benefits have gone.

One further detail may be added to the picture. It is not uncommon to find that those who do most for an old person are the least valued by them. For example, if an elderly widow has two children and lives with one of them, it is often the other for whom she has the greater regard. The relationships between cost and value discussed earlier suggest a plausible reason: The child with whom she lives does too much for her too easily and is therefore valued less than the other child whose cost: benefit ratio is less favorable.

What can be done about loneliness? Clearly, providing visitors, clubs, and other means of contact with people will have only a limited effect and not touch the hard core of the problem. What is needed is to overcome self-centeredness and conceit. These, as we have noted, are often deep-seated, and the task is therefore difficult. Two possible lines of treatment might, however, hold some promise of success. First, the fact that in earlier life the need to cooperate with others prevented loneliness, suggests that bringing lonely people to recognize that they have needs which can be satisfied only by cooperation might at least reduce their loneliness. The essential task in this case is to secure the acknowledgment of benefits not at present being realized. Second, and more fundamental, is the possibility opened up by the methods now being developed of training social skills, especially those which aim to show people the impressions they make on others and teach them how to create the impressions they intend but have been failing to achieve. Such training, if it could once be accepted by self-centered older people, might shock at least some of them into a frame of mind in which they would be better listeners and more acceptable talkers.

It may be complained that what has been said is pure speculation which adds nothing to our knowledge. In a sense this is true, but it is not the whole truth. The model outlined can be fairly claimed to do two things. First, it ties together a number of facts which would otherwise be disconnected and isolated. Second, it implies means of pinpointing, in areas which have been notably lacking in guidelines hitherto, the nature of difficulties associated with age, and thus of identifying new ways in which they might be mitigated or removed.

References

1. E. Belbin. Methods of training older Workers. *Ergonomics, 1*, 207–221, 1958.
2. E. Belbin and S. Downs. Teaching paired associates: The problem of age. *Occupational Psychology, 40*, 67–74, 1966.
3. E. Belbin and S. Shimmin. Training the middle aged for inspection work. *Occupational Psychology, 38*, 49–57, 1964.
4. R. M. Belbin. *Training methods for older workers*. Paris: O.E.C.D. 1965.
5. S. Chown, E. Belbin, and S. Downs. Programmed instruction as a method of teaching paired associates to older learners. *Journal of Gerontology, 22*, 212–219, 1967.
6. J. Botwinick, J. F. Brinley, and J. S. Robbin. The effect of motivation by electrical shocks on reaction-time in relation to age. *American Journal of Psychology, 71*, 408–411, 1958.
7. S. J. Korchin and H. Basowitz. Age differences in verbal learning. *Journal of Abnormal and Social Psychology, 54*, 64–69, 1957.
8. I. Silverman. Age and the tendency to withold response. *Journal of Gerontology, 18*, 372–375, 1963.
9. J. Botwinick. Cautiousness in advanced age. *Journal of Gerontology, 21*, 347–353, 1966.
10. F. I. M. Craik. Applications of signal detection theory to studies of ageing, in A. T. Welford and J. E. Birren (Eds.), *Decision making and age*. Basel: Karger, pp. 147–157, 1969.
11. J. N. Rees and J. Botwinick. Detection and decision factors in auditory behavior of the elderly. *Journal of Gerontology, 26*, 133–136, 1971.
12. A. T. Welford. Performance, biological mechanisms and age: A theoretical sketch, in A. T. Welford and J. E. Birren (Eds.), *Behavior, Aging and the Nervous System*. Springfield, Ill.: Thomas, pp. 3–20, 1965.
13. D. Vickers, T. Nettelbeck, and R. J. Willson. Perceptual indices of performance: The measurement of "inspection time" and "noise" in the visual system. *Perception, 1*, 263–295, 1972.
14. W. P. Tanner and J. A. Swets. A decision-making theory of visual detection. *Psychological Review, 61*, 401–409, 1954.
15. J. A. Swets, W. P. Tanner, and T. G. Birdsall. Decision processes in perception. *Psychological Review, 68*, 301–340, 1961.
16. D. McNicol. *A primer of signal detection theory*. London: George Allen & Unwin, 1972.
17. H. A. Taub and J. L. Myers. Differential monetary gains in a two-choice situation. *Journal of Experimental Psychology, 61*, 157–162, 1961.
18. L. Katz. Effects of differential monetary gain and loss on sequential two-choice behavior. *Journal of Experimental Psychology, 68*, 245–249, 1964.

19. Z. J. Ulehla. Optimality of perceptual decision criteria. *Journal of Experimental Psychology, 71,* 564–569, 1966.
20. M. Lewis. Psychological effect of effort. *Psychological Bulletin, 64,* 183–190, 1965.
21. R. B. Yaryan and L. Festinger. Preparatory action and belief in the probable occurrence of future events. *Journal of Abnormal and Social Psychology, 63,* 603–606, 1961.
22. A. T. Welford. *Fundamentals of skill.* London: Methuen, 1968.
23. J. Annett. *Feedback and human behaviour.* Harmondsworth: Penguin, 1969.
24. C. B. Gibbs and I. D. Brown. Increased production from information incentives in an uninteresting repetitive task. *Manager, 24,* 374–379, 1956.
25. A. T. Welford. *Ageing and human skill.* London: Oxford University Press, for the Nuffield Foundation, 1958. (Reprinted 1973, Westport, Conn.: Greenwood Press.)
26. A. T. Welford. *Christianity: A psychologist's translation.* London: Hodder & Stoughton, 1971.
27. A. T. Welford. *Skilled performance: Perceptual and motor skills.* Glenview, Ill.: Scott Foresman, 1976.

IV

Being Old— The Influence of the Sociophysical Environment

What makes a person what he or she is? This has been a popular question over the centuries. Answers have usually emphasized either the "nature" or "nurture" sphere of action. The controversy remains with us today although the terminology and data base continue to change both with scientific advances and shifts in the cultural attitude-belief mix. But advocates of "inner" and "outer" types of explanation seem to agree that the question is best examined in the earliest phases of development. Studies of "instinct" or "releasing mechanisms" almost always involve the very young within a given species, as do studies of environmental influence. It does make sense to begin at the beginning when attempting to clarify the nature-nurture interaction.

But it also makes sense to examine behavior and experience later in life. Neglect of the nature-nurture issue through the adult years might yield the impression that the whole story can be told very quickly: The long decades that follow early development are nothing more than a playing-out of well-established determinants. All adults have reason to protest this simplistic view of their lives, and all clinicians and scientists come off looking like rather dull folk if they permit their curiosity to be lulled by the bias. The life sciences have barely started to tell us how the nature-nurture interaction continues to operate as we move along through the adult years. Fortunately, however, gerontologists have started to make keen and useful observations about at least one side of the equation: the influence of the sociophysical environment on the aging adult. It is already evident that part of the answer to the basic question here ("What makes a person what he or she *is?*") must be based on understanding the specific sociophysical forces that dominate the immediate life situation of the older person. This section offers a variety of such explorations.

Thomas Tissue takes us into the central city where many older people live in poverty. His exploratory study produces results that will surprise some people in certain respects while appearing more predictable in others. Tissue suggests that "the central city is not merely a set of conditions to which the older persons in this study were randomly assigned. Instead, it represents the choice or destination of a special group of men whose biographies, activities, and needs set them at sharp variance from those who wind up living elsewhere." His contribution points to a more complex and sophisticated view of the relationship between individual adaptation in old age and the city environment. A fitting companion piece is Calvin Larson's study of alienation and public housing. He is concerned with the impact of the move into public housing on the elderly person's sense of social belongingness or isolation. In the words of one old person, "Isolation of the elderly is worse than cancer." The importance of the individual's ability to establish new social relationships is emphasized in this study.

The kibbutz appears to be quite a different scene for old people. Harold Wershow finds that the aged in five Israeli kibbutzim share in an active communal lifestyle whereby they escape the fate of becoming forgotten people. He sees the kibbutz as "a unique laboratory for research in aging in that it provides as totally secure a material setting for aging as can be found in the world, with the possible exception of aristocratic extended families in non-Western societies."

Nevertheless it is a fact of life in the United States and many other nations that a substantial number of old people move from the community into congregate living facilities of some kind. Such a move alters many aspects of the individual's subjective and objective world. It is appropriate to think of it broadly as an *ecology of adaptation* to a new environment. M. Powell Lawton, Beverly Patnaik, and Morton H. Kleban have studied this adaptation process in several ways. In the study offered here they concentrate on the effect of physical location, or distribution in space, on the behavior of old people who make the relatively smaller transition from one room to another within an institutional setting. The findings, interesting in themselves, also remind us that what might appear to be small changes from an outsider's viewpoint can have important effects on style and quality of life.

A familiar aspect of the older person's attempt to maintain both dignity and a sense of self-continuity is highlighted by the observations of Edmund Sherman and Evelyn S. Newman. Cherishing possessions is not limited to the elderly by any means. As aging brings with it accompanying losses in people, roles, and material possessions, however, the significance of a few personal items may become heightened. Sherman and Newman bring this question to our attention in their study of elderly people both in the community and in a nursing home. Life satisfaction in a particular environment may be related to one's success in retaining cherished objects symbolizing continuity and value. The study could well open a fruitful avenue for increased administrative and clinical sensitivity as well as research.

13

Old Age, Poverty, and the Central City

Thomas Tissue

Increasingly abandoned by younger families who flee to the suburbs, the central cities currently house large numbers of older poor persons. Their condition is frequently described as "the plight of the inner city aged." At one level, the description seems fair and accurate. To the extent that people are both old and poor, "plight" seems none too melodramatic a term to describe their circumstances. It is no secret that the society provides more penalties than rewards for sheer longevity and that poverty is an unpleasant experience regardless of the age at which one encounters it.

Considerably less clear, however, is the role of the central city itself in either intensifying or alleviating the hardship of its older inhabitants. Some have argued that the downtown area is a particularly cruel and merciless environment for the aged poor, whereas others have contended that the central city is precisely the spot at which the effects of old age and low income may be best combated.

One might best resolve the question by a comparison of the lives of the aged poor who live downtown to those of similarly old and poor persons who live elsewhere.

Background

Speaking of the manner in which the society has chosen to deal with urban centers, Jacobs (1961) remarks, "Unstudied, unrespected, cities have served as sacrificial victims" (p. 25). The sacrifice, if it be that, derives from a rich tradition of distaste and suspicion regarding the city and those who live at its center.

Many have been critical of the physical aspects of the inner city.

Reprinted with permission from *International Journal of Aging and Human Development*, 1971, 2, 235–248. This investigation was supported by Research Grant No. 93–P–75040/9–02 from the Title IV Research and Development Grants Program Administration on Aging, Social and Rehabilitation Service, Department of Health, Education and Welfare, Washington, D.C. 20201.

Traffic congestion, noise, smoke, and deteriorating structures combine to produce a central city image which drives out most of those who can afford to live elsewhere (Riesman, 1957). Equally frequent has been the assertion that urban social life is basically fragmented and shallow. Wirth's (1938) analysis of urban life contains repeated reference to anomie, nervous tension, frustration, low morale, isolation, and loneliness. The theory corresponds in part to the earlier work of Durkheim (1947) and Toennies (1963).

The theme of urban marginality and rootlessness achieves its fullest expression in reference to those who live in the central city. Nearly half a century ago, McKenzie (1925) described the downtown area as a place where "the more mobile and less responsible adults herd together" (p. 78). Hayner (1964) is even more specific regarding the restless unhappiness which prevailed among downtown hotel dwellers. Speaking of the same milieu some 40 years later, Shapiro (1966) finds that "untreated illness, hunger, loneliness, and sporadic violence are an unrelieved concomitant of existence" (p. 24).

From this perspective the plight of the aged appears specially poignant. Too poor to join in the rush to the suburbs, they remain trapped in the central city, where they are exploited by landlords, robbed by thugs, and ignored by almost everyone else (Brice, 1970). Unlikely to participate in the formal orgnizations which surround them (Bell & Force, 1956), large numbers of urban aged remain lonely and isolated in hotels, apartments, and boarding houses (Tibbitts & Schmelzer, 1965). Particularly vivid is Clark's (1971) assertion that:

> The inner city elderly are, both physically and psychologically sicker than their aged peers in other groups. They have a harder time surviving—perhaps the hardest of any elderly cohort we know. No one lovingly watches over the destinies of these tough survivors. They survive by their wits, like the rats that are often their only company. (p. 59)

The opposing point of view is one which concedes the existence of hardship and deprivation among the central city aged yet concludes that the city provides compensations unavailable to the aged poor in other locales. It is not the best of all possible worlds, yet it may be the better of those actually available to older, poor people.

It has been suggested that the downtown area is particularly well suited to the needs of its older, less robust inhabitants. In reference to the flight of younger persons from the area, Niebanck (1965) reflects:

> It is a curious thing that the high density urban areas that are being abandoned by many younger households, contain elements that make life easier and more

pleasurable for the elderly. The young are automobile users and space consumers. The elderly are quite the opposite. Many of the characteristics that
would be considered incompatible with a suburban development are for the
elderly the very things that contribute to efficiency and comfort. (p. 137)

Birren (1970) comments on the paradox involved in the fact that the
most deteriorated sections of the city are often the only places in which the
aged may piece together the goods and services they require for independent living. Such areas offer food, shelter, and drink at a cheaper price than
is found elsewhere and provide a dense concentration of service, recreation, and transportation as well (Bahr, 1967).

In view of Clark's comment (particularly the part about rats), it seems
somehow frivolous to suggest that the urban setting is "the natural habitat
of civilized man" (Park, 1925, p. 2), to hypothesize that urban dwellers "are
there because they believe that enjoyment and excitement are most easily
obtained there" (Strauss, 1961, p. 306), or to find in the city a unique
opportunity for "rich, variegated, unexpected, easy, multidimensional
contacts in the flesh" (Mead, 1957, p. 14). And yet it seems that these
peculiarly urban amenities also play a role in the lives of older people.

The downtown area is alive in a way that suburbs and farms can never
be. A constantly changing scene of the most bizarre events and people, the
central city offers an opportunity for free and spontaneous amusement,
which can be derived simply by watching what goes on around one
(Niebanck, 1965). Interesting in this respect is Frieden's (1960) research
with older women in a downtown residential hotel. For these women,
personal friendships were rare and comparatively unimportant. What did
matter was close proximity to an area in which they could observe the
activities of others within a busy downtown setting.

Finally, one may introduce a broad array of data which serve to cast
doubt upon the assumption that living alone in the central city is necessarily productive of isolation, loneliness, and unhappiness. While living alone
involves certain physical hazards, there seems little doubt that older
people generally prefer such an arrangement to living with children or
other relatives (Beyer & Woods, 1963; Donahue, 1954). Smith's (1961) data
suggest that older persons who can afford to maintain separate living
arrangements do so and that living with one's children or relatives is not
principally a matter of choice but of economic or health-related necessity.

Neither can one assume that living alone predisposes one to feelings of
loneliness (Tunstall, 1966). Loneliness sometimes appears least prevalent
among those who live alone or with a spouse only (Bond et al., 1954). To the
extent that the central city assumes the character of a geriatric ghetto, it
offers the age concentration and status homogeneity which seems important to the maintenance of friendship in old age (Rosow, 1961, 1970;
Messer, 1967). Neighbors of the same age and class appear to be of special

importance to the friendships of working-class and economically deprived older persons (Gubrium, 1970; Rosenberg, 1968).

Even when inner city aged do fail to maintain close or frequent contact with others, loneliness and low morale are not an inevitable consequence of that isolation. Speaking of a sample of central city aged in Denver, McCann (1967) reports:

> Those questioned in this study tended to be more isolated from both friends and relatives than those reported in other investigations. It was noteworthy however, that the majority of respondents stated that they were generally satisfied with the frequency and quality of their contacts with friends and relatives. Once again the pattern which appeared revealed an apparent discrepancy between the seemingly marginal situation experienced by many of those interviewed and the attitude expressed toward those conditions. (p. 38)

Similarly, a survey of Seattle's downtown aged (*Seattle's Older Population,* 1966) revealed no association between morale and frequency of contact with friends. The most consistent predictors of morale were (1) satisfaction with current income and (2) present health. In short, the central city aged may live alone and lack the close friendship bonds which sustain suburban or rural older people, yet one must exercise a certain caution in the interpretation of that condition.

How, then, does one go about reconciling such disparate interpretations of the central city and its role in the lives of old people who live there? On the one hand, it is described as a noisy, squalid ghetto in which older persons suffer alone and die unmourned. At the other extreme, the inner city emerges as a place in which the aged may achieve the maximum mileage from their admittedly slim resources—social, physical, and economic.

One might begin by acknowledging the fact that income is a pivotal element in the lives of older persons, regardless of where they happen to live. When we speak of the plight of the inner city aged, we are, at the same time, speaking principally of poor people. To compare their circumstances to those of the affluent aged in the suburbs may tell us a great deal about poverty but very little about the central city. If one is to deal seriously with the downtown area as a place to live in old age, one must compare the lives of its inhabitants to those of older persons with similar means who live elsewhere.

Second, it is imperative that one look at the central city in terms of the needs and activities of older persons who actually live there, rather than with reference to some universal standard of successful aging. Bultena and Wood (1969) observe that retirement communities are well suited to the needs of the clientele they attract. Nevertheless the authors are quick to point out that their findings will not support generalizations regarding the desirability of retirement communities for all older people. The analysis of the central city and the suburbs must proceed with the same sensitivity to the needs, preferences, and previous lifestyles of those who inhabit them.

Based on data gathered from a small sample of aged male welfare recipients, the present study explores the background, current activity, health, and morale of the central city aged, as compared to their equally poor, yet less urban, age peers. How do the downtown men differ from those in other areas, and what can be said regarding the nature and consequences of lifestyles which prevail within and beyond the central city?

Setting and Sample

The data are drawn from a study of aged welfare (Old Age Assistance) recipients in Sacramento, California. The original sample was drawn from two branch offices of the Sacramento County Welfare Department and consisted of all noninstitutional cases accepted for cash grant assistance during one summer. The only exclusions were those in which extreme poor health, language difficulty, or simple refusal made interviewing impossible.

The data reported here were gathered from the 95 men who were reinterviewed a year later. Of the 111 men in the original sample, 5 died, 4 became too ill to reinterview, 1 refused, and 6 had moved from the county prior to the second interview.

Sacramento is the principal city in a metropolitan area consisting of 800,000 people. In regard to population, the Sacramento metropolitan and suburban area ranks 41st nationally. As a middle-range city, surrounded by suburbs and rural areas, Sacramento represents an excellent site in which to examine the comparative role of the central city.

Sacramento's "old city" covers approximately 3 square miles. The area is bounded to the north and west by rivers and to the south and east by elevated expressways. At its center, it consists of the downtown shopping area, hotels, commercial offices, the state capitol and legislature, and great numbers of state office buildings. The remainder of the old city is a transitional zone, similar to that which Murphy (1966) describes as common to most urban centers. Although new office and apartment buildings are gradually supplanting the existing structures, the area presently includes large numbers of antiquated mansions that have been converted to apartments or boardinghouses; older apartment buildings; and small, single-family homes. The area also includes the West End, once the site of the homeless-men district which Bogue (1963) ranked 16th on his list of 41 American skid rows. The West End has since been razed, yet most of its former inhabitants have managed to relocate in other portions of the old city. The remainder of Sacramento County consists of sprawling suburbs, a few small towns, several semirural slums, and a great deal of relatively open country.

Of the 95 men that completed both interviews, 40 lived in the "old city" at the time of the second contact. The remaining 55 were located throughout the county, but most lived within a 6-mile radius of the central city.

Findings

At the time they were accepted for assistance, the downtown and suburban men were similar in regard to several background and demographic characteristics. The inner city men did not differ appreciably from the others regarding age, race, nativity, adult social class (Hollingshead & Redlich, 1958), or prior receipt of general relief. The age distribution is not particularly surprising—most recent approvals for Old Age Assistance can be expected to cluster at the minimum age level (65 years). More interesting is the absence of association between place of residence and the other characteristics shown in Table 13.1.

A closer look at their biographies reveals a number of important differences, however (see Table 13.2). The downtown men are more likely to have moved frequently as adults, to have worked for a great number of employers, and to have remained single throughout their lives. Even when they did marry, they produced comparatively few children.

Sharp differences emerge regarding living arrangement and type of housing as well. In the central city, almost all live in apartments, hotels, and other rentals. Roughly three of four live alone. In the suburbs, the majority live with their wives, in homes which are owned by the occupants.

An examination of the contacts maintained with other people shows that the image of central city marginality is sustained in most respects. As suggested by earlier studies, the inner city men are comparatively unin-

TABLE 13.1. General Characteristics (Percentages)

	Downtown (N = 40)	Suburban (N = 55)
1. Age: 65–66 years	53	51
2. Ethnic label: White	80	73
3. Birthplace: California	12	9
4. Adult social class: working class	57	58
5. Prior welfare status: received general relief	18	24

TABLE 13.2. Mobility, Marriage, and Living Arrangement

	Downtown (N = 40) %	Suburban (N = 55) %	p by X^2
1. Adult mobility			
Lived in 10+ different			
neighborhoods	45	22	.02
Worked for 20+ different employers	40	22	.10
2. Marriage and family			
Has married	65	93	.001
Had children (married			
only—N = 26, 51)	58	92	.001
3. Living arrangements—1970			
Alone	73	18	.001
With wife	17	62	
With others only	10	20	
4. Type of housing—1970			
Rented home, apartment	50	34	.001
Hotel, rooming house	40	2	
Owned home	10	53	
Other (trailer, etc.)		11	

volved in clubs and organizations and maintain few close friendships in the metropolitan area. Unlikely to have reproduced during their lives, they see relatively little of the children they did father. Comparatively few bought even a single present for anyone in the preceding year or entertained friends or relatives during that time.

Central city men do see other people, however (Table 13.3). As might be expected, they routinely encounter great numbers of tradespeople during a normal week. Their contact with neighbors is similar to that of the suburban men. Although they have fewer close friends than do the others, they are as likely to encounter an acquaintance of sorts each week.

The profile that emerges from these data is remarkably consistent with earlier discussions of the urban lifestyle. Living in areas of great population density, the inner city men nonetheless maintain an aloofness and reserve in their dealings with other people. Certainly, their attachment to family, friends, and voluntary organizations is less secure than is the case for older poor men who live outside the central city.

At the same time, it is obvious that the central city men participate in a greater variety of recreational activities than do the suburban men (Table 13.4.) Simple propinquity to the facilities themselves seems of considerable importance. The "old city" is comparatively small in area yet contains 9 of the county's 20 walk-in theaters; the state library; the main branch of the city-county library (and 20% of the books available in the combined

TABLE 13.3. Social Contacts

	Downtown (N = 40) %	Suburban (N = 55) %	p by X^2
A. Belongs to organization	10	38	.01
B. Has 3 or more close friends	38	67	.01
C. Has seen own child in past month (those with children only: N = 15, 47)	33	70	.02
D. Has given presents in past year	43	76	.001
E. Has entertained in past year	25	76	.001
F. Sees 10+ tradespeople per week	58	31	.01
G. Sees a neighbor weekly	60	58	> .10
H. Sees an acquaintance weekly	68	69	> .10

system); numerous shops and restaurants; Sutter's Fort (a historical monument and museum); the state capitol and legislature; the county's most opulent senior citizen's center; and nine parks. Except for the senior citizen's center, which had limited appeal for either group, the area's recreational facilities are used principally by those who live in close proximity to the downtown complex.

The downtown zone is one of the few areas within the county in which walking is a reasonably efficient means of transportation. Ironically, it is also the area in which bus service is most frequent and comprehensive. Outside the central city, the concentration of facilities (both civic and commercial) is diffuse, the distances great, the sidewalks progressively rare, and the bus service spotty at best. In consequence, the suburban men travel by automobile whereas the inner city men walk or ride the bus (Table 13.5).

TABLE 13.4. Commercial and Public Recreation

In Past Year Went to:	Downtown (N = 40) %	Suburban (N = 55) %	p by X^2
A. The state capitol	70	26	.001
B. The movies	43	16	.01
C. A park	95	60	.01
D. Sutter's Fort	45	16	.01
E. A library	45	16	.01
F. A restaurant	95	71	.01
G. The senior citizen's center	10	11	> .10

TABLE 13.5. Transportation

	Downtown (N = 40) %	Suburban (N = 55) %	p by X²
Means of transportation used			
A. Walks	80	18	.001
B. Takes bus	78	31	.001
C. Drives automobile	7	55	.001
D. Is driven by others	35	62	.01
Automobile ownership			
(owns automobile)	15	62	.001

The matter of income must be a part of any discussion dealing with the aged. The actual details of the Old Age Assistance budgeting process are awesomely complicated. In summary, however, each client has his individual need computed, item by item, according to a strict set of standard allowances. From this total need (not to exceed $200 per month), his independent income is subtracted and the agency pays the difference. Thus the total monthly income may vary from case to case, but in all instances it corresponds to the agency's uniform and strict concept of demonstrably urgent need.

That concept seems to work a greater hardship on the suburban men (Table 13.6). They were less likely to be satisfied with their income at the time aid was first granted and remained so the following year. Also, they were considerably more likely to have asked the county for a grant increase during the period between the two interviews.

One can speculate as to the reasons why the suburban men are more

TABLE 13.6. Response to Income

	Downtown (N = 40) %	Suburban (N = 55) %	p by X²
At time aid was granted,			
felt income inadequate to "get by on"	17	47	.01
At reinterview—1 year later:			
A. Feels own income lower than most age peers	22	51	.01
B. "Needs money" is a current problem	53	71	.10
Request for grant increase—			
asked for more money during year	18	40	.02

inclined to pessimism regarding their financial situation. They may, of course, have routine expenses for which the welfare budget is manifestly inadequate. The ownership of cars and houses is a case in point. Maintaining an old house and an old automobile can be a fearfully expensive enterprise, when compared to the cost of a rented room and an occasional bus ride.

Although the data are not adequate to test the proposition, it also seems likely that the suburban lifestyle is one in which a person has an obligation to keep up appearances. For the solitary men who live downtown, there are few people worth impressing. The style of life can expand and contract in accordance with this month's income. In the suburbs, men have fixed obligations which must be met, whether in terms of entertaining, giving presents, or simply maintaining a presentable home and personal appearance.

Less speculative, however, is the evidence regarding the comparative health of the downtown and suburban men (Table 13.7). The downtown men display a marked superiority in terms of health. They can perform more of the physical tasks (heavy housework, climbing ladders, etc.) that are summarized in the Functional Health Index. They are less likely to believe that they are in poor health or to consider health a current problem of consequence. Finally, they manifest fewer symptoms of mental illness, at least in regard to the variant measured by the Savage-Britton (1967) screening instrument. If one is disinclined to accept such results as indicative of mental health (either its presence or absence), one must still face the fact that the suburban men are subject to an impressive array of somatic, social, and psychological complaints (the components of the Savage-Britton scale), which are less prevalent among the inner city sample.

Two points seem worthy of mention in connection with health. The first has to do with the etiology of the differences noted above. It seems unlikely that the central city has rejuvenative powers which keep its inhabitants youthful and fit. Instead, the downtown solitary existence has a stern requirement for reasonably good health, mobility, and the capacity for taking care of oneself. When health fails, as it must inevitably, there is nowhere to turn but institutional care. Thus, the downtown men studied here represent the hardy survivors of a continuous and severe process of selection. The prospect of poor health is less ominous for suburban men, who are firmly embedded in a supportive matrix of friends and family.

The second point relates to the effects of poor health among the suburban men. To some extent one can assume that their avoidance of public transportation and out-of-home recreation is a function of physical incapacity. Poor health does not apear to be the only inhibiting factor,

TABLE 13.7.   Health

	Downtown (N = 40) %	Suburban (N = 55) %	p by X^2
Functional health			
High	55	40	.05
Medium	35	25	
Low	10	35	
Self-rated health			
Good	50	27	.02
Fair	35	33	
Poor	15	40	
Health as current problem			
Yes	12	36	.01
No	88	64	
Savage-Britton Mental Health Scale			
Positive (0–2)	55	31	.01
Intermediate (3–5)	38	33	
Negative (6–14)	7	36	

however. Considerations of money and personal preference are involved as well. When asked which activities they would increase if they were richer, 62% of the suburban men would dine out more frequently, and 80% would take more trips, poor health notwithstanding. As regards public transportation, 44% of the suburban men would ride the bus more often if the service were better, and 52% would do so if it were cheaper. Of the 25 men who simply refused to ride the bus regardless of the quality of service, only 2% mentioned health as the reason. The rest simply preferred the convenience and privacy of automobiles.

To this point, the discussion has focused on the disparities which emerge from a comparison of two basically different lifestyles. The remaining question relates to the perceived adequacy of each. How do the two groups differ in terms of morale and satisfaction with their lives?

Quite succinctly, the data show *no* difference whatsoever (Table 13.8). Despite the comparative social isolation of downtown men, they are no more likely than the others to report feeling bored or lonely. The suburban men are sicker and more worried about their financial situations, yet, as a group, they are virtually identical to the downtown men in regard to anomia (Srole, 1956); mood tone, as represented by the Affect Balance Index (Phillips, 1967); and general response to their current situation, as gauged by the Life Satisfaction Index-A (Neugarten, Havighurst & Tobin,

TABLE 13.8.   Morale, Life Satisfaction

	Downtown (N = 40) %	Suburban (N = 55) %	p by X^2
Current problems			
A. Feels lonely	25	27	> .10
B. Feels bored	40	42	> .10
Morale			
A. Anomia (high: 3–5)	58	64	> .10
B. Affect balance (low: 5–10)	37	40	> .10
C. LSIA (low: 1–9)	27	32	> .10
Life in retrospect			
A. Is willing to live life over	55	58	> .10
B. Has gotten more "breaks" than most people	25	24	> .10
C. Has achieved some or most life goals	58	57	> .10

1961). Although the two groups have led markedly different lives in the past and find themselves in quite dissimilar circumstances at present, their retrospective response to their lives is virtually identical.

Given the size of the sample, an attempt to explain the sources of morale in the two settings must remain highly tentative. Nevertheless, the results of such an attempt are provocative. On the basis of previous studies, one might hypothesize that the morale of the aged poor is dependent upon a variety of factors but that health, income, and relations with other people should predominate. The data lend only limited and qualified support to such hypotheses (Table 13.9). In the first place, reactions to income had little effect upon the morale (as measured by Affect Balance scores) of either group. Neither did age, response to neighborhood, or general self-ratings of health (i.e., good, fair, poor).

On the other hand, infrequent contact with friends, poor functional health, embarrassment at receiving welfare, and the desire to work again did predict low morale in a consistent and expected fashion—but only for the suburban men. Among the downtown men, morale was apparently unaffected by contact with friends, response to welfare, or the wish to have a job again. Since almost all were in good functional health, it was impossible to test the effect of this variable.

While hardly definitive, the findings are most interesting. Secure at a remarkably high level of functional health, the downtown men seem immune to the kinds of problems and concerns that depress morale in the suburbs. Regardless of the conditions about them and their responses to

TABLE 13.9.   Factors Associated with Morale (Affect Balance)

	Downtown (N = 40)		Suburban (N = 55)	
A. Contact with friends	Sees friends weekly	Sees friends less than weekly	Sees friends weekly	Sees friends less than weekly
High affect balance	67% (N = 27)	54% (N = 13)	74% (N = 38)	29% (N = 17)
		$p > .10$		$p = .01$
B. Functional health	High	Low	High	Low
High affect balance	* (N = 36)	* (N = 4)	72% (N = 36)	37% (N = 19)
	*distribution such that tests not indicated			$p = .02$
C. Personal response to being on welfare	Not embarrassed	Embarrassed	Not embarrassed	Embarrassed
High affect balance	65% (N = 26)	64% (N = 11)	70% (N = 37)	40% (N = 15)
		$p > .10$		$p = .02$
D. Desire for job	Does not want job	Wants job	Does not want job	Wants job
High affect balance	67% (N = 21)	58% (N = 19)	79% (N = 14)	54% (N = 41)
		$p > .10$		$p = .10$

them, downtown men appear to maintain a stable equanimity about conditions that sadden their suburban peers. In other words, the striking similarity which emerges from gross comparisons of grouped morale scores serves to mask important differences in regard to the way morale is achieved and maintained in the two settings.

Discussion

The data reveal sharp and consistent differences between older poor men who live in the central city and those who reside in the surrounding area. The groups differ in terms of biography, contacts with other people, living arrangement, recreational activity, marriage and family, response to poverty, mobility, and health.

Downtown men led mobile, marginal lives in the past. They seldom married, produced few children, and are currently unlikely to see those whom they did father. They live alone in hotels, rooming houses, and other rented quarters. They see tradespeople, neighbors, and acquaintances but have few close friends or relatives. They are, however, exceptionally healthy, find their income adequate to their needs, and take advantage of their proximity to urban facilities for recreation, amusement, and transportation.

Suburban men are family men for the most part. Nearly all have married, and most still live with their wives in owned or rented homes. They have many children and see them frequently. They own automobiles but seldom seem to go anywhere in them. They are more likely to be sick, to perceive severe financial difficulties, and to be isolated physically from the larger community's resources and activities.

Dissimilar in almost every other respect, the two lifestyles nonetheless produce strikingly *similar* levels of morale. The downtown and suburban samples are virtually identical in regard to present mood, anomia, life satisfaction, and contentment with the past. While the sources of satisfaction seem quite different for the two groups, the end result is the same.

To return to the original question—the desirability of living downtown—it is obvious that the matter cannot be resolved in a simple, apothegmatic fashion. Neither will it yield to analyses that involve buildings and services on the one hand and hypothetical people on the other. The central city is not merely a set of conditions to which the older persons in this study were randomly assigned. Instead, it represents the choice of destination of a special group of men whose biographies, activities, and needs set them at sharp variance from those who wind up living elsewhere.

With this distinction in mind, the nature of the dispute between apologists and critics of the central city becomes clearer. To some limited extent, both are right. The downtown men do live in shabby apartments and hotel rooms, do have few close friends, and do lack familial contact or support. Their circumstances seem calculated to produce unhappiness and despair among older persons as a whole. Interestingly enough, however, these conditions do not have the same effect upon those who have gravitated to the central city. As Lowenthal (1968) points out, "You do not suffer from the lack of relationships that you have long since renounced." (pp. 189–190). For the downtown men studied here, the renunciation is extensive and long-standing. Thus, one may accept the critics' contention that central city life is isolated without invalidating the apologists' claim that downtown life need not be lonely. The equation can be reversed by pointing out that the suburban lifestyle contains little out-of-home recreation and limited mobility, yet it is no more productive of boredom than is the more active, inner city pattern.

The point is not that social contact, place of residence, and recreational activity are irrelevant to the lives of the aged poor. Instead, it is suggested that such factors coalesce in reasonably well-integrated, internally consistent lifestyles, which often differ markedly from one another. They may, as in the present sample, produce virtually the same levels of satisfaction despite their profound differences in form and content.

Although the downtown lifestyle seems to "work" as well as does its suburban counterpart (at least for those who live in each locale), the central city men have the least secure prospects for the future. Attacking the use of morale or happiness as criteria for successful aging, Rosow (1963) suggests instead that adjustment be measured in terms of continuity. From this perspective, the downtown men are in the more precarious position. The downtown lifestyle is predicated on health and mobility; both will decline as time passes, with the result that independent living arrangements will be more difficult to maintain.

It is also apparent that urban renewal poses serious threats to the maintenance of the downtown lifestyle. Few attempts to revive and beautify the downtown business area have in mind the continued residence of old, low-income, single men. They are neither profitable nor scenic. Nevertheless, their ejection from the area poses severe threats to the maintenance of lifestyles based on low rent, anonymity, and immediate access to the goods and services they require. There is, of course, a sad irony in the fact that urban renewal is often justified on the grounds that it will rescue downtown pensioners from their loneliness and unwholesome surroundings, when, in fact, neither seems of particular concern to those who will be rescued from them.

In closing, one must suggest certain cautions with respect to the findings reported here. The sample is quite small and consists entirely of older men recently approved for public assistance. Caution must be exercised in the generalization of such findings to other age and income groups. More important is the qualification that derives from the site of the study. Sacramento is a middle-range city in which one is free to choose among a variety of quite different residential settings even when old and poor. The findings indicate that the choice is exercised in two remarkably consistent patterns: one group goes downtown, the other selects the outer area. The findings would not apply however to cities or areas in which there is no opportunity for differential location, either because the setting is uniform throughout or because older poor persons find themselves forced into a single locale regardless of preference. It is suggested, however, that the latter conditon is considerably less prevalent than might be imagined.

Finally, the data should not lead one to romanticize the conditions of older men who live downtown. Theirs is not an idyllic life but a different one—one in which they can achieve as much satisfaction as equally old and poor men who locate elsewhere.

Summary

This study compared the circumstances of older poor men in the central city to those of similarly aged and impoverished men who live in outlying areas. The data indicate sharp and consistent differences in the lifestyes which prevail in the two locales. The downtown men have led more mobile, solitary lives in the past and continue to maintain themselves in an independent, socially marginal fashion. While markedly different in content and form, the two lifestyles nonetheless produce nearly identical levels of satisfaction and morale. The results suggest that future analysis of the aged in the city be sensitive to the importance of selective migration, differential lifestyles, and low income itself.

References

Bahr, H. M. The gradual disappearance of skid row. *Social Problems*, 1967, *15*, (1), 41–45.

Bell, W., and Force, M. T. Urban neighborhood types and participation in formal associations. *American Sociological Review*, 1956, *21*(1), 25–34.

Beyer, G. H., and Woods, M. E. *Living and activity patterns of the aged*. Research Report No. 6, Center for Housing and Environmental Studies, Ithaca: Cornell University, 1963.

Birren, J. E. The abuse of the urban aged. *Psychology Today*, 1970, *3*(10), 37–38, 76.

Bogue, D. J. *Skid row in American cities*... Chicago: Community and Family Study Center, 1963.

Bond, F. A.; Baber, R. E.; Vieg, J. A.; Perry, L. B.; Scaff, A. H.; and Lee, L. J. *Our needy aged*. New York: Holt, 1954.

Brice, D. The geriatric ghetto. *San Francisco*, 1970, *12*(9), 70–72, 82.

Bultena, G. L., and Wood, V. The American retirement community: Bane or blessing: *Journal of Gerontology*, 1969, *24*(2), 209–217.

Clark, M. Patterns of aging among the elderly poor of the inner city. *Gerontologist*, 1971, *11*(1), 58–66.

Donahue, W. Where and how older people wish to live, in W. Donahue, (Ed.) *Housing the Aged*. Ann Arbor: University of Michigan Press, 1954.

Durkheim, E. *The division of labor in society*. New York: Free Press, 1947.

Frieden, E. Social differences and their consequences for housing the aged. *Journal of American Institute of Planners*, 1960, *26*(2), 119–124.

Gubrium, J. F. Environmental effects on morale in old age and the resources of health and solvency. *Gerontologist*, 1970, *10*(4), 294–297.

Hayner, N. S. Hotel life: Physical proximity and social distance, in E. W. Burgess and D. J. Bogue (Eds.), *Contributions to urban sociology*. Chicago: University of Chicago Press, 1964.

Hollingshead, A. B., and Redlich, F. C. *Social class and mental illness*. New York: Wiley, 1958.

Jacobs, J. *The death and life of great American cities*. New York: Random House, Vintage, 1961.

Lowenthal, M. F. The relationship between social factors and mental health in the aged. *Psychiatric Research Report No. 23*, February 1968, pp. 187–197.

McCann, C. W. *Senior Americans speak out*. Denver: Metropolitan Council for Community Services, 1967.

McKenzie, R. D. The ecological approach to the study of the human community, in R. Park, E. Burgess and R. McKenzie, *The city*. Chicago: University of Chicago Press, 1925.

Mead, M. Values for urban living. *Annals*, 1957, *34*, 10–14.

Messer, M. The possibility of an age concentrated environment becoming a normative system. *Gerontologist*, 1967, *7*(4), 247–251.

Murphy, R. E. *The American city: An urban geography*. New York: McGraw-Hill, 1966.

Neugarten, B. I; Havighurst, R. J.; and Tobin, S. S. The measurement of life satisfaction. *Journal of Gerontology*, 1961, *16*(2), 134–143.

Niebanck, P. L. *The elderly in older urban areas*. Philadelphia: Institute for Environmental Studies, University of Pennyslvania, 1965.

Park, R. The city: Suggestions for the investigation of human behavior in the urban environment, in R. Park, E. Burgess, and R. McKenzie, *The city*. Chicago: University of Chicago Press, 1925.

Phillips, D. L. Social participation and happiness. *American Journal of Sociology*, 1967, *72*(5), 479–488.

Riesman, D. The suburban dislocation. *Annals*, 1957, *34*, 123–146.

Rosenberg, G. S. Age, poverty, and isolation from friends in the urban working class. *Journal of Gerontology*, 1968, *23*(4), 533–538.

Rosow, I. Retirement housing and social integration. *Gerontologist*, 1961, *1*(2), 85–91.

Rosow, I. Adjustment of the normal aged, in R. H. Williams, C. Tibbitts, and W. Donahue (Eds.), *Processes of aging*. New York: Atherton, 1963.

Rosow, I. Old people: Their friends and neighbors. *American Behavioral Scientist*, 1970, *14*(1), 59–69.

Savage, R. D., and Britton, P. G. A short scale for the assessment of mental health in the community aged. *British Journal of Psychiatry*, 1967, *113*, 521–523.

Seattle's older population: A study of attitudes, needs and resources in King county. Planning Division, United Good Neighbors of King County, Seattle, 1966.

Shapiro, J. Single room occupancy: Community of the alone. *Social Work*, 1966, *11*(4), 24–33.

Smith, W. F. The housing preferences of elderly people. *Journal of Gerontology*, 1961, *16*(3), 261–266.

Srole, L. Social integration and certain corollaries: An exploratory study. *American Sociological Review*, 1956, *21*(6), 709–716.

Strauss, A. L. *Images of the American city*. New York: Free Press of Glencoe, 1961.

Tibbitts, C., and Schmelzer, J. L. New directions in aging and their research implications. *Welfare in Review*, 1965, *3*(2), 8–14.

Toennies, F. *Community and society*, C. P. Loomis (trans.). New York: Harper & Row, 1963.

Tunstall, J. *Old and alone*. London: Routledge & Kegan Paul, 1966.

Wirth, L. Urbanism as a way of life. *American Journal of Sociology*, 1938, *44*(1), 1–24.

14

Alienation and Public Housing for the Elderly

Calvin J. Larson

In recent years the field of social gerontology has been heavily influenced by a theoretical orientation based on the premise that aging in America is a process of social disengagement. According to its originators (Cumming & Henry, 1961), "Aging is an inevitable mutual withdrawal or disengagement, resulting in decreased interaction between the aging person and others in the social systems he belongs to" (p. 14). When a person reaches a certain chronological age (generally, the age of retirement), he or she and society are expected to sever functional interdependence and go their separate ways. Society is expected to continue on the path of "life," and the individual is expected to prepare for death.

From the vantage point of the disengagement theorist, the process of aging entails increasing estrangement (or alienation) between the aged individual and society. The reality of this separation is much in evidence. Typically, the elderly describe themselves as lonely and socially isolated. In the words of one elderly person (quoted by Niebanck, 1968), "Today, the people have no respect, sympathy, compassion or friendliness toward the old people that is needed. Isolation of the elderly is worse than cancer" (p. 45).

The concomitants of social isolation are normlessness and powerlessness. In other words, there is an absence of the direction that comes from membership in a face-to-face group with meaningful social bonds, and there is an inability to do much more than complain about the negative consequences of this condition. My primary concern here is to examine the

Reprinted with permission from *International Journal of Aging and Human Development*, 1974, 5. I wish to thank Professor Frederick Schmidt of the University of Vermont for assisting in the data collection phase of this research.

relationship between the move into public housing for the elderly and measures of alienation. It is to be hoped that the move will mitigate rather than exacerbate the effects of social disengagement in those involved.

Public Housing and the Elderly

Although considerable material is available on topics such as housing design for the elderly (e.g., Field, 1968) and the attitudes of the elderly toward aging (Shanas, 1970), surprisingly little data is available on the social and psychological effects of the move into public housing for the elderly. Carp (1966) continues to be the leading reference on the subject. Recently, Lawton and Cohen (1974) have extended Carp's work by examining the effects of the move into five different elderly housing sites located in Pennsylvania and New Jersey. Two were low-rent public housing structures, and three were lower middle–income projects. These two represent the only published studies on rehousing the elderly based on a before-and-after methodological design. In each instance, the move was found to be associated with more positive than negative effects.

The bulk of the published work has dealt with the relocation problems of the elderly displaced by urban renewal. A basic trend in this research is that the elderly are more likely than younger groups to be affected adversely by forced relocation (cf. Brand & Smith, 1974). To minimize the negative consequences of moving to a new home, the evidence indicates that the planner would be well advised to build into the design as much continuity as possible between the old and the new place of residence; for example, a structure comparable in size, type, and physical location to that to which tenants have been accustomed (cf. Niebanck, 1968, p. 44) and occupancy of the new unit by former neighbors, friends, and acquaintances (see Carp, 1966, pp. 131–139).

In her study of Victoria Plaza (located in San Antonio, Texas—a 9-story public housing structure containing 184 dwelling units), Carp (1966) found that a carefully planned apartment complex could significantly alleviate social disengagement among the elderly. The effect of the move into Victoria Plaza "seemed to be in the direction of increased activity, more frequent contact with a wider circle of people, less 'lost time' and less time spent in sleeping, in passive activities, and in solitude" (p. 143). Furthermore says Carp, "Given a comfortable and attractive physical environment and one rich in social possibilities as well, [tenants] seemed to re-engage and enjoy it" (p. 143).

Generally, the move into Victoria Plaza was accompanied by increased social participation. In particular, residents manifested an increase in number of close friends and in visits from relatives and former neighbors. Separate analyses were not made of the postmove effects of number of friendships established among fellow tenants prior to, as opposed to those developed after, the move. Further, although a distinction was made between visits from, and visits to, others, no effort was made to compare their possibly different impact on measures of adjustment to the move.

One type of social participation was not altered by the move: "Living in the Plaza had no significant effect on church attendance" (Carp, 1966, p. 136). The religious factor was an important element in the study for a number of reasons. Mostly, however, it was of interest because "religion may be an escape for people unable to adjust successfully to the demands of life, or a source of strength which enables individuals to meet life's problems more adequately" (p. 190). Frequency of church attendance was found to be highly correlated with indicators of adjustment to the move.

A perusal of this evidence suggested the central hypothesis examined in this chapter, namely: The alienating effects of the move into public housing for the elderly will *vary inversely* with the tenant's ability to maintain established social relationships and group affiliations and acquire new ones. Working hypotheses considered include:

1.   The greater the similarity between the type of housing to which an individual is accustomed and the public housing into which he or she moves, the lower the level of alienation;

2.   The greater the amount of contact with outside friends and relatives, the lower the level of alienation;

3.   As frequency of visiting with fellow tenants increases, the level of alienation decreases;

4.   The greater the number of fellow tenants known before the move, the lower the level of alienation after the move; and,

5.   The greater the amount of church attendance, the lower the level of alienation.

The Alienation Measure

To tap the respondent's attitudinal disposition prior to the move, Dean's alienation scale (Dean, 1961) was employed. This scale permits a composite measure of alienation by means of separate estimates of a individual's sense of Powerlessness, Normlessness, and Social Isolation (for a previous application of this subscale in the study of alienation among the elderly, see Ellison, 1969). By Powerlessness, Dean has in mind the Marxian concept of alienation in the sense of feeling helpless to control the forces that determine behavior and events. Representative items on this section of the scale are:

> There is little or nothing I can do towards preventing a major "shooting" war.
> We are just so many cogs in the machinery of life.

The Normlessness subscale is based on Durkheim's concept of *anomie*, or the loss of group bonds occasioned by sudden changes in social status. Typical items are as follows:

> The end often justifies the means.
> I often wonder what the meaning of life really is.

Dean's interpretation of Social Isolation is analogous to Durkheim's concept of egoistic suicide. In this case, it is "a feeling of separation from the group or of isolation from group standards." The following exemplify the nine items on this subscale.

> Sometimes I feel all alone in the world.
> One can always find friends if he shows himself friendly.

The Respondents and Their Cities

The participants of this research are those persons 62 years of age and older who entered separately administered high-rise public housing projects for the elderly in two contiguous municipalities in northwestern Vermont during the summer of 1971. The smaller of the two cities, herein referred to as "Milltown," contains approximately 8,000 persons. The population is characterized by high residential stability. A survey found that 75% of all families lived at their current address for 5 years or more. Nearly 70% of the population is of French Canadian descent. In 1974, approximately 30% of all Milltown residents lived in poverty conditions. Since 1969, the entire city has been supported by the Department of Housing and Urban Development's Model Cities program.

The second city, "Lakeside," has a population in the vicinity of 50,000, of which, 25% have been found to be existing on incomes below the poverty level. As in the case of Milltown, older citizens constitute 33% of the city's poverty households.

During the 3rd week in August 1971, the Milltown Housing Authority opened its 53-unit, 5-story, low-income housing unit for the elderly, and 1 week later the Lakeside Housing Authority's 162-unit, 11-story structure was open for its first tenants.

Data Collection

While it would have been desirable to contact prospective residents of each unit prior to the move, financial and other restrictions permitted this to be done only in the case of the Lakeside unit. The director of the housing authority provided the names and addresses of the 107 persons eligible for admission to his project. A questionnaire was mailed to each, and 87 (or 81.3%) were completed and returned. In the analysis this pretested group is identified as Lakeside 1.

After 6 months the questionnaire was administered to the tenants of the Milltown unit for self-completion, 29 of the 51 occupants (or 56.8%) provided an acceptable document. Because of physical disabilities 4 persons were not able to complete the document either by themselves or with the aid of a research assistant; 4 others were not available because of extended visits with relatives or hospitalization. The remaining 14 represent refusals and those who managed to avoid all efforts to contact them.

Concurrently with the testing of the Milltown sample, the posttest was given to the tenants of the Lakeside unit for self-completion. At this time, 61 of the 87 individuals pretested were in residence. Of these, 30 (or 49.1%) completed the posttest. In the analysis these 30 individuals are referred to as the experimental group.

In addition to the 30 persons in the experimental group, 20 not pretested returned the posttest. These 20 individuals are identified as Lakeside 2. It will be noted that this group is not represented in all phases of the analysis. Because access to tenants was restricted, the same abbreviated posttest was administered to both those pretested and those who were not.

As explanation is required for the low response rate of those pretested in the Lakeside unit. Prior to the move, a mailed questionnaire was effective because respondents had yet to be notified of their acceptance into public housing. That is, in spite of a cover sheet statement that completion of the document was not prerequisite to acceptance of their application, most felt, undoubtedly, that to be on the safe side the questionnaire should be completed and returned.

After the move no such compelling motive to complete the posttest was apparent. For this reason, an audience with tenants was requested to explain the importance of their continued participation in the study. At this time the document was distributed with every confidence that it would be completed by the end of a week's time. A social worker, hired to mediate between the needs and problems of tenants and housing authority officials, insisted that she be the one to retrieve completed documents. It was made clear that she considered the study—and the survey research of social scientists in general—to be an invasion of privacy and that her cooperation would be minimal. At the appointed time she collected 25 documents (only 5 of which were from persons who had completed the pretest) and refused to make any effort to remind the tardy to complete theirs. Furthermore, she did not wish tenants to be disturbed by a door-to-door reminder. The next step was to mail another copy of the questionnaire to those yet to respond. Of the 56 mailed to those pretested, 25 were returned in satisfactory form.

For these reasons the sample size after the move for Lakeside tenants is low and of questionable representation. In fact one may infer that those who did not take the posttest most likely would be among the most alienated members of the sample. The weight of the pretest evidence does not support this interpretation. For example, considering only the 19 individuals who are known to have been capable of taking the posttest but who either refused or failed to do so for a variety of reasons (of the 12 remaining, 2 had passed away; 2 were hospitalized; 4 were on extended visits with relatives or an ailing spouse; and 4 others were suffering the effects of advanced age), all scale scores (median) were slightly lower than those recorded by the other 68 persons who completed the pretest. The respective median scores were as follows: (1) total, 38.0 and 40.0; (2) Powerlessness, 15.0 and 16.0; (3) Social Isolation, 12.0 and 12.5; and (3) Normlessness, 9.0 and 10.5.

Notwithstanding the amount and quality of evidence of this kind, the small size of the posttest sample permits only the most restricted type of data analysis. It would appear, however, that an effort to appraise the information collected is worthwhile because (1) the topic is important and the likelihood of its being studied under less than ideal methodological conditions is exceedingly great, and (2) the opportunities for noncontrived before-and-after studies are not that abundant and, therefore, must be attempted as they present themselves.

The analysis that follows, then, is oriented toward assessing the consistency of findings rather than the precise testing of the hypotheses under examination. Thus, instead of the use of a correlation coefficient and a test of significance, the ordinal statistic *gamma* is used to measure the relationship between variables. I hope, the results are of sufficient quality to suggest a path worthy of further exploration.

The Findings

Table 14.1 contains the alienation scale scores (median) for the different respondent categories. In regard to total score, and with the exception of the figure for the experimental group before the move, the median values are higher than the mean scores evidenced by other, mostly younger and middle class, populations studied by Dean and those who have used his scale (a listing of users of the Dean scale and a summary of their major findings is contained in Miller, 1970, pp. 323–326). This is not unexpected, as scale scores have been found to be (1) negatively correlated with socioeconomic indicators (income, education, and occupation), and (2) positively correlated with age (Dean, 1961, p. 757).

Milltown respondents recorded the highest median total score and the highest median Powerlessness score. The experimental group manifested the lowest median Normlessness score both before and after the move. The Lakeside 1 and Lakeside 2 populations evidenced virtually the same median scores on all four measures.

Controlling for sex of respondent (women constitute two-thirds of Milltown respondents and nearly 59% of those from both Lakeside categories) does not account for the relatively high total score registered by Milltown respondents. Even so, with but one exception (Milltown women on the Social Isolation scale) males recorded higher scores than females. In regard to total median scores, for example, and comparing men to women, the Lakeside 1 scores were 46.5 and 37.5; Lakeside 2, 40.0 and 35.5; and Milltown, 48.5 and 42.0. Examination of the findings in regard to each of the five working hypotheses sheds additional light on these data.

  1. *The greater the similarity between the type of housing to which an individual is accustomed and the public housing into which he or she moves, the lower the level of alienation.* From this hypothesis we might expect those accustomed to apartment living to be less alienated by the move than those who are not. Even though it is assumed that alienation scores will be higher generally for apartment dwellers than residents of

TABLE 14.1. Alienation Scale Scores (Median)

	Median Scores				
	Experimental Group (N = 30)				
Alienation Measures	*Before*	*After*	*Lakeside 1 (N = 87)*	*Lakeside 2 (N = 20)*	*Milltown (N = 29)*
Total score	38.5	37.7	39.0	39.3	42.5
Powerlessness	17.2	16.5	16.6	16.0	19.5
Social Isolation	13.5	12.5	13.8	14.0	10.8
Normlessness	9.8	10.0	10.2	10.2	10.5

single-family dwelling units, the expectation is that the move into the type
of public housing under discussion would be more alienating to those most
accustomed to the latter than the former type of living unit.

Each respondent was asked to identify the type of housing lived in
most of his or her life from a list of specified alternatives. Over 60% (61.5) of
Lakeside 1 respondents indicated having lived in a structure containing
two or more dwelling units most of their lives. The comparable statistic for
Milltown was 45.5%. The remaining 54.5% had lived most of their lives in a
single-family dwelling unit. Not one indicated having lived in housing
containing more than four dwelling units most of their lives. Nearly 13%
(12.8) of the Lakeside 1 category had lived most of their lives in an
apartment complex of five or more separate dwellings. For the experimental group the figure was exactly 12%. Also a slightly larger proportion (68 as compared to 61.5%) of those in this group as compared to those
in Lakeside 1 had lived in a building containing two or more dwelling units
most of their lives. Finally, slightly more than 38% (38.4) of those in
Lakeside 1 and 32% of those in the experimental group were most accustomed to residence within a single-family dwelling.

Consistent with hypothesized expectations, scores were lower after
the move for those accustomed to living in multiple dwellings but higher
for those more familiar with living in a single-family unit.

To get a broader and different slant on those findings, "type of dwelling unit lived in most of life" was treated as an ordinal variable and related
to the four possible scale scores. The expectation is that scale scores would
decrease from those respondents accustomed to living in a single-family
dwelling unit to those most familiar with residence in an apartment complex of five or more units. As indicated in Table 14.2, the measures of
association for Milltown respondents are the highest with the exception of

TABLE 14.2. The Relationship (Gamma) between Type of Dwelling Unit Lived
in Most of Life and Alienation

Alienation Measures	Experimental Group (N = 30)		Lakeside 1 (N = 87)	Milltown (N = 29)
	Before the Move	After the Move		
Total score	.27	.10	−.10	.38
Powerlessness	.25	.09	.12	.51
Social Isolation	.51	.35	.28	.29
Normlessness	.09	−.05	−.001	.59

the statistics on Social Isolation for the experimental group. Consistent with the trend indicated by total median scores, the "after" figures for the experimental group tend to be lower than those in the "before" column.

2. *The greater the amount of contact with outside friends and relatives, the lower the level of alienation.* Table 14.3 reports the relationship between alienation and frequency of visiting with and being visited by nontenant friends and relatives. All of the statistics for the experimental group are higher for visiting than being visited. The statistics for Lakeside 1 and Lakeside 2 are inconsistent. Those for Milltown are evenly split. The total alienation and Powerlessness statistics are higher in the visited than the visiting column, while the remaining figures are higher in the opposite direction. Consistently negative statistics suggest that frequency of contacts with outside friends and relatives has a positive influence on the tenant's state of mind. The fact that the only positive statistics appear in the pretested group (Lakeside 1) further implies that such contacts are more effective in mitigating sense of alienation after than before the move into public housing.

3. *As frequency of visiting with fellow tenants increases, the level of alienation decreases.* Frequency of contact with fellow tenants has the same positive effect as frequency of contact with outside friends and relatives.

4. *The greater the number of fellow tenants known before the move, the lower the level of alienation after the move.* It would appear that frequency of visiting with fellow tenants is influenced by the number known before the move. Data on this variable are available for the Lakeside 2 and Milltown samples, as the posttest called for respondents to identify the number of fellow tenants known before and after the move. With one exception (the Normlessness subscale statistic for the experimental group), as number of fellow tenants known both before and after the move increases, alienation scores decrease. The weight of the evidence suggests that number of friends is related to a decrease in level of measured alienation.

5. *The greater the amount of church attendance, the lower the level of alienation.* Because only two Milltown respondents are not Catholic, and since Catholics generally attend church more regularly than Protestants, separate computations were made for Catholic respondents for all groups except Lakeside 2. The trend of the data is generally consistent with the expectations of the hypothesis. That is, of the 40 statistics, 35 indicate that, as church attendance increases, alienation scores decrease. In spite of sharing this pattern, respondents in the experimental group and Milltown manifest certain differences when subscale statistics are compared (Table 14.4).

TABLE 14.3. The Relationship (Gamma) between Visiting with Nontenants and Alienation

| | Visiting with Nontenant Friends and Relatives | | | | | | | |
| | Experimental Group (N = 30) | | Lakeside 1 (N = 87) | | Lakeside 2 (N = 20) | | Milltown (N = 29) | |
Alienation Measures	Visited	Visiting	Visited	Visiting	Visited	Visiting	Visited	Visiting
Total score	-.18	-.32	.05	.02	-.19	-.33	-.35	-.23
Powerlessness	-.19	-.21	-.002	.05	-.17	-.17	-.45	-.06
Social Isolation	-.04	-.34	-.08	-.01	-.31	-.53	-.20	-.31
Normlessness	-.12	-.23	-.005	.03	-.11	-.11	-.21	-.22

TABLE 14.4. The Relationship (Gamma) between Church Attendance and Alienation

	Frequency of Church Attendance									
	Experimental Group				Lakeside 1		Lakeside 2		Milltown	
	Before the Move		After the Move				Before the Move	After the Move	Before the Move	After the Move
Alienation Measures	(N = 15)/(N = 30)		(N = 15)/(N = 30)		(N = 54)/(N = 87)		(N = 20)/(N = 20)		(N = 29)/(N = 29)	
	C^a	T^b	C	T	C	T	T	T	C	C
Total score	-.48	-.11	-.49	-.28	-.24	-.19	-.22	-.27	-.16	-.38
Powerlessness	-.52	-.32	-.85	-.39	-.22	-.23	-.22	-.35	-.16	-.19
Social Isolation	-.24	-.34	-.27	-.13	-.07	-.13	-.35	-.17	-.77	-.24
Normlessness	-.80	-.12	-.28	-.03	-.44	-.27	.12	.04	-.73	-.54

[a] Catholic respondents only.
[b] Total respondents.

For the experimental group, only the Social Isolation statistic indicates a negative aftereffect of the move. For Catholic respondents, only the Normlessness subscale statistic is inconsistent with the generally prevailing positive influence of the move. In the case of Milltown Catholic respondents, frequency of church attendance is related to expressions of greater Social Isolation and Normlessness after than before the move.

Summary and Interpretation

For the experimental group, only the Social Isolation statistic indicates a negative aftereffect of the move. For Catholic respondents, only the Normlessness subscale statistic is inconsistent with the generally prevailing positive influence of the move. In the case of Milltown Catholic respondents, greater frequency of church attendance is related to expressions of greater Social Isolation and Normlessness after than before the move.

The major hypothesis examined in the study concerning the relationship between level of alienation and the maintenance of established— and the acquisition of new—social relations was modestly but consistently supported. The five working hypotheses stating an expected negative relationship between alienation scale scores, and the following variables were supported in varying degrees by the findings:

1. Type of housing lived in most of life,
2. Frequency of visiting with "outside" friends and relatives,
3. Frequency of visiting with fellow tenants,
4. Number of fellow tenants known before the move, and
5. Frequency of church attendance before and after the move.

More than one factor may be invoked in order to account for these findings. Weaknesses in the experimental design and a relatively low response rate for both the experimental group and Milltown populations readily come to mind. On the positive side they may be mostly the product of the move into an age-segregated housing unit. Recent research (for example, Teaff et al., 1978) has shown that the elderly who live in age-segregated environments evidence a greater sense of social and psychological well-being than those who do not. On the negative side is the possibility that alienation among the elderly is extremely difficult to mitigate because of the overwhelming impact of physical deterioration and social isolation from the mainstream. In spite of the importance of these and other possibilities, the most important factor may be the different conceptions of and administrative responses to the move by officials of the two housing authorities.

Those in charge of the Lakeside unit assumed that considerable planning for the needs of its occupants was in order because many would be giving up a familiar way of life for a new and unfamiliar one. This led them to hire a social worker *before* the move to anticipate, and identify, tenant problems and relate them to the administration and vice versa.

Milltown officials had a different conception of the move into their 5-story 53-unit building. For them, the unique feature of the move was that it would enable people to maintain, if not strengthen, established relationships and habits by providing them with the security of quality housing near to their previous homes and at a price they could afford. Church services, for example, are held in the Lakeside unit, while it is assumed that Milltown tenants will continue to attend the church of their choice. Furthermore, it was not thought necessary to facilitate social interaction because most Milltown tenants were well acquainted with each other prior to the move. It is possible that a different administrative definition of the situation might have led to a lower level of measured alienation in Milltown respondents after the move. Alienation scale scores were mitigated more by relationships established before than after the move. This suggests that it might have been helpful for administrators to show a greater concern for social organization with the unit.

That different administrative responses can influence degree of alienation among the elderly is demonstrated by the recent work of Dudley and Hillery (1977). They studied the relationship between degree of perceived freedom and alienation among the residents of homes for the aged. Alienation (as measured by the Dean scale) was lowest among those who perceived their basic freedoms to be the least curtailed by administrative practices. "At a minimum," they emphasize, "our research suggests that, in addition to the physical and social characteristics of the residents of homes for the aged, we must begin to consider the structural characteristics of their feeling of alienation and deprivation of freedom" (p. 145). It remains to be determined which types of administrative response can best fulfill the needs and expectations and alleviate the fears and doubts of the tenants of homes for the aged. It is becoming increasingly clear, however, that what administrators think and do can influence the degree of alienation experienced by the elderly in public housing.

References

Brand, Frederick N., and Smith, Richard T. Life adjustment and relocation of the elderly. *Journal of Gerontology*, 1974, *29*, 336–340.

Carp, Frances M. *A future for the aged*. Austin and London: University of Texas Press, 1966.

Cumming, Elaine, and Henry, William E. *Growing old: The process of disengagement*. New York: Basic Books, 1961.

Dean, Dwight G. Alienation: Its meaning and measurement. *American Sociological Review*, 1961, *26*, 753–758.

Dudley, Charles J., and Hillery, George A., Jr. Freedom and alienation in homes for the aged. *Gerontologist*, 1977, *17*, 140–145.

Ellison, David L. Alienation and the will to live. *Journal of Gerontology*, 1969, *24*, 361–367.

Field, Minna. *Aging with honor and dignity*. Springfield, Ill.: Thomas, 1968.

Lawton, M. Powell, and Cohen, Jacob. The generality of housing impact on the well-being of older people. *Journal of Gerontology*, 1974, *29*, 194–204.

Miller, Delbert C. *Handbook of research design and social measurement*. New York: McKay, 1970.

Neal, Arthur G., and Rettig, Salomon. On the multidimensionality of alienation. *American Sociological Review*, 1967, *32*, 54–64.

Niebanck, Paul L. *Relocation in urban planning: From obstacle to opportunity*. Philadelphia: University of Pennsylvania Press, 1968.

Rhode Island Council of Community Services. *An analysis of the social functioning of elderly residents relocated from the central-classical area of Providence, Rhode Island*, 1966.

Shanas, Ethel. A note on restriction of life space: Attitudes of age cohorts. *Journal of Health and Social Behavior*, 1968, *9*, 86–90.

Shanas, Ethel. Aging and life space in Poland and the United States. *Journal of Health and Social Behavior*, 1970, (Sept) *11* (3), 183–190.

Simmons, J. L. Some intercorrelations among alienation measures. *Social Forces*, 1966, *44*, 370–372.

Teaff, Joseph D.; Lawton, M. Powell; Nahemow, Lucille; and Carlson, Diane. Impact of age integration on the well-being of elderly tenants in public housing. *Journal of Gerontology*, 1978, *33*, 126–133.

15

Aging
in the Israeli Kibbutz:
Where the Old
Are Not Forgotten

Harold J. Wershow

The kibbutz is a unique laboratory for research in aging in that it provides as totally secure a material setting for aging as can be found in the world, with the possible exception of aristocratic extended families in non-Western societies. Initial findings in a continuing investigation of aging in the Israeli Kibbutz were reported in an earlier paper.[1] This chapter is a further attempt at quantification of the success of the kibbutz in producing a healthy gerontic population.

The Participants and the Research Setting

The participants studied were residents of five long-established kibbutzim of varying size and organizational affiliation. There are several kibbutz movements, which differ in their devotion to strict communitarian ideology and religious observance. The five kibbutzim all belonged to two more middle-of-the-road, nonreligious movements. Three kibbutzim were among the larger ones; one with 600–1,100 inhabitants; one with less than 500; and the fifth with a bit over 250. It was hoped that the total universe of those over 65 in the five kibbutzim would participate in the study; actually only 45% did: 55% of the males, and 37% of the females ($N=77$ men and 60 women).

Reprinted with permission from *International Journal of Aging and Human Development*, 1973, *4*, 211–227. This study was supported by the University of Alabama Research Grants Committee and International Opportunity Program. The aid of the Union of the Kibbutz Movements, Mr. Shlomo Rozen, M. K., Chairman, and the Union's Committee on Aging, Mr. Eli Freier, past Chairman and Mr. Shmuel Schachar, present Chairman, are gratefully acknowledged, as is the assistance of Miss Shoshana Shomer and Miss Sima Rafelovitch, who worked indefatigably as research assistants.

Two questions arise: How representative are the respondents of their kibbutzim and of the kibbutz aged in general, and what generalizations may be made beyond the kibbutz aged? Kibbutz aged are, in some respects, very much like those Jewish aged studied in the United States. They came from traditional Jewish homes, either Orthodox or less Orthodox but Yiddish-speaking; from the Pale of Settlement of the old Russian Empire (the Pale included small towns and villages of the western territories of Imperial Russia—the Baltic states and Poland, where Jews could live with less restriction than in Russia proper); and from the eastern provinces of the Austro-Hungarian Empire, Galician Poland, Carpatho-Ukraine, and the Bucovinian area of Rumania.[2] In this respect, they are similar to the Jewish aged studied by other American investigators.[3-5].

In other respects, this is a group *sui generis*. First, they are remarkably well-educated. Over 40% speak at least three languages (Hebrew, Yiddish, and the language of their country of origin), and a half of those speak four or five. Virtually all came to what was then Palestine in their teens or early 20s and have been in their present kibbutz or a predecessor for at least 30 years. This is a generation of "George Washingtons," who drained swamps, endured privation which killed many of their comrades,[6] integrated into newly born Israel the unprecedented immigration from concentration camps and feudal Arab monarchies, and were, for a long time, the elite of the Yishuv (the Jewish community of Israel). They were leaders and role models for the entire society—a distillate of 40 years of pioneering (for about five times as many people went through the kibbutz as "stuck it out," finding it, or themselves, wanting).

How representative are these aged of older people in kibbutzim? As Bettelheim recognizes, kibbutzim differ greatly in many respects—size, proportion of population of different ages, child-rearing practices, etc.[7] However, all adhere to the precepts of economic egalitarianism, providing the aged with security, dependence on the community (not offspring) for major assistance, and the assurance of continued living (barring only the contingency of extreme chronic disability) in the community which they founded.

The kibbutzim which were investigated were more prototypical than typical. They are among the oldest kibbutzim and have appreciable proportions of older people. Of the 50 kibbutzim surveyed, only 2.5% of the population is over 65 compared with 7% to 12% in these five kibbutzim. By 1975 the proportion of the aged in the kibbutzim as a whole will rise to 15%.*

*This projection preceded the Six-Day War, with its consequent revival of pioneering ideals and the need to establish many kibbutz outposts in the Golan Heights and the Judean desert.

In this sense, the five kibbutzim are prototypical. The kibbutz aged are atypical of the Western aged, in that males are a majority in the 65+ (59%) age group of the three older movements.[8] Of the respondents, 59% are similarly male, though only 49% of the aged in these five kibbutzim are male. Half of the respondents are 70 years of age or older, somewhat more than their proportion in the population of these five kibbutzim, in which 44% of the aged are 70 or older. So the respondents are not unduly unrepresentative in age and sex distribution of either their kibbutzim or their movements, to the limited extent that comparative data exist. The only other data available in the two reports of the Union of Kibbutz Movements concern occupational distribution.[8,9] In this respect, a smaller proportion of respondents are active in agriculture, trades, and industry (40% of the males and 22% of the females), whereas in the 50 older kibbutzim older people comprise 40% (breakdowns by sex are not reported) of those active in these "productive" branches, and a smaller proportion work in services.[8] Other aspects of the occupational roles of *vatikim* are discussed in a later section. In other respects, the problem of ascertaining the representativeness of volunteers needs no explanation. We suspect that those *vatikim* (a kibbutz veteran is known as a *vatik*, "an old hand"—plural, *vatikim*) who consented to be interviewed were among the mentally healthier, more secure people in the kibbutz, who felt that they could honorably represent their kibbutz, and kibbutz aged in general, to a foreign (even though known to be sympathetic) investigator. We also suspect that their answers to questions with mental health parameters, which tend to elicit anxiety, were often answered counterphobically, with a fearful denying "Never!" where "hardly ever" or "not often" would have been an appropriate reply. Nevertheless, this study has value in establishing some hypotheses for more intensive investigation with another sample employing more sensitive measuring instruments.[10]

Method

Having previously experienced difficulty with conducting long interviews in the hustle and bustle of the summer work schedule in agricultural communes plagued with a chronic labor shortage, the investigator prepared a highly structured questionnaire largely based on the work of Kutner.[11] It was hoped it could be administered in groups. The questionnaire had to be employed as a highly structured interview schedule, as numerous errors and omissions were made in group administration.

However noncomparable this group may be to any other group, it is of interest to make certain comparisons with certain other groups, which are described in Appendix A, to establish some bench marks of morale, health, etc., relative to aged living in other societies.

Findings

The respondents appear to be generally alert, interested, and healthy. Similar to Spanish-American War veterans,[12,13] they appeared to be younger than their chronological age and physically vigorous, striding uphill and down faster than the investigator, who could hardly keep up with them. Many, (30% of the men and 12% of the women,) work in agriculture, and only 2% are retired. In all the kibbutz movements, 7% of those 65+ are retired; in Denmark 62% of the males 65+ are retired; in Great Britain, 72%; in the United States, 68%.[14] Their work history and attitudes toward work are discussed in greater detail in a later section.

Marital Status

The marital status of the respondents corresponds more nearly to that of urbanized Western societies than it does to that of even Westernized sectors of the Israeli population. A smaller proportion is currently married and there are twice as many single people as in the urban Israeli population of Western origin of the same age group.

Educational Level

The *vatikim* are well educated for their generation by any standards (see Table 15.1), even that of surviving U.S. Spanish-American War veterans, an elite group of octogenarians.[13] Only two men (3%) and one women (2%) have no formal education, in contrast with the U.S. urban population's illiteracy rate of 7%. It cannot be assumed, as it can in the United States, that these respondents are therefore illiterate. Those who were not educated in the Czarist and Bolshevik Siberian exile have attended many kibbutz courses in the slack winter season.

Occupational Status

The modal first employment upon migrating to Palestine in the immediate post–World War I years was road building. The British mandatory power's first task was to establish an economic infrastructure in the desolate backwash of the Ottoman Empire, and a road system was imperative. As kibbutzim were founded and grew, members gradually learned specialized jobs in various work areas and often sought expertise in branches of agriculture, especially the valued, income-producing branches—grain

TABLE 15.1.   Comparative Educational Level of Respondents (by Percentages)

Level	Vatikim	U.S. 1960 Census 65 and Over [a]	Spanish-American War Veterans
Less than 12 grades	40	79	
High school graduate	37	12	
Some college[b]	22	10	17

[a]Urban whites only.
[b]Includes rabbinical training in a Yeshiva (seminary of European vintage).

crops, dairy, fruits and vegetables, fodder, and poultry. Of the men, 62%, and of the women, 32%, worked in various agricultural branches in their prime productive ages of 40–50. Another 37% of the women worked in child rearing and education.

Even in the kibbutz, aging leads to occupational downgrading. The proportion of men in agriculture has halved and the proportion in services has quadrupled, from 6% to 27%. In the kibbutz value system, agriculture is the highest calling, because of its role in redeeming the land; income-producing activities are also highly valued, but service occupations are held in lower esteem.[15] Services include those non-income-producing activities necessary to keep the commune functioning—feeding and cloth-ing the inhabitants. Even those who remained in the agricultural area have largely been downgraded from managerial and technical experts to such mundane tasks as picking olives. The women have moved into services to a greater extent then the men; their agricultural role has decreased to 12%; in education and child rearing, to 8% (change in the kibbutz child-rearing philosophy, particularly the role of the mother, aiding this change by deposing the older child-rearing personnel who could not adjust); and in service occupations, from 18% to 65%—a large increase. Despite their downgrading, and even though people over 65 are not required to work more than 3 hours daily and may freely exercise their option to work fewer hours, 21% of the men work 8 hours a day or more; 27%, from 6 to 8 hours. (Corresponding figures for women are 3% and 19%.) Half the men and 75% of the women work 3–6 hours daily; only one man works less than 3 hours, and one man and two women do not work at all. It is curious to note that at one time there was a group of nonmember parents of kibbutzniks resident in the kibbutz who were brought over from Europe in the depression 1930s or the immediate postwar years—then often younger than the *vatikim* are today—who were not expected to work and many did not do so. This set no precedent for the action of these old pioneers.

Despite their downgrading in work responsibility and status, this is a generation of Jews imbued with the Protestant ethic, who enjoy work as a calling, which can be seen in the replies to the question, "How much do you enjoy your work now? How much did you enjoy it between ages 40 and 50?" These replies are tabulated in Table 15.2.

It is evident that most enjoyed their work either "very much" or "fairly well" today and also in the past. How does this compare with other aged? In the Yorkville sample, of those still working, 86% enjoy their work very much or fairly well (an identical proportion of our respondents give the same replies, when sexes are merged). In the Cross-National Study, 73–77% of the not-retired men want to work till the end; 79% of the Spanish-American War veterans worked at least parttime beyond the age of 65; 1% are still working in their late 70s and 80s. It is of interest to note that, while the Yorkville sample was heavily weighted to a lower socioeconomic strata who required work to maintain life, the Spanish-American War veterans, or almost half of them, had more nearly an adequate income. The evidence suggests that work is of some importance to the well-being of older people raised in the Protestant ethic, and these Jews were raised that way, at least as far as the work ethic is concerned.

Work has a different meaning to men and women on the kibbutz, which may be significant in the differential adjustment of the sexes. In the beginning, women worked alongside the men; they tilled the fields, rode the tractors, and participated directly in redeeming the land. As time wore on, as children arrived, women were drawn into child rearing and household maintenance functions. Some came to feel

> that the kibbutz did not provide opportunity for the kind of family life which they desired—the opportunity for the wife to keep her own house, raise her children by herself and provide for her husband's personal needs. In the kibbutz, they felt, this work was dull and uninteresting; it had meaning only if it was done in one's own home. The women of the family felt this difference most keenly. (pp. 184, 162–166)[15]

What the kibbutz refers to as "the Problem of Women" should be kept in mind when the questions of morale are discussed in a later section.

TABLE 15.2. Respondents' Enjoyment of Work (By Percentages)

Extent of Enjoyment of Work	Males		Females	
	Age 40–50	*Now*	*Age 40–50*	*Now*
Very much	63	44	67	33
Fairly well	33	47	32	48
Not so much or not at all	3	6	1	15

Health Status

The health self-rating of the kibbutz respondents is high in relation to all of the comparison groups (Table 15.3). The kibbutz *vatikim* rate themselves in "good" or "excellent" health more than the urban Israeli sample and rate themselves "fair" more and "poor" less than the samples from the Western countries. The difference between the other samples (even the United States) and Yorkville may be owing to the lack of health care for the medically indigent in the 1950s when Kutner did his study and to the relatively more adequate provision in the European "welfare states" and the United States a decade later.[11]

Again, it must be remembered that the kibbutz respondents are a highly selected group, the survivors who remained in a rigorous environment which drove off or killed off more people than survived to the present relatively affluent society of the older kibbutzim.

It may be of interest to mention the respondents' view of their health care. In common with 75% of the Israeli population, the kibbutzim are served medically by Kupat Cholim, the Worker's Sick Fund of the General Federation of Labor (Histadruth). An additional 9% of the populace is served by other sick funds. The fund is modeled on the British system of medical care, in which day-to-day medical care is carried out by general practitioners in neighborhood clinics and extraordinary measures in hospitals by specialists, with less than optimal liaison between the two groups. One striking observation is the lack of understanding of the concept of preventive health care in Israel (not limited to kibbutzim). A majoritiy of the respondents (51% of the males, 58% of the females) did not feel that an annual health checkup was advisable. However, members of the Sick Fund, and all residents of the kibbutz are automatically enrolled and have virtually unlimited access to their local general practitioner, who is either

TABLE 15.3.   Health Self-rating, Kibbutz *Vatikim* and Various Other Groups

Self-rating of Health	Respondents		Israel		Denmark		Great Britain		United States		Yorkville	
	M	F	M	F	M	F	M	F	M	F	High	Low[a]
Good or excellent	53	46	28	16	56	49	61	54	55	51	67	46
Fair	41	47	45	45	29	35	27	31	28	31		
Poor	6	7	27	39	15	16	12	16	17	18	33	54

[a]High and low status group.

resident in the kibbutz (if a larger one) or has office hours there several days a week. Being old and therefore possessed of several chronic complaints, they may see their physician frequently and see no reason for special checkups. Practically all who avail themselves of the medical care view it as either "excellent" or "good"; a negligible two men see it as "poor." However, a third of these kibbutz elders never get a medical checkup, and an additional 15% of the men (and 3% of the women) never make use of the health care available. It became obvious to us that a number of men are health faddists of one kind or another, a curious phenomenon in view of their acceptance of the most modern practices in agriculture: weighing and measuring every egg laid, or pail of milk drawn, and following the latest research findings in agriculture, yet indifferent to modern medicine for their own needs. It takes a stubborn individualist to choose this pioneering life, evidence for which appears in several contexts.

Loneliness and Isolation

It was unexpected that evidences of loneliness would exist in the organic community of the kibbutz, where people have lived in close proximity for decades. As an example, 50% of the men and 42% of the women spend no time visiting with close friends in the kibbutz. Among the men, 18%, and among the women, 7%, never had a close friend; an additional 8% of the men and 7% of the women claim that their close friends have either left the kibbutz or died. Thus, a total of 25% of the men and 15% of the women presently have no close friends. An identical proportion (with probably a good deal of overlap) have no friends outside the kibbutz. Tea time (the kibbutz social hour par excellence) is spent alone by 19% of the men and 34% of the women. There are 25% who do not visit children and grandchildren (this figure probably includes many who are either unmarried or without issue). At least 14% of the men, and 9% of the women, with spouses, claim to spend little or no time conversing with them. This section again attests to their stubborn individualism and to a measure of orneriness.

Changes in Activity

Respondents were asked whether they engaged in certain activities more, less, or the same as they had 5 years ago (or if they never engaged in that activity). Activities were classified (a modification of Bengtson's scheme[16]) as:

> *Familial-intimate*—sitting and chatting with spouse, visiting children and grandchildren, visiting with friends in or out of the kibbutz.

Individual—reading, listening to the radio, gardening, letter writing, engaging in a hobby.

Group—attending meetings of the kibbutz, one's political party, or other associations; going to lectures, movies, classes.

With a small number of elders and a large number of permutations of increases and decreases in these activity constellations, it was possible to do no more than count the individuals whose acitivity increased or decreased in each constellation. In all constellations, more people lose activities than gain, except for individual activities, where more women gain than men. Though none are statistically significant, the relative losses are greatest for group activities and greater for men than for women (as women engage in these activities less at all ages)—another indication of the "Problem of the Women" in the kibbutz.

As might be expected of older people, they listen to the radio more (TV was then still a very new and sometime thing in Israel) and read less than they did 5 years ago, when their vision was presumably better. Many who can do so continue to garden. They engage less in politics and running the kibbutz, though 42% of both men and women continue to attend the weekly kibbutz general meeting (the town meeting which is the ultimate governing body of the kibbutz).

Morale and Self-image

The attempt to employ Kutner's "morale" and "self-image" scales was disappointing and led us to question the utility of scales consisting of questions chosen without regard for a coherent theory of personality structure and unvalidated by factor analysis even when the items scale by Guttman techniques, as Kutner's do, with the population he employed.[11] For example, the extent to which one plans ahead has no necessary relationship to the degree to which one regrets the chances one missed to do a better job of living. As McNemar pointed out long ago,

> The burden of proof as to whether an attitude as measured does follow a single dimension falls upon the one who constructs the measuring scale . . . that individuals may give similar responses but for different reasons is an obvious possibility. . . . It seems obvious that morale is not an entity, that there are many "morales," that there has been an open season for calling a wide variety of things by the name of morale . . . and that much of the available research on morale suffers from a lack of hard-boiled critical mindedness.[17]

Perhaps the dramatic setting of beleaguered Israel brought out more clearly the problems raised by hit-or-miss questions. For example, when asked, "On the whole, how satisfied would you say you are with your way of life today?" the responses were often, "How can I be satisfied, with the problems on our frontiers?" or "What does my personal dissatisfaction matter, with the establishment of the State of Israel in my lifetime?" The various dimensions that this question might arouse are reminiscent of the famous question reported in Jahoda, Deutsch, and Cook: "After the war, would you rather have the country remain pretty much as it was before the war?"[18] There is no way of knowing, with a "yes" or "no" answer and no further probing, whether respondents referred to foreign or domestic policy, to continuation of wage and price controls, to reversion to prewar depression, or to some other aspect of society.

When some "old chestnuts" designed to evoke responses of "morale," are closely examined, weaknesses of the individual items become apparent. "As you get older, would you say things are better or worse than you thought they would be?" What things? In an American context, prices are higher, but we have social security today. We have the atom bomb, but we have virtually conquered childhood epidemic diseases. Any of us gerontologists would probably answer such a question differently, using a different frame of reference, if we were asked it every 5 minutes. Where do we get the chutzpah* to score a multidimensional question as though it had some consistent meaning?

"How often do you" . . . "regret the chances you missed"; . . . "feel bitter"; . . . "feel there's no point in living?" etc. Don't we all on one occasion or another "feel bitter" . . . or "regret the chance" not to have become department head, or dean, or joined the faculty of Prestigious U? How often is often?

And is it necessarily a negative symptom that one did "regret chances," "feel bitter," or "find unhappiness" on occasion?

"How much do you plan ahead the things you will be doing next week or the week after?" In our work-structured schedules, we plan to be in class next week, and the week after, and every week of this semester. But how much do we plan for the use of vacation time, which is more analogous to the structure of retirement? Is the person who plans more rigidly for the use of his or her vacation mentally healthier, or does he or she have higher morale than the person who makes fewer vacation plans and prefers a more spontaneously structured day? We can conjecture that this question is meant to discover the apathetic, withdrawn individuals, but may it not also tap an unknown quantity of creative, spontaneous souls who do not fit into our stereotypes of aging? Is our model of mental health the simple, unconflicted, bovine individual? And is this a valid model, at any age?

*"Chutzpah = gall, brazen nerve . . . presumption—plus—arrogance such as no other word, and no other language, can do justice to" (pp. 92–93).[19]

A further caution is necessary about accepting at face value "yes" or "no" questions about morale items. It was readily apparent in our questioning that a number of Israeli responses to such questions as have been mentioned were exercises in massive denial. There is nobody who "never" experiences unhappiness, bitterness, or regret; yet, there were a number of respondents who completely denied ever having had such feelings. To lump those together with others who admit having experienced mildly negative feelings is to lump together the sicker and the well; yet this goes on all the time in our research on aging.

These caveats may help to explain the wild fluctuations of morale and self-image of the two sexes, various age groups, and Yorkville[11] and kibbutz comparisons, when controlled for health and age self-perception, marital status, having friends, spending tea time alone, and visiting with children. The only statistically significant relationships are: Kibbutz men have higher morale than women (but not self-image) in both the married and other (usually widowed) states. Nonmarried kibbutz women have lower morale than married women; male morale does not differ between the marital statuses. Morale is related to good health self-perception for kibbutz males but not for females. More men of 70 and older have medium morale in the kibbutz than in Yorkville; kibbutz women have higher morale at ages 65–69 and 70+. There are no significant relationships between morale or self-image and having positive relationships with friends, children, or tea-time companions. We suggest that morale questions evoke more counterphobic responses in the kibbutz than in Yorkville and that kibbutz elders are less vulnerable to the loss of friendship and family ties than those living in other societies. The kibbutz "automatically" provides at least minimal social relationships in the mess hall, cinema, and at work, which almost makes impossible the stark isolation which can affect the aged in the urban West.

About the only consistent finding is that in virtually all attitudinal measures (health self-perception, morale, self-image) kibbutz respondents tend to cluster in the median ranges. People whose origins are in cultures in which notions of the "evil-eye" flourish do not court ill-fortune by suggesting that their situation is overly auspicious. No matter how rational and emancipated they may be, language patterns persist, to the point that one hears frequently and quite naturally such phrases as, "I, thank God, am an atheist." Few would answer "excellent" when quizzed; the more usual answer is a guarded circumlocution such as "Praise the Lord, it could be worse," or "Not bad, all things considered." "Excellent, good, fair, or poor" are exactly translatable into Hebrew or Yiddish, but the connotations are quite different. Comparisons with "stiff upper lip" cultures, in which "Fine" or "Excellent" is the expected answer should be made with the greatest caution.

Some rationalizations can doubtless be contrived to explain away the contradictory findings. Social scientists are adept at the game of post hoc explanations. It is better to leave the reality unencumbered with jargon. Many of the *vatikim* may be relatively solitary and stubborn, even a bit sour in spite of the success of their youthful endeavor, yet demonstrate unquestioned competence in livng. As Lawton wrote in discussing an earlier draft of this chapter, "You very rightly question the meaning of a 'low morale' response—to me, this is a fascinating illustration of how success in living may be relatively independent of 'morale,' as traditionally measured."[20] We have elsewhere suggested that "sweetness and light," with the amount of psychic energy spent in the denial that such a stance demands, is an inappropriate affect for the elderly.[5] Our culture may foster it, but far more appropriate is a "bitter-sweet" stance that recognizes and deals with undeniable realities of aging. We should, perhaps, question some of the WASP-ish assumptions that go into our scales about which those of us who stem from circum-Mediterranean or east-European ethnics should know better.

This research experience has convinced us that research endeavors employing questionnaires based on no more than casual familiarity with the populations studied are quite futile. The more seminal studies of American society that have (in our estimation) advanced our understanding of this society the most, are not those studies with many respondents and great methodological rigor, but rather are those which have resulted from a longer period of immersion in the milieu with the respondents, achieving some insights, which may then become the basis for more rigorous hypothesis testing. Often, these much-touted consequences of methodological rigor do not occur. The contributions of Lynd and Lynd, of Hollingshead, of Whyte, and of Liebow fructify our understanding in three dimensions as do few methodologically traditional investigations.[21-25] If this is true for our own culture, how much more necessary is an immersion in a foreign culture to produce a piece of research that can pass muster? It might not be a bad idea to require investigators to replicate their studies in another cultural milieu before publication. This type of replication can turn up deficiencies in method and raise questions as to conclusions that can be provided in no other way. This test would be more rigorous than is a large number of people superficially examined. As McNemar pithily stated a generation ago, "A consensus of worthless opinion is a worthless consensus of opinion."[17]

We would also suggest that kibbutz aged are good subjects for studying factors contributing to longevity. Studies of Spanish-American War veterans indicate that longevity seems to be related to:

1. Higher educational attainment.
2. Late retirement, after many years in the same occupation.

3. Adequate financial status.
4. Having few children.
5. Coming from families of origin with many children.
6. Living in one's own home.
7. Belonging to at least one social organization.
8. Keeping up with current events.
9. Tending to minimize, repress, and deny disappointments and trauma.
10. Marriage at mature age (i.e., not a teenager) to a girl several years younger of similar social, ethnic, and religious background, and of similar interests.
11. Youthful participation in a patriotic and venturesome experience.[12,13]

The kibbutz aged generally fulfill all these criteria. We would suggest that they are excellent subjects for a prospective study of longevity. Many variables, including diet, can be controlled, as living conditions are quite invariant from one kibbutz to another. The additional requirement of longevous parents cannot be fulfilled, as most of their parents perished in the Holocaust.

Anecdotal Observations

Each kibbutz has an individual flavor with regard to its concern for the problems of the aged. We suggest, in general, and on the basis of our limited observation, that ability to cope with problems of aging is directly related to the size of the kibbutz. The largest kibbutzim have even started to absorb their older labor force—although not always successfully. First of all, *vatikim* who have spent their productive years in agriculture, the kibbutz ideal, do not always take easily to the noises and artificial rhythm of the factory. Second, if the factory is a profitable industry, it tends to be run by the most qualified; if it is unprofitable, it is not worth the investment of capital.

The larger kibbutzim with a greater volume of service and consumption needs (laundry, clothing and shoe fabrication and repair, warehousing, etc.) have found suitable work slots for the aged more readily than did the smaller, and this seemed to be the major factor in whether the aged were, or were not, considered a problem in the kibbutz. Also, it may be that smaller kibbutzim, because they are more *gemainschaftlich* in character, are more aware of the problems of oldsters. An additional factor may be the sheer number of aged. The larger, long-established kibbutzim contain 70 or 80 people over 65; the medium and smaller from 20 to 40. The percen-

tage of aged in these five kibbutzim ranges from 7% of the total population
to 12%, compared with 5.5% and 8.5% of the population of 36 older
kibbutzim in the two movements.[8]

Our perception of the relationship of size and problems of aging may
have been colored by a fortuitous circumstance. The smallest kibbutz was
founded by followers of A. D. Gordon, a Socialist-Zionist philosopher who
extolled the simple life of working in the fields with one's hands and who
deemphasized labor-saving devices. Some elders here feel particularly
betrayed by their children's attraction to farm machinery and labor-saving
devices in general. The other *vatikim*, who also began with primitive
agricultural implements, say rather good naturedly:

> It took our children to teach us that there is no great virtue in breaking your
> back. We came out of the ghettos of Eastern Europe in which Jews were
> prohibited from owning and working on the land, so to us work was an ideal.
> To our children work is no longer an ideal, it's the way you earn your living.

There are some minor tragedies associated with the contrasting viewpoints of the *vatikim* and their sabra (Israeli-born) children. The first
generation built a sheep and goat's milk (from which Levantine cheeses are
made) industry. As King David, they delighted in being shepherds in the
renewed land of Israel. Agricultural experts come from all over the world to
learn, from these children of Russia's ghettos, how to raise milch sheep and
goats. This industry, born in romance, will die with this generation, for the
sabras have not the patience to spend their lives herding sheep. There will
be no more emulators of King David when the present generation can no
longer perform this task, and they will feel the loss keenly.

In our earlier paper, we commented on the observations of Yonina
Talmon.[26,27] She found a *vatik* population that seemed to be suffering the
pangs of aging beyond our own observations. We explained the discrepancy in our findings as lying

> in the delay between Dr. Talmon's research and this effort, a period of
> approximately 10 years. At that time, her Ss were in their mid-fifties, going
> through the difficult process of getting out of the driver's seat and handing
> over the kibbutz administration to younger people. That process is now
> completed.[11]

We can comment further on the accuracy of Talmon's observations, that,
where the process of generational succession is still uncompleted, problems are created. The supervisor of one work branch in the "Gordonist"
settlement confided that he would like to retire from such responsibility
but he dared not. He would be succeeded by "youngsters" (probably in

their 40s) who cared not about seeing that a full day's work was done by all. He was hanging on, as he put it, by his fingernails for as long as he could.

Another incident: The Secretariat of a kibbutz consulted with us about this problem. An elder was in charge of an agricultural work branch which he had developed. He taught himself English and statistics so that he could understand American agricultural manuals, and he adapted U.S. methods to this subtropical climate. He was indeed a pioneer in his time, but today there are younger men, fully trained graduates of agricultural schools, waiting to step into his shoes. What to do? I suggested the kibbutz might want to institutionalize the American rite de passage of the farewell banquet and the gold watch, to which the Secretary replied, "We can't do that! If we do not employ more humane methods than the rest of the world, what reason is there for the kibbutz?" Thus does the kibbutz act toward its elders, so that they may end their years with a modicum of respect and dignity too often denied old people in the larger society. No social system can shield one from the eventualities of illness, loss of spouse, and death, but the kibbutz can provide social security (in the fullest sense of the term *social* and absorb the problems of aging with less problem than an individual's children are able to do.

Appendix

Composition and Source of Comparison Groups

Older Population of 22 Kibbutzim[9] is a statistical survey of all the aged (women 50+ and men 55+) in 22 older kibbutzim, including the 3 large kibbutzim from which most of the subjects of this report were drawn. This report deals almost exclusively with the occupational distribution of the older workers. Certain data were abstracted out for the 12 kibbutzim, which belong to the same movements as do the 5 kibbutzim studied.

Older Population of 50 Kibbutzim[8] is a statistical survey of all the aged (same ages as the 1966 report) of 50 kibbutzim, including all 41 of the oldest and 9 additional older kibbutzim. Included are all 5 kibbutzim from which the respondents of this report are drawn. This report also deals largely with the occupational distribution of the older workers.

Urban Jewish Aged of Israel[28] is part of the Cross-National Study of aging. It includes an area-probability sampling of 1,500 persons drawn from voter lists (supplemented by house-to-house screening for elders not on the lists) who were Jewish, over 65, and lived in nonrural areas.

This study, in addition to the focuses dealt with in the Cross-National Study, dealt with questions of time of immigration and culture of origin. Comparisons have herein been made only with Jews of European extraction, as there are virtually no kibbutz *vatikim* from North Africa or Asiatic countries.

Cross-National Sample of Ages in Denmark, Great Britain, and the U.S.A.[14] comprises an area probability sample of 2,500 persons in each country, aged 65+ and noninstitutionalized. The focus of this study was much broader than the Israeli kibbutz occupational focus, as it concentrates on level of physical functioning, retirement, social and financial supports, services needed, and interrelationships of these factors.

The Spanish-American War Veterans Study[12,13] is a study of 149 octogenarian males, veterans of the Spanish-American War, who attended the Boston Veterans' Administration Outpatient Clinic. This is a largely native American, New England group; it is employed because it gives some hints of factors involved in longevity which may apply to the kibbutz aged.

The Yorkville Study[11] is a survey of a sample of 500 aged 65+, who lived in the area of New York City served by the Yorkville–Kips Bay Health District. This is a sample of great heterogeneity of religion, income, and nationality, and they are in an area of great density of population of elderly (the five kibbutzim has a total of 300 older people; Yorkville has an average of 138 per city block). The sample was deliberately weighted toward the lower socioeconomic strata; but wherever data were available, kibbutz comparisons were made with the high-status Yorkville group, as kibbutznikim were very high-status people indeed in their prime and, to an extent, still are.

References

1. Wershow, H. J. Aging in the Israeli kibbutz. *Gerontologist*, 1969, *9*, 300–304.
2. Zborowski, M., and Herzog, E. *Life is with people: The culture of the shtetl*. New York: International Universities Press, 1952.
3. Abrams, A.; Tobin, S. S.; Gordon, P.; Pechtel, C.; and Hilkevitch, A. The effects of a European procaine preparations in an aged population: I. Psychological effects. *Journal of Gerontology*, 1964, *20*, 139–143.
4. Lieberman, M. A.; Prock, U. N.; and Tobin, S. S. Psychological effects of institutionalization. *Journal of Gerontology*, 1968, *23*, 343–353.
5. Wershow, H. J. The older Jews of Albany Park: Some aspects of a subculture of

the aged and its interaction with a gerontological research project. *Gerontologist*, 1964, *4*, 198–202.

6. Baratz, J. A. *A village by the Jordan: The story of Degania*. New York: Sharon, 1957.

7. Bettelheim, B. *Children of the dream*. New York and London: Macmillan, 1969.

8. Union of Kibbutz Movements. Research in the kibbutzim on the problems of aging. Part II, November 1967, Tel Aviv, mimeo, in Hebrew.

9. Union of Kibbutz Movements. Research in the kibbutzim on the problems of aging. Part I, August 1966, Tel Aviv, mimeo in Hebrew.

10. Wershow, H. J. On asking questions meaningfully in gerontological research on morale, unpublished manuscript, 1970.

11. Kutner, B.; Fanshel, D.; Togo, A. M.; and Langer, T. S. *Five hundred over sixty*. New York: Russell Sage Foundation, 1956.

12. Rose, C. L. Social factors in longevity. *Gerontologist*, 1964, *4*, 27–37.

13. Nichols, M., and Cummins, J. Social adjustment of Spanish-American War veterans. *Geriatrics*, 1961, *16*, 641–646.

14. Shanas, E.; Townsend, P.; Wedderburn, D.; Friis, H.; Milhøj, P.; and Stehouwer, J. Old people in three industrial societies. New York: Atherton, 1968.

15. Weingarten, M. *Life in a kibbutz*. New York: Reconstructionist Press, 1959.

16. Bengtson, V. L. *Differences between sub-samples in level of present role-activity*, in R. J. Havighurst, J. M. A. Munnichs, B. Neugarten, and B. Thomae (Eds.), *Adjustment to retirement: A cross-national study*. The Netherlands: Von Gorcum, 1965.

17. McNemar, Q. Opinion—attitude methodology. *Psychological Bulletin*, 1946, *43*, 289–374.

18. Jahoda, M.; Deutsch, M.; and Cook, S. W. *Research methods in social relations*. New York: Dryden, 1951.

19. Rosten, L. *The joys of Yiddish*. New York: McGraw-Hill, 1968.

20. Lawton, M. Powell. Personal communication, 1971.

21. Lynd, R. S., and Lynd, H. M. *Middletown, a study in American culture*. New York: Harcourt, Brace, 1929.

22. Lynd, R. S., and Lynd, H. M. *Middletown in transition*. New York: Harcourt, Brace, 1937.

23. Hollingshead, A. B. *Elmtown's youth*. New York: Wiley, 1949.

24. Whyte, W. F. *Street corner society: The social structure of an Italian slum*. Chicago: University of Chicago Press, 1955.

25. Liebow, E. *Tally's Corner*. Boston: Little, Brown, 1968.

26. Talmon, Y. Aging in Israel: A planned society. *American Journal of Sociology*, 1961, *67*, 284–295.

27. Talmon, Y. Aging in collective settlements in Israel, in C. Tibbetts and W. Donahue (Eds.), *Social and psychological aspects of aging*. New York: Columbia University Press, 1962.

28. Weihl, H.; Nathan, T.; Avner, U .; Finkelstein N.; and Getter, N. Investigation of the family life, living conditions and needs of the noninstitutionalized urban Jewish aged 65+ in Israel. Jerusalem: Social Welfare Ministry, n.d.

16

The Ecology of Adaptation to a New Environment

M. Powell Lawton
Beverly Patnaik
Morton H. Kleban

The way people distribute themselves in space, like any other behavior, must be assumed to be purposeful. Yet, it is a relatively recent phenomenon to have been studied by the methods of social science, beginning with geography and now including the broad interdisciplinary science of human-environment relations.[1-3] Such behavior as crowding,[4] the search for privacy,[5] the distancing of people in relation to one another,[6] and the choice of specific locations for specific behaviors[7] have been studied by anthropologists, sociologists, and psychologists both as the cause of other behaviors and as the result of antecedent conditions. The broadest view of such behavior sees it as a part of the total behavioral system, where human needs not only are satisfied in a particular location but may be blocked or facilitated by the use of space, objects, and other people in the space. Furthermore, the individual is seen as utilizing space in a characteristic style that is consonant with his or her behavior in other spheres.

The present study examines some aspects of the use of space and objects by people faced with the demand to adapt to an environmental change not of their own choosing. The most general hypothesis was that they would alter such spatial behavior in a manner that would help them deal with an ostensibly stressful experience.

The occasion for the study was the intrainstitutional room transfer of 24 residents of a long-term care institution for the elderly, which required the vacating of 24 other room spaces—a total of 48 residents requiring relocation. The moves were mandated by implementation in Pennsylvania of Public Law 92–603 as of January 1, 1973. Long-term care thereby was

Reprinted with permission from *International Journal of Aging and Human Development,* 1976, 7, 15–26.

placed under Title 19 of the Social Security Act instead of under Public Assistance, as had been the case prior to that date. Separate and distinct areas for the categories of skilled nursing care and intermediate care were required, each with its own specified uniform staffing pattern and level of reimbursement. Prior to January 1, the monthly maintenance charge was uniform throughout the institution, but residents were grouped in five different areas in accordance with their need for care. The staffing patterns of the areas had varied appropriately. The net effect of the change would be homogenization of residents and more even distribution of staff within the two broad levels ("skilled" and "intermediate"). The skilled nursing care area, of course, was to be for residents requiring more skilled nursing care than those in the intermediate area, and the staffing requirements are greater. The homogenization was thus accomplished by transferring some relatively independent residents to floors that had been serving the more dependent residents, and vice versa. The relocation was accomplished after a period of careful planning by the entire staff of the institution, working together with both residents and their families. The 48 moves were made on a single day, with the mobilization of the entire staff, particular care being taken in such matters as counseling, preparation, and support of the movers; moving familiar furniture; scheduling elevator use; and reorienting the resident to his or her new surroundings. Whatever could have been done to moderate the well-documented stress of environmental change was accomplished.

This relocation was utilized as a natural experiment by the social work and behavioral science research staffs. While there have been many studies of relocation between institutions,[8-10] and of housing relocation,[11,12] the only studies of relocation within an institution have utilized younger mental patients,[13,14] and none of these has dealt explicitly with the effects of the relocation on spatial behavior.

The institutional milieu is known to minimize opportunities for privacy and to restrict grossly the range of space and objects that are definable as one's own. Whatever territory can become personalized is jealously guarded, and a variety of compensatory means of establishing one's private world are utilized: the staking out of a chair or part of a public room as one's own; the exchange of avoidance behaviors with a roommate; or the "turning off" of interactive behavior in a crowded public space.[15] The attachment to one's own room or floor is a part of such attempts to preserve the self in both a psychological and a spatial sense. An essential ingredient of this state of institutional adjustment is clear knowledge of where such things as furniture, staff offices, bathrooms, exits, and familiar faces are located. Thus, the loss of these sources of stability would be expected to activate new behaviors and new uses of space whose purpose would be to minimize the stress of the change.

We hypothesized that behavior would change in such a way as:

1. To maximize the opportunity for reorientation to a new environment and

2. To minimize the risk of anxiety-arousing consequences of too-sudden exposure to new environmental stimuli.

Method

Participants

Of the total of 48 residents being relocated, 11 from the first floor of the institution were exchanged with a similar number from the topmost floor, and 13 others were shifted from one first-floor room to another on the same floor. With very little time to plan the study and to gather data, it was decided to limit the study to these two physical areas, involving the majority of the relocations. The total number of residents moving to or within the first floor was 31 (including 7 from the other floors not mapped), while 11 moved to the top floor. Individual assessment of the relocated residents in terms of health and functional capacity could not be performed within the time limits. However, the net effect of the moves was clearly to populate the first floor with more independent residents than it previously housed, and conversely for the top floor. The total resident bed census on the first floor was 54; on the top floor, 74.

Procedure

The data reported here were gathered exclusively from direct observation of the behavior occurring in the two physical areas of the institution, in the form of behavior maps.[16] A map of the entire floor was reproduced, and the position and behavior of every individual was noted by research assistants trained in the mapping technique. The observer began at a predetermined point on the floor and followed a prescribed routine of gazing successively at each area of the ward, walking or pausing as required to be able to code the following individual behavior.

Individual characteristics. All residents were mapped whether the person was a resident, staff member, volunteer, or visitor and regardless of whether or not they were involved in the move. Individuals were not identified by name.

Physical location of the individual. Each person's location was marked on the map; but for coding, locations were classified as bedroom, hall (closed end), hall (nearest the elevator and exit), and lounge.

Position of the individual. Each person's position was noted as lying down, sitting, standing, walking (with or without cane or walker), in wheelchair (self-propelled) or in wheelchair (being pushed by another person). For analysis, walking and wheelchair ambulation were considered a single category.

Behavior of the individual. Behavior was classified as social, effectance (i.e., nonobligatory constructive behaviors such as reading, watching TV, engaging in occupational therapy, and so on), instrumental (eating, dressing, housekeeping, for example), sleeping, or null behavior (the apparent absence of any activity, though awake). Since walking was both a position and a behavior, those who were walking appear only in the totals for positions.

The observer thus attempted to obtain a photographic image of the total pattern of behavior, though the picture had to be composed in serial fashion over time. The time required to do each behavior map was about 30 minutes. All areas of each floor were covered, except for resident and staff rooms whose doors were closed. A closed resident's door was treated as an item of data, but in order not to intrude further on the resident's privacy, no attempt was made to enter such rooms.

Behavior maps were done on two occasions:

1.   During the 2 weeks before the move, before residents had been notified that they were to move. The last maps were done on the 6th day before the move.
2.   During the 2 weeks following the move, beginning 1 day after the move took place. 5 times of day were sampled: 9:00 a.m., 10:30 a.m., 1:00 p.m., 2:30 p.m., and 4:00 p.m.

An attempt was made to obtain equal numbers of maps for every time on each floor for each occasion, but because of problems in scheduling enough personnel time, there were 39 maps done on the first and 43 on the top floor prior to the move, 45 on both floors following the move.

Following the completion of the maps, each map was coded in terms of the number of residents and staff in each physical area, the number of open doors, the position of each resident, and the behavior each was observed to be engaged in at the time.

Results

Total Number of Residents Observed

One aspect of reorientation to a new environment by a person of low competence involves the person's restricting his or her behavioral range, that is, remaining close to his or her home territory. Therefore, we expected that more residents would be counted on the floor area following the move. The mean number of residents observed on each mapping on the first floor prior to the move was 16.9, and following the move, 18.3. This difference was not significant ($t = 1.39$, 83 df, $p > .05$). On the top floor the premove mean of 10.4 did not differ significantly from the postmove mean, 11.8 ($t = 1.40$, 87 df, $p > .05$).

Open Doors

Another aspect of reorientation is the need to survey the new environment—to gain a maximum amount of information about the physical and social aspects of life in a new location. We thus hypothesized that relocated residents would be more likely to leave their doors open, so as to be able both to survey activity in the hall from their rooms and also to be able to monitor their own rooms from a position outside the room. We also reasoned that nonmovers would experience heightened interest in what went on after such a major change in the complexion of their floors. Since it was easy to determine which rooms housed any resident who was to move, separate counts of open doors were made for "affected" (i.e., rooms containing a mover) and "unaffected" (rooms containing no movers) rooms. Table 16.1 shows the excess of open doors in the postmove as compared to the premove occasion at each time period for each floor, with separate totals for affected and unaffected rooms. It can be seen that, while differences were sometimes small, the predicted relationship occurred 10 times out of 10 occasions in the affected rooms ($p = .001$ by the binomial test) and 9 out of 10 occasions for the unaffected rooms ($p = .004$).

Location of Body Position and Behavior of Staff and Residents

The percentage distributions of staff and residents observed on all behavior maps both prior to and following the move were computed, using as a base the total number of residents or staff observed over all occasions (the infrequently occurring staff categories are omitted). The significance of the

TABLE 16.1. Percentage Excess of Open Doors on Postmove as Compared to Premove Condition at Five Observation Occasions

	First Floor		Fourth Floor	
	Affected Rooms	Unaffected Rooms	Affected Rooms	Unaffected Rooms
9:00 a.m.	13	11	11	4
10:30 a.m.	23	14	10	3
1:00 p.m.	12	14	7	1
2:30 p.m.	8	12	13	6
4:00 p.m.	11	−2	9	1

p (affected rooms) = .00097.
p (unaffected rooms) = .0039.

differences between the pre- and postrelocation percentages was calculated by z scores; a negative z indicates that the prelocation percentage was higher. One-tailed tests were used where the category had been hypothesized to change in a particular direction; otherwise, two-tailed tests were used.

We hypothesized that more passive behavior would be the dominant response to the dislocation, on the theory that these relatively dependent residents would attempt to conserve energy and avoid immediate entry into more demanding and complex types of behavior. Specifically, we expected that residents would be:

1. More likely to be found in bedrooms rather than in halls, in common spaces, or in the vicinity of the nurses station;
2. More likely to be lying down, sitting, or standing, than walking; and
3. More likely to exhibit null behavior and sleeping, rather than instrumental, effectant, or social behavior.

Predictions for staff were roughly that the reverse would be true, namely that the demands of coping with the residents' relocation would result in more active behavior. However, for location, it was thought that, if staff's locational patterns changed, they would change in the same direction that residents' patterns would change, since presumably some of the additional job-related tasks would require them to be with residents wherever they were.

Residents' Patterns

Location. On the first floor, lounge population decreased significantly, as was predicted, while bedroom population increased on both floors. The busiest part of the hall on the top floor decreased in population, with the same effect barely missing significance on the lower floor. No change occurred in the population of the closed end of the hall.

Position. On the first floor, three hypothesized changes occurred: An increase in the percentage lying down and standing, and a decrease in the percentage walking. On the fourth floor, there was a marginal increase in the percentage sitting.

Behavior. On the first floor, the hypothesized increase in null behavior and decrease in effectance occurred to a significant degree, while on the fourth floor, null behavior increased and social behavior decreased, as hypothesized. We hypothesized that instrumental behavior would also decrease, on the theory that greater passivity should be reflected in all behaviors. To the contrary, instrumental behavior increased significantly on the top floor (two-tailed test).

Staff Patterns

Location. In conformity with our expectation, staff population in resident bedrooms increased on both floors, indicating that they tended to be wherever residents needed them. The same parallelism was seen in the decreased staff population of the elevator end of the hall on the top floor. Staff also showed a significant redistribution into the closed end of the hall on the top floor, which did not parallel any resident trend (two-tailed test).

Position. No significant changes were found in the distribution of staff over the three relevant body positions.

Behavior. Only two types of staff behavior occurred with great enough frequency to be analyzed. The heavy preponderance of social behavior results from the arbitrary restriction of categorizing each behavior only once; much staff activity involved simultaneous instrumental and social behavior, in which case the more complex (i.e., social) was tallied. The instrumental behavior increase on the top floor was expected since residents had shown a similar increase, this difference was significant using a one-tailed test. The complementary decrease in social behavior, while it paralleled resident behavior, was not covered by a hypothesis, and therefore, even though z was, naturally, the same size as the z for instrumental behavior, application of the two-tailed test left this value short of significance.

Discussion

Out of all predictions made regarding changes in residents' behavior, 12 were supported, 13 were not, and 1 changed significantly in a direction opposite to that predicted. The 12 supported predictions indicate very strongly the increase in passive types of behavior and space occupancy. The very clearcut findings showing more open bedroom doors following the relocation support the idea that a first task for the relocated is to reestablish their orientation to their physical and social surroundings.

Almost as interesting as the predicted effects was the one that ran opposite to prediction: the increase in instrumental behavior that occurred in one floor and barely missed significance on the other floor. Most observed instrumental behavior occurred in the resident's room: grooming, housekeeping, washing, and so on. Important among these behaviors were rearranging one's possessions, tidying clothes, and so on, tasks that were specific to being in a new location. Thus, though this interpretation is necessarily a post hoc conclusion, one gets the larger picture of a relatively adaptive response to a most stressful change. While restriction of behavioral range and greater passivity are generally considered undesirable behaviors over the long run, they may well have allowed the individuals to reconstitute their resources for future more active dealings with their environment. The open doors and other signs of reorientation are necessary preludes to later increased mobility. The increase in instrumental behavior was not only appropriate to the personal rearrangements that go with any move but also indicates the residents' continued ability to be active in a safe, spatially restricted way.

Making this argument for the positive adaptive quality of the behavior changes seen immediately after moving implies additionally that behavior should return to normal after the initial adjustment period. A few months later, fewer bedroom doors should be open; there should be less null behavior, less sitting, less standing, and less bedroom use; there should be more effectance and social behavior, more walking, and more use of halls and lounges. Unfortunately, there was no way to test this hypothesized outcome, since the complexions of both floors continued to change as further transfers to and from these floors were made in the normal course of institutional management, this time spread out over time rather than being concentrated in a single day.

One is struck by the greater number of changes occurring on the first floor as compared to the top floor. We are inclined to attribute this to the fact that the total number of room changes on the first floor was much greater—again a further validation of the notion of a relocation effect. Very little seems explainable on the basis of simple change in the types of residents housed in the two areas. The net change in resident characteristics on the lower floor was toward higher competence and on the top floor toward lesser competence; yet, most changes in behavior and location on both floors were consistent with a lowered level of functioning, temporary though we believe it to be.

Finally, as might be expected, staff behavior changed less than resident behavior. Furthermore, in those five instances where it did change, it was always congruent with patient change, even if all such changes were not originally predicted. Thus, we can conclude that the less vulnerable group, staff, maintained more stable behavior and space-use patterns following the disruption and that their competence was expressed in their alteration of behavior, where necessary, so as to be of maximum assistance to residents.

This study of the adaptation process in relatively dependent older people constitutes only one aspect of the more general problem of relocation as discussed with respect to migration of groups of all ages,[17] of individual moving[18] and relatively healthy older people living in the community.[19] Passivity and cognitive restructuring are only two of the possible means that may be utilized. Beck et al. have discussed a number of possible adaptive styles that people may utilize in anticipation of a move, in the process of moving, and following a move.[20] While Holmes and Holmes present evidence of the stressful quality of relocation for all people, there seems to be a greater effect on older people than on young.[18] This phenomenon seems consistent with the "environmental docility hypothesis," which suggests that the behavior of individuals of reduced competence (such as the mentally ill, aged, or economically deprived) is more susceptible to determination by environmental influences than is true for those of higher competence.[21] Further study of the conditions of environmental impact from the point of view of both individual and environment seems warranted in order to foresee, plan for, or minimize negative effects in a number of situations.

References

1. J. Wohlwill. The emerging discipline of environmental psychology. *American Psychologist*, 25, 303–312, 1970.
2. K. H. Craik. Environmental psychology, in *New directions in psychology, 4*. New York: Holt, Rinehart & Winston, 1970.
3. L. A. Pastalan and D. H. Carson (Eds.). *Spatial behavior of older people*, Ann Arbor: University of Michigan, Institute of Gerontology, 1970.
4. J. B. Calhoun. The role of space in animal sociology. *Journal of Social Issues*, 22, 46–58, 1966.

5. N. Marshall. Environmental components of orientation toward privacy, in J. Archea and C. Eastman (Eds.), *EDRA 2*. Pittsburgh: Carnegie-Mellon University, 1970.

6. E. T. Hall. *The hidden dimension*. New York. Doubleday, 1966.

7. I. Altman, P. A. Nelson, and E. E. Lett. *The ecology of home environments*. Salt Lake City: Psychology Department, University of Utah, 1972 Final report, Grant OEG–8–70–0202, U.S. Office of Education, mimeo.

8. C. K. Aldrich and E. Mendkoff. Relocation of the aged and disabled: A mortality study. *Journal of the American Geriatrics Society, 11,* 185–194, 1963.

9. E. Markus, M. Blenkner, M. Bloom, and T. Downs. The impact of relocation upon mortality rates of institutionalized aged persons. *Journal of Gerontology, 26,* 537–541, 1971.

10. E. C. Killian. Effect of geriatric transfers on mortality rates. *Social Work, 15,* 19–26, 1970.

11. F. M. Carp. *A future for the aged*, Austin: University of Texas Press, 1966.

12. M. P. Lawton and S. Yaffe. Mortality, morbidity, and voluntary change of residence by older people. *Journal of the American Geriatrics Society, 18,* 823–831, 1970.

13. M. Zlotowski and D. Cohen. Effects of environmental change upon behavior of hospitalized schizophrenic patients. *Journal of Clinical Psychology, 24,* 470–475, 1968.

14. D. L. DeVries. Effects of environmental change and of participation on the behavior of mental patients. *Journal of Consulting and Clinical Psychology, 32,* pp. 532–536, 1968.

15. A. Lipman. A socio-architectural view of life through old people's homes. *Gerontologia Clinica, 10,* 88–101, 1968.

16. W. H. Ittelson, L. G. Rivlin, and H. M. Proshansky. The use of behavioral maps in environmental psychology, in H. M. Proshansky, W. H. Ittelson, and L. G. Rivlin (Eds.), *Environmental psychology*. New York: Holt, Rinehart & Winston, 1970.

17. E. B. Brody (Ed.). *Behavior in new environments*. Beverly Hills, Calif.: Sage, 1970.

18. T. S. Holmes and T. H. Holmes. Short-term intrusions into the life style routine. *Journal of Psychosomatic Research, 14,* 121–132, 1970.

19. K. K. Schooler. The effects of changes in residential environment. *Proceedings of the Ninth International Congress of Gerontology,* Kiev, U.S.S.R., July 1972.

20. R. J. Beck, S. B. Cohen, K. H. Craik, M. Dwyer, G. F. McCleary, and S. Wapner. Studying environmental moves and relocations. *Environment and Behavior, 5,* 335–349, 1973.

21. M. P. Lawton. Ecology and aging, in L. A. Pastalan and D. H. Carson (Eds.), *The spatial behavior of older people*. Ann Arbor: University of Michigan, Institute of Gerontology, 1970.

17

The Meaning of Cherished Personal Possessions for the Elderly

Edmund Sherman

Evelyn S. Newman

The intent of this study was to explore the meaning of cherished personal possessions for the elderly in their adjustment to old age and in some cases to institutionalization. There appears to have been no substantial published empirical work done in this area, although there has been speculation and discursive writing regarding the fact that the elderly will often value a particular possession or possessions far beyond all others, as well as beyond the actual monetary value.

The strong attachment to such a possession suggests that it may serve a purpose in the life of the aged person that is analogous to the "transitional object" of early childhood which enables some children to undertake a degree of independence from the mother and to move into another developmental stage of their lives. If this analogy holds to any extent, the valued possession of the aged person, with its symbolic meanings and associations, may assist her or him in coming to terms with the past and moving into another developmental stage of life, the most mature of Erickson's eight stages, ego integrity, with its particular concerns and tasks.[1] The importance of the cherished possession for the transition from independent living to nursing home or some other form of institutional care is readily apparent, if there is any substance to the analogy with the transitional object.

In addition, Goffman has pointed out that in total institutions such as mental hospitals, certain possessions take on extreme importance. He notes that clothing and cosmetic supplies in particular form a person's "identity kit," and the loss of this identity equipment prevents the indi-

Reprinted with permission from *International Journal of Aging and Human Development*, 1977, 8, 181–192.

vidual from presenting the usual self-image to others.[2] Although Goffman is particularly interested in possessions that bear on presentation of self, he is also cognizant of the fact that possession of other kinds of objects is also extremely important "because persons invest self feelings in their possessions" (p. 18).

Simone deBeauvoir sees ownership of certain possessions as a guarantee of ontological security for the elderly. As she notes, "thanks to his possessions the old person assures himself of his identity against those who claim to see him as nothing but an object" (p. 699).[3] Frankl has commented on this particular meaning of possessions for persons in their reactions to unaccustomed and unusual environments, notably the concentration camps of World War II. He observed that, when all possessions were taken away, except perhaps for eyeglasses, the person had nothing with which to form an external link with his or her former life (p. 76).[4]

Butler and Lewis have observed that cherished possessions provide a sense of continuity, comfort, security, and satisfaction; and the fear of their loss is a frequent preoccupation among older persons. They also note that some institutions are now recognizing the therapeutic value of encouraging people to bring some of these possessions with them (pp. 24–25).[5] Various negative effects of failing to take cherished possessions into account in relocation of the elderly were noted in Carp's study of Victoria Plaza:

> The surrender of furniture and other possessions was important, not only because the objects were missed, both as items in themselves and as reminders of the family events associated with them, but also because their absence and the substitution of cheaper and less distinguished furnishings was a continual reminder of general loss of status. (p. 89)[6]

Thus, it is abundantly clear that cherished possessions are important in the lives of the elderly, particularly in regard to relocation. Yet there is little evidence in the literature of any systematic exploration of the kinds of possessions and their particular meanings for the elderly. Consequently, this study was undertaken to shed some light on the following questions:

1.   What proportion of the elderly claim to have a most cherished possession?

2.   What kinds of possessions tend to be cherished the most?

3.   Do different kinds of possessions have different meanings and referents?

4.   Are there any associations between cherished possessions and life satisfaction?

Method

Given these somewhat general and speculative concerns, the study was quite exploratory in nature and design. The method of data collection consisted of interviews with 94 aged persons conducted in seven different Senior Service Centers in and around the city of Albany, New York, as well as in one nursing home in the same area. There were 62 respondents interviewed in the service centers and 32 interviewed in the nursing home. Respondents in the nursing home were selected on the basis of their being ambulatory and sufficiently well oriented to respond meaningfully to the questions asked. A number of interviews with respondents from both types of settings were deleted from the sample because of evident mental deterioration or disorientation and therefore questionable validity of responses.

Individual interviews were conducted by graduate social work students from the School of Social Welfare at the State University of New York at Albany. The students obtained the interviews by prearrangement with program staff in the various settings. The time most generally selected was a midday when the largest numbers of elderly were at the centers for the lunches being offered under the Hot Meals programs.

The nursing home setting was a large (200-bed) modern facility with attractive private rooms available for the ambulatory residents. The administration and programming in the home were progressive and allowed considerable latitude to residents in the kinds of personal possessions they could bring with them, even including items as large as a favorite chair. The home was selected in part because of this policy, so that responses about cherished possessions would not be constrained by enforced limitations on their retention.

The selection of the sample was thus purposive rather than random in nature, and it cannot in any sense be considered a probability sample. Given the exploratory nature of the study, the intent was simply to obtain adequate numbers of interviews with ambulatory, nonsenile elderly persons living in the community and in a residential setting so as to note any contrasts that might be indicated in cherished possessions between institutional and community living.

Participants

The respondents were predominantly white (only 6 nonwhites out of $N = 94$), and female (63 females to 31 males). As for marital status, 67% were widowed, 17% married, 9% single–never married, 5% divorced, and

2% separated. The Hollingshead Two-Factor Index of Social Class Position was obtained for the majority of the sample, and it showed the following distribution (p. 387 ff.):[7] Class I (upper) 2%, Class II (upper middle) 6%, Class III (middle) 21%, Class IV (upper lower) 36%, Class V (lower lower) 20%, undetermined 15%. It was therefore a lower middle and lower class sample, by and large. The occupational groups represented were predominantly lower white-collar (clerks and sales personnel) and skilled and semiskilled trades. Educationally, the largest grouping were those with less than 7 years of grammar school (23%) and those with between 7 and 10 years (23%). Another 12% claimed some high school; 13%, high school graduation; 8%, some college; 6%, college graduation; and 15%, unknown. Although we did not collect data on religion, it should be pointed out that the nursing home residents were predominantly Jewish, whereas the community group was more heterogeneous.

The mean age of the total sample was 74.7 years, with a range of 60–95 years. The nursing home subsample had a mean age of 81.2, with the same range; and the senior center subsample had a mean age of 71.4, with a range of 61–85 years. Thus, the nursing home group was almost 10 years older on the average than the community group.

Procedure

The interview schedule was a semistructured instrument with a few open-ended items allowing for probes, particularly in the area of cherished possessions. There were also some fully structured items. The interviews generally took 20–30 minutes and began with factual, demographic data. Names were not recorded, and the respondents were assured that confidentiality would be observed. They were told what the study was about, and the introductory statement began as follows:

"This is a study about the meaning of cherished possessions or personal objects to the people who own them. Most of us have certain objects or possessions that we value above all others. In this study we are interested in learning more about what these objects are and what they mean to people who have retired."

After the demographic questions were posed, the respondents were asked, "Is there one personal possession you value above all others?" This was followed by, "Could you tell me what it is?" If the answer to the first question was "no," the interviewer was asked to probe as to the reason why, for example, "can't think of one object," or "prefers not to."

The next question, asked only if a possession was identified, was "Would you tell me why it has such a special meaning for you?" This was followed by, "If you were allowed to take only one personal possession into a nursing home or institution, what would that be? The same (as above) or something else?" Then, "Why is that?"

The participants were then asked what their next-most valued possession was, and if they had one, the same series of questions were asked about it.

When the subject of personal possessions had been fully explored, the interviewer administered the 20-question Life Satisfaction Index A developed by Neugarten, Havighurst, and Tobin (p. 141.)[8] If respondents were capable of filling our the index themselves, they did so; otherwise, the interviewer asked the questions sequentially.

The analysis of the resulting data required the development of a classification scheme from the total inventory of identified cherished possessions. Cross-tabulations of this classification were then made with all the other variables in the study, including the Life Satisfaction Index. The chi-square test was applied to the data in these cross-tabulations, and the .05 level of significance was used to determine potential relationships. This was not a probability sample, so the intent of this statistical analysis was not to generalize beyond the sample but to explore promising relationships for future hypotheses in this area of study.

Results

Extent of Cherished Possessions

A striking majority (81%) of the sample were able to identify a most cherished possession, with only 18 of the 94 respndents claiming none. By contrast, only 45 respondents (48%) were able to identify a second-most cherished possession. It generally took little or no probing on the part of the interviewers to obtain a response identifying (or disclaiming) a most cherished possession, whereas it took somewhat more probing to identify second ones. It is therefore rather clear from these findings that the concept of a most cherished possession is a viable one in an elderly population such as this.

Types of Cherished Possessions

The range of items identified as most cherished possessions was quite extensive, going all the way from objects as small as a piece of jewelry (ring, brooch, etc.) to one as large as a home. Given the total inventory of 76 identified possessions, it was necessary to develop a classification scheme that would be economical enough in the use of categories to allow for cross-tabulation but at the same time be descriptive of the variety of items. A set of categories was developed that appeared to be descriptive of the objects and in which different members of the project staff were able to classify individual items from this particular study in an unambiguous and consensual manner.

The categories that were developed were religious items, symbolic jewelry, personal performance items, photographs, consumer items, and other. Religious items included such objects as Bibles, Torahs, rosaries, crosses, and prayer books. "Symbolic jewelry" denotes items that were given by or associated with an important person or associated with significant events in the life of the respondent. The term *symbolic* was used to distinguish this type of jewelry from the kind cherished primarily for its material value, which was included under consumer items. Further if a piece of religious jewelry (e.g., cross, pendant, or necklace) was cherished primarily because of its religious value rather than its associative value, it was included in religious items.

Personal performance items included such possessions as musical instruments, art materials, or any item that denoted a creative or performance function in the life of the respondent. Photographs, which were the most frequently identified possession, are self-explanatory. Consumer items included such things as entertainment items (TV, radio), books, expensive (nonsymbolic) jewelry, and furnishings. Lastly, the category "other" included pets, homes, documents (e.g., military discharge), and enabling items such as eyeglasses, hearing aids, and canes. These latter items were not numerous enough in this sample to warrant separate categories. Table 17.1 shows the distribution of responses according to this classification scheme by sex of respondent.

Interestingly, there was no difference between men and women in identification of a cherished possession. If there was any expectation that women would more commonly show a sentimental attachment to personal possessions, it was not borne out in these findings. There was, however, a significant difference in the types of possessions identified (X^2 = 18.24, 6 df, p < .01) Perhaps the most remarkable differences were in the greater relative identification of photographs by women and consumer items by men as most cherished possessions. The greater identification of symbolic jewelry by women was, of course, to be expected.

There were no significant findings with regard to social-class position and cherished possessions. Lower class respondents (Hollingshead's Classes IV and V) tended to identify consumer items and symbolic jewelry with greater relative frequency than middle-class respondents, but the numbers involved were not enough to suggest statistical significance. On the other hand, age made a considerable difference as to whether or not an

TABLE 17.1. Cherished Possession and Sex of Respondent

Possession Identified	Male N (31)	Percentage	Female N (63)	Percentage	Total N (94)	Percentage
None	6	19	12	19	18	19
Religious item	2	6	9	14	11	12
Symbolic jewelry	1	3	10	16	11	12
Personal performance	4	13	2	3	6	6
Photographs	2	6	17	27	19	20
Consumer items	8	26	5	8	13	14
Other	8	26	8	13	16	17

individual claimed to have a cherished possession. Neugarten's delineation of the "young-old" (under 75) and the "old-old" (75 and over) turned out to be a significant demarcation in this respect.[9] Table 17.2 gives this breakdown.

The statistical findings with regard to Table 17.2 indicate statistical significance ($X^2 = 14.83$, 6 df, $p < .05$). It is quite remarkable that the category in which the difference between the young-old and old-old is most

TABLE 17.2. Cherished Possession and Age of Respondent

Possession Identified	Under 75 N (48)	Percentage	75 and Over N (46)	Percentage	Total N (94)	Percentage
None	4	8	14	30	18	19
Religious item	9	19	2	4	11	12
Symbolic jewelry	7	14	4	9	11	12
Personal performance	1	2	5	11	6	6
Photographs	11	23	8	17	19	20
Consumer items	8	17	5	11	13	14
Other	8	17	8	17	16	17

marked is "none." It is also interesting that the second-largest relative difference in the two groups is the lesser identification of religious items among the old-old. Unfortunately there is no way of knowing whether this is a real difference or the result of an atypical sample.

Although it appeared in this sample that the old-old were less apt to have a cherished possession, this finding was initially somewhat clouded by the fact that the nursing home subsample was made up predominantly of the old-old, whereas the reverse was true of the community subsample. Thus, it was possible that the difference was mostly due to the setting rather than to age. Since in this particular nursing home residents were permitted to have personal possessions, a possible explanation might be that persons in nursing homes see themselves as at "the end of the line" and are decathecting significant objects in their lives.

In order to control for the possible influence of the setting factor, chi-square tests were run separately on the community subsample and the nursing home group by age and whether or not a cherished possession was identified. Remarkably, the relationship between age and cherished possession in the community subsample not only held up but was enhanced $(X^2 = 9.93, 1\ df, p < .01)$. The results in the nursing home group, on the other hand, were not significant, but this was probably due to the fact that there were too few persons under 75 in that group to make the statistical results meaningful. Essentially, in both subsamples the direction of the findings was the same: markedly fewer old-old respondents claiming to have a cherished possession.

Meanings of Cherished Possessions

The third major area of inquiry in the study had to do with the question of whether there were different referents and meanings for different possessions. As far as the issue of referents was concerned, the most meaningful classification of the interview responses we were able to develop consisted of a list of persons, including self and significant others. The list of persons, with the frequency of responses, was as follows: self (25), child (18), spouse (15), parents (5), grandchild (4), friend (1), grandparent (1), aunt (1), other relative (1), other nonrelative (1).

When this list was cross-tabulated with type of cherished possessions, certain clusterings of referents with types of possessions became apparent. Religious objects most often had the self as referent. Symbolic jewelry most often was associated with a spouse; photographs most often with a child (14 out of 19 responses). Personal performance items were all identified with the self, and consumer items and the "other" category were almost always associated with the self.

As for the particular meanings of the possessions for the respondents, it is almost impossible to give the full range, richness, and poignancy of the responses. Perhaps the following brief samples will give some flavor and serve to illustrate a number of representative responses:

Female respondent: my Bible. It has been my guide and has sustained me through life. Its message is particularly relevant for today's time.

Male respondent: violin. I am a musician and the violin means everything to me.

Female: gold cross. It was a gift from my son when he was a youngster. He had a paper route and worked and saved very hard to get it for me.

Female: pictures (photos). You renew your life with your children's pictures. They can appease your loneliness.

Female: pictures (photos). They mean I was a woman. I had children and built my life around them. Happy memories.

Female: bracelet. My husband gave it to me 60 years ago. My feelings for him add much meaning to the object.

Female: paintings. Painting keeps my mind off the nursing home.

Female: ring. It was my mother's wedding ring. She gave it to me before she died.

The last general area to be explored was the possible relationship between cherished possessions and life satisfaction among the elderly. With a maximum possible score of 20 on the Life Satisfaction Index A, the median score for this sample was 12. The old-old and the nursing home group had lower index scores, but the main concern of this analysis was with the relationship of the scores and cherished possessions. Table 17.3 portrays this relationship.

A number of interesting points came to light in Table 17.3. There is a significant relationship between life satisfaction scores and cherished possessions in this study group ($X^2 = 23.76$, 6 df, $p < .001$). There were very few persons with no cherished possession who had a high life satisfaction score, far fewer than the expected frequency would be. Therefore it can be said for this sample that lack of a cherished possession is associated with a lower life satisfaction score.

Among the other points to be noted was the fact that those who identified symbolic jewelry as a cherished possession had high satisfaction scores in considerably greater frequency than might be expected statistically. The same thing was true to a somewhat lesser degree for those with

TABLE 17.3.   Cherished Possession and Life Satisfaction Score

Possession Identified	Low Score (Under 12)		High Score (12 and Over)		Total	
	N (51)	Percentage	N (43)	Percentage	N (94)	Percentage
None	14	27	4	9	18	19
Religious item	5	10	6	14	11	12
Symbolic jewelry	1	2	10	23	11	12
Personal performance	5	10	1	2	6	6
Photographs	14	27	5	12	19	20
Consumer items	7	14	6	14	13	14
Other	5	10	11	26	16	17

possessions classified in the "other" category. It should be noted that this category included pets and homes as most frequently mentioned possessions. These persons are still living in the community rather than the nursing home, and they are for the most part young-old rather than old-old. Their more favorable life circumstances, including the fact that they can still have such possessions, should make for higher life satisfaction. The persons who identified symbolic jewelry were also, with only three exceptions, in the young-old category and living in the community.

A remaining point illustrated in Table 17.3 is the relatively high number of persons with photographs as cherished possessions who have low life satisfaction scores. The answer to this finding would appear to lie in their life circumstances. They were for the most part old-old who were living in the nursing home rather than the community. More than two-thirds of those who had photographs as cherished possessions were living in the nursing home, which is markedly disproportionate for the total sample, in which only slightly more than a third of the respondents were in the nursing home. This raises the interesting possibility that photographs might more often be the possession of choice for those who see themselves as at the "end of the line," in the old-old category and in institutions.

By contrast, some of these factors did not play a role in the low life satisfaction scores among those who had no cherished possessions. Those persons were for the most part living and functioning in the community. This clearly suggests that *lack* of a cherished possession is a meaningful fact in lives of elderly persons. These findings also suggest that cherished possessions provide a vehicle for what Butler has identified as the adaptive and constructive manifestations of reminiscence in the life review process (p. 68).[10]

Discussion

Since this was an exploratory study with a nonrandom sample, the findings are suggestive rather than conclusive in any sense. The .05 level of significance was used to explore potential relationships for future research rather than to make inferences about the elderly population in general. Within the limits of this sample, however, a number of points concerning the meaning of cherished possessions for the elderly came through rather clearly. First, the concept of a most cherished possession appeared to be a viable one in the lives of these elderly. A dominant majority (81%) of them were able to identify rather readily a particular possession that they cherished above all others.

Second, there were certain characteristic kinds of possessions that were identified as most cherished. The most frequent was photographs, but religious items (e.g., Bibles, rosaries, Torahs), symbolic jewelry (e.g., wedding rings), and consumer items (TV, radio, books) were also fairly common. On the other hand, the lack of a cherished possession took on certain significance in the findings. It was generally the old-old who lacked a cherished possession. This raises the interesting question as to whether cherished possessions are decathected along with other significant objects and persons in a more general process of disengagement among certain elderly. The place of cherished possessions in the relationship between personality types and aging patterns could prove a fruitful area for further research.

There were particular referents and meanings for different kinds of cherished possessions. Symbolic jewelry was almost always associated with the memory of a spouse, while photographs were almost invariably associated with children. There appeared to be a poignant, hanging-on quality to the meanings attached to photographs. The fact that the old-old were disproportionately represented in the photograph group also suggests a direction for further research.

Finally, the exploration of the relationship between life satisfaction and cherished possessions turned up some promising findings. In this study group it was clear that the lack of a cherished possession was associated with a lower life satisfaction than those who had such possessions. This suggests that the lack of such possessions might serve as an indicator of (or be symptomatic of) a poor adjustment to old age. It also raises the possibility that at least some kinds of cherished possessions might indeed serve as adaptive objects of reminiscence in the life review process, allowing elderly persons to make a positive adjustment to and come to terms with old age.

References

1. Erikson, E. *Identity and the life cycle*. New York: International Universities, 1959.
2. Goffman, E. *Asylums: Essays on the social situation of mental patients and other inmates*. Garden City, N.Y.: Doubleday, Anchor, 1961.
3. deBeauvoir, S. *The coming of age*. New York: Warner Paperback Library, 1973.
4. Frankl, V. *The doctor and the soul*. New York: Bantam, 1955.
5. Butler, R., and Lewis, M. *Aging and mental health: Positive psychosocial approaches*. St. Louis: Mosby, 1973.
6. Carp, G. *A future for the aged: Victoria Plaza and its residents*. Austin: University of Texas Press, 1966.
7. Hollingshead, A., and Redlich, F. *Social class and mental illness*. New York: Wiley, 1957.
8. Neugarten, B., Havighurst, R., and Tobin, S. The measurement of life satisfaction. *Journal of Gerontology*, 1961, *16*, 134–143.
9. Neugarten, B. Age groups in American society and the rise of the young-old. *Annals of the American Academy*, 1974, *415*, 187–198.
10. Butler, R. The life review: An Interpretation of reminiscence in the aged. *Psychiatry*, 1963, *26*, 65–75.

V
Vulnerability and Death

When are we vulnerable? As infants, as children, as adults, as aged adults. When are we exposed to the possibility of death—our own or the death of others significant in our lives? The same, all-encompassing answer prevails. Vulnerability is ever associated with life. Perhaps it is a mistake to single out the vulnerabilities of old people. There is a risk of exaggerating the situation of the aged, setting one subpopulation apart from the rest. We do well to bear in mind the needs, desires, and vulnerabilities that characterize all humans, indeed, all living creatures, if we are to avoid portraying the aged as different from all the rest.

Nevertheless many risks to health, well-being, and life itself tend to increase with advancing age. Those hazards that are largely biomedical in nature are not addressed directly here. Instead we concentrate on ways in which other people influence the safety and survivial of the elderly person in our society.

The retirement village is one of the newer developments on the scene of old age. Victor Marshall discerns an implicit conflict in the socioeconomic structure of at least some retirement villages that may have significant impact on vulnerability and death. Taking his clue from game theory, he examines the potentially serious conflict between investors earning a handsome return on their money and the length of survival ("turnover rate") in privately developed housing for the aged.

The widely cited statistics to the effect that only a relatively few old people live in institutions tend to lead attention away from their vulnerabilities. Because it would appear that so many old men and women are living independently in the community, one is then tempted to persist in a pattern of ignoring serious disability and terminal illness. This is part of what Robert Kastenbaum and Sandra E. Candy characterize as "the 4% fallacy." Their study (the results of which have since been supported by other investigators) indicates that many more people die in nursing homes than were supposed to be living there in the first place. "The misleading usage of extended care facility population statistics tends to draw attention away from the fact that many of our elders end their lives among strangers in an environment that offers little true 'nursing' and scarcely resembles a 'home.' "

Death can occur prematurely even for the elderly. Self-injurious behavior is one of the modalities through which a person can place his or her own life in excessive jeopardy. Robert Kastenbaum and Brian L. Mishara find that the environment within which geriatric medical inpatients must function can itself encourage self-injurious behavior. Some of the practical suggestions made in this chapter have since been taken up in demonstration programs that indicate that, given a chance, many geriatric patients are willing and able to replace self-injurious behavior with more positive forms.

18

"Betting on Death": A Retirement Village Dilemma

Victor W. Marshall

Retirement communities are a relatively recent and rapidly growing alternative for the aging individuals as they decide what kind of living arrangement will best provide the security and supports they might need for their last years. A feature of many such facilities is the provision of a "life-care" contract which guarantees lifetime residency in the community, including care in an affiliated or attached extended care facility should this become necessary. In the "life-care" arrangement residents typically pay a substantial entrance fee and sign a contract which commits them to pay monthly rental or maintenance fees for the duration of their lives. From the perspective of the owners and administrators of such communities, the entrance fees can be applied to the amortization of the mortgage on the physical plant, while the monthly rental payments can be utilized to cover operating expenses. This situation can be described as one of conflict of interest between the administistiration and the residents. I draw on game theory to elucidate a particular case and suggest its wider applicability. Additionally, I hope to demonstrate the value of a game-theoretical approach to some other issues relating to gerontology.

Game theory may be defined (Rapoport, 1959) as

> an attempt to bring within the fold of rigorous deductive method those aspects of human behavior in which conflict and cooperation are conducted in the context of choices among alternatives whose range of outcomes is known to the fullest extent by the participants.

My own use of game theory is nonmathematical but involves the following assumptions which are common to all game theories:

Reprinted with permission from *International Journal of Aging and Human Development*, 1973, *4*, 285–291. The assistance of The Canada Council, Princeton University, and the residents and administration of Glen Brae is gratefully acknowledged.

    1.   Participants (or "players") in a game formulation are viewed as seeking to maximize utility (the excess of rewards over costs), or at least to "satisfice," or gain a quantity of rewards satisfactory enough to make playing the game worthwhile (Simon, 1957; American Behavioral Scientist, 1964).

    2.   Each player knows the preference patterns or preferred strategies of the other player. "Awareness that other social actors have goals, and a varied but finite set of means through which to realize them, constitutes the primary prerequisite for game action" (Lyman & Scott, 1970, p. 31).

    3.   Each player is fully informed of the rewards and costs of alternative lines of action both for himself or herself and for other players (American Behavioral Scientist, 1964; Rapoport, 1960, p. 10).

Game-theoretical analysis attempts to construct a model of decision making under the above conditions. The emphasis is on players basing their decision strategies on not only their own conception of goals and the means to their realization but also on a complete knowledge of the perspective of the other player. That is, interaction is viewed as *strategic,* as a "cycle of two players taking into consideration their consideration of each other's consideration, and so forth" (Goffman, 1970, p. 137; see also O. K. Moore & Anderson, 1963). As most game theorists themselves admit (Luce & Raiffa, 1957, p. 10; Ofshe & Ofshe, 1970, p. 2; Boguslaw, 1965, pp. 56–58), the above conditions, which constitute a definition of "pure rationality," seldom if ever obtain in the real world, if only because the human mind does not have the information-processing capacities required (March & Simon, 1958, p. 139; Simon, 1957, p. 198). Nonetheless, human beings or players are generally recognized as intending to act rationally (Simon, 1957, p. 199) even if they must act practically on the basis of incomplete knowledge of the situation at present and at some future time (Schutz, 1953). While a game-theoretical analysis can never give us an accurate picture of the real world, it can sensitize the observer to departures from pure rationality and their causes, especially as these involve the interplay between two or more persons each with limited knowledge and each making assumptions about the other, neither of which may be highly accurate.

    It is possible to use real data to see whether they fit the implications of a game theory model (Morgan, 1963). My real data come from observation, interviewing, and documents gathered in a life-care retirement community I will call Glen Brae (Marshall, 1972), where approximately 400 residents have paid entrance fees ranging between $14,500 and $45,000 and have committed themselves to a contract specifying monthly maintenance fees upward of $330 for the rest of their lives, "or such larger or smaller amount per month as may from time to time be determined to be necessary by the Corporation" (statement appearing in the contract). The entrance fee is lost on a 2% monthly calculation such that any resident desiring to leave the community after 50 months, or dying at any time, will have lost his or her entire investment.

Because of the initial high payment, a move to Glen Brae would not be a good investment should people not live very long; they might well find better ways to spend their money. On the other hand, because monthly payments extend for the duration of their lives, the move to Glen Brae will not be a good investment should people live too long and run out of money. A rational decision to enter Glen Brae thus depends fundamentally on an accurate prediction of life expectancy, and secondly on an accurate estimate of any raises in monthly rental fees which might stem from inflation or mismanagement.

These two elements are also crucial to the rationality of the management. In order to establish a mortgage payment schedule, a resident death rate must be predicted, for only when someone dies (or moves permanently to the infirmary) does an apartment turn over and yield another entrance payment. In game-theoretical terms, the management (as one player) bets that any individuals entering Glen Brae (as other players in this retirement-community game) will die according to a predicted rate. Having recruited to the community a population with finite financial resources, the management also bets that the operational costs of maintaining community services will not be inflated to an extent that residents cannot cover them with their monthly rental fees.

These two elements, prediction of life expectancy and estimation of operating costs, are common to both parties and establish entry to Glen Brae as a gamelike situation. Both players, residents and management, have demonstrated gross departures from pure rationality on both elements.

Management established a 25-year mortgage schedule on the basis of a predicted death rate calculated, from mortality tables on its insurance company policyholders, by the insurance company which holds the mortgage. This estimate was overly "optimistic," as residents did not die as quickly or as frequently as predicted. During the first full year of operation, management predicted that apartment turnover from death would yield $250,000; actual turnover yielded only $79,000. An administration committee investigating the consequent financial crisis frankly stated:

> One of the problems . . . accrues from the fact that residents are outliving the insurance company statistics for life expectancy. . . . Actual deaths have run about 60% of the actuarily expected rate.

Management had defined the situation as, in game theory terms, a "game against nature" (Williams, 1966, p. 13; Burger & Freund, 1963, p. 68–69). In such games one plays the odds against a nonthinking, nonstrategic other; in this case against a statistical death rate. But this game is in fact a two-person mixed-motive game (Schelling, 1960, p. 100), with each party acting strategically; and rationality necessitates a taking into account of the other. In establishing a new prediction of death rate to accompany a shift from a 25- to a 30-year mortgage, the insurance company recognized that:

> the occupants would probably exercise selection similar to that of purchasers of annuities. That is to say, an individual or couple in ill health would probably not pay the relatively large sum required as [an entrance fee] since there would be no refund in the event of their early death. (Internal management document)

Purchasers of annuities are investors, different from the typical purchasers of insurance policies. They expect to live long enough to realize a return on their investment and are thus probably healthier than average for their age. Further, in order to make an investment on this large a scale, they are likely to have been so economically privileged as to have received better-than-average health care. Management erred in not considering the decision of an individual to move to Glen Brae as a strategic decision which would disconfirm the prediction of death rate. I suspect this error was compounded by a failure to recognize that in the case of a couple, the apartment, as specified in the resident's contract, reverts upon the death of one member, not to the corporation, but to the surviving spouse.

For their part, the residents, faced with the more complicated necessity of predicting a life expectancy long enough but not too long, have frequently erred as well. Their judgments of life expectancy are based on age and perceived health, but also inordinately on the age to which their parents lived, making little allowance for the greater life expectancy of each successive generation (treated in detail in Marshall, 1972). The words of one resident recognized the typical error of most: "I've lived beyond the time I thought I would."

The second common element in this retirement-community game is the prediction of inflationary effects on the monthly rental fees. Residents assumed the administration would provide an efficient and careful management, holding rental fees as low as possible, given inflation. Undoubtedly, few residents anticipated inflation would be as great as it has been. In any case, the effects of inflation were compounded by two errors on the part of management. The community was built on the basis of an *unwritten* agreement that it would not be taxed by the locality. Glen Brae is now taxed, and the additional operating expenses have been thrown back at the residents in the form of increased rental payments. Secondly, the costs of medical care were severely underestimated, and the proportion of the monthly rental fee devoted to the provision of medical care has increased more than threefold in a 5-year period. Since high-quality medical care presumably both costs a great deal and prolongs life, this conflict of interest situation represents a twofold financial threat to the corporation which runs Glen Brae, increasing outlfow and holding back inflow. As one resident put it,

> I've heard you get such beautiful care here you haven't a chance of dying. Here is the administration wanting you to die because they want to sell apartments, and the medical staff wanting you to live.

Monthly rental payments have increased at a rate of 18.6% a year over a 5-year period; this is an increase which could not have been foreseen by the most intendedly rational person deciding to move to Glen Brae.

In a mixed-motive game, neither player can win unless he behaves as the other expects him or her to do (Schelling, 1960, p. 100). Neither of the players has acted according to the expectations of the other, and there have been many losers. At a mundane level, for many residents it means what is expressed in this statement of a spinster over 80:

> I just got my bank statement, and it isn't too high. I'll have to be careful from now on. If you knew how long you had [to live] you could figure it out to the cent. But you can't.

Or, as another said:

> I think with the rapid increase in rates here that there are people in great anguish that they will not die until they've spent everything they've got—you see if you could just make it come out even it would be very nice.

Many of the residents have had to leave Glen Brae. Others have found it as difficult to leave as to remain. A discerning resident describes this entrapment as follows:

> There is a terrible feeling amongst the residents that we are caught. It was a great decision—physically and emotionally—to come. We got rid of many possessions, and paid our fees. Now if we've been here 5 years, we haven't much strength. There's that awful feeling of having been caught.

The administration as the other player has lost as well. Glen Brae was established by a church on a nonprofit basis, as a ministry to a segment of the aged population. An administration statement of philosophy notes that "it was realized that the middle income elderly have great needs just as those who are less affluent—needs of companionship—medical care and freedom from worry." In terms of freedom from worry, this experiment failed.

It should be clear that game theory, with its assumptions of full rationality on the part of both players, does not describe what has actually happened at Glen Brae. What then is its value? Game theory (Luce & Raiffa, 1957)

> can be used normatively to tell a person that this is the knowledge he should acquire, and, once he has it, the theory establishes the decisions he should make in order to achieve specified ends. (p. 49)

In its normative function, game theory provides a strong suggestion that one try one's best to take the perspective of the other and that failure to do so leads to a failure to maximize or satisfy utility. These imperatives to gaining full knowledge and taking the perspective of the other apply to other gerontological situations as well. I cannot extensively delve into these here, but would suggest its applicability to the understanding of failures in retirement planning along several dimensions. What intendedly rational person in planning for his or her later years could have successfully predicted inflation in property taxes and costs of medical care? Was not a person who planned, 30 years ago, on being cared for by his or her children in old age as rational as possible, even though now caught by a shift in the expectations regarding the flow of services between the generations (W. E. Moore, 1966)? I think game theory leads us to recognize that retirement planning in its immediate and long-range aspects is not likely to be characterized by high levels of rationality. This recognition should be helpful in directing us to policy implications. As the game theorist Rapoport suggests (1966):

> Rational analysis, for all its inadequacy, is indeed the best instrument of cognition we have. But it is often at its best when it reveals to us the nature of the situation we find ourselves in, even though it may have nothing to tell us how we ought to behave in this situation . . . Game-theoretical analysis, if pursued to its completion, *perforce* leads us to consider other than strategic modes of thought. (p. 214)

References

American Behavioral Scientist. A current appraisal of the behavioral sciences, Behavioral Research Council Bulletin, March 1964, Sect. 7, Vol. 7.

Boguslaw, R. *The new utopians*. Englewood Cliffs, N.J.: Prentice-Hall, 1965.

Burger, E., and Freund, J. *Introduction to the theory of games*. Englewood Cliffs, N.J.: Prentice-Hall, 1963.

Goffman, E. *Strategic interaction*. Oxford: Blackwell, 1970.

Luce, R. Duncan, and Raiffa, H. *Games and decisions*. New York: Wiley, 1957.

Lyman, S., and Scott, M. *A sociology of the absurd*. New York: Appleton-Century-Crofts, 1970.

March, J., and Simon, H. *Organizations*. New York: Wiley, 1958.

Marshall, Victor W. Continued living and dying as problematical aspects of old age. Unpublished doctoral dissertation, Department of Sociology, Princeton University, 1972.

Moore, Omar K., and Anderson, A. R. The structure of personality, in O. J. Harvey (Ed.), *Motivation and social interaction*. New York: Ronald, 1963, pp. 167–186.

Moore, Wilbert E. Aging and the social system, in John C. McKinney and Frank T. DeVyver (Eds.), *Aging and social policy*. New York: Appleton-Century-Crofts, 1966, p. 23–41.

Morgan, James N. Planning for the future and living with risk. *American Behavioral Scientist*, 1963, *40* (May:52–54).

Ofshe, L., and Ofshe, R. *Utility and choice in social interaction*. Englewood Cliffs, N.J.: Prentice-Hall, 1970.

Rapoport, Anatol. Critiques of game theory. *Behavioral Science*, 1959, *4*, 49–66.

Rapoport, Anatol. *Fights, games, and debates*. Ann Arbor: University of Michigan Press, 1960.

Rapoport, Anatol. Two-person game theory, in The essential ideas. Ann Arbor: University of Michigan Press, 1966.

Schelling, Thomas C. *The strategy of conflict*. Oxford: Oxford University Press, 1960.

Schutz, Alfred. Common-sense and scientific interpretation of human action. *Philosophy and Phenomenological Research*, 1953, *14*, 1–37.

Simon, Herbert. *Models of man*. New York: Wiley, 1957.

Williams, J. O. *The compleat strategyst*. New York: McGraw-Hill, 1966.

19

The 4% Fallacy:
Many Die
Where Few Have Lived

Robert Kastenbaum
Sandra E. Candy

It is often said that only 4% or, at the most, 5% of the elderly in the United States are to be found in nursing homes and other extended care facilities. Evidence to support this statement is not lacking. Riley and Foner used United States census data for 1960 to show that only 2.4% of Americans over the age of 65 were residing in homes for the aged and dependent.[1] The percentage of institutionalized could be increased to 3.7% if other kinds of group quarters and extended care facilities are included in the total. It could be increased again to 4.8% if those in mental hospitals are also included. Population data for 1965, also summarized by Riley and Foner, yielded a similar picture. Slightly less than 4% of Americans over the age of 65 were residing in group facilities or institutions. This information is adequate for the purposes of this chapter, although more recent population statistics are becoming available.

Most gerontologists appear to be familiar with the figures that have been cited here. References to the 4% figure are encountered frequently in journals, books, classes, conferences, and governmental deliberations. This statistic has many implications. Perhaps the most common usage has been to emphasize the overwhelming percentage of elders who are *not* institutionalized. This, in turn, spins off other implications, for example, "Conditions may be deplorable in many extended care facilities, but it is more practical to concentrate our attention elsewhere because so few elders are institutionalized."

It seems to us that a very elementary kind of error is being perpetuated here, the sort we teach our students to avoid. Our utilization of these population statistics is often fallacious because we fail to recognize that *the data are cross-sectional*. Knowing how many elders are institutionalized at

Reprinted with permission of *International Journal of Aging and Human Development*, 1973, 4, 15–21.

this moment, no matter how accurate a statement, does not tell us how many people will have resided in extended care facilities at some time in their lives. It does not give us the probabilities for an individual; only a series of longitudinal studies could answer that question satisfactorily.

Assume for sake of simplicity that the percentage of institutionalized elders at a particular point in time remains constant. Are we in a position to conclude that only 1 person in 25 who reaches old age will become institutionalized? We can conclude nothing of the sort. Common sense urges that the probabilities must be higher. How *much* higher is an empirical question.

Perhaps it is sufficient just to have called attention to a popular fallacy in generalizing from population data in gerontology. However, we felt that a small exercise in the gathering of corrective data might be appropriate. A pair of small studies were conducted to satisfy our own curiosity and encourage others to carry out more extensive and sophisticated work on this problem. For those who are cost conscious, it might be mentioned that the total budget was 25¢ (not supported by a grant).

Study 1

The first study was based upon the premise that, if a person *died* in a nursing home or other extended care facility, then it is reasonable to conclude that he or she had indeed *been* there. The method was to read all the obituaries reported in the *Detroit News* ("Detroit Area Obituaries" rubric) for a 1 year period (January 3, 1971–January 2, 1972). Place of death was the critical item noted, although other information was abstracted as well.

This method resulted in the identification of 1,184 deaths. Slightly more than half of this sample (52.7%) died in hospitals, according to the obituary notices. Interestingly, place of death was not specified in more than 20% (21.79%) of the entries. Approximately 13% were reported to have died in private homes, and a little over 10% in nursing homes. About 2% died in other locations, for example, in automobile accidents.

If we eliminate obituaries that did not specify places of death, we then have 926 cases remaining. Of these, 13.3% died in nursing homes. Deaths in private homes remained slightly more common (16.4%), and hospital deaths proved even more dominant, rising to 67%.

This reduced sample thus consists of all deaths of persons over the age of 65 reported in the daily newspaper of a large metropolitan area with places of death specified. We see that more than three times as many elders died in nursing homes than are reported as existing in same by cross-sectional population counts. The discrepancy becomes even more pronounced if we compare deaths with the figures for elders said to reside only in homes for the aged and dependent. Our method of data classification seems to justify this comparison. We now find that 13.3% died where only 2.4% lived—a discrepancy ratio that approaches 6:1.

One of the obvious difficulties with this study was the high percentage of deaths in which place was not, specified. Another difficulty was the question of possible missing cases, i.e., elders whose death may not have been reported in the form of a newspaper obituary. For these and other reasons we moved on to the second study.

Study II

Our premise remained the same—use the fact of death to establish place of residence. The difference was in source of information. This time we went directly to the death certificate.* Access was obtained to the microfilm records of all death certificates filed in the metropolitan Detroit area during the 1971 calendar year. These mortality records included 28,755 entries for persons aged 50 and over. This report is limited to those 65 and over, a population that numbered 20,234.

One could ask how many of these people died in a nursing home; this would not be identical with those who died in institutions of every type. We report separately upon deaths in nursing homes, in extended care facilities of all types, and in hospitals. The focus is upon the first two categories. The first is limited strictly to those who died in a place that could be positively identified as a nursing home. The second includes nursing home deaths and adds those which occured in other types of extended care facilities as well. If there was doubt concerning the nature of the facility, the death was not included in either of these categories. Typically, this meant recording a death in the hospital category, although the medical facility in question could perhaps be described more accurately as a nursing home with delusions of grandeur. Any errors in classification therefore should have resulted in an *under*estimation of deaths occurring in nursing homes and other extended care facilties.

Results

We find that approximately 20% of all deaths in the 65+ age range occurred in nursing homes, and approximately 24% occurred in the larger category that included all identifiable extended care facilities. The basic data are represented in Table 19.1.

*We are grateful to the Michigan Cancer Foundation for use of their microfilm records.

TABLE 19.1.   Place of Death for All Persons Aged 65 and Over in Metropolitan Detroit Area, 1971 (N = 20,234)

Place of Death	Number	Percentage of Total
All extended care facilities	4,796	23.70
Nursing homes only	4,099	20.02
Hospitals	12,631	62.43
Other	36	.18

Make a point-by-point comparison now with the usual cross-sectional population data. More than eight times as many elders died in nursing homes than were assumed to be living there. Six times as many people died in extended care facilities (the larger category) than the population data would have led us to believe.

Look at the same data from the perspective of the individual. When population data are used carelessly we assume that the odds of a person entering an extended care facility of some type are only 1 in 25. If we at least reasoned fallaciously with the appropriate figures, we would set the odds at about 1 in 40 for a person taking up residence in a home specifically designated for the aged and dependent. The present data offer a radically different set of odds: 1 chance in 4 of being in an extended care facility; 1 chance in 5 for a nursing home.

We should immediately acknowledge another factor that influences the data. Any person who resided in a nursing home but did not die there would not be counted among those deceased in institutions. This is an additional source of underestimation; More people have lived in nursing homes than have died there. The opposite is not true. Everybody who did expire in a nursing home was a resident, whether long- or short-term.

Discovery was made of 72 documented instances in which an elderly person sustained an injury in a nursing home, was transferred to a hospital, and died soon thereafter of pneumonia, pulmonary emboli, myocardial infarction, or some other form of heart disease. These individuals obviously had been in a nursing home although they died elsewhere. How many other old men and women were transferred from nursing homes for other medical reasons and subsequently died in the hospital? No information was available on this point, although moving out a terminally ill resident to die elsewhere is a well-known practice.

All the circumstances that affect the way in which death certificates are completed and in which this study was conducted veer in the direction of underestimating the number of people who spend some time as a resident of a nursing home or other extended care facility.

Sex and Race

Are there differences in place of death between men and women, and between blacks and whites? Whites comprised 87% of the total sample, blacks 13%. There was a slight predominance of males over females: 53%:47%. The ratio of men to women was approximately the same for blacks and whites; there were about seven male deaths for every six female deaths in both samples. Data on sex and race are presented in Table 19.2.

It is clear that place of death was not equally distributed by sex. Males were underrepresented in nursing home and extended care facilities and overrepresented in deaths recorded in hospitals and private homes. More women (58%) than men (42%) died in nursing homes, a difference of 23% from statistical expectations. This finding will not surprise those who are familiar with geriatric institutions. We would like to emphazise, however, that the present data do not include information on length of residence. We cannot say that the observed differences are related entirely to the predominance of female admissions to nursing homes. It could be that more men than women are removed from nursing homes to die elsewhere.

There is another finding that is worth pausing over. Of more than 20,000 deaths, only 36 were listed as occurring in some place other than an extended care facility, hospital, or private home. It is striking that 29 of these fatalities (about 80%) involved males. We have the impression that most of these deaths were sudden or traumatic, but our information is not complete.

The picture is quite different for race. The percentage of blacks in each

TABLE 19.2. Place of Death by Sex and Race for Persons Aged 65 and Over in Metropolitan Detroit Area, 1971

Group	Total	Extended Care Facility	Hospital	Private Home	Other
Women	9,541	2,789	5,350	1,305	7
Black	1,197	325	709	161	2
White	8,245	2,463	4,634	1,143	5
Other	9	1	7	1	0
Men	10,761	2,004	7,272	1,456	29
Black	1,398	277	943	170	8
White	9,363	1,727	6,329	1,286	21
Other	22	3	9	10	0
Black	2,595	602	1,652	331	10
White	17,608	4,190	10,963	2,429	26

of the major place-of-death categories was close to the total percentage of blacks in the study population. Remembering that 13% of all deaths in this sample involved black elders, we find 12.6% in nursing homes, 13% in hospitals, and 12% in private homes. There was a difference, however, in the fractional category of "other" deaths: Here 10 of the 36 fatalities, about 28%, were black.

It remains to examine sex-by-race combinations. The tendency for a higher percentage of the women to die in nursing homes was approximately equal for both blacks and whites. There were no instances in which the relative proportion of deaths by sex was reversed for blacks and whites. On the basis of the death certificate information, then, sex appears to be a more differentiating variable than race.

Discussion

If we are concerned about "death with dignity," to use the now-popular phrase, then perhaps the hospital should be our primary concern. Almost two out of every three deceased elders (62.4%) in the metropolitan Detroit area died in a hospital. (In all, 86% died in some kind of institution.) However, there is also much reason to be concerned about the nursing home as a final environment. We have seen that approximately one elder in four dies in an extended care facility, the odds being slightly higher for women. How many of these facilities are equipped to provide physical, social, and emotional comfort to the terminally ill old man or woman? Whether we choose to emphasize quality or duration of life for the terminally ill person, it is highly doubtful that nursing homes are providing adequate services for either goal.

Many old people die in nursing homes and other extended care facilities. In the Detroit metropolitan area alone, no fewer than 336 and as many as 476 men and women died *every month* during 1971. Yet relatively little attention is given, even by nursing home activists, to improving the quality of terminal care. Federal and local governments have also been remiss. Governmental policies and practices have done little to encourage minimally acceptable care within institutions. This failing is all the more unfortunate in view of a similar lack of attention to the development of realistic alternatives to the nursing home as a final environment.

The reluctance to become involved in terminal care and the 4% fallacy tend to fuel each other. Dying is so unimportant or unworthy that a person should not really be counted as "living" in an extended care facility if he or she is in a process of terminal decline. Similarly, the misleading usage of extended care facility population statistics tends to draw attention away from the fact that many of our elders end their lives among strangers in an environment that offers little true "nursing" and scarcely resembles a "home." Perhaps abandonment of the 4% fallacy will also contribute to the abandonment of destructive attitudes and practices.[2,3]

The most general implication of this study is its reinforcement of every problem that gerontologists have already identified in the nursing home. All the painful shortcomings of the inadequate extended care facility must be regarded as of even greater consequence than previously noted. This statement perhaps should be amended to: of greater *social* consequence. Despair and indignity are as real if only one person is affected. We have known that many thousands are affected. And now we must face the fact that the true extent of the institutional care problem is of greater magnitude than usually assumed. To look at the same facts from a brighter perspective, every action that is taken to improve the quality of life in extended care facilities will be a blessing to a very considerable number of our fellow citizens.

We hope that the 4% fallacy will now be retired—gracefully or otherwise—and give rise to a renewed determination to understand and overcome the problems of institutional care for our elders. Follow-up studies by other researchers have confirmed and extended the basic findings of the original study reprinted here.[4,5]

References

1. Riley, M. W., and Foner, A. *Aging and society. V. 1: An inventory of research findings,* New York: Russell Sage Foundation 1968.
2. Markson, E. W., and Hand, J. Referral for death: Low status of the aged and referral for psychiatric hospitalization, *Aging and Human Development,* 1970,*1,* 261–272.
3. Kastenbaum, R., and Aisenberg, R. B. *The psychology of death,* New York: Springer, 1972.
4. Palmore, E. Total chance of institutionalization among the aged, *Gerontologist,* 1976, *16,* 504–507.
5. Wershow, H. The four percent fallacy. *Gerontologist,* 1976, *16,* 52–55.

20

Premature Death and Self-injurious Behavior in Old Age

Robert Kastenbaum

Brian L. Mishara

Assume a physician intends to do right by his elderly patients. He has freed himself from the cultural bias that regards those of advanced years as second-class citizens. Without condescension, begrudging, or sloughing off, he does what can be done with existing medical capabilities to maintain health and forestall death. When inescapable death is in prospect, the physician remains as involved and helpful as ever. Now he acts in the interest of reducing discomfort and preserving the human integrity of his dying patient.

Even when all these assumptions are entirely justified, it remains possible that the elderly patient will die "too soon" or "prematurely." This chapter is concerned with the concept and the reality of premature death in old age. Attention is directed especially to those psychosocial factors that may counteract the physicians's efforts to maintain life and health.

Premature Death As a Concept

Premature birth is an established concept. Why? Perhaps this is because our society places strong (and mostly positive) values on birth and the young. By contrast, premature death is a concept that has been around in various forms but cannot be said to have become established. It has scarcely even been defined. The concept of premature death may seem especially vague, if not downright alien, when applied to old age. Death and the aged do not strike the same responsive chord in our society as birth and the young.

From *Geriatrics*, 1971, *26*, 70–81. Reprinted with permission of *Geriatrics*. The authors wish to acknowledge the cooperation of staff members of Northville State Hospital and a critical reading of the manuscript by Beatrice Kastenbaum.

Some of the differences between premature birth and premature death in old age are suggested in Table 20.1. The first three points of comparison remind us that we know more about the conception-to-birth sequence than we do about the events from the onset of dying to death. Typically, one cannot specify precisely when the dying process began or how long a course it should run. Furthermore, a death may be premature in either of two senses: (1) The expected temporal course from inception of the terminal phase to death has been foreshortened, or (2) the inception of the terminal phase itself has come too soon. One could, of course, also speak of a "surprise" or unwanted baby as a premature birth even though the gestation period proved to be normal.

But our culture's selective attention to birth and inattention to the death of the aged show up more clearly when we consider the context in which these events occur. Perhaps it can even be said that premature birth is an event while the premature death of an old person is a nonevent. A medicosocial system cradles the woman who is on the verge of bringing forth a premature baby. She is not spurned or neglected. The system makes special human skills and technical facilities available for the care of her child as well as for herself. It seems almost superfluous to add that usually there is somebody there with her, witnessing and sharing the experience. Postpartum care is maintained with reference to criteria for the well-being of both mother and child. Physicians and nurses know the characteristics of a healthy neonate. "A good delivery" and a "healthy baby" are appropriate concepts for a premature as well as for a normal birth.

Old people die alone. This proposition cannot be documented with hard data at the moment, but it is consistent with many observations.[1-3] Even when the death of an old person is expected, we are not very likely to be at his or her side. We have more important duties to perform elsewhere,

TABLE 20.1.   Premature Birth Compared with Premature Death in Old Age

Factor	Premature Birth	Premature Death
Onset	Often specifiable	Seldom specifiable
Term of process	Gestation time well established	Duration of dying process not well established
Temporal variation	Small range	Large range
Context of event	Usually social-technical, directly witnessed	Often solitary, noted retrospectively
Criteria	Standards for normal birth and condition of neonate well established	Standards for "appropriate death" vague, conflicting, not established

anywhere else. The dying elder is to be screened off from the world of the living—at least in this regard his or her existence receives a negative sort of acknowledgement.

Yet the persons who succumb to a premature death are even more isolated. The solitary nature of their existences may be related intimately to the timing of their deaths, as in the suicide of a lonely man. He may pass unnoticed although others are in the vicinity. His death's prelude of withdrawal from social relations may serve as an effective emotional screen to conceal his mortal move.

Whether or not there are witnesses to the death of an old person, the "appropriateness" of his or her demise may be far from clear. The concept of an appropriate death was introduced by Weisman and Hackett.[4] Essentially, an appropriate death is that which one might have chosen for oneself if given the opportunity. Timing is one but only one dimension of the appropriate death. A person might have chosen either an earlier or a later death, either alone or in the company of intimates, either in bed or "with his boots on," etc. The concept of an appropriate death remains controversial in general. It may be especially difficult to apply in geriatrics since our culture remains deficient in its conception of what constitutes an appropriate life for the aged. The ambiguity as to what is good, acceptable, or appropriate death for an old person makes it difficult to judge whether a particular death was premature. More significantly, it also hobbles our efforts to improve the quality of the terminal phase of life. How can we be enablers of good deaths without the guidance and motivation provided by acceptable criteria?

The concept of premature death in old age cannot be separated entirely from the concept of premature death at any age. Premature birth is, of course, a concept that is specific to a particular segment of the total life-span. There is a tendency to regard premature death in a parallel manner. At the extreme, one might hold that any death of a young person is premature while every old person is ripe for death. Careful evaluation of ths view would require working through the multiple and sometimes conflicting bases for establishing definitions of young and old. Furthermore, we would have to take into account the fact that some young people face death with equanimity and readiness, as well as the fact that some elders give every indication of not being prepared to leave this life. Age per se may not be the most enlightened criterion to employ when considering the timeliness of death.

Perhaps at this stage of our ignorance it is enough to admit that premature death is a concept we can neither crystallize nor abandon. We have accustomed ourselves to regarding some deaths as premature or untimely without having developed adequately the images of a mature or a timely death. It may now be time to take such concepts seriously. Until we have thought, observed, and experimented our way through the question of mature death, it might be wise to follow the course of least mischief. This course itself may be nothing more or less than a reading of the Hippocratic oath within a special context: Physician or Layperson, we will avoid inflicting, enabling, or abetting the cessation of human experience. Less mischief is to be done if we assume that *all avoidable deaths are premature,* regardless of what may be written in faded ink upon the individual's birth certificate. If we are not certain of the opposite proposition, then it might be the most reasonable course to direct our influence to the prevention of preventable death even in old age. As we see below, the patient may not have been ready to die, despite external readings of his or her condition and even his or her own protestations.

Premature Death As a Reality

Suicide is perhaps the most obvious type of avoidable death at any age. The victims would still be alive had they not raised their own hands against themselves. It is gradually becoming recognized that suicide is a major threat to life in the later years. Statistics in the United States regularly display a progressively higher suicide rate with advancing adult age.[5] Men appear to be especially vulnerable. Not only do many more elderly men take their own lives in comparison with elderly women and younger men but the ratio between attempt and completion narrows alarmingly. Suicidal old men seldom miss.[6]

In expert opinion,[7] reported suicides underestimate the true incidence by a large margin. At meetings of the American Association of Suicidology and in intensive suicide prevention workshops, for example, the estimate most often given is that the true incidence is at least twice as great as the 20,000–25,000 deaths that are officially recorded as suicides each year. The reasons for this disparity include such factors as insurance claims, religious sanctions, and differential practices among coroners and pathologists. There is no reason to believe that certification of suicide as cause of death is any more accurate for the elderly than it is in general. If anything, we might expect that even less care is taken to develop the full picture. Less seems to hinge upon the final diagnosis, and one may still be ready to believe that some people die of old age per se. Until and unless firm contradictory evidence is unearthed, it will be difficult to shake the impression that suicide is even more of a menace to the lives of elderly Americans than the available figures proclaim.

But suicide is just the begining. Rather, suicide is just the most identifiable, classifiable form of avoidable death in old age. When we consider "subintentional suicide" or "life-threatening behavior," we must depend largely upon case material. Intensive, multifaceted, and persuasive as some of this material may be, it does not permit us to make sound estimates of prevalence. Rightly or wrongly, however, the present writers have come to believe that the number of self-aided deaths in old age that cannot be classified as suicidal equals or exceeds those which properly would be classified as suicidal were all facts known.

The pioneering suicidologist Shneidman has offered a classification of orientations toward the cessation of one's own life based upon extensive case material.[8] The subintentional orientation is of most relevance here. The person who increases the probability of his or her own demise without conscious knowledge of this disposition or uses methods that are indirect may be said to have a subintentional suicidal orientation. Death can result sooner than necessary without any instrumental action being performed that ordinarily would be labeled as suicidal—the wrist is not slashed, the noose is not strung, the gun is not fired, yet the person is dead before his or her time.

Some of the most interesting supportive material for Shneidman's propositions has emerged from several series of psychological autopsies. The psychological autopsy is an intensive multidisciplinary case approach introduced by Shneidman and Farberow to investigate instances in which the cause of death was difficult to determine by traditional means.[9,10] It soon became apparent that the traditional cause-of-death categories themselves are insufficient to represent the complex psychosociobiologic processes that lead to some deaths. Whether or not the existing classification system is ever modified, there has been an increasing awareness among those who study suicide or death in general that understanding and prevention require a broader and more differentiated approach than what is afforded by the present system.

A modified form of the psychological autopsy method was developed by Weisman and Kastenbaum to study a sampling of all deaths that occurred in a geriatric hospital population.[11] The emphasis here was less upon achieving an improved final diagnosis than upon searching for points of possible intervention in working with those who are still alive and upon advancing our knowledge of the preterminal and terminal processes. The observations tend to support Shneidman's thesis that individuals often play a greater role in their own demise than what the suicide statistics per se would indicate—and these observations were made entirely upon a geriatric population. A related study at the same facility yielded suggestive data that elders who were seen as manifesting a "will to die" did, in fact, succumb sooner than what would have been expected from medical criteria alone (although the ratings themelves were made by physicians).[12,13] The evidence, however, remains fragmentary. It can only be asserted that, if we look carefully, we are likely to find that some elders (and some of their juniors) advance the date of their death without executing an overtly suicidal action.

As Weisman has noted, "The most disturbing fact . . . is that frank suicide attempts may be only a minor example of the overall prevalence of equally destructive, life-threatening behavior." (p. 1)[14] He rejects the dynamics of depression as an adequate basis for understanding self-inflicted death and also holds that the theory of implicit or subintentional suicide has not really been proved. He prefers the alternative concept of life-threatening behaviors, which encompasses a broader range of individuals and contexts. Weisman suggests that

> we can combine our knowledge of the psychosomatic aspects of organic illnesses and death with what we know about suicide. . . . We shall turn away from the "causes" of death and toward the "contexts" of death. A comprehensive theory of death and what it means to people, how it articulates with events, crises, and conflicts, and how factors in communication both incite and relieve lethal behavior may repay efforts to suspend our habitual methods of formulation. (pp. 1–2)[15]

Subsequent publications by Weisman and his colleagues will present his views and preliminary findings in detail. Here we report a wisp of an independent exploratory study that might have a little heuristic value.

Self-injurious Behavior among Geriatric Medical Inpatients

Life-threatening behavior may be regarded as comprising a continuum from the almost certainly lethal action to the action, or nonaction, that subtly nudges one along the path toward damage and destruction. An attempt was made to sample all instances of life-threatening behavior that could be observed during a short time period in a population of elderly men and women. This preliminary study was undertaken both as a test of the feasibility of conducting such research on a more systematic basis and as a gathering of at least a taste of baseline data to provide some foundation for subsequent work.

Participants

The participants were 64 male and 142 female inpatients who were residing on two male and four female wards at a state mental hospital. These men and women were not classified as psychotic. Rather, they were hospitalized on the basis of chronic and presumably irreversible medical problems. The mean ages of the men and women were 70.3 and 72 years, respectively.

Procedure

Charge attendants on each of the three shifts for the six wards involved were asked to make note of all self-injurious behaviors observed during a 7-day period. Each behavior was to be described briefly and the frequency of its occurrence recorded. Repeated self-injurious behaviors (S-IBs) by the same individual were recorded as such.

A random sample of 20 men was observed for 3 days by the nursing personnel. The Psychotic Inpatient Profile (PIP) Form (Lorr) was completed on these patients to confirm their nonpsychotic diagnoses at a behavioral level.

Results

The PIP ratings of the 20 men in the subsample indicated abnormal behaviors on only 1 of the 12 scales. They were rated as high on "care needed." It would appear, then, that the geriatric patients for whom the following data were obtained do not constitute a psychiatrically deviant population.

Of the men, 28, or 43.8%, engaged in at least one S-IB during the observation period. Of the women, 31, or 21.8%, engaged in self-injurious behaviors. No women and only 2 men displayed more than one S-IB. Each of the 2 men engaged in aggressive behaviors toward each other twice.

The relative number of men and women who engaged and did not engage in S-IB during this period was compared. The chi-square value of 9.887 (with 1 degree of freedom) was significant at the .01 level. The men were more likely to exhibit behavior rated as self-injurious.

Frequencies with which various types of S-IBs were recorded are given in Table 20.2. A male-female comparison was made between the proportions of S-IB which involved more than one person. The observations for the men consisted almost entirely of fighting, pushing, or pulling incidents. The 18 incidents noted for the men clearly exceeded the 3 stepping, tripping, or assaulting incidents observed for the women. A test of the difference between proportions of behaviors involving others for men and women (z test, corrected for continuity) was significant beyond the .0001 level.

Discussion

A serious deficiency of this study is the lack of an adequate control group to determine if the high frequency of S-IB reported here is peculiar to the institutionalized geriatric population observed. This, of course, is also a deficiency of the entire field, since no comparable data seem to have been collected elsewhere. Even so, the alarmingly high incidence of S-IB or, in Weisman's term, life-threatening behavior, is important in itself. Serious

TABLE 20.2.   Enumeration of Self-injurious Behaviors for 1-week period among Chronic Geriatric Inpatients

Behavior	Number of Patients Engaging in Behavior at Least Once	
	Men	Women
Injury from inability to walk adequately or feebleness, for example, falling down	1	5
Bumping into object such as a wall	1	4
Climbing out of wheelchairs and falling	0	3
Scratching self	0	2
Undressing self	0	2
Injury due to "careless" use of cigarettes	2	4
Scalding hands by turning on hot water	0	2
Eating foreign object	1	3
Choking from eating too fast	0	2
Fighting, pushing, etc., another	18	1
Tripping over another and being injured	0	1
Injury from being tripped over	0	2
Striking solid immovable object such as a wall or window with arm	4	0
Injury caused by hostility evoked by stealing another's cigarettes	1	0
Total	28	31

questions about the quality of the lives of those individuals must be raised when the incidence of S-IB is 43% for men and 21% for women in a 1-week period. Multiplying this frequency by the many weeks which make up the many years of residence of a large number of patients is staggering to the imagination. Also, the realization that this is not a psychiatric population but, rather, a group of people with "organic" problems leads one to question the practice of making dichotomous organic-psychiatric classifications. It is difficult to relate organic deficits or dysfunctions to self-destructive behaviors unless intervening psychosocial variables are considered.

This preliminary sampling of S-IB among medical inpatients raises a number of questions. Could it be that within the institutional environment destructive behaviors may lead to increased survival potential because they provoke the much-wanted attention of nursing personnel? Is it possible that the same dynamics might be found in the home and the community as well as the institution? Might it be the case that the special care given an injured patient serves as a social reinforcer to increase the probability of further S-IB? In other words, the same action may have opposite effects: leading to higher probability of survival because of additional care received, which in turn bolsters self-esteem, dependency cravings, and will to live, but also leading to the strengthened tendency to repeat self-destructive acts, any of which may prove to be the one that introduces the preterminal process. This would indeed be a species of the double-bind situation. Elderly patients may feel, and *be* ignored if they do not do something to draw attention to themselves every week or so; yet every such action introduces a new risk factor.

Precisely how do specific S-IBs lead to deaths that might have been prevented? Who are the greatest threat to themselves, elders who have fallen into a pattern of self-jeopardy or the ones who suddenly manifest their first S-IB? What is to be made of the apparent sex differences—and how are these differences in S-IB related to actual death? One should not assume that elderly women are less lethal than their male peers simply because they seem to exhibit fewer S-IBs.

Speaking of frequency, it must also be kept in mind that an unknown number of S-IBs were not observed. It would be naïve to treat the obtained reports as exhaustive records of all the actions that might have been classified as S-IB. Not only do we have an underestimation but there is no way of determining the selective factors that might have been involved—by shift, by sex of the patient, by type of incident, by age or personality of the observer, etc. The obtained frequency of S-IB, if anything, is probably an underestimation of the amount and perhaps the intensity of potentially life-threatening behavior exhibited during this 1-week period.

Furthermore, there may well be systematic biases that conceal some of the most significant behaviors. Consider the following list of life-threatening maneuvers:

1. Refuses medication
2. Fails to follow specific order of the physician
3. Smokes or drinks against medical advice
4. Refuses to eat or, more subtly, seems to accept food but ingests and retains very little
5. Situates oneself in a hazardous environment (near a drafty window, for instance)

Behaviors such as these have at least three characteristics in common: (1) Singly or in combination they can hasten death; (2) they are relatively passive and "untrouble making" compared with obvious self-aggressive actions; and (3) none of these items was recorded as S-IB by the charge attendants.

Trained observers or those with other frames of reference might have compiled a record of S-IB of this general type that rivaled or exceeded the information summarized above. The differential peception implied here is also likely to affect prevention and intervention. One cannot very well attempt to alter the course of elderly persons who are threatening their own lives unless one notices what is happening and makes the relevant interpretation.

The possible inadvertent reinforcement of S-IB and the likely differential perception of hazaradous actions have been cited. These are two of the general ways in which the social environment may contribute to injuries, failings, and deaths that could have been forestalled. But these observations merely stake out two lines of needed investigation and modification. The total picture of the life-and-death ecology of the elderly person is in urgent need of development.

Some Implications for the Physician

Each reader's own professional and personal experiences will enrich the implications she or he draws from what has been presented above. Here we simply touch upon a few considerations that seem to merit further attention. These are divided into implications for the physician as a physician and for the physician as a vector in the social life space of elderly patients.

As a Physician

Some medical practioners have an exquisite awareness of the messages which the patient is attempting to communicate on the wavelength of the presenting symptoms. They recognize that a symptom-oriented reading of the patient's condition may be inadequate in the broad sense, even if technically accurate. While this sensitive practice of medicine is welcome throughout the age spectrum, it is especially desirable in the geriatric range. The physician may be the first, and last, professional to whom an elderly person turns before turning on himself or herself.

As a general rule, it is suggested here that every elderly patient be evaluated by his or her physician in terms of potential suicide or life-threatening behavior. This additional dimension of evaluation does impose still another burden upon the already busy and burdened practitioner. However, this surveillance is a natural implication of the high known suicide rate among the elderly and the even higher suspected rate, as well as the suspected death rate through subintentional and other indirect methods.

Assessment of suicide potential is an art and science that has received substantial attention during the last few years. It is by no means an easy or automatic procedure. One expects to make mistakes of both the false-positive and the false-negative type. Yet an awareness of typical clues to suicide and an appreciation of some of the contextual factors which dispose toward attempts at self-destruction can prevent many preventable deaths. The interested physician will find an expanding literature on the identification of suicidal clues. The actual uncovering of potentially lethal trends requires more in the way of being "tuned in" to this wavelength than it does an inordinate investment of time.

It is relevant to emphasize the significance of the physical distress signals which the aged patient brings to his or her physician. These signals may foreshadow premature death either of the suicidal or nonsuicidal type. A condition need not pose an imminent threat to life in the purely medical sense in order to serve as a critical element in the lethal sequence. Lipsitt reminds us that "the anguish arising from emotional starvation is profound and lingering, and it ultimately leads to despair, preoccupation with bodily functions, reliance upon others, physical and mental deterioraton, hospitalization, and even death. *Before giving up* [italics added], geriatric individuals often turn pleadingly to their physician for the alleviation of their misery and pain."[15] He adds that physicians too often reject the patient when they reject the medical significance of his or her symptoms, failing sometimes even to offer the tenuous support of a return appointment. Having ruled out the presence of a serious organic disease, the physician leaves the aged patient alone with his or her anguish—and that much closer to a desperate solution. From our own clinical research, it was found that even the successful treatment of organic problems in aged patients can result in regressive and life-threatening behavior.[16] Organic illness or no, treated successfully or no, the patient seems to require sensitive support to remain interested in surviving.

There is the further implication that assessment of lethal potential be made continuously. The orientation toward self-destruction is no more constant in most people than other sentiments. While people at any age may have their self-hating days, the more precarious physical and environmental status of many elders should raise the red flag in our minds whenever such a mood is detected. The oft-noted fluctuation in alertness, vigor, and mood among some aged people is still another indication for the physician to stand ready to revise her estimate of lethal potential from contact to contact. The alert physician will identify maneuvers on the part of each patient in her care that may have idiosyncratic life-threatening implications.

As a Vector

By what he leaves unsaid and undone as well as by what he says and does,
the physician exerts substantial influence over the quality and duration of
his patient's life. For example, the implicit attitudes that being old and sick
is as "good as dead" has its way of becoming part of the medical care system,
even if the attitude is just a subconscious stowaway in the mind of a
conscientious physician.

The distinguished geriatrician Goldfarb, asks,

> Why do we see aged persons who have suffered stroke or cardiac failure
> admitted to long-term facilities and left without blankets in a drafty corridor,
> or kept sitting in a wheelchair for a long period of time before they are placed
> on a stretcher, and then roughly handled from stretcher to bed? Because
> attendants have heard a physician say, with seeming compassion, "We can't do
> much for this poor fellow except let him die." Here we see rationalized
> hostility and justification of medical neglect. Translated in terms of staff
> activity, it may encourage inhumane and harmful attitudes.[17]

More specifically, the physician can use her influence to reduce the
likelihood of premature death in such ways as the following:

1. *Encourage continuity of care*. Supportive emotional relationships
that sustain the patients through those times when they are tempted to
give up or to turn against themselves are more apt to exist when the
"system" makes possible the stable assignment of personnel to patients.
Shifting personnel about for reasons that are not directly related to patient
care may have some administrative advantages but is apt to deprive patients of the informed attention and support they require at points of
special vulnerability.

2. *Discourage relocations*. Research continues into the apparent
relationship between relocation and sudden death in elderly patients. It is
difficult to draw firm conclusions at present. Nevertheless, concern about
the effects of "transplantation shock" appears eminently well justified.
Even small moves, say from one type of accommodation to another within
the same facility, may have major implications for the patient. The specific
advantages to be derived from each proposed move should be weighed
carefully against the possibility of an "unhinging effect" that could reach
lethal extremes.

3. *Foster interpersonal mutuality*. Elderly patients too often are cast
in the role of powerless beings who must accept what is "good for them"
with scarcely a whimper. As Clark and others have pointed out, this is
exacting a high price indeed for having one's legitimate dependency needs
met.[18] But the price may also include life itself. The high incidence of

self-destructive behaviors noted in our little study could be interpreted as a natural reaction to the one-sidedness of old people's role in the medical care system. When one becomes stirred up or enraged, one is not likely to vent one's feelings directly. It is too risky to antagonize those powerful people upon whose goodwill one's survival seems to depend. Therefore, one "takes it out" on oneself or one's equally inconsequential peers. How many suicides and other acts of life-threatening behavior could have been avoided if old people felt free to express themselves directly without fear of retaliation? It must be understood that the mere subjective conviction that one is operating a benign and open system is not equivalent either to the objective facts of the situation or to what comes through to the patients themselves.

4. *Reinforce comfort-giving behaviors.* So long as cure or rehabilitation remain the only really acceptable goals to the medical system (including nurses, social workers, etc.), we cannot expect that consistent attention will be given to the comfort of those who seem beyond cure. The physician can set appropriate examples by his own behavior and by identifying and approving the examples he notices in others. By establishing comfort-giving behavior as an entirely legitimate activity, the physician will be moving closer to two desirable goals: (1) He will actually be improving the survival potential of patients who appear to be hopelessly ill or deteriorated, since what comforts may also restore the will to live, and (2) he will have an opportunity to transcend the popular controversy between "saving" and "letting go" of a failing life. Adequate provision of comfort requires the same degree of sensitivity and commitment that one would bring to straightforward life-extending interventions. One must take the trouble to know the patient if either the life-extending or comforting efforts are to be intelligently conceived. Because a patient may at a particular point in time express an inclination to die does not necessarily alter the picture that much. There is some evidence on hand that aged patients with a dominant death-seeking mood may change their orientation after appropriate comfort and stimulation are offered.[19] There is an obvious parallel here with suicidal individuals at any age—no matter how self-destructive a person may be today, tomorrow he or she may be deeply grateful for the fact that his or her feelings were respected but not obeyed.*

References

1. Glaser, B. G., and Strauss, A. *Awareness of dying*. Chicago: Aldine, 1965.
2. Sudnow, D. *Passing on*. Englewood Cliffs, N.J.: Prentice-Hall, 1967.

*Follow-up clinical programs by Mishara and his colleagues have now demonstrated that it is possible to reduce the frequency of self-injurious behavior among geriatric patients by changing the expectations and reinforcements available in the milieu.[20]

3. Kalish, R. A. The aged and the dying process: The inevitable decisions. *Journal of Social Issues, 21,* 1965, 87–96.

4. Weisman, A. D., and Hackett, T. The dying patient. *Forest Hospital Publication, 1,* 1962, 16–21.

5. *Vital statistics of the United States, 1968.* Vol. 11. *Mortality,* Part B. U. S. Department of Health, Education, and Welfare, 1968.

6. Farberow, N. L., and Shneidman, E. S. Suicide and age, in E. S. Shneidman and N. L. Farberow (Eds.), *Clues to suicide.* New York: McGraw-Hill, 1967.

7. Shneidman, E. S. New developments in the psychological autopsy method. Address given at Northern New England Conference on Suicide Prevention, April 1967.

8. Shneidman, E. S. Orientations toward death: A vital aspect of the study of lives. *International Journal of Psychiatry, 2,* 1966, 167–200.

9. Litman, R. E.; Curphey, T. J.; Shneidman, E. S. et al. Investigations of equivocal deaths. *Journal of the American Medical Association, 184,* 1963, 924–929.

10. Shneidman, E. S. Sample investigations of equivocal deaths, in N. L. Farberow and E. S. Shneidman (Eds.), *The cry for help.* New York: McGraw-Hill, 1965.

11. Weisman, A. D., and Kastenbaum, R. *The psychological autopsy: A study of the terminal phase of life.* New York: Behavioral Publications, 1968.

12. Kastenbaum, R. The realm of death: An emerging area in psychological research. *Journal of Human Relations, 13,* 1965, 538–552.

13. Kastenbaum, R. The interpersonal context of death in a geriatric institution. Presented at the 17th Annual Scientific Meetings, Gerontological Society, Minneapolis, October 30, 1964.

14. Weisman, A. D. Suicide, death, and life-threatening behavior. Presented at "Suicide Prevention in the Seventies," Phoenix, January 30–February 1, 1970.

15. Lipsitt, D. R. A medico-psychological approach to dependency in the aged, in R. A. Kalish (Ed.), *The dependencies of old people.* Ann Arbor: Institute of Gerontology, University of Michigan, 1969, pp. 17–26.

16. Kastenbaum, R. The crisis of explanation, in R. Kastenbaum (Ed.), *New thoughts on old age.* New York: Springer, 1964, pp. 316–323.

17. Goldfarb, A. I. The physician and the chronic care institution. *Gerontologist, 10*(Part 2), 1970, 45–49.

18. Clark, M. Cultural values and dependency in later life, in R. A. Kalish (Ed.), *The dependencies of old people.* Ann Arbor: Institute of Gerontology, University of Michigan, 1969, pp.59–72.

19. Kastenbaum, R. and Weisman, A. D. Application of the psychological autopsy method to geriatrics, in D. P. Kent, R. Kastenbaum, and S. Sherwood (Eds.), *Research, action, and planning for the elderly.* New York: Behavioral Publications, 1972.

20. Mishara, B. L. and Kastenbaum, R. Wine in the treatment of long-term geriatric patients in mental institutions. *Journal of the American Geriatrics Society,* 1974, *22,* 88–94.

VI

Vitality and
Self-actualization

Despite all the problems that have been explored in this book—and others that might have been—old age is proving to be a rewarding time of life for many people today. But why not for *more* people? How can the blessings of vitality and self-actualization be enjoyed by a greater number of men and women in their later decades? Few responsible observers would offer a single answer. There has been such a promising development of personal growth opportunities through the cultivation of life-long learning, however, that this approach deserves special attention.

Maggie Kuhn, the indomitable founder of the Gray Panthers, places the potential of America's elders in broad context in her observations of learning by living. She sees our older and therefore more experienced echelons of citizens as excellent advocates not only for themselves but also for "a more humane and just society" for everybody, especially those who traditionally have been oppressed and powerless.

Formal educational opportunities for older people are examined by Jeanne E. Bader, who also provides a useful selective bibliography for those interested in starting, evaluating, or participating in such programs. Bader finds that in recent years the opportunity for formal education has become "quite generally available, frequently cost free, and has been designed to appeal, in one form or another, to a substantial proportion of the elder community."

Hyman Hirsch, director of the Institute for Retired Professionals at the New School for Social Research, describes his innovative program that is now serving as a model for others. At the IRP educated retirees have found a new way of spending much of their time in dignified and valuable roles as teachers, leaders, administrators—and participants—in their own "inner university."

Mental health of the elderly in general is not always supported by our culture's attitude toward what is and is not "mentally healthy." Robert Kastenbaum wonders: "Is it possible that what often passes for mental health is a precondition to much of the despair and excessive focus on a high-noon vision of the human condition in which time and change, shadow and sorrow are ignored?" It is argued that a more mature attitude in culture and in our mental health establishment can enrich all who are here today and gone tomorrow.

Vitality and self-actualization

21

Learning by Living

Margaret E. Kuhn

Old people too often are seen by gerontologists as objects of scholarly inquiry like mice in laboratories or butterflies impaled on pins in cases or case histories. It is time we were recognized as living, breathing collaborators in and contributors to society's understanding of aging. We have important contributions to make to the new patterns of thinking and research which are emerging and which fully take account of all who have a part in this age of self-determination and liberation—including us. Too long have gerontologists studied *about* us instead of *with* us.

The Gray Panthers is an emerging national movement which emphasizes the relationship of personal growth and self-development to the pursuit of larger social goals such as self-determination and liberation from stereotypy. As a coalition of old people and young people working together for social change and in the larger public interest, we also demonstrate interactional lifestyles and actions which counter age-ism in all its oppressive forms.

Our movement has three characteristics which distinguish it from other groups of so called "senior citizens" (a euphemism which we reject!):

1.   We are people and young people working as an action coalition for change—not adjustment or accommodation to the existing order.

2.   We are concerned about all forms of injustice and oppression, including unjust treatment of citizens because of their age.

3.   We are experimenting with new, flexible structures and with multiple leadership, believing that human relationships are more important than bureaucratic hierarchies; our network does not depend on a lot of machinery to keep oiled and running.

Our long-range goals are directed toward social change and in the direction of a more humane and just society—and toward the liberation and empowerment of all persons who are oppressed and powerless—among them, nonwhite people, women, and the aged.

More immediate objectives include the following:

Reprinted with permission from *International Journal of Aging and Human Development*, 1977/78, *8*, 359–365.

   1.   To eradicate age-ism and all forms of discrimination on the basis of age.

   2.   To build a new, supportive community of the old and the young, which will have power and influence in society and enhance personal growth.

   3.   To develop and test new models and lifestyles.

   4.   To build coalitions for political and social action.

   5.   To use our experience, wisdom, and skills to humanize our society and its structure.

The educational process must characterize the implementation of each of these objectives. Certainly the liberation of people from stereotypes of any kind requires intensive reeducation to counter the brainwashing which society has imposed upon us and which we ourselves have incorporated in many cases as just. The Gray Panthers have proved to be one movement successful in the reversal of such stereotypes. What is required is that we be students of change as well as teachers. It is fortunate indeed that the eldest among us are by definition free to initiate change, rattle cages, and rock boats. We have only to gain!

The Elimination of Age-ism and Discrimination Based on Age

An important element in age-ism is the segregation of people by age, the herding and ghettoizing of the elders away from the young and middle aged. Some of this segregation occurs in our minds and is reflected in our attitudes about age and aging and in our age-based self-deceits and self-hate.

Young people, too, are powerfully conditioned by society to accept all sorts of age stereotypes:

Never trust anybody over 30.

Old people are cranky and hard to get along with.

Young people are just irresponsible these days; you can't depend on them for anything.

Old people don't change; you can't teach an old dog new tricks.

As we reflect on this segregation and our isolation from other age groups, we realize that old people and young people have much in common. When we are kept apart by society or imprisoned by our own fears, we deprive ourselves, and we also deprive the young. Our society is correspondingly weaker because we have not lived together. Without interacting as we were intended to do, young and old rarely communicate, share experiences, or give each other mutual support. Instead, we mistrust one another, often vote against measures which favor other age groups, and act as if they fully accepted the stereotypes relevant to other age groups.

The Development of
Mutually Supportive Communities
of Young and Old

The Gray Panthers, based in Philadelphia and fanning out in a national network,[1] and a like-minded group of elders and youth called "The Collective" in the Brighton-Alston area, are experimenting with new forms of education in the public schools of Greater Boston. One of several approaches taken in the Boston area was entitled "History through Life Experience" and was initiated in the winter of 1972 by the Brighton-Alston Area Planning Action Council and the Boston School Committee. The following excerpt suggests the creativity with which the project was undertaken and indicates its success in terms of community impact:

> Age segregation in our communities means, among other things, that young people and elderly people rarely talk together. Both groups miss the opportunity to break down stereotypes of each other and realize their common interests. Last winter an attempt was made to begin communication between the ages by a course given in the Flexible Campus Program of Brighton High School. The course was planned and taught by elders from the Allston-Brighton Federation of Elders and was called "History Through Life Experience." Each week for six weeks an elder gave a short talk about such topics as "Entertainment in the Twenties (Vaudeville)," "Organizing Working People in the Twenties and Thirties," "The Depression." Then elders and students just talked. The course was tremendously popular with students and really exciting and challenging for the elders.
>
> The progress is an attempt to build a new role for elders in our community—a role which says YOU ARE IMPORTANT, YOUR EXPERIENCES GIVE NEW MEANING TO THE LIVES OF ALL IN OUR COMMUNITY. We can begin to integrate our common needs for belonging and create a community with concern and compassion. These values were predominant during the lives of elderly people, and if we reach back to them and return them to our lives, we can overcome the fractured existence that so many suffer.
>
> The Boston School Committee likes the idea and hopes to expand the program to other Boston High Schools. If you are interested in starting such a program in your high school, church, or community center, or if you would be interested in teaching or participating in a program like this, contact the Allston-Brighton Area Planning Action Council.

One Philadelphia-based effort brought together young inner city students from the public schools and older people attracted by a newspaper article in which the opportunity to hear about the Gray Panthers was announced. The process of mutual education was crystal clear: Stereotypes were shattered and bridges built across 50-year-wide expanses.

Another approach taken by four Philadelphia Gray Panthers was to organize and guide a highly successful consciousness-raising group composed of young people and old people. Between 20 and 30 people meet weekly, on Saturday mornings, to become aware of the multiple forms of discrimination directed by our society toward both young and old. The leadership is shared and flexible; participants take turns as conveners or moderators. The goals of the groups have been:

1. To identify the problems of our personal lives and to come to understand the degree to which such problems are, in fact, socially—and not just individually—determined:

2. To end the isolation of the generations;

3. To *listen* to each other and learn from each other. Often the art or practice of listening is a new one to many of us;

4. To increase self-esteem and confidence;

5. To find valid ways to deal with our anger and frustration and direct it toward action; and

6. To learn to enjoy and support one another.

During these sessions, extraordinary things have been revealed about attitudes and depths of suffering. Prejudices formerly unrecognized have surfaced and been neutralized. Sensitivity and openness have characterized the discussions. Homosexuality, fear of sexual impotence, and continuing sexual interest-without-opportunity-for-involvement are topics frankly discussed by all. Because young and old often suffer crises of identity, some hostile and negative feelings about youth and age were inevitable and were discussed with candor and understanding.

The wide age range of the group members has been a distinct asset; the youngest is 14 years of age and the oldest is 78. In one instance, for example, compulsory education in classrooms where little learning takes place was compared to compulsory retirement. It was 14-year-old Matt who first suggested the analogy: He really *heard* what 67-year-old Rene was saying about being "put out at 65."

The Development and Testing of New Models and Lifestyles

The Gray Panthers are encouraging several novel approaches to learning by living. Some have addressed chapters of the American Association of University Women, asking them to be our advocates in urging their alma maters to open courses for audit by older adults.

Apprenticeships of young people working with retirees are being considered in a number of settings. Old people who remember their own apprenticeship days are interested and involved in experimental planning.

In addition, the Gray Panthers are sponsoring the development of a new residence in West Philadelphia in the center of University City to house older and younger adults. It will be operated on a cooperative, nonprofit basis by the residents. Plans include commercial facilities for the convenience of residents and the community, a community information center, and opportunities for social involvement with the people living near the University (of Pennsylvania).

One of the major concerns of older adults, and, therefore, of the Gray Panthers, is health. We therefore constantly update analyses and critiques of our present health care nonsystem and frequently testify at national, state, and local hearings and meetings on our findings and in favor of a national health program. Recently we participated as a national group by conducting an alternative to the annual meeting of the American Medical Association in New York City. The New York branch of the organization did a splendid job of organizing the alternative meeting with less than a month's lead time.

The Development and Support of Coalitions for Political and Social Action

Several specific examples of such coalition building have been given above; one more is given here.

Everyone knows that the lack of public transportation is a national disgrace and a major cause of the social isolation of many old people. But it often requires pointing out the obvious to make younger people recognize that many elderly citizens are completely dependent on public transport. In fact, in those thousands of American communities which lack public transportation, old people are the chief victims and losers.

In Philadelphia, where public transportation is available (but less than adequate), a coalition of groups of older people took stock of their need for safe, economical transport and pressed for reduced fares for riders over 65 and for rescheduled bus routes. Hard data about declining ridership and increased fares and costs were secured by research teams who also studied what other communities were doing with dial-a-ride services and free rides in non–rush hours. When the board of the Transportation Authority met, older residents packed the meeting and demanded consideration of their request for reduced fares. Mass media covered the meeting, and spokespeople argued their case from the facts—hard facts—based on inventories of human needs, dollars and cents, and ridership tables. A carefully reasoned argument and mass action won the day!

Older Philadelphians have, in the past year, demonstrated their approval by greatly increasing their use of buses and trolleys. Thus, by their example, they helped restore public confidence in a transportation system which had been deemed a "*non*system" by the majority of Delaware Valley residents.

The Humanizing of Society and Its Structure

Our Gray Panther Living History project is one example of how one might put experience, wisdom, and skill to work toward the betterment of all. It was begun by two Bryn Mawr College undergraduates and two graduate students in the Bryn Mawr College School of Social Work. They interviewed six old people living in a retirement community in nearby Swarthmore. The project had three important results which persuaded us to plan further experiments of this sort—in particular, by interviewing patients in nursing homes (who are just as special and "experienced" as the old people whose names appear in TIME), as a means of engaging them in patients' rights committees and advocacy groups.

The results were:

1.   Warm, mutually enhancing relationships developed between interviewers and interviewees. The old people had lived extremely interesting lives and their own histories proved to be instructive to the students.

2.   The materials taped were relevant and important to contemporary social issues. Examples: Tapes recording memories of the Great Depression of the 30s, the political battles to get unemployment measures adopted, and the debates preceding the enactment of social security legislation gave important insights into the persistent poverty of the 1970s and the sickness of our present welfare system.

3.   The taping of personal histories was a positive factor in giving the retirees a new appreciation of what they could contribute to the resolution of contemporary problems.

One graduate student has delved especially deeply into the social and political reforms of urban society. Her taped interviews with a former U.S. senator, one of the great liberals of the 1950s and 1960s, started the senator on his memoirs, which, when complete, will comprise an autobiography in its own right significant to social analysis and commentary.*

*The senator is Joseph S. Clark, first mayor of Philadelphia under a reform charter adopted in 1950 and the distinguished Senior Senator of Pennsylvania for two eventful terms.

Another set of tapes was made by a student deeply involved in the women's movement. She interviewed one of the suffrage leaders who helped to organize the first suffrage parade in Philadelphia. Both interviewer and interviewee developed new insights into the present women's movement and into the far less than equal status in which most women today find themselves.

An undergraduate with Jewish background interviewed three elderly women in a Jewish home for the aged. They had been born and reared in Russia and Poland. Poignant memories of their childhoods and coming to America—the "melting pot"—were expressed. Their comments also pointed up the need to foster and enhance cultural roots for the young and for the old to safeguard personal emotional health as well as societal strengths.

The Gray Panthers have taken other approaches to this issue, too. In all cases, it should be noted that we strive to be well informed before acting. We are, for instance, currently developing a data bank about community resources: people, organized groups, service agencies, community concerns and needs. (We believe that what turns people on may also be considered a "community resource.")

Finally, in this regard, we undertake a role not usually attributed to older Americans: We are political activists. Our thesis, too, may surprise many onlookers: We are expendable. Every index of status, quality of life, and measure of support reinforces this thesis. Therefore, we believe that we, too, should join ranks with the (mostly) young in the struggle for justice—in all arenas.

In summary, we believe that learning is indeed a function of living and that the more of the one, the more likely is the other. Old people are said to be wise. They have accepted the challenge to learn from life. Many wish to continue to do so—but the lessons that society wishes to teach older people are usually painful ones: poverty, indignity, and isolation.

If we are to liberate ourselves from the oppressive age stereotypes which society imposes on us—at all ages—we must involve ourselves in social action. And effective strategies for social change invariably require knowledge of the past and present state of the issue as well as knowledge, in most cases, of power, politics, and economics. Our thesis, then, is that action and mutual education are interlocked and that knowledge becomes power only when it is informed and informs our action.

Reference

1. Gray Panthers. *Network organizing manual*. Philadelphia, 1974.

22

Formal Educational Opportunities for Older Adults

Jeanne E. Bader

Executive branch support has many years been focused on volunteerism as a way of life for older Americans. During the same period, however, Congress has often been hard pressed to obtain administrative support for the provision of payments and baseline services which would permit lower income older citizens (of whom there are many) time out from "just scraping through." While it is true that some older people can afford to participate in elaborate leisure activities, others can afford little else but enforced stationary leisure. Still others continue to work long years after their friends and colleagues have retired.

In recent years, however, a new opportunity has become available to older Americans—an opportunity which is quite generally available; frequently cost free; and has been designed to appeal, in one form or another, to a substantial proportion of the elder community: educational opportunities for older adults.

Educational opportunities for older adults have generally taken one of three forms: training, recreation, or more formal academic course work. However, according to a new book on the subject, "hobbies and recreation, consumer education, health related subjects, home and family life. . .are the most popular subjects in almost every agency serving the older population."[1] It is important to note that these are among the very options which have been promoted *for* the older learner. Because our national experience to date has not for the most part included encouraging older people to compete with younger ones in the classroom, to attempt to pursue "heavy" subjects "even" in the company of other older people, or to

Reprinted with permission from *International Journal of Aging and Human Development*, 1977/78, *8*, 339–344. The author wishes to note that the materials for this chapter were culled when she was Project Associate to the Alfred & Hanna Fromm Fund. The inspiration for and resources to research the literature found in this introductory statement and the bibliography (Chapter 23) were provided by Hanna and Alfred Fromm of San Francisco.

attempt to complete the requirements for academically sound correspondence courses, we do not know how the scattered individuals currently engaged in such activities are doing. We do, however, have anecdotal evidence of success: newspaper articles by individual older learners; scholarly papers and creative works by seniors; and rapidly increasing numbers of educational opportunities for them.

Articles about training, recreational, and more formal educational opportunities for older Americans may be found in the selected bibliography which follows this chapter. Older articles among those listed should not be overlooked when they lack key words in their titles, as it is only a recent development that education *for* aging, education *of* the aged, and education *for work with* the aged have generally become distinguishable by the titles of articles dealing with these subjects. Even a recent and very fine volume entitled *Learning for Aging* continues to mix these specialty approaches.[2]

The Consumers

In a nation where the median number of years of formal schooling of those 65 or older was only 8.7 years in 1969/1970.[3] current estimates claim that only 2.4% of the 65+ population are now "attending school."[4] (This figure may be expected to increase in the years to come if such opportunities become more widespread and if the median educational level of the larger community continues to rise.) While one might ask *why only* a half million older Americans are attending classes of one sort or another, one might also ask *why so many* seniors are "in school."

This relatively new trend—back to school—represents a philosophical advance, it seems to me, among older people—at once in the direction of belief in one's worth and also toward a desire for and belief in one's lifelong potential for intellectual growth and personal development.

The Sponsors

The upsurge in the availability of opportunities for older persons at colleges and universities throughout the country probably not only represents the desire of such institutions to serve their communities better but also may signal the beginning of a national recognition of the increased number of healthy older adults and of their potential market value as consumers of educational as well as other commodities and as influencers of consumers of all ages. It is not clear, however, that such explanations as these tell the full story. Both the fact that many educational institutions are experiencing

declining enrollment rates among younger students[4] and, might, therefore, be looking toward new educational markets and the fact that older
people are highly motivated[5] and able students ("attractive consumers")
have undoubtedly contributed to the current emphasis on developing
educational opportunities for seniors.

The explanatory link with which one might begin to trace the history
of this surge of educational programs for seniors lies not only in fiscal or
humanitarian motives, however, but also in the goals and objectives,
strengths and hard work of the leaders in this movement. It is of particular
interest to note that most formal educational opportunities for older adults
have arisen primarily in response to the hard work of senior educators
themselves: Kaufman in Kentucky (now in Florida); Hirsch in New York;
the Fromms in San Francisco; Ferber in Minnesota; Western at Fairhaven,
Bellingham, Washington; Carp in Marin County, California. Neither
gerontologists nor academic staff members have assumed as much responsibility for these developments in most cases as have emeriti and other
educators. But in those instances in which they have done so, the motivations and talents of younger leaders in this field must also be noted in order
better to understand the roots of this movement: e.g., Beatty in Syracuse
and Carlson in Bakersfield, California.

Exemplary articles by two older leaders in this movement—Hyman
Hirsch and Maggie Kuhn—are published in this section. The range of ways
in which older people are participating as educators and as students
encompasses both Hirsch's and Kuhn's philosophies and programmatic
activities—and many more besides.

A book by Korim details another philosophy and system of education.[6]
This volume is particularly significant because it deals with educational
opportunities for seniors provided by community colleges in this country—
the very institutions which many believe should, because they are publicly
financed and generally available, strive to meet the bulk of the educational
needs and desires of older Americans.

Assessment

Both Kuhn and Hirsch are providers and monitors of educational opportunities for seniors. In no formal instance have less committed and invested
older students themselves been the evaluators and analyzers of the programs in which they are participating.

The call for professional evaluation of educational programs for older
Americans by nonparticipants in the target programs has been clearly
sounded by the authors of a comprehensive report on educational programs for older Americans.[7]

Nor has there been a full blown study of learning by older adults in the "natural" settings of ongoing course work. It is remarkable that, in the context of the vast literature on cognitive functioning by older adults, no such naturalistic learning study has been undertaken. Nor do we have any solid information as to how best to present materials to be learned by seniors, how best to design learning environments for seniors, nor to reinforce their learning.[8] Such deficiencies in the literature are all the more remarkable considering the emphasis frequently placed on the importance to seniors themselves of sensory (especially visual) changes accompanying aging and in view of the recent surge of interest in physical-environmental and social-environmental issues.[9]

It would seem appropriate for gerontologists to initiate studies of learning as it takes place outside the laboratory in the near future since:

1.   Many communities are only now planning educational programs for their older residents, and before-after longitudinal investigations are, therefore, still possible;

2.   Such programs have, in almost every case, been designed, promoted, and carried out by nongerontologists—thereby guarding against the accusation of conflict of interest;

3.   Most gerontologists are already in academic settings and many would find educational programs for seniors to be conveniently located on their own campuses; and

4.   The opportunity for researchers to respond creatively to other taxpayers' cry for "relevance" could surely be partially met by conducting formal research in the arena with which he or she is most personally familiar—the American educational institution.

It would seem an oversight not to round out the literature on cognitive functioning—the largest single area of investigation in gerontology—with a study of short- and long-range learning as it originates in the classroom, training session, or formal discussion group.*

Finally, current interest in the construction or conversion of dormitories for seniors—whether dwelling alongside or apart from younger residents—is high and may only be expected to increase as the application rates of younger students drop and as more younger students seek community, rather than dormitory, living arrangements.[10] Given the many

---

*The long-range benefits of training older people to become better consumers, more efficient housekeepers, or safer pedestrians and drivers are, however, equally unknown. Furthermore, considering the mandatory requirement for all area agencies on aging to have advisory bodies of seniors, a further opportunity for the investigation of learning as it accrues through training programs in which they participate is also available.

issues which must be considered in the establishment of such living arrangements, one might reasonably expect to find a sophisticated study of the effects of such arrangements on both older and younger neighbors— and in both groups' experiences as residents of congregate housing and as students.[11] The possibility that residency alone may not necessarily promote increased educational activities among older tenants of on-campus, intergenerational housing might also have been expected to lead to a comparative study of similar housing sites on and off campuses.[12] This author was unable, however, to locate any such study, although a proposal on this subject was submitted but not funded.*

References

1. R. DeCrow. *New learning for older Americans: An overview of national effort.* Washington, D.C.: Adult Education Assoc., 1975.
2. S. Grabowski and W. D. Mason (Eds.). *Learning for aging.* Washington, D.C.: Adult Education Assoc. and ERIC Clearinghouse on Adult Education, 1975.
3. *Current population report, series P-23, No. 43.* Washington, D.C.: USDC, 1973.
4. Colleges face decline in applicants. *New York Times,* April 15, 1973.
5. C. Carlson. Serving the needs of retired persons. *Community and Junior College Journal,* pp. 22–23, March 1973.
6. A. S. Korim. *Older Americans and community colleges: A guide for program implementation.* Washington, D. C.: American Assoc. of Community and Junior Colleges, 1974.
7. Academy for Educational Development. *Never too old to learn.* New York, 1974.
8. K. Rindskopf and D. C. Charles. Instructor age and older learner. *Gerontologist, 14,* 479–482, 1974.
9. B. A. Goodrow. Limiting factors in reducing participation in older adult learning opportunities. *Gerontologist, 15,* 418–422, 1975.
10. C. A. Lowe Sanderson. The week after next. . . *Gerontologist, 11(2),* whole issue, 1971.
11. L. J. Hedden. Intergenerational living in university dormitories. *Gerontologist, 14,* 283–285, 1974.
12. G. McKibben. Bridging educational opportunities of young and old with university-community resources. Presented at 26th Annual Meeting, Gerontological Society, Miami Beach, 1973.

*It may well prove interesting to compare further the effects of intergenerational living in relation to their sponsors: colleges and universities (e.g., Syracuse University or Fairhaven's The Bridge) vs. others (e.g., the Gray Panthers in Philadelphia or the community group assembled for this purpose in Berkeley, California).

23

Education for Older Adults: Selected Bibliography

Jeanne E. Bader

Abrams, Albert J. Librarians and Our Senior Citizens. In *Young at Any Age* (Legislative Document No. 12). Albany: New York State Joint Legislative Committee on Problems of the Aging, 1950 (166–172).

Abstracts of Papers Presented to the National Seminar on Adult Education Research (Toronto, February 9–11, 1969). Syracuse, New York: Syracuse University, ERIC Clearinghouse on Adult Education, 1969.

Aging and Learning. Chicago: Mayor's Office for Senior Citizens, 1972.

Adams, Arthur S. The Challenge of Later Maturity to Education (Address to National Pilot Institute on Education for the Aging, Exeter, New Hampshire, January 28, 1967). (Occasional Papers 2.) Durham, New Hampshire: New England Center for Continuing Education, 1967.

Adams, Arthur S. To Keep on Keeping on. *Adventures in Learning: Proceedings of Two Conferences on Education for the Aging.* Rhode Island: University of Rhode Island, 1969.

Adult Education: An Overview of Adult Education and a Summary of the Survey of Adult Education in Minnesota Public Schools and Junior Colleges, 1953–54. St. Paul: State of Minnesota Department of Education, 1955.

Adult Education Associations and Organzations. Washington, D.C.: National Advisory Council on Adult Education, 1972.

Adult Education for the Aging and the Aged (Bulletin No. 6). Albany: The University of the State of New York, State Education Department, Bureau of Adult Education, 1950.

Adult Leadership, 9: 1, May 1960 (whole issue on problems of education for aged and aging).

Adult Learning Characteristics (Current Information Sources, No. 21). Syracuse, New York: ERIC Clearinghouse on Adult Education, 1968.

Aker, George F. (Comp.). *Adult Education* (a classified and annotated bibliography), 1953–1963. Syracuse, New York: Library of Continuing Education, 1965.

Alford, H. J. *Continuing Education in Action; Residential Centers for Lifelong Learning.* New York: Wiley, 1968.

Reprinted with permission from *International Journal of Aging and Human Development,* 1977/78, *8,* 345–357.

Ampene, Emanuel K. Teaching Styles in Adult Basic Education. *Literacy Discussion, 4:* 3, 1973. (191–205).

Andrus, Ethel P. Education As the Retired See It. *Adult Leadership, 9,* May 1960 (whole issue).

Andrus, Ruth. Personality Change in an Older Age Group. *Geriatrics, 10,* 1955 (432–435).

Anonymous. Center Brings Education They Want to the Elderly. *Aging,* 1971 (8–9).

Anonymous. Education, Learning, and Retirement. *Adult Leadership, 17,* 1969 (381–391)

Archer, Sara K. Aesthetics Education for the Elderly. *Journal of Education, 152:* 2, 1969.

Annual Report. Washington, D.C.: National Advisory Council on Adult Education, yearly (March).

Annual Report. Washington, D.C.: National Advisory Council on Extension and Continuing Education, yearly (March).

Atwood, H. Mason. Diagnostic Procedure in Adult Education. *Viewpoints, 49:5,* 1973 (1–6).

Atwood, H. Mason, and Joe Ellis. Concept of Need: An Analysis for Adult Education. *Viewpoints, 49:5,* 1973 (7–16).

Auer, Mary A. A Grandmother on Campus. *Journal of the National Association of Women Deans and Counselors, 36:3,* 1973 (137–138).

Bader, Jeanne E. Education for Older Adults: A Review of the Literature, Some Commendations, and Some Predictions. Paper presented at 26th Annual Meeting of the Gerontological Society, Miami Beach, 1973.

Baker F. Never Too Late to Learn. *Harvest Years,* July 1968 (34–36).

Barnes, John O., Jr. A Program of Adult Education for the Marshall County High School Service Area, Lewisburg, TE (M.S. thesis). Knoxville: Tennessee University, 1963.

Barnes, Robert E., and Andrew Hendrickson. The Role of Colleges and Universities in the Education of the Aged. Columbus: Ohio State University, 1964.

Belbin, R. Meredith. Retirement Strategy in an Evolving Society, In Frances Carp (Ed.), *Retirement.* New York: Behavioral Publications, 1972 (175–196).

Birren, James E., and Diana S. Woodruff. Human Development over the Life-span through Education. In Paul B. Baltes and K. Warner Schaie (Eds.), *Life-span Developmental Psyhcology: Personality and Socialization.* New York: Academic, 1973.

Blake, Clarence Napoleon. *A Descriptive Analysis of the Adult Education Methodology and the Non-threatening Approach to Adult Education as Practiced by the Institute of Lifetime Learning.* Washington, D.C.: George Washington University, 1969.

Boyd, R. Basic Motivations of Adults Enrolled in Non-credit Programs. *Journal of Adult Education, 11,* 1961 (91–96).

Bradley, Harry M., et al. *A Program for the Educational Enrichment of the Senior Citizens of Polk County.* Bartow, Florida: Polk Junior College, 1967.

Bradley, Harry M., and Leland R. Cooper. Retirees Assist in Developing Programs for Educational Enrichment. *Adult Leadership, 17,* 1969 (383–385).

Bromley, D. B. Age and Adult Education. *Studies in Adult Education, 2:2,* October 1970 (124–138).

Brown, G. T. Never Too Old to Learn. *School and Society, 74,* 1951 (279–281).

Brunner, Edmund De S., et al. An Overview of Adult Education Research. Chicago: Adult Education Association, 1959.

Brunner, Edmund De S., and Coolie Verner. Adult Education. In D. L. Sills (Ed.), *International Encyclopedia of the Social Sciences* (1). New York: Macmillan, 1968.

Burkett, Jesse E. Comprehensive Programming for Life-long Learning. *Adult Education, 10,* 1960.

Buswell, Christa H. Reading and the Aged. *Wilson Library Bulletin, 45,* 1971 (467–476).

Butler, R. N. New Colleges for All Ages. *International Journal Aging and Human Development, 5,* 1974.

Calloway, Pauline, and others. *A Survey and Pilot Project to Meet the Educational Needs of Senior Citizens in an Urban Area—Brevard County, Florida.* Gainesville, Florida: Florida Cooperative Extension Service, University of Florida, 1970.

Canadian Association for Adult Education. The Mature Student Clause. *Continuous Learning, 4:5,* 1965 (205–215).

Carlson, Charles R. California Commission on Colleges and Education of the Aged (Ed. D. thesis). Los Angeles: University of Southern California, 1972.

Carlson, Charles R. Serving the Needs of Retired Persons. *Community and Junior College Journal* (March) 1973, (22–23).

Carlson, William S. The Role of the Modern University in an Aging Society. In *Brightening the Senior Years.* New York State Legislative Document, No. 81, 1957.

Chamberlin, Martin N. *Education for Older Persons: An Overview.* Seattle: University of Washington, Division of Adult Education, Extension Services, 1954.

Charles, D. C. The Older Learner, *Educational Forum, 35,* 1971 (227–233).

Chiasson, Joseph T. Residential Adult Education and the Condition of Participation in Learning (Master's thesis). Saskatoon, Sask.: University of Saskatchewan, 1971.

Cleugh, M. F. *Educating Older People.* London: Tavistock, 1962. (Reprinted in 1970.)

Cole, K. C. Golden Oldies: Senior Citizens Go Back to School. *Saturday Review: Education, 1:1,* 1973 (41–44).

Community and Junior Colleges That Offer Courses for Cultural Enrichment. Washington, D.C.: American Association of Community and Junior Colleges, 1973.

Comprehensive Bibliography on Educational Gerontology, Parts 1–20. Ann Arbor and Detroit: Institute of Gerontology, University of Michigan and Wayne State University, 1971.

Conference on the Role of Education for Aging and the Aged. Proceedings, November 30—December 2, 1961, at the Center for Continuation Study, University of Minnesota, Minneapolis.

Conference on the Role of Education in the Field of Aging. Proceedings, November 27 and 28, 1961, Charlottesville, University of Virginia.

Crabtree, Arthur P. Education—The Key to Successful Aging. *Adult Education*, 1967 (157–165).

Crosman, Arthur M., and Alice Gustav. Academic Success of Older People. *Psychology in the Schools*, 3:3 1966 (256–258).

Davis, George. Background Paper on Education for Aging. Washington, D.C.: Planning Committee on Education for Aging, WHCoA, 1961.

DeGabriele, Eugene H. *A Review of Present Educational Programs Available to Older Adults in California's Public Adult Education Program*. Sacramento: State Department of Education, 1967.

Department of Adult Education. *Education for Senior Adults*. Leadership Institute. Tallahassee: Florida State University, 1959.

Directory of Consultants for Planning Adult Learning Systems, Facilities and Environments, 1973–74. Washington, D.C.: Adult Education Association of U.S.A., 1973.

Dixon, J. C. (Ed.). *Continuing Education in the Later Years*. Gainesville: University of Florida Press, 1963.

Dobson, Catherine. *Education of Adults: A Bibliography*. Ann Arbor: University of Michigan, 1973.

Donahue, Wilma. Experiments in the Education of Older Adults, In *Participants in Adult Education*. Washington, D.C.: Adult Education Association, n.d.

Donahue, Wilma. *Education for Later Maturity: A Handbook*. New York: Whiteside and William Morrow, 1955.

Donahue, Wilma. Learning, Motivation and Education of the Aging. In John E. Anderson (Ed.) *Psychological Aspects of Aging*. Washington, D.C.: American Psychological Association, 1956 (200–206).

Dubin, S. S. Obsolescence of Lifelong Education: A Choice for the Professional. *American Psychologist*, 27:5, 1972.

Education for Later Maturity in the U.S.A. In *Old Age in the Modern World* (Report of the Third Congress of the International Association of Gerontology, 1954). Edinburgh and London: E&S Livingston; and Balitmore: Williams & Wilkins, 1955 (610–617).

Education of Aging and Aged. Albany: New York State Education Department, 1950.

Eklund, Lowell. Aging and the Field of Education. In Mathilda W. Riley (Ed.). *Aging and Society* (11). New York: Russell Sage, 1969 (324–351).

Evaluation of LSCA Services to Special Target Groups: Excerpts from Draft of Final Report. Washington, D.C.: System Development Corporation, Education and Library Systems Department, 1973.

Extending Educational and Cultural Opportunities for Older People. New York: Central Bureau for the Jewish Aged, n.d.

Fahey, Patricia MacDonald. Shattering the Myths of Age. *News Hunter, 3*:3, 1974 (1–3).

Federal Activities in Support of Adult Education. Washington, D.C.: National Advisory Council on Adult Education, 1972.

Federation Employment and Guidance Service. *Resources for the Employment of Mature Women and/or Their Continuing Education.* New York, 1965.

Field, Minna. *Aging with Honor and Dignity.* Springfield, Illinois: Thomas, 1968.

Fitch, William C. Lifetime Learning. Paper Presented at the National Conference of State Executives on Aging, Washington, D.C., 1965.

Fleming, Elizabeth. Senior Citizens Pose Educational Challenge. *Extension Service Review,* 1973 (3–7).

447 Junior Colleges Offer Courses Relating to Elderly. *Aging, 226,* 1973.

Froelicher, Francis M. Education for Older Adults. *Baltimore Bulletin of Education, 33*:3 (28–31).

Gardner, John W. Education As a Way of Life. *Science,* February 1965.

Garfunkel, Florence R., and Gabriele H. Grunebaum. A New Use of Education in Programming for the Aged. *Journal of Jewish Communal Service, 45,* 1968 (102–110).

Geist, Harold. Education, Research and Conclusions. In *Psychological Aspects of Retirement.* Springfield, Illinois: Thomas, 1968.

Gerontological Society Committee on Research and Developmental Goals in Social Gerontology. Work, Leisure and Education: Toward the Goal of Creating Flexible Life Styles. *Gerontologist, 9,* 1969 (17–36).

Giambattista, Robert N. They Yearn to Learn. *Business Education Forum, 27*:8, 1973 (45–46).

Giordano, Enrico A., and D. F. Seaman. Continuing Education for the Aging—Evidence of a Positive Outlook. *Gerontologist, 8*:1, 1968 (63–64).

Goldberg, Richard. Goddard's Adult Degree Program. *Change, 5*:8, 1973 (15–20).

Grabowski, Stanley M. ERIC Materials—Education for Leisure. *Adult Leadership, 18*:3, 1969 (99–100).

Grabowski, Stanley (Ed.) *Research and Investigation in Adult Education: 1972 Annual Register.* Washington, D.C.: Adult Education Association, 1973.

A Great University Studies Educational Needs of Older People. *Adult Leadership, 16*:1, 1967 (2–4).

Griffith, William S. Introduction to Research in Adult Education. *Adult Leadership, 20*:7, 1972 (270).

Groombridge, B. *Education and Retirement: An Inquiry into the Relevance of Education to the Enjoyment of Leisure in Later Life.* London: National Institute of Adult Education, 1960.

Haak, Leo A. *A Comparative Analysis of the Institute Programs of the Oliver Wendell Holmes Association, 1963–68.* New York, 1969.

Hand, Samuel E. What It Means to Teach Older Adults. Presented at Institute for Education for Senior Adults Leadership, Tallahassee, Florida State University, Department of Adult Education, 1959.

Harding, Gene. Writing Workshops for Older Adults. *Adult Leadership: 19*:10, 1971 (329–330).

Havighurst, Robert J. Social Roles, Work, Leisure, and Education. In Carl Eisdorfer and M. Powell Lawton (Eds.), *The Psychology of Adult Development and Aging*. Washington, D.C., American Psychological Association, 1973.

Havighurst, R. J., and B. G. Neugarten. *Society and Education* (3rd edition). Boston: Allyn & Bacon, 1967.

Hawkinson, William; E. Percil Stanford; Rolf Monge; and David Dowd. Survey of Gerontologists' Opinions on White House Conference on Aging Issues on Education and Training. *Gerontologist, 12*, 1972 (79–84).

Helling, John F. Senior on Campus. *Adult Leadership, 21*:6, 1972 (203–205).

Hendrickson, Andrew. The Role of Colleges and Universities in the Education of the Aging. In O. Bruce Thomason (Ed.), *Potentialities for Later Living*. Gainesville: University of Florida, 1968.

Hendrickson, Andrew, and George F. Aker. *Education for Senior Adults*. Tallahassee: Florida State University, Department of Adult Education, 1969.

Hendrickson, Andrew, and George F. Aker. *Education for Older Citizens: Second Leadership Development Institute*. Tallahassee: Florida State University, Adult Education Department, 1971.

Hendrickson, Andrew, and George F. Aker. *Report on Education for Older Citizens*. Tallahassee: Florida State University, Department of Adult Education, 1971.

Hendrickson, Andrew, and George F. Aker. *Improving Education for Older Adults: Third Leadership Development Institute*. Tallahassee: Florida State University, Department of Adult Education, 1972.

Hendrickson, Andrew, and Robert F. Barnes. *The Role of Colleges and Universities in the Education of the Aged* (mimeo). Columbus: Ohio State University, Center of Adult Education, 1964.

Hendrickson, Andrew, and Barnes, Robert F. Educational Needs of Older People. *Adult Leadership, 16*:1, 1967 (2–5).

Hicks, John W. Changing Environments of Continuing Education: Politics and Pressures. *NUEA Spectator, 37*:12, 1973 (9–12).

Hiemstra, R. P. Continuing Education for the Aged: A Survey of Needs and Interests of Older People. *Adult Education, 22*:2, 1972 (100–109).

Hiemstra, R. P. Educational Planning for Older Adults: A Survey of "Expressive" Versus "Instrumental" Preferences. *International Journal of Aging and Human Development, 4*:2, 1973 (147–156).

Hirsch, Hyman. The Liberal Arts and the Older Adult (mimeo). New York, 1968.

Hirsch, Hyman. Adult Education in the Retirement Years. Presented at the 26th Annual Meeting, Gerontological Society, Miami Beach, 1973.

Hixson, Leroy E. Formula for Success: A Step-by-step Procedure for Organizing a Local Institute of Lifetime Learning. Long Beach, California: American Association of Retired Persons, 1968.

Hixson, Leroy E. Non-threatening Education for Older Adults, *Adult Leadership, 18*:3, 1969 (84–85).

Hodgkinson, H. L. The Next Decade of Higher Education. *Journal of Higher Education, 41*:1, 1970 (16–28).

Hodgkinson, Harold L. Changing Roles in Higher Education. Paper prepared for conference: "The Role of the Institutions of Higher Learning in the Study of Aging," Newport Beach, California, 1972.

Holden, J. B. A Survey of Participation in Adult Education Classes. *Adult Leadership, 4,* 1958.

How to Teach Adults (Leadership Pamphlet #5). Washington, D.C.: Adult Education Association, 1955.

Jacobs, H. Lee. *Report of a National Survey of Programs in Education for Older Adults.* Minneapolis: University of Minnesota, Center for Continuing Education, 1961.

Jacobs, H. Lee; W. Dean Mason; and Earl Kauffman. Education for Aging: A Review of Recent Literature. Syracuse, New York: ERIC Clearinghouse on Adult Education, 1970.

Johnson, E. A. Education Comes to You. *Florida Adult Educator, 21,* 1971.

Johnstone, W. C. *Volunteers for Learning: A Study of the Educational Pursuits of American Adults.* Chicago: University of Chicago Press, 1963.

Johnstone, W. C., and Ramon J. Rivera. *Volunteers for Learning: A Study of the Educational Pursuits of American Adults.* Chicago: Aldine, 1965.

Kaplan, Jerome. *A Social Program for Older People.* Minneapolis: University of Minnesota, 1953.

Kauffman, Earl. *Continuing Education for Older Adults: A Demonstration in Method and Content.* Lexington: University of Kentucky, Council on Aging, 1967.

Kauffman, Earl. Education in Later Life. *Adult Leadership, 17,* 1968 (7–8; 42–43).

Kauffman, Earl. Educare: An Investigation of a Method for Continuing Engagement. Paper presented for the Eighth International Congress of Gerontology, Washington, D.C., 1969.

Kauffman, Earl. The Older Adult as a University Student. Paper presented at National Seminar on Adult Education Research, Toronto, 1969.

Kempfer, Homer. Education for a Long and Useful Life (Bulletin 6). Washington, D.C.: U.S. Office of Education, n.d.

Kent, Donald P. Current Development in Educational Programming for Older People. *American School Board Journal, 149,* 1964 (27, 30).

King, Robert Henry. *Identification of Educational Needs of Older Adults in Three Congregate Facilities: A Diagnostic Study.* Bloomington: Indiana University, School of Education, 1969.

Kleis, Russell J. *Bibliography on Continuing Education.* East Lansing: Michigan State University, Office of Studies in Continuing Education, 1972.

Knowles, Malcolm S. (Ed.). *Handbook of Adult Education in the United States.* Chicago: Adult Education Association of the USA, 1960.

Knowles, Malcolm S. *The Adult Education Movement in the United States.* New York: Holt, 1962.

Knowles, Malcolm S. *Higher Adult Education in the United States.* Washington, D.C.: American Council on Education, 1969.

Knowles, Malcolm S. The Relevance of Research for the Adult Education Teacher/Trainer. *Adult Leadership, 20*:7, 1972 (270–272; 302).

Knox, A. B., and R. Videbeck, Adult Education and Adult Life Cycle. *Adult Education, 8,* 1963.

Koch, Moses S., and Saul E. A. Lilienstein, Community College Attracts the Aging. *Junior College Journal, 35,* 1964 (26–27).

Korim, Andrew. The Role of the Community College in Extending Opportunities to Senior Citizens. Presented at 26th Annual Meeting of Gerontological Society, Miami Beach, 1973.

Kramer, Mollie W. *A Selected Bibliography on the Aging, and the Role of the Library in Serving Them.* Urbana: Illinois University, Graduate School of Library Science, 1973.

Kreitlow, W. B., and Associates. Liberal Education in an Age of Leisure: Exploration in the Development of Educational Programs for Older People (Research proposal dated Sept. 23, 1957). Madison: University of Wisconsin, College of Education, 1957.

Kuhlen, Raymond G. (Ed.). *Psychological Backgrounds of Adult Education.* Chicago: Center for the Study of Liberal Education for Adults, 1963.

Kuhn, Margaret. Learning by Living. Presented at the 26th Annual Meeting of Gerontological Society, Miami Beach, 1973.

Kuplan, Louis. Building a Philosophy towards Aging. *Occasional Papers on Adult Education.* Vancouver, B.C.: University Extension, British Columbia University, 1958.

Kushner, Rose E., and Marion E. Bunch. *Graduate Education in Aging within the Social Sciences.* Ann Arbor: University of Michigan, Division of Gerontology, 1967.

Kuypers, Joseph A., and Vern A. Bengston. Social Breakdown and Competence: A Model of Normal Aging. *Human Development, 16*:3, 1973 (181–201).

Learning for the Aged. *Time,* July 17, 1972 (48).

Lee, Raymond E. The Opportunity for a Lifetime: A Look at Continuing Education and What the Washington Community Colleges Are Doing About It. Pullman: Washington State University, 1973.

Lenzer, Anthony. The Role of the University in Gerontological Training. *Gerontologist, 6,* 1966 (105–110).

Lewinski, Austin J. Continuing Education for Adult Learners in Empire State College. New York: Empire State College, 1972.

Linton, Thomas E., and Donald L. Spence. The Aged: A Challenge to Education. *Adult Leadership, 12,* 1964 (261–262; 270; 280).

Londoner, Carroll A. Survival Needs of the Aged: Implications for Program Planning. *Aging and Human Development, 2,* 1971 (1–11).

Look Who's Going Back to School. *After 40,* January 1968 (6–10).

Los Angeles County Superintendent of Schools and California State Department of Social Welfare. *Understanding the Older Adult: A Teacher's Manual,* 1966.

Lowy, Louis. *Training Manual for Human Service Technicians Working with Older People. I, Trainers. II, Trainees.* Boston: Boston University, 1968.

Malassis, Louis. Forms and Strategies. *Prospects, 3*:2, 1973 (219–230).

McCloskey, Mark A. Education for Senior Citizens in New York City. In *Growing with the Years* (Legislative Document No, 32). Albany: New York State Joint Legislative Committee on Problems of Aging, 1954 (128–130).

McKibbin, Glen. Bridging Educational Opportunities of Young and Old with University-Community Resources. Presented at the 26th Annual Meeting of Gerontological Society, Miami Beach, 1973.

A Measure of Success: Federal Support for Continuing Education. Washington, D.C.: National Advisory Council on Extension and Continuing Education, 1973.

Miller, Charles Edward. *The Utilization of an Adult Education Program of Group Discussion with Participation Training to Meet Selected Needs of Aged Persons.* Bloomington: University of Indiana, 1963.

Miller, J. A., Jr. Who Needs Higher Education? In W. T. Furniss (Ed.), Higher Education for Everybody? Washington, D.C.: American Council on Education, 1971 (94–105).

Miller, Merle. School for Students Age 60. *Nation's Business, 41,* 1953 (98–102).

Mills, Beatrice Marie. The Educational Interests and Needs of Older Adults in Selected Presbyterian Churches (Ed.D. thesis). Cleveland: Case Western Reserve University, 1968.

Moberg, David O. Life Enrichment—Educational Needs of Older People. *Adult Leadership, 11,* 1962 (162–164; 185).

Moshey, Kathleen M. The Retired Adult Reader: His Reading Interests and Choices and the Readability of Them (Master's thesis). New Brunswick, New Jersey: Rutgers University, 1972.

Murchison, John. Never Too Late to Learn. *American Education, 9:8,* 1973 (28–31).

Myran, Gunder A. et al. *Community College Services for Senior Citizens.* East Lansing: Kellogg Community Services Leadership Program, Michigan State University, 1971.

National Organizations and Voluntary Associations with Adult Education Concerns in the United States. Washington, D.C.: National Advisory Council on Adult Education, 1971.

National Pilot Institute on the Education of the Aged. *A Selected Bibliography.* Exeter, New Hampshire, 1967.

New York Central Bureau for the Jewish Aged. *Proceedings of a Conference on Extending Educational and Cultural Opportunities for Older People.* New York, 1971.

Newberry, John S., Jr. Participants and Participation in Adult Education. In Edmund de S. Brunner (Ed.), *An Overview of Adult Education Research.* Washington, D.C.: Adult Education Association, 1959.

Norton, Paul G. Consideration of How Levels of Achievement and Anxiety toward Education Affect Older People's Participation in Adult Education Programs. Paper Presented at the Adult Education Research Conference, Minneapolis, Minnesota, February 27–28, 1970.

Norton, P. G. A Study of How Levels of Achievement and Anxiety toward Education Affect Older People's Participation in Adult Education Programs (Ed.D. thesis). Boston: Boston University, 1970.

Ohliger, John. Integrating Continuing Education. *Journal of Higher Education*, 40:7, 1960 (555–562).

Ohliger, John, and Joel Rosenberg (Comp.). *Compulsory Adult Education*. Columbus: Ohio State University, College of Education, 1973.

Opportunity for the Aging. Bloomington. University of Indiana, Division of Adult Education, n.d.

Other Issues Concerning Education for the Aging. *Florida Adult Educator: 21*, 1971.

Pattison, Rose Mary. Senior Citizen Renewal Action Program. *Adult Leadership*, 22:2, 1973 (59–60; 84).

Peterson, David A. Education and the Older American. *Adult Leadership, 19:8*, 1971 (263).

Phinney, Eleanor (Ed.). Library Services to the Aging. *Library Trends*, January 1973 (whole issue).

Pressey, Sidney L. Major Problems—and the Major Problem—Motivation, Learning, and Education in the Later Years. In J. E. Anderson (Ed.), *Psychological Aspects of Aging*. Washington, D.C.: American Psychological Association, 1965.

Pressey, Sidney, and Raymond G. Kuhlen. Education through the Life-span. In Sidney Pressey and Raymond G. Kuhlen (Eds.), *Psychological Development through the Life-Span*. New York: Harper, 1957 (122–164).

Proceedings: Conference on the Role of Education for Aging and Aged. Minneapolis: University of Minnesota, Center for Continuing Study, 1961.

Public School Adult Education Classes for the Elderly, 1971–72. Connecticut State Department of Education, Bureau of Elementary and Secondary Education, 1973.

Pulling, R. J. Education for the Elderly. In *Birthdays Don't Count* (Legislative Document No. 61). Albany: New York State Joint Legislative Committee on Problems of the Aging, 1948 (290–295).

Rabe, Henrietta F. Educational Needs of the Older Adult in Rural New York State. In *Young at Any Age* (Legislative Document No. 12). Albany: New York, State Joint Legislative Committee on Problems of the Aging, 1950 (160–165).

Rabe, Henrietta F. Public School Educational Programs. *Adult Education, 1:2*, 1950 (56–60).

Rabe, Henrietta F. Grandma's Going to School Again. *New York Education, 38*, 1951 (324–326).

Rabe, Henrietta F. Recreation and Education Services for the Aging and Aged. In Irving L. Weber (Ed.), (title, unknown). Gainesville: University of Florida, 1957.

Reals, Willis H. Education of the Aging in Institutions of Higher Learning. *School and Society, 79*, 1954 (177–184).

Report of a Special Committee on Learning Opportunities for Older Adults. Ottawa: Canadian Welfare Council Division on Aging, 1973.

Report of the Committee on Leisure Time and Adult Education Activites. Hackensack, New Jersey: Bergen County Citizens Committee on the Needs and

Problems of the Aging, the Bergen County Tuberculosis and Health Association, 1957.

Retirees Return to School. *Aging*, December 1962 (1–3).

Robinson, Phileon B., Jr. Socio-cultural Characteristics of Senior Citizen Participants in Adult Education Activities. *Adult Leadership, 20:7*, 1972 (234–236; 258).

Sanfield, Ronald. Senior Studies: An Adult Education Program for the Elderly of the Chicago Uptown Area. City of Chicago: Department of Human Resources, 1971.

Sarvis, Robert E. Educational Needs of the Elderly. Lynnwood, Washington: Edmonds Community College, 1973.

Savicky, I. (Comp.). European Selective Bibliography on Adult Education (1966–1971) (Bibliographic Series 6). Prague, Czech.: European Centre for Leisure and Education, 1973.

Schonfield, David. Family Life Education Study: The Later Adult Years. *Gerontologist, 10*, 1970 (115–118).

Schultz, C. B., and H. A. Aurbach. The Usefulness of Cumulative Deprivation As an Explanation of Educational Deficiencies. *Merrill-Palmer Quarterly, 17*, 1971 (27–39).

Scott, Frances G. Innovative Educational Opportunities for Older Persons. *Adult Leadership*, April 1974 (337–343(.

Sixth Annual Report of the National Advisory Council on Extension and Continuing Education, Pursuant to Public Law 89-329. Ninety-second Congress, Second Session. Washington, D.C.: House Committee on Education and Labor; National Advisory Council on Extension and Continuing Education, 1972.

Smith, Jeffery J. Education for the Rest of Your Life. Presented at 26th Annual Meeting of the Gerontological Society, Miami Beach, 1973.

Smith, R. M.; G. F. Aker; and J. R. Kidd. *Handbook of Adult Education*. New York: Macmillan, 1970.

Soop, Everett J. Proposed Programs in Education for the Aging Propulation. In Wilma Donahue and Clark Tibbitts (Eds.), *Growing in the Older Years*. Ann Arbor: University of Michigan Press, 1951 (127–145).

Stanford, E. Percil. Education and Aging: New Task for Education. *Adult Leadership, 20:8*, 1972 (281–282; 292–294).

Stern, Bernard H. *How Much Does Adult Experience Count: A Report of the Brooklyn College Experimental Degree Project*. Chicago, Illinois: Center for Study of Liberal Education for Adults, 1955.

Sundholm, Tertta. Course Activity among the Old. *Adult Education in Finland, 8:4*, 1971 (14–16).

Survey of Urban Education in State Colleges. *Urban Affairs Newsletter*. Washington, D.C.: American Association of State Colleges and Universities, 1973.

Sweeney, Sean M. *Working with the Senior Citizen as an Adult Learner*. Durham, New Hampshire: Cooperative Extension Service, University of New Hampshire, 1973.

Tanner, Francis H. Adult Education and the Aged in Wyoming. *Journal of Adult Education* (Mountain Plains A.E.A.), *1*:1, 1972 (46–52).

Tanner, Francis H. Educational Activities of Wyoming Adults Aged 65 and Over. Laramie: University of Wyoming, Department of Adult Education, 1972.

Thomason, O. B. *Potentialities for Later Living*. Gainesville: University of Florida, 1968.

Thompson, F., Jr. Adult Under-education. *Adult Leadership, 12*, 1963 (49–50).

Thumin, Frederick J., and Nancy Burnett. Academic Correlates of Chronological Age. *Journal of Gerontology, 18:4*, 1963 (376–377).

A Time for Learning. *Harvest Years,* June–August 1968.

Trow, M. Admissions and the Crisis in Higher Education. In W. T. Furniss (Ed.), *Higher Education for Everybody?* Washington, D.C.: American Council on Education, 1971 (26–52).

Turnbull, W. W. Dimensions of Quality in Higher Education. In W. T. Furniss (Ed.) *Higher Education for Everybody?* Washington, D.C.: American Council on Education, 1971 (126–136).

University of Indiana. *Opportunity for the Aging*. Bloomington, Indiana: Division of Adult Education, n.d.

University of Maryland. *State Leadership in Action for Education in Aging*. Washington, D.C.: U.S. Office of Aging and U.S. Office of Education, 1963.

University of Minnesota. *Proceedings on the Role of Education for Aging and Aged*. Minneapolis: Center for Continuing Study, 1961.

Uphaus, Ruth M. Educating Retirees. *Adult Leadership, 20:1*, 1971 (17–19).

Van Ommen, L. B. Adult Education in the Netherlands. *Convergence, 6:1*, 1973 (28–36).

Vanderbilt, Amy. Older People are Fast Learners. *Arizona Republic,* 1969 (M–7).

Verner, Coolie, and Thurman White. *Participants in Adult Education*. Washington, D.C.: Adult Education Association, 1965.

Videbeck, Richard, and Alan B. Knox. Alternative Participatory Responses to Aging. In Arnold M. Rose and Warren A. Peterson (Eds.), *Older People and Their Social World*. Philadelphia: Davis, 1965.

Wallin, J. E. Wallace. The Psychological Education and Social Problems of the Aging As Viewed by a Mid-octogenarian. Smyrna, Delaware: Division of the Aging, State Welfare Home, 1960.

Ward, Betty Arnett. Education on the Aging: A Selected Annotated Bibliography. Washington, D.C.: Department of Health, Education, and Welfare, 1960.

Waters, John. You're Never Too Old for a Scholarship. *Retirement Life,* 1955 (10).

Wesman, Alexander G. Standardizing an Individual Intelligence Test on Adults: Some Problems. *Journal of Gerontology, 10,* 1955 (216–219).

White, Ruth M. (Ed.). *Library Services to an Aging Population*. Chicago: American Library Association, 1960.

White, T. J. Adults: From the Wings to Center Stage. In W. T. Furniss (Ed.), *Higher Education for Everybody?* Washington, D.C.: American Council on Education, 1971 (173–182).

Wientge, King M. A Model for the Analysis of Continuing Education for Adults. *Adult Education, 16:4,* 1966 (246–251).

Williams, Richard H., and Claudine G. Wirths. *Lives Through the Years: Styles of Life and Successful Aging*. New York: Atherton, 1965.

Wolfe, Lloyd Mathias. A Study of the Relationship between Lifelong Learning and Adjustment of Older People (Ph.D. thesis). Ann Arbor: University of Michigan, 1963.

Wray, R. P. An Interdisciplinary Non-credit Community Course in Adult Development and Aging. Bethesda, Maryland: ERIC Document Reproduction Service, 1971. [Abstract: *Industrial Gerontologist, 13*, 1972 (152–153).]

Zatlin, Carole E.; M. Storandt; and J. Botwinick. Personality and Values of Women Continuing Their Education after 35 Years of Age. *Journal Gerontology, 28:2*, 1973 (216–221).

24

Higher Education
in Retirement:
The Institute for Retired
Professionals

Hyman Hirsch

Live and Learn is a basic tenet of the Institute for Retired Professionals, an adult education program at the New School for Social Research in New York City. The program's enrollees, who are retired from professional, administrative, and executive careers, have found in this learning community new answers to the use of retirement leisure. The IRP, as the program is called, has made it possible for its more than 600 members to study in the non-age-segregated classes of a university as well as to conduct, under its own leadership, an extracurricular program of almost 60 groups in many learning areas. Thus, with this participatory and integrated concept of adult education, the retiree has made real the adage to Live and Learn as well as its reverse—to Learn and Live.

Retirement Leisure

One of the seven cardinal principles of education on which generations of secondary school teachers have been reared is to inculcate in students the worthy use of leisure.[1] Without probing into the meaning of the word *worthy*, few will dissent from the observation made by Robert J. Blakely, a former vice-president of the Fund for Adult Education at White Plains in New York, who remarked to a symposium on free time in 1957: "In the United States we have educated and are educating quite well for working for a living, but we are betrayed by our inadequate education for the periods in which we do not work."[2] If we are so little prepared for the use of part-time leisure during our working years, is it any wonder that many

Reprinted with permission from *International Journal of Aging and Human Development*, 1977/78, *8*, 367–374.

retirees have difficulty adjusting to full-time leisure? But even if we were able to educate for the "worthy" use of free time while at work, we would still fall short of providing adequate programs to meet the needs of the retired.

People who retire today are faced with a situation where they must abandon one conformity for another: the work ethic for total idleness. This is especially true of the educated professional and the executive who have retired from careers of some status. It becomes necessary for them to find a substitute for the previous challenges and absorbing interests provided by their work. Deprived of the important satisfactions of their previous occupations, the adjustment to retirement often becomes traumatic. In the light of this, there is a compelling need for the establishment of a new ethic, perhaps the leisure ethic, to supply the kind of motivating support that work had hitherto provided. By no means is this intended to limit itself, by definition, to recreational activities current during part-time leisure, a relief and antidote to the strains of work life.

This new ethic is more fundamental in its demands, much broader in its scope, and could be viewed as encompassing the mental and social well-being of the retired person. It is my purpose to prove that this idea can best be implemented as a program in continuing education, preferably at a university. Though they may now only dimly perceive it, universities have a crucial role to play in the planning and development of the emerging leisure ethic.

Where adult education noncredit programs do exist at universities, they are often limited to avocational and recreational aims. For the retired educated person who no longer wishes to pursue courses for a degree, there is a need for a new type of adult learning program which makes it possible to integrate the skills, experience, and talents of the educated retiree in an atmosphere of learning. Such programs should give opportunities for retirees to function—they key word here is *function*—as leaders and teachers as well as students. There is a give-and-take in this which purports to make use of abilities of a lifetime of garnering. Learning for its own sake, not for job use, can thus be a realizable ideal; and in sharing with others one's skills and interests, the retired person finds a raison d'être.

The IRP Program

This type of adult learning program has been in operation at the IRP since 1962. Its uniqueness can be spelled out in two major ways: going back to school as students plus the more significant participation in an "inner university," a kind of do-it-yourself institute where volunteers function as leader-teachers in a proliferation of courses.

Each member is required to enroll in a New School course each semester; thus retirees function in a non-age-segregated classroom where students of all age groups rub shoulders. Both learn from each other. But merely taking courses would not be enough to attract the numbers who fill the waiting lists. They are drawn in by the lure of the "inner groups," or courses presided over by the retirees themselves, some of whom have never taught but function very ably as teachers. They bear full responsibility for curriculum planning, assignments, and discussions—all in an atmosphere of educational democracy. Former teachers find this an unusual opportunity to continue work within a new context and with a receptive student body (which is, after all, a teacher's all-time dream). Thus, skills fostered by so many years of experience are not lost but flourish in an atmosphere of enthusiasm and appreciation. The desk is no longer the divisive symbol which separates the learning from the learned.

A talent pool of members is crucial to the program's success. A selective process of admission where hundreds apply and only 70–75 can be admitted annually makes this possible. The members are, by and large, a participating and enthusiastic group of retirees whose average age is close to 70 (males 72+ and females 67+).

Because of the varied interests and abilities of the membership, the IRP program is rich in variety. History, poetry, playreading, foreign languages, music, literature, and current affairs represent a few of the subjects in this inner university. There are open discussion groups as well as small study groups and seminars to meet the differing interests and participatory needs of the members.

As to leadership, there is a great variety—former teachers make up 50% of the volunteer chairmen. Other professionals as well as former business executives find their "second chance," as some have called it, directing discussion groups as well as teaching in their life-long areas of avocational interest.

In the IRP, aspiring writers are given the chance to be read and see their work in print. Members publish and edit a magazine, *The IRP Review*, which the IRP finances and which is read with interest and appreciation by friends in widely scattered centers throughout the country.

Parallel to this involvement in learning is a social program. This is very important for the older person whose circle of friends is gradually narrowing. New friends are acquired when one believes that the time for that is over. Similarities of interest draw members together and where there are contacts with diverse careers, the association is that much more meaningful. Opportunities for socializing are encouraged in group parties, periodic membership meetings, and chartered bus trips to various points of interest.

There is also no lack of volunteering for community services. Some find a creative outlet in activities such as recording for the blind, acting as aides at museums, teaching remedial reading at a nearby elementary school, working with retarded children, giving talks at senior citizen centers, manning telephones at city consumer offices, and educational TV.

While the cooperative spirit as demonstrated is the key to the program, the leadership of an enthusiastic and imaginative director is paramount. Without this the program might well disintegrate. As in all working groups of any size, somebody must make certain decisions and accept the buck. The assurance of the democratic process, however, is found in an elected council, chairman's conferences, semiannual membership meetings, etc. A set of by-laws sets the guidelines, and there is accountability to the dean of the New School, as is required from other departments.

Participants' Evaluation

To many members of the institute, the IRP has become a way of life. They look to it for their intellectual and even social sustenance. This is evidenced by the low drop-out rate, which is 10%. Those who leave often do so compelled by circumstances or when forced to move to a warmer climate. Even when out of New York, as in Florida for the winter, their sense of belonging draws them together to form discussion groups or other sharing activities. They know how to be self-starters wherever they are geographically.

To demonstrate what the institute means to its members, we can best illustrate it in their own words.

> From a former director of communications for a national organization: "The IRP program has reopened old skills and interests so that I can produce at my own pace. . . . Having a course at the university with old and young together is stimulating and shows me that there is less of a generation gap than I thought. The gap is largely between antagonistic individuals."

> A retired research physicist remarks, "Teaching a class at the IRP for the first time in my life, I have come to an appreciation of the ideal of learning for its own sake and thus feel richly rewarded."

> A former expert on foreign trade gives her experience after her first year at the IRP: "As a paper giver I experienced the joy of being creative—a new one for me since college. After having done almost routine tasks during my so-called interesting career, I have at last a chance for self-expression."

> A retired high school teacher after 11 years at the institute is still able

to say, "Leading a group in literature, paper giving, studying something in depth, the give-and-take in discussions with people retired from different walks of life, are truly stimulating and broadening experiences."

A former fashion editor for a well-known newspaper and a first year member writes, "I find it stimulating to meet several times a week with such bright contemporaries. . . . The academic atmosphere is especially appealing to me in striking contrast to my newspaper days and my domestic tasks. It also has been great fun to work on the *IRP Review*. Here's to the back-to-school idea of the IRP."

From a retired principal, also a first year member, "The overriding benefit at the IRP is that a member can accommodate the program to his own pace. I know of no other educational institution that offers such flexibility. Also I found the research I did for the five papers I gave last year was very rewarding to me, emotionally and intellectually. The comments and praise of my fellow students were a source of deep gratification. This is all too rare for many like me who have retired from a profession where what I said and thought had some meaning to many."

Some Observations

After more than a decade of experience as director of the institute, I feel qualified to make some observations about retirement leisure as it affects the retired professional.

In the first place, the hobby or course or concert which served a re-creative purpose while at work is not enough to fill the total retirement leisure time of the educated. A leisure ethic must take the place of the work ethic and provide some of the same motivational satisfactions.

Second, the lifestyle, educational background, and status of the retiree must be taken into account in the design of programs. There is no reason to suppose that the educated retiree will find much in common with retirees in general. This was brought home to me when I encountered a distinct lack of enthusiasm in response to the following question asked of a group of directors of senior citizen centers: "How many of you plan to join a senior citizen center when you retire?"

Third, the retired person must be brought into the planning, direction, and operation of programs for older people. This was recognized in the organization of the 1971 White House Conference on Aging. The need for having the aging themselves involved as "insiders" was stated in the preamble to the legislation setting up the conference: "It is essential that in all programs developed for the aging, emphasis should be upon the right and obligation of older persons to free choice and self-help in planning their own futures."

Fourth, and lastly, the IRP has shown that there is a need for similar programs. The university can do much to dispel the sense of isolation of the educated retiree as well as help in creating some kind of intercommunication between generations.

Discussion

A number of questions were raised at the time this chapter was presented as a paper and at the informal sessions held spontaneously later that day. A summary of these issues and IRP responses to them follows:

Q: Must such a program be part of a university? Can't it be started at community centers?

A: The IRP program is directed toward the educated retiree. This does not necessarily mean only those who have been to college. But the intellectually motivated person looks to a university rather than to a community center.

I have helped several centers around New York City get started with programs, and I have found that in the absence of a university's non-age-segregated environment, the development of standards which will appeal to the educated retiree are made very difficult.

Q: How is your organization financed?

A: Since the IRP is primarily a middle–class–oriented program, it has little difficulty supporting itself from its fees and contributions. That does not mean to say that the university has no role to play. To get an IRP started, some seed money is required during the first year or two for space, clerical help, and direction.

Q: Your fees, I understand, are almost $200.00 a year. Can retirees, living on fixed incomes, afford this?

A: The vast majority of retirees are quite willing to meet this fee since what they are getting is of far greater value. Where a hardship exists, there is little difficulty in obtaining a partial scholarship, which comes from a fund created by our affluent members.

Q: How do you get so many volunteers? I believe you mentioned the figure of 80 co-chairmen.

A: Let's not forget that the volunteers are really teaching at a college, even though they are not on the regular staff of the institution. I hold faculty meetings with them every 2 months where we discuss teaching and administrative problems of the IRP. We determine policies at these meetings by a consensus.

Here again, the volunteer has a new sense of identity as well as pride in being linked with a university as a "teacher." Perhaps retired faculty have no need of such an image, but many educated people find a feeling of accomplishment in this new role. It leads them to become real students and to grow intellectually. What's wrong with that?

Q: What are your criteria for admission to the institute?

A: Our requirements are a background of education, not necessarily with a degree, and recent retirement from a professional or equivalent career after at least 20 years of practice. An equivalent career may include a corporate executive, an official in a union, a director of a public service organization, as well as a recognized artist, musician, lecturer, reporter, etc.

A committee screens the applications, and then they are given an interview by the director. In the interview he tries to determine whether the applicant will profit from the program rather than whether he will, in fact, become a leader. The emphasis is always on the individual.

Q: What you are doing may be all right for the educated, but what about the many who hated school and have not been able to get over that feeling? Don't they need education too?

A: No educational program can succeed if it tries to meet all educational needs of the entire senior citizen population. There is no doubt that much can be learned from our experience to help in the education of all senior citizens. But what we have to offer is a new approach to learning—a self-involvement. Let me illustrate this concept. The other day a TV crew taped one of our groups called "Fun with Words." The chairman or teacher had lists of "bad" words that were at one time "good" and the reverse. The wit, humor, folkways, etc., of German, Jewish, Russian, French, and even ancient Latin and Greek background of the participants made great fun.

Since this program will be shown on cable TV at senior citizen centers, it is hoped that self-motivated "Fun with Words" groups will be formed. As a concerned group the IRP will help just as it is doing now by sending volunteers to such centers to show slides, demonstrate art techniques, give papers, conduct discussions, etc.

Q: How can anyone get started to form an institute?

A: I will be glad to help in any way. I have done just this in Boston, Philadelphia, Cleveland, and San Francisco. Many universities have requested information, and they were always answered in detail. I have been asked to come out to address groups of retirees. This has been a very successful approach, for there is no substitute for example and enthusiasm.

Addendum

The roster of members has reached the limit of 650. Currently there are 80 groups, staffed by 110 volunteers from among the membership. Nearly half of the members serve as leaders, teachers, reporters, social secretaries, or in an administrative function. A number of council committees have assumed some of the administrative tasks hitherto performed by the director. The IRP Educational Services Committee selects reporters who repeat their talks at senior citizen centers throughout the city. In November of 1976, 70 college and university officials attended an IRP "Observation" Conference. This is bearing fruit in the many programs that are being started on college campuses. Since the IRP consists of volunteers, the program pays for itself.

References

1. *Report of the Commission on the Reorganization of Secondary Schools.* Washington, D.C.: National Education Association, 1918.
2. W. Donahue, *et al.* (Eds.). *The way of a liberal education—Free time—A challenge to later maturity.* Ann Arbor: University of Michigan, 1958.

25

. . . Gone Tomorrow

Robert Kastenbaum

Mental health at any age implies more than the absence of serious disturbance. We look for positive characteristics as well. Zest; confidence; ability to learn, to communicate, to share with others; specific skills and competencies; and a general receptivity to experience are among the characteristics we might expect to find in a person who radiates well-being.

Aging and dying imply the opposite. Taken separately or together, these terms bring to mind images of frailty, diminishing competence, increased dependence, and attenuated contact with the sociophysical environment. Furthermore, while the "mentally healthy" person enjoys, the aging or dying person suffers. But even this sharp contrast does not go far enough. It is not just that one person functions, prospers, and enjoys while another falters, loses, and suffers. The crucial difference is a matter of time (or the way we are inclined to think about time). Both people are "here today." One will be "gone tomorrow."

A central question is implied: *How can we orient ourselves throughout life both to the immediate challenges of being "here today" and to the mind-bending prospect of being "gone tomorrow"?* This chapter focuses selectively on the life situation of the older person and the challenges posed to family, physician, and society in general. Some of the more familiar issues and materials will be neglected in order to explore dimensions that have received less systematic attention. Although what follows is grounded in my clinical and research experience, it should be stated at the outset that we will be venturing rather far from the snug harbor of secure documentation at several points.

Mental Health As a Cause of Despair

Is it possible that what often passes for mental health is a precondition to much of the despair suffered by the aging, the dying, and those close to them? Absurd as this proposition might sound, I offer it here for consideration.

From *Geriatrics*, 1974, 29, 127–134. Reprinted with permission of *Geriatrics*.

The usual image of mental health is supported by psychosocial maneuvers that can be described as either denial or selective focusing. Denial has long been recognized as a significant type of coping process, sometimes operating to our advantage, sometimes to our disadvantage. Both the concept and the phenomena involved are complex, with various observers arriving at rather different interpretations. Recently, for example, Kübler-Ross,[1] Weisman,[2] and Becker[3] have all dealt extensively with denial phenomena within the context of terminal illness. Roughly speaking, we might say that denial has gone too far when aspects of reality crucial for competent functioning or survival itself have been treated as though nonexistent. Because *denial* is a loaded term, we might think instead of selective focusing. Pathology is not necessarily implied in the concept of establishing priorities for which phenomena are to receive the most attention.

I suggest here that mental health often focuses selectively (and excessively) on a high-noon vision of the human condition. The person characterized in the opening paragraph is young or youthful-appearing and in good physical health. The sun is shining now and, by implication, will always do so. We do not picture the mentally healthy person as ill or tormented, as burdened, stressed, or forced to the absolute limits of capacity. She or he smiles wholesomely in the sunlight.

The focus is so selective that the dimension of time and change is scarcely acknowledged. Shadows will not lengthen; darkness will not descend. Like a bubble, the image dissolves if pricked by nettlesome realities that have been carefully excluded. "There *will* be a tomorrow. You will be different then. The world will be different. Much of what you take for granted will be gone. And then you will be gone as well." This kind of message would be intolerable. Mental health depends too heavily on a vein of naïve optimism, which in turn depends on a romanticized episode selected from the entire human life cycle. I am suggesting, in other words, that there is nothing accidental about the frequent association between mental health and the noonday vision of life. Mental health is not only for the young and healthy; it is for those who will remain young and healthy. Time and change might give the lie to this vision, so they must be ignored or distorted.

The high-noon vision does recognize certain forms of challenge and adversity, but it is not prepared for problems that continue and deepen. A person must either solve or get over the problems that come his or her way.

Bereavement is one particularly relevant example. When a wife becomes a widow, society may tolerate the acute or transitional phase. She is entitled to special understanding and assistance. In fact, she can even be depressed and people will not necessarily hold it against her—for a while. Social allowances for the widow's sorrow, loss, and altered behavior often terminate, however, while the grief process is still active.[4,5] Why? One plausible answer is that life must go on, after all. The bereaved herself, as well as those close to her, feel obligations and pressures to get back to normal.

I suggest that another factor also contributes: our inclination to regard death as just one more problem or interruption. We acknowledge some of the temporary correlates and sequelae of death, but we turn away from what is most distinctive: permanent and total loss. This is an example of selective focusing. It is acceptable for the widow to be upset for a while, to pass through a phase of acute mourning. It is not acceptable for her to continue to live with the mark of this bereavement on her. "Cry; get it out of your system" is familiar mental health advice. Why is this expression of anguish tolerable? Because it is thought to facilitate return to normal (i.e., high-noon) functioning. But it is seldom considered "healthy" to go through life with a measure of sorrow and other heavy affects in consequence of the severe interpersonal loss that has been suffered. Sorrow, grief, and suffering have no value or validity per se but are tolerable only if these states can be used in the service of "mentally healthful" goals.

We seem unable to comprehend that a person can both sorrow and be "mentally healthy" over a prolonged period of time. We seem unwilling to acknowledge that death can signify a drastic and permanent change in the quality of life for those who remain (as well as a reminder of the full meaning of the death that lies in prospect for each of us). The person who chooses to acknowledge the full weight of death thereby relinquishes claims on full mental health. One either steps back into the sunlight and smiles or goes off into the shadows as a failure, weakling, or deviant.

The antagonism between current conceptions of mental health on the one hand and of aging, death, and suffering on the other can be seen in many other ways. Consider these brief illustrations:

1. Fear of death has been belittled, reviled, and pathologized. We are not supposed to fear death. It is somehow morally weak or neurotic to be concerned with personal annihilation, unless this concern is disguised in a sociably acceptable form.[6] It is acceptable to fear that crabgrass will invade our lawns or that inflation will undermine our finances. It is not acceptable to fear (or even to think much about) death. Further, this bias against thinking and feeling about death cannot be dismissed as a characteristic of the "unenlightened lay person"; it has been a signal feature of professionals in both mental and physical health fields.

2. We edge away from those whose lives have been marked strongly by suffering, aging, or death. Survivors of concentration camps, prisoner-of-war internment, and nuclear holocaust often find "normal" people un-willing or unable to interact with them. We do not seem to know how to

relate to people whose experiences with suffering and loss so decisively explode the fragile high-noon vision of the human condition.

Reluctance to be close to those who are old or dying has been observed and discussed extensively in recent years. [7-9] The person who has suffered, the person who is suffering, and the person who will continue to suffer all threaten a vision of mental health that requires problems to be temporary and resolvable. Given the choice, often we retain the vision and reject the people.

3. The educational system in the United States has been influenced in many ways by our conceptions of mental health, although many other influences are operative as well. Whatever else it might be, education is much concerned both with transmission of past knowledge and traditions and with preparation of the young for the future. Despite or because of mental health input, very little attention is devoted to those dimensions of past or future that lie beyond pleasure and achievement. The phenomena of reflection, meditation, and reminiscence—of *using* the past—are given short shrift by a surging emphasis on futurity. Yet, the future is limited to between now and being grown up. A career from kindergarten through college can be completed without the broad topics of aging, death, and suffering ever coming into focus. It is as if they said, "We are preparing you to grow up—not to grow old, not to face vulnerabilities in yourself or others, not to live with the keen awareness of mortality."

The high-noon vision purveyed by our schools is seldom convincing in its entirety to either teachers or students. Life continues to swirl about them, and even the youngest know something of loss, death, and distress. [10] The official stance of the school system and the persistent shaping that takes place, however, tend to alienate the participants from their own life experiences. They are obliged to grow up achieving, socializing, and smiling; but they also observe, in various ways, the side of life that is not included in either the formal or informal curriculum. This dichotomy is perhaps most evident in schools of the type that led Kozol to speak of death at an early age, [11] but few children anyplace inhabit a world in which suffering is unknown.

We have been suggesting here that the mainstream vision of mental health in the United States selectively focuses on a small range of phenomena as comprising the total human condition. Suffering, aging, and many aspects of dying and death cannot be accommodated in this vision. It is not just that our notion of mental health fails to prepare people for adversities that are common or universal—it actually sets us up to be demolished when the other side of reality intrudes. We cannot believe what has hit us. It is not just that we fail to prepare ourselves and others to live within limits and, when necessary, to dwell with suffering and loss.

The point is that we *dare not* make such preparations. To preserve our fragile optimism, we must keep aside or neutralize reminders that life includes seasons other than spring, summer, and early autumn. People find themselves unemployed, old, widowed; physically impaired, or terminally ill. "How could this happen, how could this really happen to *me?*" they cry. Although to some extent a willing participant *in* the deception, they have been tricked and have a right to be angry.

It is important to remind ourselves that suffering and despair are not identical states. Many people, young and old, have demonstrated the ability to maintain or even deepen their sense of selfhood and worth in the midst of suffering. Despair has something to do with the collapse of values. There is nothing to suffer *for* or the suffering itself is wrong (antiself, antisociety, or anti-God). Those who purvey and accept the high-noon version of mental health make it difficult to accept pain, loss, suffering, and death as dimensions of the human condition. Flights into psychosis, senility, and other forms of psychic suicide (as well as physical self-destruction itself) are options sometimes chosen by people who see utter despair as the only other alternative. One old person tries desperately to "sell a symptom" to a physician. If the physician "buys it," then the person at least has something certifiable and of social value. Another old person, who says he has "nothing to kick about," has, in fact, nothing to feel either good or bad about. Responsivity has been dulled and affectivity shallowed out because to feel is to feel despair.

On Time, Age, and Death

It is possible that a more comprehensive appreciation and cultivation of psychological time might enable us to move beyond the limited image of mental health that has been sketched here. Our society is future oriented, but only in a highly selective fashion. It is typical for young adults to clip off their future projections before the years of physical decline are reached. [12,13] Intensive contact with the aged can be astonishing to them and produce at least a temporary reorganization of personal time structure. [14] Meanwhile, old people function within a time frame that is the rejected future of the young, while themselves often thinking most of the past. Not often do we come upon a person of any age whose thoughts and feelings are oriented to past, present, and future in a fully encompassing manner.

One significant clue has been provided by Butler, whose concept of the life review is now well known. [15] He interprets the life review as

a naturally-occurring universal mental process characterized by the progressive return to consciousness of past experiences, and particularly, the resurgence of unresolved conflicts; simultaneously, and normally, these revived experiences and conflicts are surveyed and reintegrated. It is assumed that this process is prompted by the realization of approaching dissolution and death, and by the inability to maintain one's sense of personal invulnerability. Although the process is initiated internally by the perception of approaching death, it is further shaped by contemporaneous experiences and its nature and outcome are affected by the lifelong unfolding of character.[15]

This is an important contribution for several reasons. It recognizes an active (as contrasted with merely reactive) psychological process in the old person, and one that "binds time," being responsive to past-, current-, and future-oriented inputs. Further, as a normal (nonpathological) process, the life review represents a "mentally healthy" activity. The process itself ranges from relatively serene to relatively disturbing while still being worked out and can have an outcome that is more or less favorable.

The concept of a life review, then, offers one of the few available links between mental health and the problems of aging and death. It would be useful to build further upon this concept and to explore practical applications. Before making a few suggestions along this line, however, I would like to call attention to several other retrospective modalities. The processes that are described briefly here emerge from my research and clinical experience but are not grounded in point-by-point relationships to particular data. These modalities are discussed more extensively elsewhere.[16]

Validation. The individual "returns" to the past for reassurances that he or she once was (and by implication still might be) a competent and worthwhile person. "I was a strong, competent, beloved person once. Therefore, I am still worthwhile, capable of further survival and adaptation." Young people are more likely to attempt validation by projecting themselves into a future state in which they will have arrived at full powers and have achieved some measures of worldly success.

Boundary setting. "What is over and done with, and what can still be a part of my life?" This is a question that the boundary-setting process attempts to resolve. The move into a nursing home, for example, may occasion an evaluation of past life to determine what should be given up and what should be retained.

Perpetuation of the past. The past is treated as though it were the present. This is "living in the past" in its purest form. While this process can easily become too dominant and pervasive, it also can have adaptive value when kept within limits. To some extent, perpetuation of the past is a function the old person can perform for society at large; but in the contemporary United States, this often shrinks to an individualistic, isolated mechanism.

Replaying. Selected past experiences are taken out of their time frame and repeated again and again. The time sequence in which they originally occurred is no longer important. The old person has shaped a highly personal self-history comparable in some ways to an artistic production. Replaying may reduce concern about death, because the person to some extent now lives outside of the usual past-present-future time frame. (This does not necessarily imply disorientation to time, places, and persons; it can be an alternative mode of functioning set alongside competent awareness.) Because, in a sense, time does not flow significantly from the past through the present into the future; the person has no death "ahead." The future has been abolished, and therefore, death has been abolished as well.

A particular individual can be working with more than one of these time modalities simultaneously. Obviously, it does little justice to the richness and complexity of an old person's relationship to time to simply say that he or she is "living in the past." This could mean many things, from selective replaying of significant experiences to a concerted effort to integrate all past experiences with the prospect of death. Greater sensitivity to the way in which people orient themselves to time would improve communication among the young and the old, to the mutual benefit of all.

If aging and death could be incorporated into our vision of mental health, then the burden of orienting ourselves would not fall so heavily upon those who are already suffering physical, psychological, and social loss. A life review might still be necessary and appropriate in advanced age, for example, but it would have been preceded by a life *preview* many years in advance. And it would be pursued in a contemporaneous context in which other people appreciate what is going on. Today, one often has the impression that a person who engages in the life review of any of the other modalities for preserving and transforming identity through psychological time must do so on his or her own, receiving little understanding from the environment. Required of us is a willingness to consider past, present, and future at *every* point in our life cycle, both independently and in dialogue with others.

"Here Today and Gone Tomorrow"

I have argued that "mental health" often has come to mean a state of affairs that can exist only under favorable circumstances: youth, health, good prospects. It involves a process of selective focusing in which the dimension of time and change must be treated as though unreal or unimportant. The mentally healthy person is here today. Period. This orientation provides a cruel disservice when the person eventually meets with certain kinds of adversity. Acute problems can be accepted, but conditions that will continue and worsen may strike a person as unbelievable or unfair. People are not really prepared for this kind of change. Furthermore, society tends to reject those whose suffering undermines the fragile optimism of the high-noon vision.

Despair is a possible outcome, although the person usually will engage in other protective actions before succumbing (actions which themselves can be quite disturbing and deleterious). The prospect of being gone tomorrow may be anguishing beyond the specific pain and loss that is experienced. One is isolated from others and from one's own previous life experiences and values, trapped in what might be called, after Nietzsche, the midnight vision.

It is neither necessary nor acceptable to divide reality into these two partial visions. The field of gerontology and geriatrics is beginning to appreciate what some individuals have always known: that joy and sorrow are both dimensions of the human condition at all age levels. By insisting that time, change, age, suffering, and death have their place in our image of mental health, we can enrich both the high-noon and the midnight visions. The prospect that one of us may be gone tomorrow will be not a precipitant of withdrawal or alienation. Our being here today can encompass an orientation that does justice both to immediate experience and to the estates of time remembered and time anticipated that stretch forth around us.

References

1. Kübler-Ross, E. *On death and dying*. New York: Macmillan, 1969.
2. Weisman, A. D. *On dying and denying*. New York: Behavioral Publications, 1972.
3. Becker, E. *The denial of death*. New York. Free Press, 1973.
4. Lopata, H. *Widowhood in an American city*. Cambridge, Mass.: Schenkman, 1973.
5. Mathison, J. A cross-cultural view of widowhood. *Omega, 3,* 201–218, 1970.
6. Kastenbaum, R., and Aisenberg, R. B. *The psychology of death*. New York: Springer, 1972.
7. LeShan L., and LeShan, E. Psychotherapy and the patient with a limited life-span. *Psychiatry, 24,* 318–323, 1961.
8. Kastenbaum, R. The reluctant therapist. *Geriatrics, 18,* 296–301, 1963.
9. Quint, J. *The nurse and the dying patient*. New York: Macmillan, 1967.
10. Kastenbaum, R. The kingdom where nobody dies. *Saturday Review of Science,* January 1973, pp. 33–38.

11. Kozol, J. *Death at an early age*. New York. Bantam, 1967.
12. Doob, L. *Patterning of time*. New Haven, Conn.: Yale University Press, 1971.
13. Kastenbaum, R. Time and death in adolescence, in Feifel, H. (Ed.), *The meaning of death*. New York: McGraw-Hill, 1959, pp. 99–113.
14. Kastenbaum, R. Impact of experience with the aged upon the time perspective of young adults. *Journal of Genetic Psychology, 101,* 159–167, 1967.
15. Butler, R. N. The life review: An interpretation of reminiscence in the aged. *Psychiatry, 26,* 65–76, 1963.
16. Kastenbaum, R. Time, death and ritual in later life, in J. T. Fraser (Ed.), *The study of time,* Vol. 2. New York: Springer-Verlag, 1975.

Index

Index